hagstrom® New York ATLAS

W9-APG-535

In celebration of the Millennium

Stephan Van Dam presents the first

innovation in urban cartography in 50 years:

"...A sophisticated resource..." **NEW YORK TIMES**

"The best innovation in map design since the

globe was flattened onto paper!" **DIVERSION**

...For savvy travelers..." **PLAYBOY**

NYAtlas

While the area of today's New York had been settled by the Manates for millennia, it was first settled by the Dutch in 1626. The City of New York, incorporating the five boroughs of the Bronx, Brooklyn, Manhattan, Queens and Staten Island, is a more recent invention and dates back only to 1898.

NYAtlas organizes the metropolis into three easily accessible parts:

Basics: neighborhoods, hospitals, schools, streets, and the like.

Top 100: the best in dining, attractions, architecture, hotels, performing arts, nightlife, shopping, sports, natural resources, theatre, education & more.

Histories: Ten diagrammatic spreads illustrate how NYC has shaped global pop culture.

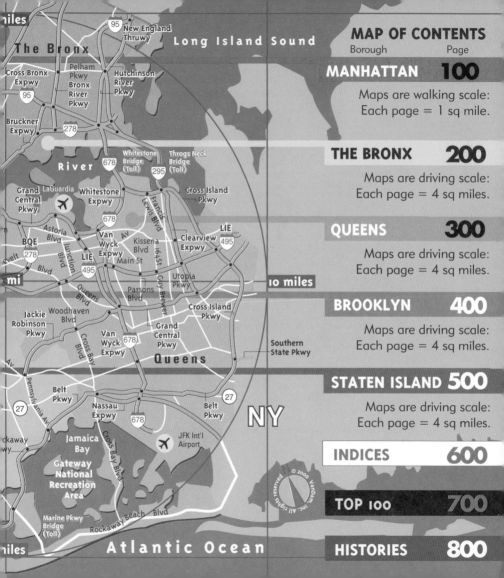

MAP OF CONTENTS

Borough | Page

MANHATTAN 100

Maps are walking scale:
Each page = 1 sq mile.

THE BRONX 200

Maps are driving scale:
Each page = 4 sq miles.

QUEENS 300

Maps are driving scale:
Each page = 4 sq miles.

BROOKLYN 400

Maps are driving scale:
Each page = 4 sq miles.

STATEN ISLAND 500

Maps are driving scale:
Each page = 4 sq miles.

INDICES 600

TOP 100 700

HISTORIES 800

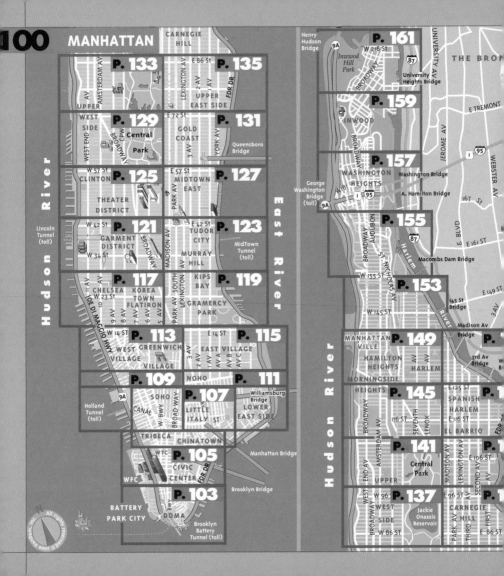

nhattan's Best

is the ultimate vertical city
e "the Culture of Congestion"
.

tral Park is the city's
d public square. Treasured
ocals and visitors alike, it is
ocus for play, pastoral love,
e—back riding, jogging,
ing, biking, rollerblading &
ics. Its Metropolitan Opera
Philharmonic concerts in
ummer and the NY Marathon
ovember are living proof of
the uniquely American
an experiment can work. **129A**

inbow Grill Uniquely NY!
rve for dinner and dancing in
clouds. The "Fred & Ginger"
s an Art Deco stunner as is Ł
orix fixe. The best views are
the Promenade Bar. 30 Rock.
a, 65th fl, 212-632-5100. **126A**

rld Financial Center

rica's most successful urban
elopment of the 1980s opened
city to the Hudson & reinvented
ntown as a destination.
ffing the breezes on the
anade, one is tempted to forsake
country for the city. The free
ing mambo and guajira
certs in the summer have made
t strides in unwelding
herners at the hip. **104C**

The Metropolitan Museum of Art

Covering five millennia, this is the
world's encyclopedia of the arts
with collections too numerous to
list. Favorites include the Rockefeller
wing, the Egyptian galleries and
the Lehman Wing. Allow for more
than one visit to drink in the views
of Central Park from the Roof Terrace
Bar. 5 Av @ 82 St, 212-535-7710. **133B**

Lever House This classic of
Corbusian modernism marked the
beginning of what has become a
virtual museum of modern
architecture on Park Avenue. **126B**

TriBeCa Once the poor cousin
of SoHo, TriBeCa (Triangle below
Canal St) is now the rich Hollywood
uncle. Robert de Niro's Tribeca Grill,
Drew Nieporent's Montrachet and
Nobu as well as Chanterelle and
Danube are the temples of
haute cuisine downtown.
(Check top 100 Dining for
details). **106C**

Chrysler Building

Despite recent plans to turn
it into a hotel, William Ł
Van Alen's classic Deco Ł
tower remains the
pièce de resistance of
1930s American skyscraper
design. 405 Lexington Av,
212-682-3070. **126C**

**Manhattan Stats
Population:**
1.4 million
Area: 24 sq miles

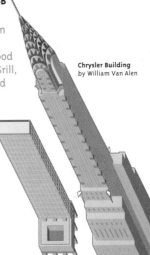

Chrysler Building
by William Van Alen

Lever House
by Gordon Bunshaft

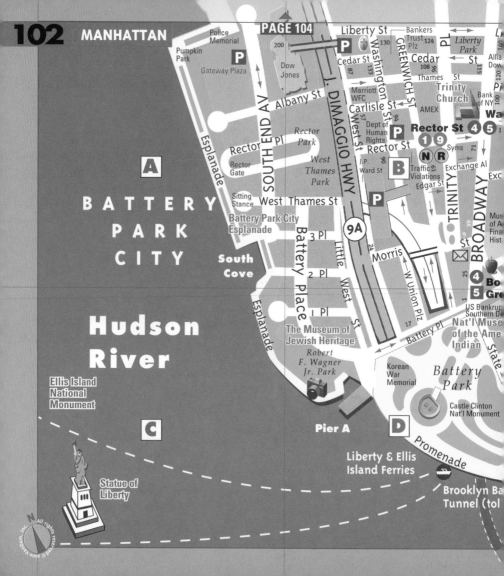

PAGE 104

Police Memorial

Pumpkin Park

Gateway Plaza

Liberty St

Bankers Trust Plz 124

Liberty Park

Cedar St 130

Washington St

GREENWICH ST

Cedar St 108 96

Thames St

Trinity Church

Allia Dow

Bank of NY 100

115

120

200

Dow Jones

Albany St

J. DIMAGGIO HWY

Carlisle St

West St

Marriott WFC

133

87

Dept of Human Rights

AMEX

Wa

Rector St 4 5

1 9

N R

Rector St

South End Av

South Pl

Rector Park

West Thames Park

Rector Gate

J.P. Ward St

90

B

57

94

Syms 71

Exchange Al

EXC

Sitting Stance

West Thames St

Battery Park City Esplanade

Traffic Violations

Edgar St

TRINITY

BROADWAY

Mus of A Fina Hist

BATTERY PARK CITY

A

3 Pl

9A

Morris

24

W Union Plz

Hudson River

South Cove

Battery Place

Little West St

2 Pl

1 Pl

Battery Pl

25

4 5

Bo Gr

US Bankrup Southern D

Ellis Island National Monument

The Museum of Jewish Heritage

17

Nat'l Muse of the Ame Indian

Robert F. Wagner Jr. Park

Korean War Memorial

Battery Park

Castle Clinton Nat'l Monument

C

Pier A

D

Promenade

Liberty & Ellis Island Ferries

Brooklyn Ba Tunnel (tol

Statue of Liberty

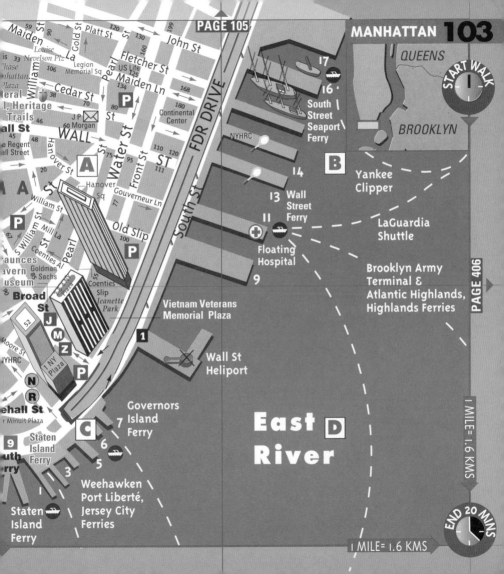

QUEENS

START WALK

BROOKLYN

Maiden La
Louise Nevelson Plz
59
80
Gold St
Platt St
120
130
199
John St

is 33
hase
hattan
Plaza
eral
I, Heritage
Trails 46

Fletcher St
160
Legion Memorial Sq
Pearl
US Life
106
125
Maiden Ln
134
168

Chase Manhattan Plaza
William St
Cedar St
38

JP
60 Morgan
St
80
Continental Center
180

WALL
Water St
ST
110
120
95
111

45
48
e Regent
all Street
Hanover St
20

A
Hanover Sq
Gouverneur Ln
75
77

NYHRC

B
Yankee Clipper

LaGuardia Shuttle

17

16
South Street Seaport Ferry

William St
Old Slip
100

14

13 Wall Street Ferry

11

P

S William St
Coenties Al
Pearl St
55
Coenties Slip
Jeanette Park

Mill La

Goldman & Sachs

aunces
avern
useum

Broad St

52

J
M
Z

Moore St

NYHRC

N
R

ehall St
r Minuit Plaza

9
uth
rry

Staten Island Ferry

P

1 NY Plaza

Floating Hospital

9

Brooklyn Army Terminal & Atlantic Highlands, Highlands Ferries

Vietnam Veterans Memorial Plaza

1

Wall St Heliport

C

Governors Island Ferry

7

6

5

3

Weehawken Port Liberté, Jersey City Ferries

Staten Island Ferry

East River

D

PAGE 406

1 MILE = 1.6 KMS

END 20 MINS

1 MILE = 1.6 KMS

FDR DRIVE

South St

PAGE 106

T R I B E C A Y

N Moore St
Franklin St
Finn Square
Chanterelle
Leonard St
Knitting Factory
NY Law School
WORTH ST
Bell Atlantic
Harrison St
Independence Plaza
Jay St
Staple St
HUDSON ST
BROADWAY
74 The Odeon
Thomas St
Duane Park
Bouley Bakery
Duane St
Trimble Pl
Tribeca Performing Arts Center
Reade St
CIVIC
Tribeca Park
Chambers St
Chambers St

J. DIMAGGIO HWY
107
88
366
355
2
Boro of Manhattan CC
West St
64
62
40
124
46
71
102

A Stuyvesant HS
North Esplanade
Tribeca Bridge
1 WTC
Windows on the World, Greatest Bar on Earth
B

The Real World
Rockefeller Park
Pavilion
CHAMBERS ST
CHAMBERS ST
160
285
138 95
132
A C
3 9
Chan
143

Park House
Warren St
Il Giglio 67
Warren St
81
126
WEST
CHURCH

W F C
Park Pl West
College of Insurance
2 WTC
Observation Deck
Murray St
57
41
62
253
109
Ci Ha

Esplanade
River Terrace
Play ground
Murray St
9A
World Trade Center
Park Pl
Park Pl
2 3
Wool Bldg
21
47
94
U.S. Customs
Barclay St
Venator Grou
Kinney Shoe Corp 219

Lilly Pool
Mercantile Exchange
North End Av
Amex
Merrill Lynch
Lehman Bros
7 WTC
6 WTC
W T C
Vesey St
St. Pau Chape

Belvedere
Vesey St
Vesey St
Borders
5 WTC
C ✉
E
Fulton St
Millenium Hilton
N

C WFC Plaza
Winter Garden
Merrill Lynch
D
Dey St
Century 21
R

Ferries to Hoboken, Liberty Science Ctr & State Park
Manhattan Sailing School
3 WTC Marriott Hotel
4 WTC Commodities Exch.
Cortlandt S
Cortlandt St
1 9
One Liberty Plaza
NYL Care Health Plans

World Financial Center
Police Memorial
Liberty St
Bankers Trust Plz 124
Liberty Park
130

North Cove
Pumpkin Park
Gateway Plaza
P
S End Av
225
200
Dow Jones
Cedar
87
Washington St
Greenwich St
133
P
108 96
Thames St

Hudson River

26
25

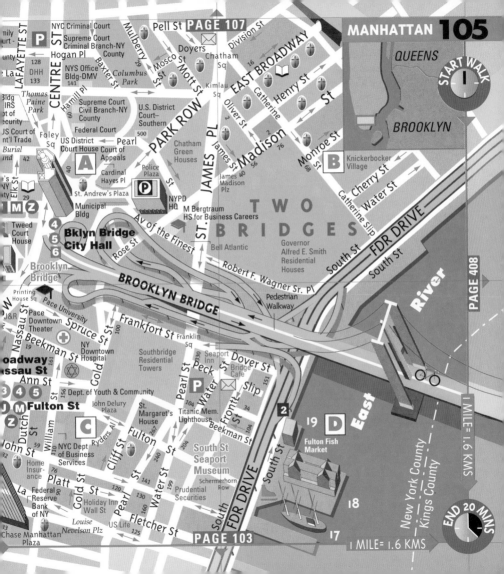

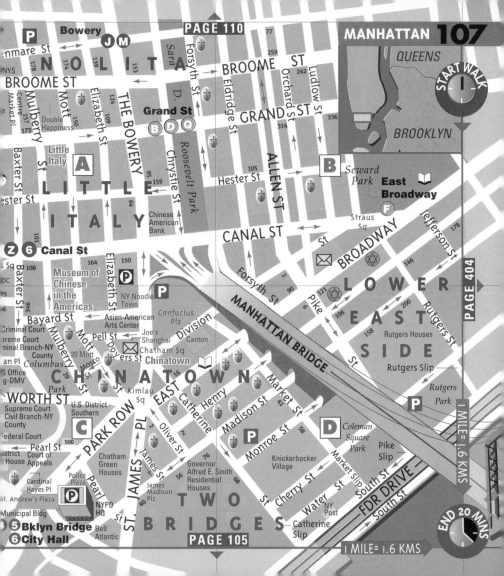

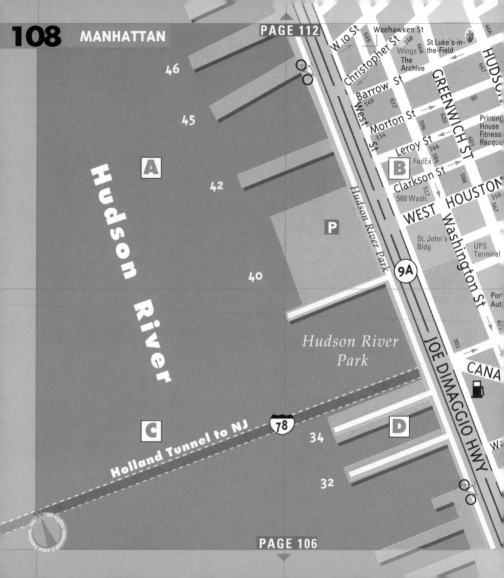

PAGE 112

Hudson River

Hudson River Park

Hudson River Park

A

B

C

P

D

46

45

42

40

34

32

W 10 St

Weehawken St

Christopher St

Wings

The Archive

St Luke's-in-the-Field

Barrow St

West St

Morton St

Leroy St

Clarkson St

560 Wash.

FedEx

GREENWICH ST

HUDSON

Printing House Fitness Racque

WEST HOUSTON

Washington St

9A

St. John's Bldg

UPS Terminal

Por Aut

JOE DiMAGGIO HWY

CANA

Holland Tunnel to NJ

78

PAGE 106

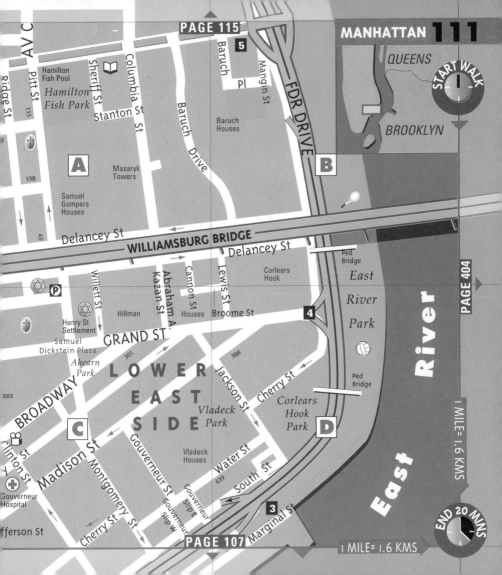

AV C

Ridge St

Pitt St

115

198

45

Sheriff St

Hamilton Fish Pool

Hamilton Fish Park

Stanton St

Columbia St

A

Masaryk Towers

Samuel Gompers Houses

Baruch Pl

Baruch Drive

Mangin St

Baruch Houses

5

PAGE 115

FDR DRIVE

START WALK

QUEENS

BROOKLYN

B

Delancey St

WILLIAMSBURG BRIDGE

Delancey St

Ped Bridge

Corlears Hook

East River Park

PAGE 404

Willett St

P

Abraham A. Kazan St

Cannon St

Hillman Houses

Lewis St

Broome St

4

Henry St Settlement

Samuel Dickstein Plaza

GRAND ST.

Ahearn Park

301

388

L O W E R

E A S T

S I D E

BROADWAY

Jackson St

Vladeck Park

Cherry St

Corlears Hook Park

Ped Bridge

D

ses

C

Clinton St

Madison St

Montgomery St

Vladeck Houses

Water St

639

South St

Gouverneur St

Gouverneur Slip E

Gouverneur Slip W

East River

Gouverneur Hospital

Cherry St

fferson St

3

Marginal St

PAGE 107

1 MILE= 1.6 KMS

1 MILE = 1.6 KMS

END 20 MINS

PAGE 116

W 14 St
VanDam | The Cooler

14 St Ⓐ Ⓒ Ⓔ Ⓛ 14 S
8 Av   Nell's

Mother Bldg Baktun 400
Patisserie Chicago
Lanciani B.L.U.E.S. Jackson
St

MEAT
W 13 St Fressen

MARKET Pastis

Little W 12 St
Florent
LeGans

Bloomfield St

Ⓐ

Gansevoort St

Horatio St

Jane St

9A

W 12 St
Ⓟ
Ⓟ
Bethune St

Westbeth Theater

Bank St

Ⓑ

Jason Croy

Abingdon Sq

Biography Bookshop

White Horse Tavern Ⓟ

Ⓟ

WEST

W 11

Perry St

VILLAGE

Eighty Eight's

Lucille Lortel

Charles La

Charles St **Christopher St** Bedf

W 10 St Ⓓ

Hudson River

51

50

Ⓒ 48

46

45

Christopher St

Weehawken St

Wings The Archive

St Luke's-in-the-Field

Barrow St

Morton St

Leroy S

JOE DIMAGGIO HWY

West St

PAGE 108

PAGE 118

PAGE 113

PAGE 110

L 1 Av

E 14 St
92   Variety Arts   106   Kiel's   213   300   Agrotikon   350   219   444   500
NY Eye & Ear Infirmary   210

E 13 St
100   CSC Rep   142   Airmarket   246   Ukrainian Museum   192   Detour 356   198   448   500

E 12 St
Webster Hall   67   242   Iso   Angelica Kitchen   Brownies   500
FOURTH AV

E 11 St
124   NY Central Art Supply   232   Dancespace at St Mark's Church–in–the–Bowery   158   Izzy Bar Standard   **B**   500 Tompkins Sq

E 10 St
Wanamaker Pl   756   98   St Mark's Book Shop   128   145   Col Legno   2 Av Deli   Theater for the New City   147   Russian & Turkish Baths PS 122

Lafayette Ct   115   Hasaki Around the Clock   Alt.Coffee

E 9 St
746   **6** Astor Pl   138   Jules   134   129   **E A S T**

Tompkins Square Park

Astor Pl   Cooper Union   119   Saint Mark's Pl   Alphabets

Astor Wines & Liquors   McSorley's   Orpheum   Pearl Theater Co   115   **V I L L A G E**

Joe's Pub   THIRD AV
Joseph Papp Public Theater   E 7 St
YWCA   2   Taras Shevchenko Pl   36   48   86   100   University of the Streets   95   Sidewalk Cafe

Stella Adler Conservatory   E 6 St   Pyramid Club

Audobon Society   Village Voice   200   87   E 5 St   Village View Houses   Opaline   74   **A L P H A B**

Stable   Cooper Sq   Ct   NY Theater Workshop   300   59   185   **C I T Y**

Old Merchant's House   E 4 St

Fez   684   44   Bowery Bar   Duo   La MaMa E.T.C.   53   86   130   Little Rickie   138   50   First Houses   180   42   Brisa la Ce

Great   Jones St   Pioneer Theater

Shinbone Al   Jean Cocteau Rep   **C**   E 3 St   Internet Cafe   Two Boots   Context   **D**

670   Bouwerie Lane Theater   19   Bond St   **N O H O**   E 2 St   42   86   Mekka   225

644   Jones Al SoHo B & B   Bleecker St   Amato Opera   Anthology Film Archives   13

Crosby St   **6**   32   Mott St   304   Elizabeth St   BOWERY   Extra Pl   CBGB   E 1 St   Yonah Schimmel   Peretz Sq   Orchard St   Ludlow St   207   Essex St   Mercury Lounge   Norfolk St   Suffolk St   151

Broadway Lafayette St
B D   **F Q**   2 Av   **F**   EAST   HOUSTON ST   208   73

PAGE 110

QUEENS

START WALK

BROOKLYN

East

River

East
River
Park

FDR

6

P

213
700
199

700
198

P
654
740

Szold Pl

650
162
P A
147

394
145
700
448
134

La Plaza
Cultural
Community
Garden

550
126
700

107

Jacob Riis
Houses

Jacob Riis
Houses

90

90
77

60

& B

700
752

Lillian Wald
Houses

301
41

AV C

300
33

360

AV D

B

5

D

ican
Cafe

C

1

1 MILE= 1.6 KMS

Ridge St
139

Pitt St
115

Hamilton
Fish Pool

Hamilton
Fish Park

Sheriff St

Columbia St

Stanton St

Baruch Dr

Baruch
Pl

Baruch

Mangin St

DRIVE

Baruch
Houses

END 20 MINS

1 MILE= 1.6 KMS

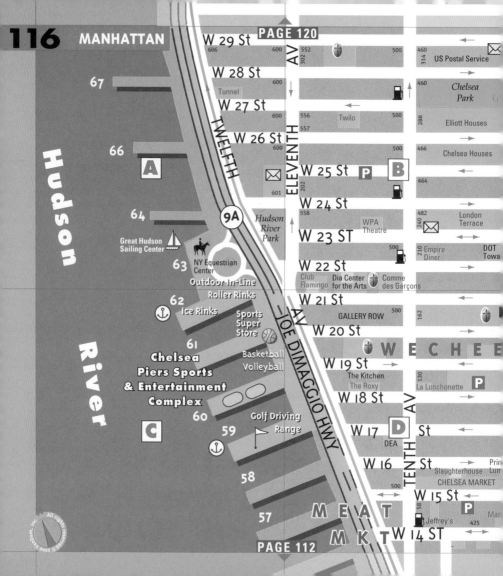

116 MANHATTAN

PAGE 120

W 29 St
606   600

W 28 St
600

Tunnel

W 27 St
600

W 26 St
600

W 25 St   **P**

W 24 St

Hudson River Park

W 23 ST
WPA Theatre

W 22 St

Club Flamingo   Dia Center for the Arts   Comme des Garçons

W 21 St

GALLERY ROW
W 20 St

W E C H E E

Sports Super Store

W 19 St
The Kitchen
The Roxy   La Lunchonette

Basketball Volleyball

W 18 St

Golf Driving Range

W 17   **D**   St
DEA

W 16   St
Slaughterhouse   Prin Lum
CHELSEA MARKET

W 15 St

Jeffrey's   Mar

W 14 ST

552   302   500
US Postal Service

460   314

460   *Chelsea Park*

556   557   500   288   Elliott Houses

466   Chelsea Houses

464

482   London Terrace
240

210   Empire Diner   DOT Towa

162

130   **P**

TENTH AV

ELEVENTH AV

TWELFTH

9A

Great Hudson Sailing Center

NY Equestrian Center

Outdoor In-Line Roller Rinks

Ice Rinks

Chelsea Piers Sports & Entertainment Complex

JOE DIMAGGIO HWY

MEAT MKT

A

B

C

D

67

66

64

63

62

61

60

59

58

57

601
202
558
500
500
500
500
500
58   425

PAGE 112

Hudson River

All rights reserved © 2000 Vandam, Inc.

START WALK

QUEENS

BROOKLYN

Catch A Rising Star

P

Fashion Institute of Technology
FIT - Haft Auditorium
Goodman Resource Center

nn Station uth Houses

American Jewish

1 **9** **28 St**

Currican

Ubu Repertory

F L O W E R

TADA!
28 St Theatre

Brecht Forum

M A R K E T

W 26 St

F A S H I O N

A

High School of Fashion Industries

McBurney YMCA

Chelsea Hotel, Serena

Chelsea Savoy

D I S T R I C T

P

(Fashion Av)

Chelsea Antiques Market

P

SIXTH AV

B

W 24 St

Worth Sq

Madison Square Park

C **E** **23 St**

1 **9** **23 St**

F **23 St**

N **R** **23 St**

St Martin's Press

Flatiron Bldg

C H E L S E A

Bright Food Shop

ter's h

Chelsea Int'l Youth Hostel

Atlantic

Rocking Horse Cafe Mexicano

Dance Theater Workshop

Joyce Theater

Irish Repertory

Gotham Comedy Club Ohm

Cheetah
Caffe Bondi

Periyali

P

BWY

Metronome

E 20 St

F L A T I R O N

P

G Lounge

AV OF THE AMERICAS

Gauntlet

E 19 St

Hackers, Hitters & Hoops v Holtzbrink

Bed Bath & Beyond

E 18 St

1 **9** **18 St**

Judy's Chelsea

C

Actor's Playhouse

Poster America

SEVENTH AV

Barnes & Noble Exec. Offices

D

SoHo Arts Group

NY Foundling Hospital

YIVO Institute for Jewish Research

Disney

B&N Paragon Main

E 17 St

Union Square Cafe

Rebar

uthority Bldg

St Vincent's Cancer Center

ead El Cid

EIGHTH AV

Paul Smith
Mesa Grill

P

E 16 St

Coffee Shop

E 15 St

NY State Armory

P

14 St

E 14

END 20 MINS

14 St **A** **C** **E** **L** **8 Av**

1 **2** **3** **9** **14 St**

6 Av **L**

F **14 St**

PAGE 113

I MILE= 1.6 KMS

1 MILE= 1.6 KMS

PAGE 118

I MILE= 1.6 KMS

PAGE 122
PAGE 117
PAGE 114

E 29 St
W 28 St (N)(R) 28 St · E 28 St · 6 28 St
Mavalli Palace
Jai-Ya Thai
LITTLE INDIA
W 27 St · E 27 St
Reportorio Español
BROADWAY
NY Life · The Jazz Standard
W 26 St · E 26 St
Madison Sq N
Madison Sq Plz
Supreme Appellate Court - First Division
W 25 St · E 25 St
A · Worth Sq
SUNY - College of Optometry
B
Madison Square Park
Tabla · Met Life · 11 Madison Park
Baruch College
New York Comedy
W 24 St · E 24 St
Met Life
School of Visual Arts
F 23 St · W 23 ST · (N)(R) 23 St · E 23 ST · 6 23 St
Baruch College
St Martin's Press
Flatiron Bldg · Bolo · E 22 St
Gramercy Park Hotel
W 22 St
Gotham Comedy Club · Ohm · Centro Fly
Gramercy Park North
W 21 St
Cheetah · Metronome · E 21 St
GRAMERCY PARK
Police Academy
FLATIRON
Periyali · Caffe Bondi
Gramercy Park South
Gramercy Tavern · Patria
W 20 St · E 20 St
Theodore Roosevelt Birthplace
Cabrini
W 19 St · E 19 St
Bed Bath & Beyond
Harvey's · ABC Home & Carpet
W 18 St · E 18 St
Barnes & Noble Exec. Offices
B & N Paragon Main
Barnes & Noble
Guardian Life
Verbena · Inn at Irving Place
IRVING PL · THIRD AV
W 17 St
YIVO Institute · SoHo Arts Group
E 17 St
The NY Film Academy
C · D
NY Foundling Hospital
Union Square Cafe
Union Square Theater
W 16 St · E 16 St
Paul Smith · Mesa Grill
Coffee Shop
Union Square Park
Lee Strasberg Theater Institute
NY Friends Meeting
W 15 St · E 15 St
Daryl Roth · Century
UNION SQ
6 Av · 14 St · W 14 St
Union Sq 14 St · L N R · 4 5 6
E 14 ST
Irving Plaza · Con Edison · 14 St BID
Bambou
F 14 St · W 14 ST
Virgin Superstore
Beth Israel Ambulatory Care
L 3 Av

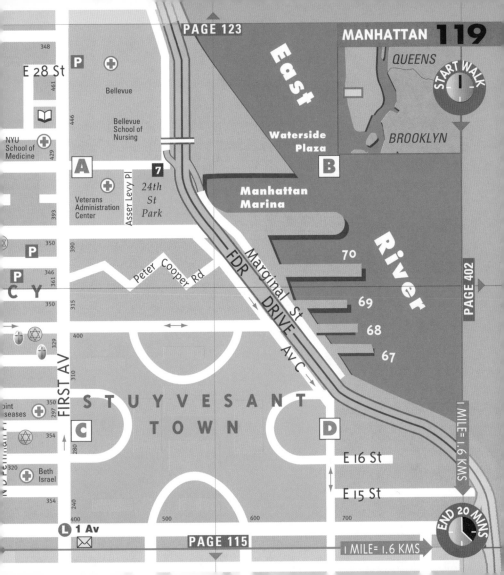

QUEENS

START WALK

BROOKLYN

East

River

E 28 St

348

461

P

Bellevue

446

Bellevue
School of
Nursing

429

NYU
School of
Medicine

Waterside
Plaza

B

A

393

Veterans
Administration
Center

7

24th
St
Park

Asser Levy Pl

Manhattan
Marina

Manhattan
Marina

390

70

P

350

Peter Cooper Rd

FDR

Marginal St

DRIVE

346
361

P

315

69

C Y

350

68

329

400

Av C

67

FIRST AV

310

S T U Y V E S A N T

int
seases

350
297

T O W N

D

354

C

280

E 16 St

320

Beth
Israel

E 15 St

354

240

400

500

600

700

L 1 Av

PAGE 115

PAGE 402

1 MILE = 1.6 KMS

END 20 MINS

1 MILE = 1.6 KMS

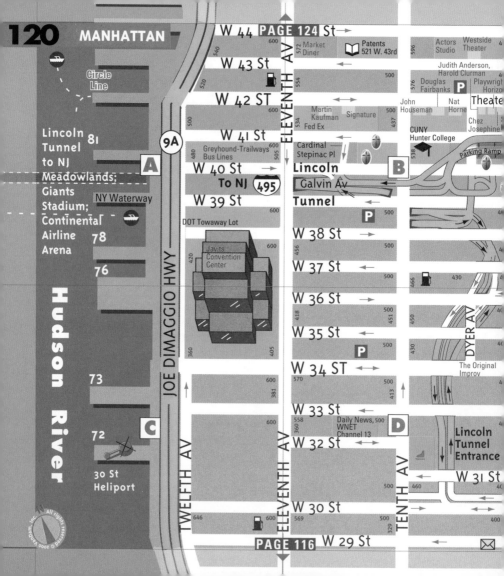

Circle Line

Lincoln Tunnel to NJ Meadowlands; Giants Stadium; Continental Airline Arena

81

78

76

NY Waterway

Hudson River

73

72

C

30 St Heliport

JOE DIMAGGIO HWY

9A

W 44 PAGE 124 St →

W 43 St

W 42 ST

W 41 St

Greyhound-Trailways Bus Lines

W 40 St →

To NJ 495

W 39 St

DOT Towaway Lot

Javits Convention Center

TWELFTH AV

600
540
520
500
480
505

600
500

420
600

360
405

600
381

600

646

A

ELEVENTH AV

Market Diner
572
554

534
Martin Kaufman Fed Ex

Signature

Cardinal Stepinac Pl

Lincoln

Galvin Av

Tunnel

P

W 38 St →

W 37 St ←

W 36 St

W 35 St ←

W 34 ST ←→

P

W 33 St ←

Daily News, WNET Channel 13

W 32 St ←→

W 30 St

W 29 St ←

Patents 521 W. 43rd

500

500

500

437

500

500
456

500
418
451

500
430

500
570
413

500
558
360

500

500
460

500
569
329

400

B

D

Actors Studio
596

Westside Theater

Judith Anderson, Harold Clurman
Douglas Fairbanks
576

John Houseman

Playwright Horizo

Nat Horne

Theate

Chez Josephine

CUNY Hunter College
538

Parking Ramp

DYER AV

466
430

450

430

The Original Improv

Lincoln Tunnel Entrance

TENTH AV

W 31 St

30 St Heliport

PAGE 116

✉

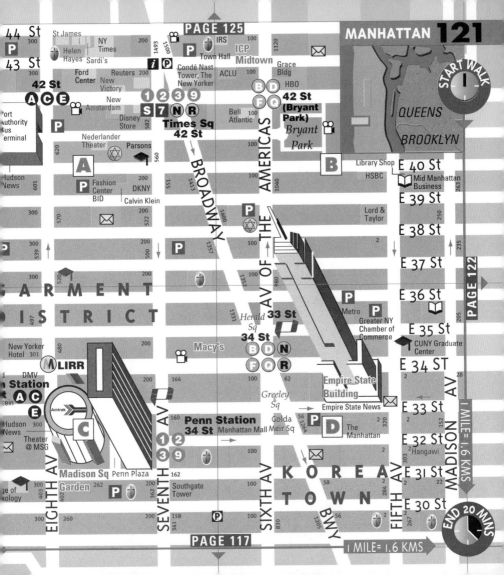

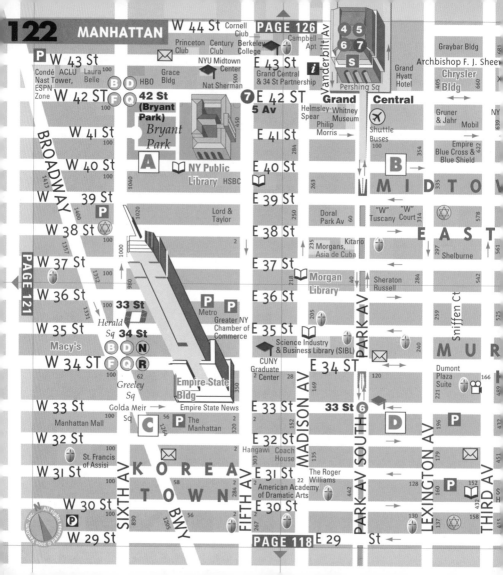

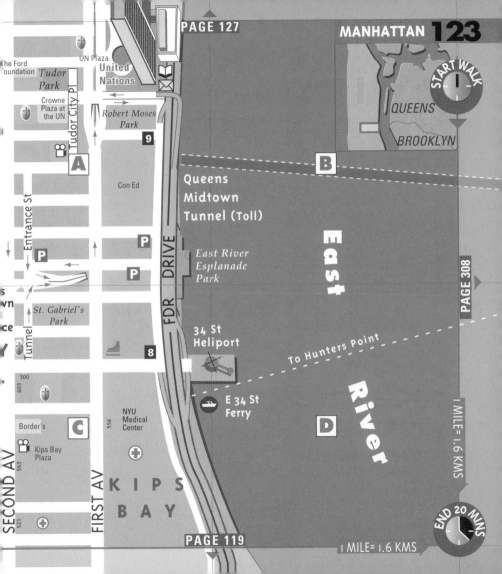

START WALK

QUEENS

BROOKLYN

The Ford Foundation

UN Plaza

Tudor Park

United Nations

Crowne Plaza at the UN

Robert Moses Park

A

9

B

Con Ed

Queens
Midtown
Tunnel (Toll)

East

Entrance St

P

P

P

FDR DRIVE

*East River
Esplanade
Park*

St. Gabriel's Park

Tunnel

8

34 St
Heliport

To Hunters Point

PAGE 308

River

300
603

NYU
Medical
Center

556

E 34 St
Ferry

D

C

Border's

Kips Bay
Plaza

563

I MILE= 1.6 KMS

FIRST AV

SECOND AV

521

K I P S

B A Y

END 20 MINS

I MILE= 1.6 KMS

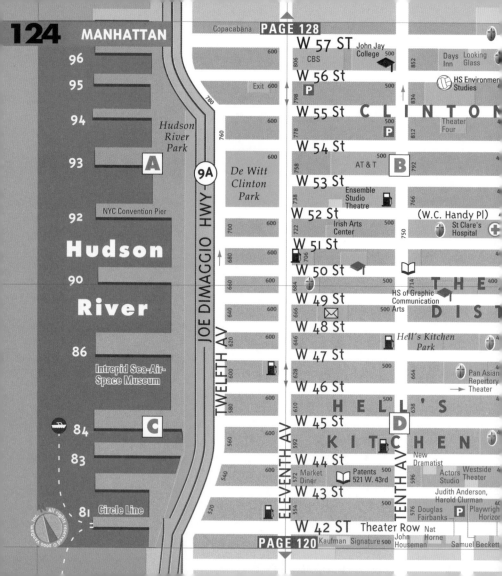

Copacabana

PAGE 128

96
95
94
93
92
90
86
84
83
81

Hudson River Park

9A

JOE DIMAGGIO HWY

NYC Convention Pier

Hudson

River

Intrepid Sea-Air-Space Museum

Circle Line

780
760

De Witt Clinton Park

TWELFTH AV

700
680
660
640
620
600
580
560
540
520

600
600
600
600
600
600
600
600
600
600
600

W 57 ST
W 56 St
W 55 St
W 54 St
W 53 St
W 52 St
W 51 St
W 50 St
W 49 St
W 48 St
W 47 St
W 46 St
W 45 St
W 44 St
W 43 St
W 42 ST

Exit 600

ELEVENTH AV

592
572
554

John Jay College
CBS
806

P
798

CLINTON
778

AT & T
758

Ensemble Studio Theatre
738

Irish Arts Center
722

706
684
666
646
628
610

Market Diner

Patents 521 W. 43rd

Theater Row

PAGE 120 Kaufman Signature 500

852
834
812
792
766
750
714

Days Inn
Looking Glass

HS Environmental Studies

Theater Four

B

(W.C. Handy Pl)
St Clare's Hospital

THE
DIST

HS of Graphic Communication
Arts

Hell's Kitchen Park

Pan Asian Repertory Theater

HELL'S

KITCHEN
638
664

D

New Dramatist
Actors Studio
Westside Theater

Judith Anderson, Harold Clurman

596
576

P
Playwright Horizo

John Horne Houseman
Nat
Douglas Fairbanks
Samuel Beckett

TENTH AV

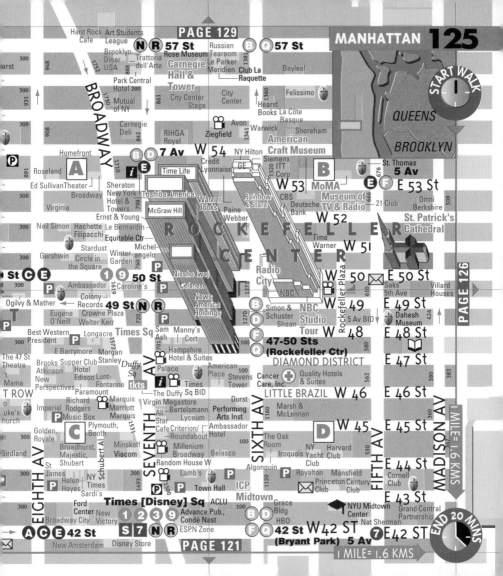

START WALK

QUEENS

BROOKLYN

Hard Rock Cafe
Art Students League
N R 57 St
Rose Museum
Russian Tearoom
Le Parker Meridien
B Q 57 St
Brooklyn Diner USA
Trattoria dell'Arte
Carnegie Hall & Tower
Club La Raquette
Bayleaf
Park Central Hotel 200
Mutual of NY
City Center Stage
City Center
Felissimo
Carnegie Deli
RIHGA Royal
Avon
Ziegfeld
Hearst Books
La Côte Basque
Warwick
Shoreham
NY Hilton
American Craft Museum
Homefront
A
B D 7 Av W 54
Credit Lyonnaise
GE
Siemens ITT Corp
St. Thomas
B 5 Av
Roseland
i
Time Life
W 53
MoMA
E F E 53 St
Ed Sullivan Theater
Sheraton New York Hotel & Towers
Toshiba America
Warner Books
Rainbow & Stars
CBS
Deutsche Bank
Museum of TV & Radio
21 Club
Omni Berkshire
Broadway
Virginia
McGraw Hill
Paine Webber
W 52
St. Patrick's Cathedral
Ernst & Young
Neil Simon
Hachette Filipacchi
Le Bernardin
Equitable Ctr
Time Warner
W 51
Stardust
Michelangelo
Gershwin
Winter Garden
Radio City
W 50
E 50 St
Saks 5th Ave
Villard Houses
St C E
Circle in the Square
1 9 50 St
Nissho Iwa
Celanese
NBC
Ambassador
Colony Records
49 St N R
News America Holdings
Simon & Schuster Shaan
NBC Studio Tour
W 49
E 49 St
5 Av BID
Dahesh Museum
Ogilvy & Mather
Eugene O'Neill
Crowne Plaza
Walter Kerr
Caroline's
W 48
E 48 St
Best Western President
Longacre
Times Sq
Sam Ash
Manny's
Hampshire Hotel & Suites
47-50 Sts (Rockefeller Ctr)
The 47 St Theatre
E Barrymore
Morgan Stanley
Cort
American Place
Stevens Tower
DIAMOND DISTRICT
E 47 St
Mama
Brooks
Atkinson
Supper Club
Edison Hotel
Lunt-Fontanne
Duffy Sq
Palace
Times
Cancer Care, Inc.
Quality Hotels & Suites
New Perspectives
Paramount
Richard Rodgers
Marquis
Marriott Marquis
tkts
The Duffy Sq BID
Virgin Megastore
Durst
LITTLE BRAZIL W 46
Marsh & McLennan
Imperial
Music Box
Minskoff
Viacom
All-Bertelsmann Lyceum
Performing Arts Inst
W 45
E 45 St
Luke's church
Golden, Royale
Plymouth, Booth
Broadhurst, Majestic, Shubert
All-Star Cafe
Criterion/ Roundabout
Millenium Broadway
Ambassador Hotel
Belasco
The Oak Room
D
NY Yacht Club
Harvard Club
E 44 St
Cornell Club
Birdland
St James
Random House W
Lamb's
Iroquois
Algonquin
Royalton
Mansfield
Princeton Club
Century Club
E 43 St
Helen Hayes
NY Times
Sardi's
Town Hall
ICP
Midtown
Grace Bldg
NYU Midtown Center
Nat Sherman
Grand Central Partnership
Times [Disney Sq]
ACLU
HBO
Ford Center
New Victory
Broadway City
1 2 3 9
Advance Pub., Condé Nast
B D
F Q
42 St W 42 ST
7 E 42 St
A C E 42 St
S 7
N R
ESPN Zone
(Bryant Park) 5 Av
New Amsterdam
Disney Store

BROADWAY

SEVENTH AV

EIGHTH AV

SIXTH AV

FIFTH AV

MADISON AV

R O C K E F E L L E R C E N T E R

PAGE 126

1 MILE = 1.6 KMS

END 20 MINS

1 MILE = 1.6 KMS

E 57 ST

E 56 St

P

E 55 St

E 54 St

11

E 53 St

Lipstick
Bldg

A

Casa Brasil

(Swing St)

B

Av/3 Av

T U R T L E

ckwick
ms

B

Zarela

E 51 St

B A Y

E 50 St

y & Grill

FIRST AV

Beekman
Tower

hin Chin

E 49 St

Mitchell Pl

E 48 St

*MacArthur
Plaza*

10

P
Japan
Society

N

E 47 St

Peace
Garden

anderbilt
MCA

*Dag Hammar-
skjold Plz*

Peace
Statue

Sparks

E 46 St

Marichu

SECOND AV

U.N. Plaza

C E 45 St

Palm

Palm
Too

Regal
UN Plaza
Hotel

P

E 44 St

E 43   St

D

Tudor City Pl

Ford
Foundation

*Tudor
Park*

United
Nations

ox

Pfizer

Crowne Plaza
at the UN

E 42 ST

Sutton Pl S

E 52 St

*Peter
Detmold
Park*

Beekman Pl

FDR DRIVE

B

START WALK

QUEENS

BROOKLYN

River

PAGE 308

East

D

1 MILE= 1.6 KMS

END 20 MINS

1 MILE= 1.6 KMS

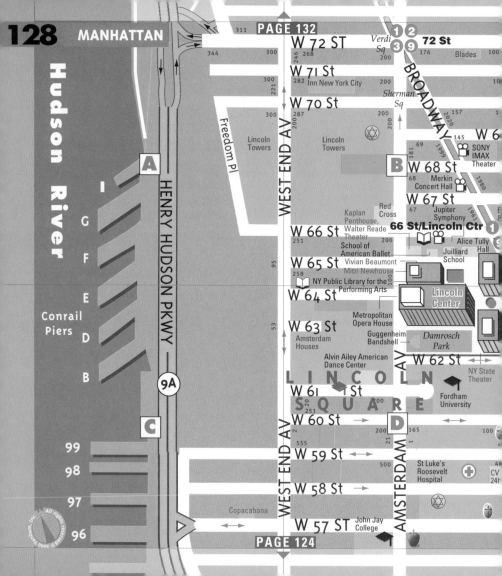

311   PAGE 132

Hudson River

HENRY HUDSON PKWY

Conrail Piers

Freedom Pl

WEST END AV

AMSTERDAM AV

BROADWAY

W 72 ST

Verdi Sq

72 St

Blades

W 71 ST

282 Inn New York City

Sherman Sq

W 70 ST

Lincoln Towers

Lincoln Towers

W 6

SONY IMAX Theater

W 68 ST

Merkin Concert Hall

W 67 ST

Jupiter Symphony

Kaplan Penthouse, Walter Reade Theater

Red Cross

66 St/Lincoln Ctr

W 66 ST

Alice Tully Hall

School of American Ballet

Juilliard School

W 65 ST

Vivian Beaumont

Mitzi Newhouse

NY Public Library for the Performing Arts

W 64 ST

Lincoln Center

Metropolitan Opera House

W 63 ST

Amsterdam Houses

Guggenheim Bandshell

Damrosch Park

Alvin Ailey American Dance Center

W 62 ST

LINCOLN

NY State Theater

W 61 St

SQUARE

Fordham University

W 60 St

W 59 St

St Luke's Roosevelt Hospital

CV 24H

W 58 St

Copacabana

W 57 ST

John Jay College

PAGE 124

99

98

97

96

9A

PAGE 134
PAGE 129
PAGE 126

Inventors' Gate

Terrace Drive

Naumburg Bandshell

Rumsey Playfield

Singer Lilac Walk

Mineral Springs Concessions

Roller Skating

The Mall

Literary Walk

East Drive

A

C e n t r a l

P a r k

Sheep Meadows

Balto

65 St Transverse

Ballplayers Houses

The Carousel

Heckscher Ballfields

The Dairy

Chess & Checkers House

Central Park Zoo Wildlife Conservation Center

Children's Gate

The Arsenal

Heckscher Playground

Wollman Mem. Rink

Center Drive

Umpire Rock

Puppet House

Gapstow Bridge

Hallett Nature Sanctuary

Cop Cot

C

The Pond

Scholars' Gate

9 W 57

Artisans' Gate

Artists' Gate

CENTRAL PARK SOUTH

5 Av
N R

Grand Army Plz

Pulitzer Fountain

Essex House Les Célébrités

Inter Continental

St Moritz

The Plaza Hotel

W 58 ST

Petrossian

Wyndham

Bergdorf Goodman

Van Cleef & Arpels

W 57 ST

B Q 57 St

Warner Bros Studio Store

FAO Schwarz

Madison Av BID

E 72 ST

E 71 St
Frick Collection

E 70 St

E 69 St

E 68 St

E 67 St

E 66 St

E 65 St

E 64 St

E 63 St

E 62 St

E 61 St

E 60 St

E 59 St

E 58 St

E 57 ST

Ralph Lauren

Asia Society

Paul Mellon House

Spanish Institute

Union Club

The Sylvia & Danny Kaye Plathouse

NY Sch Interior

68 S
Hun
6 Coll

The Americas Society

B

Council on Foreign Relations

Hunter College

7th Regiment Armory

Armani

Sarah D. Roosevelt Mem House

China House Gallery/ China Inst. in America

India House

Chase Manhattan

Daniel

Plaza Athénée

Berwind Mansion

Museum of American Illustration

Jo Jo
Lexington

Post House

The Lowell

The MAFCO

Circus

B

Helmsley-Carlton House

Sherry Lehmann

The Regency

Feinstein

Trum

C

The Pierre

Barneys NY

Loew's

DK

Aureole

Delmonico

140

N R Lexi

Bloomingd

Calvin Klein

Crate & Barrel

French Institute

Florence Gould Hall

4 5 6 5

Sherry-Netherland

Estée Lauder

Vidal Sassoon

G M Bldg

Au Bar

Argosy

Le Col

The Four Seasons

Borders

Hammacher Schlemmer

NikeTown Tourneau

FIFTH AV

MADISON AV

LEXINGTON AV

PARK AV

7 AV

6 AV

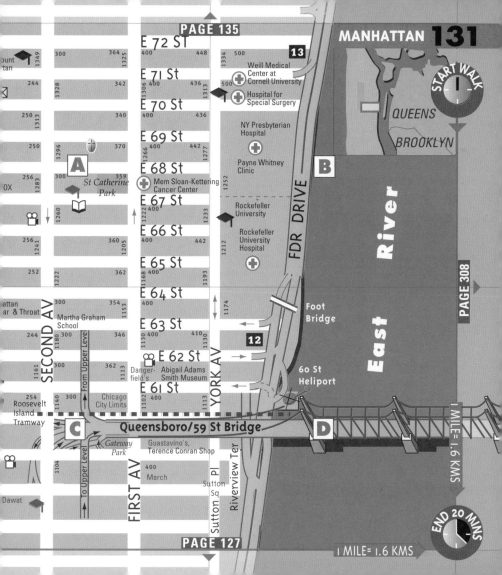

START WALK

QUEENS

BROOKLYN

E 72 ST

E 71 ST

E 70 ST

E 69 ST

E 68 ST

E 67 ST

E 66 ST

E 65 ST

E 64 ST

E 63 ST

E 62 ST

E 61 ST

13

Weill Medical Center at Cornell University

Hospital for Special Surgery

NY Presbyterian Hospital

Payne Whitney Clinic

B

Rockefeller University

Rockefeller University Hospital

Mem Sloan-Kettering Cancer Center

St Catherine Park

A

C

D

FDR DRIVE

East River

Foot Bridge

60 St Heliport

12

SECOND AV

YORK AV

FIRST AV

Martha Graham School

Danger-field's

Abigail Adams Smith Museum

Chicago City Limits

Roosevelt Island Tramway

attan ar & Throat

Gateway Park

Guastavino's, Terence Conran Shop

Queensboro/59 St Bridge

March

Sutton Pl

Sutton Sq

Riverview Ter

Dawat

From Upper Level

To Upper Level

1 MILE= 1.6 KMS

END 20 MINS

1 MILE= 1.6 KMS

300 364 400 448 1334 500
1349 1325
244 342 1328 1306 436 1313
250 340 1313 400 436
250 370 1296 1266 400 442 1277
256 359 1283 300 400 1252
1260 1222 400 1233
256 360 1241 1205 400 442 1212
252 362 1222 1168 400 1193
300 354 1174 400 1153
244 300 346 1180 1130 400 410 1130
300 362 1161 1113 400
254 300 1140 1102 400 1113
1104 400 1266

OX

PAGE 136

Hudson River

Boat Basin

HENRY HUDSON PKWY

Riverside Drive

Riverside Park

WEST END AV

BROADWAY

AMSTERDAM AV

9A

A

B

C

D

UPPER WEST SIDE

W 86 St — 1 9 86 St
Barney Greengrass

W 85 St
The Red House

W 84 St
(Edgar Allan Poe St)
Mannes College of Music

W 83 St
Mt. Tom Edgar Allan Poe's Perch
Barnes & Noble
Children's Museum of Manhattan

W 82 St
EJ'S Luncheonette

W 81 St
Zabar's
Cafe Con Leche
Monsoon

W 80 St

W 79 ST — 1 9 79 St

W 78 St
Stand-Up NY
Upper West Side B & B

W 77 St
Promenade Theater

W 76 St

W 75 St
Citarella
Fairway
Beacon Hotel
Shark Bar

W 74 St
Beacon Theater

W 73 St
Islamic Cultural Center of NY

W 72 ST — Verdi Sq — 1 2 3 9 72 St
Blades

PAGE 128

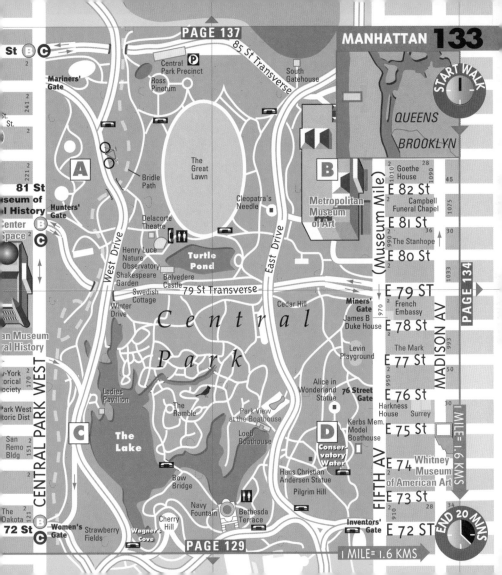

START WALK

QUEENS

BROOKLYN

St B C

Mariners' Gate

Central Park Precinct

Ross Pinetum

85 St Transverse

South Gatehouse

81 St
useum of
l History

enter
pace

A

Hunters' Gate

Bridle Path

The Great Lawn

Delacorte Theatre

Henry Luce Nature Observatory

Shakespeare Garden

Belvedere Castle

Swedish Cottage

Winter Drive

West Drive

Turtle Pond

79 St Transverse

Cleopatra's Needle

B

Metropolitan Museum of Art

(Museum Mile)

East Drive

Goethe House

E 82 St

Campbell Funeral Chapel

E 81 St

The Stanhope

E 80 St

E 79 ST

French Embassy

an Museum
ral History

v-York
orical
ociety

ark West
toric Dist

San Remo Bldg

The Dakota

72 St

CENTRAL PARK WEST

Ladies Pavillion

The Ramble

C

The Lake

Bow Bridge

Cherry Hill

Women's Gate

Strawberry Fields

Wagner's Cove

Central Park

Cedar Hill

Miners' Gate

James B Duke House

E 78 St

The Mark

Levin Playground

E 77 St

Alice in Wonderland Statue

76 Street Gate

E 76 St

Park View at the Boathouse

Loeb Boathouse

Harkness House

Surrey

Kerbs Mem. Model Boathouse

E 75 St

D

Conservatory Water

Hans Christian Andersen Statue

Pilgrim Hill

E 74 St

Whitney Museum of American Art

E 73 St

Navy Fountain

Bethesda Terrace

Inventors' Gate

E 72 ST

END 20 MINS

MADISON AV

FIFTH AV

PAGE 134

1 MILE = 1.6 KMS

1 MILE = 1.6 KMS

85 St Transverse

PAGE 138

Central Park Precinct
Ross Pinetum
South Gatehouse

The Great Lawn

A

Bridle Path

Delacorte Theatre

Cleopatra's Needle

Henry Luce Nature Observatory
Shakespeare Garden
Swedish Cottage
Winter Drive

Belvedere Castle

Turtle Pond

79 St Transverse

Cedar Hill

C e n t r a l

P a r k

Ladies Pavillion

The Ramble

C

Parkview at the Boathouse
Loeb Boathouse

Alice in Wonderland Statue

76 Street Gate

Kerbs Mem. Model Boathouse

Conservatory Water

Hans Christian Andersen Statue

The Lake

Bow Bridge

Pilgrim Hill

Bethesda Fountain
Bethesda Terrace

Cherry Hill

Wagner's Cove

Ancient Playground

Metropolitan Museum of Art

Goethe House

Frank E. Campbell Funeral Chapel

The Stanhope

Miners' Gate

French Embassy

James B Duke House

The Mark

Levin Playground

The Carlyle
Cafe Carlyle w/Bemelmans Bar

Daniel
Harkness House Surrey

Inventors' Gate

Madison Av BID
Ralph Lauren

(Museum Mile)

E 86 ST

E 85 St

E 84 St

E 83 St

E 82 St

E 81 St

E 80 St

E 79 ST

E 78 St

E 77 St

E 76 St

E 75 St

E 74 St

E 73 St

E 72 St

Church of St. Ignatius Loyola

B

Lewis Spencer Morris House

Junior League of the City of N

Lenox Hill Hospital

D Whitney Museum of American Art

FIFTH AV

MADISON AV

PARK AV

77 S

8

4

1165 48 78 100 128
1030 38 74 1000 132
35 1248
1109 132
1010 28 72 132
1090 45 960 1210
1075 72 100 136
941
2 36 30 64 126
The Stanhope 916 1166
2 40 76 142
1033 903 1030
970 82 100 142
39 878 1120
993 72 138
863
950 50 86 100
840
930 58
821
940 100 136
1036
921 30 58 142
910 34 68 140
760 1004
2 84 100 140

PAGE 133

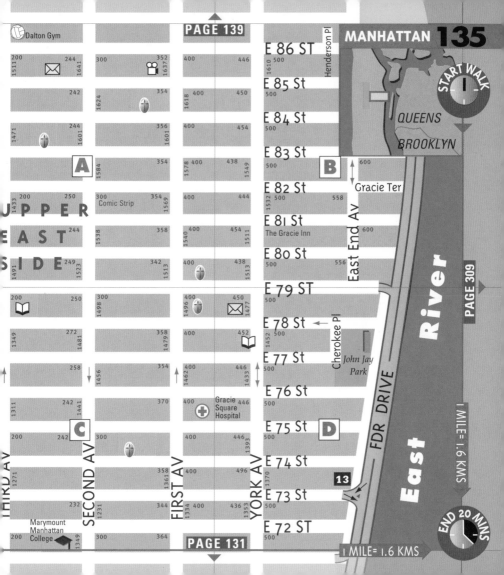

Dalton Gym

START WALK

QUEENS

BROOKLYN

E 86 ST

E 85 St

E 84 St

E 83 St

E 82 St

Gracie Ter

E 81 St
The Gracie Inn

E 80 St

E 79 ST

E 78 St

Cherokee Pl

E 77 St

John Jay Park

E 76 St

E 75 St

E 74 St

E 73 St

E 72 ST

UPPER EAST SIDE

Comic Strip

Gracie Square Hospital

Marymount Manhattan College

THIRD AV

SECOND AV

FIRST AV

YORK AV

East End Av

Henderson Pl

FDR DRIVE

East River

1 MILE= 1.6 KMS

13

END 20 MINS

A

B

C

D

PAGE 309

PAGE 131

1511 1641 200 244
1624 300 352 1637
400 446 1610 500
242 354 1618 400 450
1471 1601 244 356 400 454
1584 354 1578 400 438 1549
1433 200 250 300 354 1569 400 444 1532 500 558
244 1538 358 1540 400 454 1511
1491 249 1523 342 1513 400 438 1513 500 556
200 250 300 1498 400 1496 500 450 1477
1349 272 1481 358 1479 400 452 1452 500
258 1456 354 1462 400 446 1433 500
1311 242 1441 370 400 446 500
200 242 300 1393
1271 358 13618 400 496 1370 500
232 344 1231 400 436 1353 500 1334
200 300 364 1349 500

1 MILE= 1.6 KMS

← PAGE 140

W 99 St

Park West

W 98 St

Village

W 97 St

W 96 ST

① ② ③ ⑨ 96 St

The Latin Quarter

B

W 95 St

← Thalia Theater

Pomander Walk

Symphony Space

UPPER

W 94 St

Joan of Arc Statue

WEST

W 93 St

SIDE

W 92 St

Duane Reade 24hr

Trinity House

W 91 St

W 90 St

(Henry J Brow

Claremont Riding Academy

WEST END AV

BROADWAY

AMSTERDAM AV

W 89 St

Soldiers & Sailors Monument

W 88 St

W 87 St

D

Barney Greengrass

HENRY HUDSON PKWY

W 86 ST

① ⑨ 86 St

C

W 85 St

The Red House

Mannes College of Mus

Riverside

W 84 St

(Edgar Allan Poe St)

Hudson River

Riverside Park

A

9A

Drive

PAGE 132

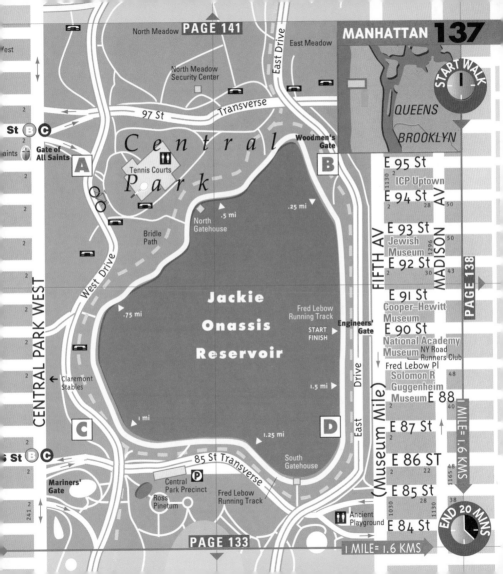

North Meadow

PAGE 141

East Drive

East Meadow

START WALK
1

QUEENS

BROOKLYN

North Meadow
Security Center

West

St B C

aints

Gate of
All Saints

97 St

Transverse

A

Central

Park

Tennis Courts

Woodmen's
Gate

B

E 95 St

1130 ICP Uptown

E 94 St

2   28   50

E 93 St

Jewish   50
Museum 1296

E 92 St

2   30   43

PAGE 138

.5 mi

.25 mi

North
Gatehouse

Bridle
Path

West Drive

E 91 St

Cooper–Hewitt
Museum

E 90 St

National Academy
Museum NY Road
           Runners Club

Fred Lebow Pl

Solomon R   48
Guggenheim
Museum E 88

.75 mi

Jackie

Onassis

Reservoir

Fred Lebow
Running Track

START
FINISH

Engineers'
Gate

Claremont
Stables

CENTRAL PARK WEST

C

1 mi

1.5 mi

East Drive

40

1 MILE = 1.6 KMS

D

E 87 St
2

s St B C

1.25 mi

E 86 ST

2   22

3151

Mariners'
Gate

241 2

85 St Transverse

South
Gatehouse

E 85 St

1030   28   1130

Central
Park Precinct

Ross
Pinetum

P

Fred Lebow
Running Track

(Museum Mile)

FIFTH AV

MADISON AV

38

END 20 MINS

Ancient
Playground

E 84 St

PAGE 133

1 MILE = 1.6 KMS

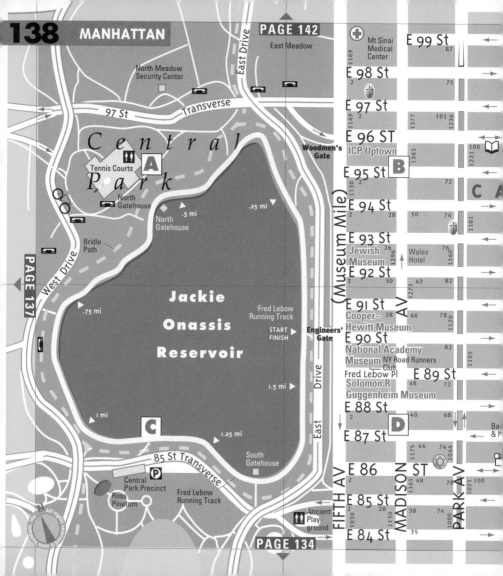

PAGE 142
East Meadow

North Meadow
Security Center

97 St Transverse

Central

Tennis Courts A

Park

North
Gatehouse

North
Gatehouse

.5 mi

.25 mi

Bridle
Path

West Drive

East Drive

Jackie

Onassis

Reservoir

.75 mi

Fred Lebow
Running Track

START
FINISH

1.5 mi

Engineers'
Gate

1 mi

C

1.25 mi

85 St Transverse

South
Gatehouse

Central
Park Precinct

P

Ross
Pinetum

Fred Lebow
Running Track

Ancient
Play-
ground

PAGE 134

PAGE 137

Mt Sinai
Medical
Center

E 99 St
87
1169

E 98 St
75

E 97 St
1149   1377   101   1236

E 96 ST
ICP Uptown

Woodmen's
Gate

E 95 St
1130   2   1361   72   1221   100

B

E 94 St
2   28   50   76   1181

(Museum Mile)

E 93 St
Jewish
Museum   26   1296   Wales
Hotel   76   1160

E 92 St
30   43   82   1273

E 91 St
Cooper–
Hewitt Museum   28   46   78   1120

E 90 St
National Academy
Museum   NY Road Runners
Club   82   1105

Fred Lebow Pl   E 89 St
Solomon R
Guggenheim Museum   48   72

E 88 St
2   40   68

D

E 87 St
2   1175   44   74   1046

E 86   ST
MADISON   1165   48   78   1021   100

FIFTH AV   E 85 St
1030   2   28   1130   38   74   1000

E 84 St
35

PARK AV

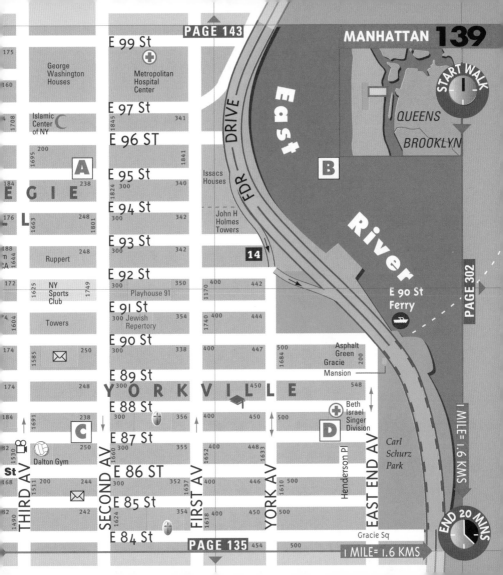

START WALK

QUEENS

BROOKLYN

East

River

B

14

E 99 St

George
Washington
Houses

Metropolitan
Hospital
Center

Islamic
Center
of NY

175

160

1708

E 97 St

341

1845

E 96 ST

200

1695

1841

A

E G I E

238

184

1824

E 95 St

300

340

Issacs
Houses

FDR — DRIVE

1663

L

176

248

1801

E 94 St

300

342

John H
Holmes
Towers

1644

188

A

Ruppert

248

E 93 St

300

342

1625

172

NY
Sports
Club

1749

350

E 92 St

400

442

Playhouse 91

1170

1604

4

Towers

E 91 St

300 Jewish
     Repertory

354

1740

400

444

E 90 St

300

338

400

447

E 90 St
Ferry

PAGE 302

1585

174

⊠

250

1684

500

Asphalt
Green
Gracie
Mansion

200

E 89 St

174

248

Y O R K V I L L E

300

450

548

E 88 St

184

1691

238

300

356

400

450

500

Beth
Israel
Singer
Division

C

E 87 St

250

300

355

1652

400

448

1633

D

82

1530

⊠

Dalton Gym

St

E 86 ST

168

1511

200

244

300

352

1637

400

446

1610

500

1 MILE= 1.6 KMS

THIRD AV

1490

82

242

SECOND AV

1624

E 85 St

354

FIRST AV

1618

400

450

YORK AV

500

Carl
Schurz
Park

Henderson Pl

EAST END AV

END 20 MINS

E 84 St

454

500

Gracie Sq

1 MILE= 1.6 KMS

PAGE 144

W 110 ST ① ⑨ CATHEDRAL PKWY ← Cathedra

501 419

Cathedral Pkwy (110 St)

224 995

Hudson

River

9A

A

HENRY HUDSON PKWY

Riverside Park

Riverside Drive

C

W 109 St
300
354 Bloomingdale
House Of Music 2799
261 200 174 10

W 108 St
Nicholas Roerich Museum
247 200 196 10

W 107 St
328 300
340
B 174

Straus Park

W 106 St
338 300
919
256 Smoke 200 (Duke Ellington B
160 10

W 105 St
327 300
318
258
916 200 U P P E
176 10

W E S T

W 104 St
324 Equity Library
Theatre 303
266 234 200
235 S I D E
10

W 103 St
324 ① ⑨ 103 St
296 916
303 254 235 216 200 203
NY International American Youth Hostel (AYH)

W 102 St
316 303
879
309
254 216 200
229
Frederick Douglas

W 101 St
316 300
280
244 216 200
916 Trinity Theatre
AMSTERDAM AV

W 100 St
Men of Fire Memorial 300
799
256 244 243 216 200
168 Park P
D 10

W 99 St
315 300
262 230 200
West
243

WEST END AV

BROADWAY

W 98 St
321 300
777
300 230 200
West
241 Village

W 97 St
321 300
300 230 200
178 10

W 96 ST ← → ① ② ③ ⑨ 96 St
738 275 214 200 731
2541

PAGE 136

©2000 Vandam, INC. All rights reserved

PAGE 146

Central Park N (110 St)

CENTRAL PARK NORTH

Ellington Circle

Douglass Circle

235
348

East

Warriors' Gate

Farmers' Gate

Charles A. Dana Discovery Center

Pioneers' Gate

W 109 St
22 2

Blockhouse No. 1

Duck Island

Harlem Meer

E 109 St
2 28

Drive

W 108
18 2

Nutter's Battery Site

E 108 St

61

McGowan's Pass

W 107
20 2

A

Lasker Rink & Pool

Fort Clinton Site

E 107 St
2 48

63

B

W 106
42 2

Huddlestone Bridge

Fort Fish Site

E 106 ST
260
1550

51

Great Hill

E 105 St

W 105 St
2

The Mount

Conservatory Garden

53

El Museo del Barrio

W 104 St
20 2

The Loch

Ravine

E 104 St
Museum of the City of N

PAGE 141

103 St B C
18

E 103 St

NY Academy of Medicine

W 102 St
20 2

Central

Girls' Gate

E 102 St
22

W 101 St
20 2

Park

East Drive

E 101 St
20

W 100 St
2

The Pool

Bridle Path

1189

Mt Sinai Medical Center

W 99 St
2

C

North Meadow

D

East Meadow

1169

W 98 St
2

North Meadow Security Center

E 98 St
2

W 97 St
2

97 St Transverse

E 97 St
2

1149

96 St
B C
2

Woodmen's Gate

E 96 ST
2

Tennis Courts

PAGE 138

MANHATTAN AV

CENTRAL PARK WEST

FIFTH AV (Museum Mile)

MADISON AV

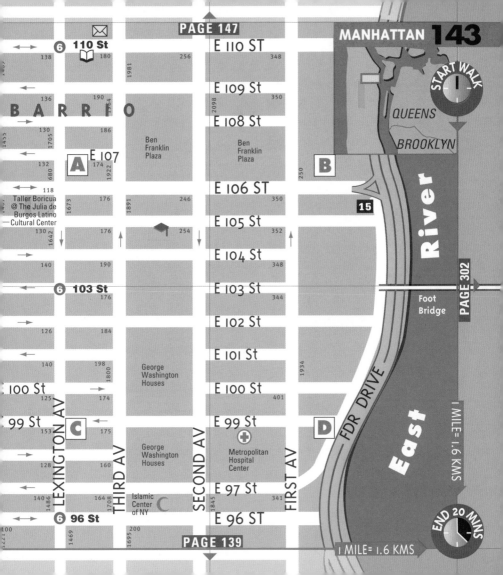

PAGE 147

START WALK

QUEENS

BROOKLYN

⊠

6 **110 St**
138   180

B A R R I O

136   190   1981
1455   1984

130   186   256
1705

A E 107
132   174   1922
680   1891

118
Taller Boricua
@ The Julia de
Burgos Latino
—Cultural Center
130   176   246
1642   1673

176   254
176

140   190

6 **103 St**
176

126   184

140   198
1800

100 St
125   174

99 St
153   175

128   160

C LEXINGTON AV   THIRD AV

140   164
1486   1708

6 **96 St**
200   1695
1469

100
1421

Ben
Franklin
Plaza

Ben
Franklin
Plaza

250   **B**

E 110 ST   348

E 109 St   350
2098

E 108 St

E 106 ST   350   **15**

E 105 St   352

E 104 St   348

E 103 St   344   Foot
Bridge

E 102 St

E 101 St

E 100 St   401

George
Washington
Houses

E 99 St   **D**

SECOND AV   FIRST AV

Metropolitan
Hospital
Center

George
Washington
Houses

Islamic
Center
of NY

E 97 St   341
1845

E 96 ST
200

1934

River

East

FDR DRIVE

1 MILE = 1.6 KMS

PAGE 302

END 20 MINS

1 MILE= 1.6 KMS

PAGE 139

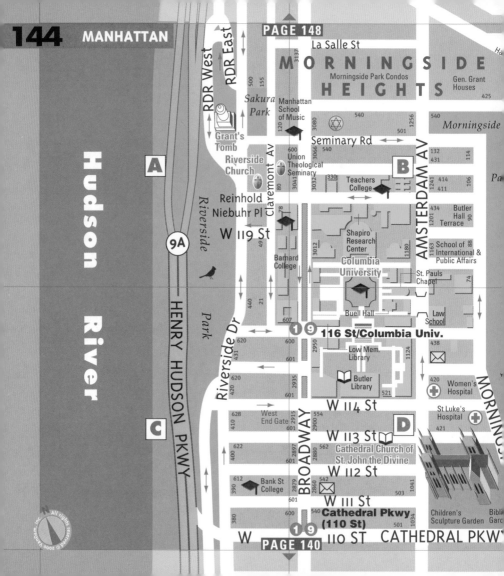

PAGE 148

La Salle St

MORNINGSIDE

Morningside Park Condos

Gen. Grant Houses

HEIGHTS

Sakura Park

Manhattan School of Music

Morningside

Grant's Tomb

Seminary Rd

Riverside Church

Union Theological Seminary

A

B

AMSTERDAM AV

Reinhold Niebuhr Pl

Teachers College

W 119 St

Butler Hall Terrace

Shapiro Research Center

9A

Barnard College

Columbia University

School of International & Public Affairs

St. Pauls Chapel

Riverside Dr

Buell Hall

Law School

HENRY HUDSON PKWY

Hudson River

Park

1 **9** 116 St/Columbia Univ.

Low Mem. Library

Butler Library

Women's Hospital

C

W 114 St

West End Gate

BROADWAY

St Luke's Hospital

W 113 St

D

Cathedral Church of St. John the Divine

Bank St College

W 112 St

MORNINGS

W 111 St

Children's Sculpture Garden

Bibl Gard

1 **9** Cathedral Pkwy (110 St)

W PAGE 140
110 ST CATHEDRAL PKW

PAGE 149

B ✉ 351
D 125 St

W 125 ST

PAGE 149

2 3 125 St

Studio Museum in Harlem

New Heritage Repertory

Lenox Lounge

THE BRONX

START WALK

W 124 St

Mt Morris Pk West

QUEENS

A

B

Marcus Garvey Memorial Park

SAINT NICHOLAS AV

(Adam Clayton Powell Jr Blvd)

A. Philip Randolph Sq

B C 116 St

2 3 116 St

FREDERICK DOUGLASS BLVD

African-American Wax Museum

W 114 St

SEVENTH AV

Martin Luther King Jr Towers

Sen R. Taft Houses

FIFTH AV

MADISON AV

C St

W 113 St

W 112 St

LENOX AV

D

Arthur A Schomburg Plaza

W 111 St

Cathedral Pkwy (110 St)

Central Park North (110 St)

1 MILE = 1.6 KMS

Douglass

B C CENTRAL PARK Circle

PAGE 141

2 3 NORTH

Ellington Circle

END 20 MINS

1 MILE= 1.6 KMS

PAGE 146

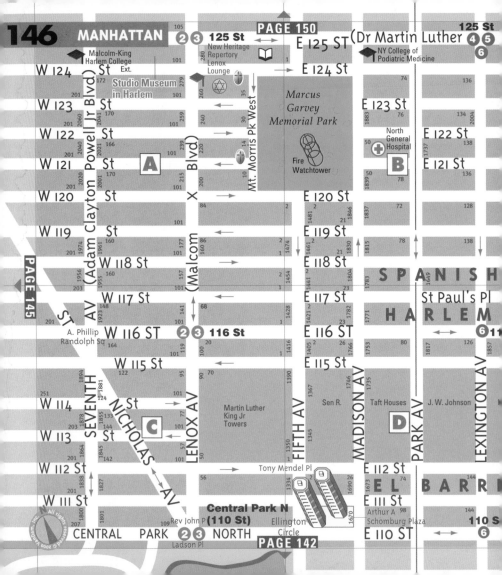

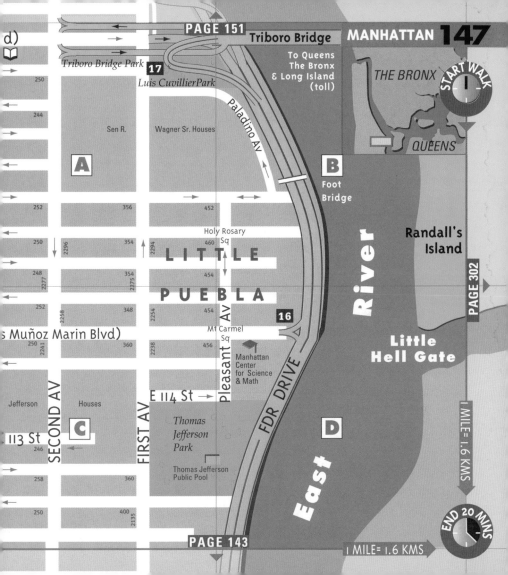

To Queens
The Bronx
& Long Island
(toll)

THE BRONX

START WALK

Triboro Bridge Park **17**

Luis Cuvillier Park

QUEENS

250

244

Sen R.

Wagner Sr. Houses

Paladino Av

A

B

Foot
Bridge

Randall's
Island

252

356

452

River

250

2296

354

Holy Rosary
Sq

460

L I T T L E

PAGE 302

248

2277

354

2375

454

P U E B L A

Little
Hell Gate

252

2258

348

454

16

s Muñoz Marin Blvd)

250

2241

360

2238

456

Mt Carmel
Sq

Manhattan
Center
for Science
& Math

1 MILE= 1.6 KMS

Jefferson

SECOND AV

Houses

FIRST AV

E 114 St

Pleasant Av

FDR DRIVE

D

113 St

C

246

Thomas
Jefferson
Park

Thomas Jefferson
Public Pool

258

360

2135

East

END 20 MINS

250

400

1 MILE= 1.6 KMS

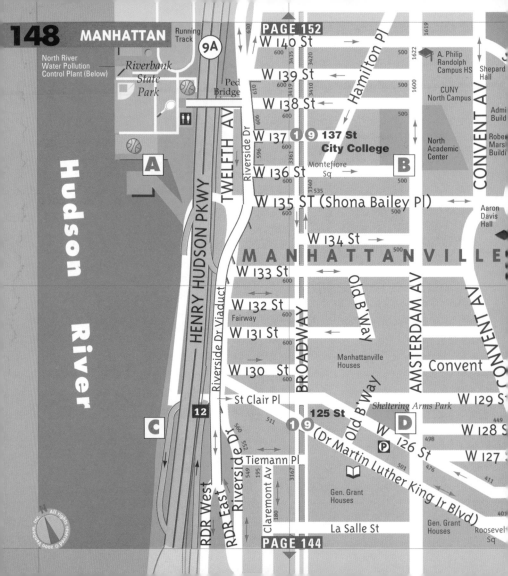

Running Track

9A

North River
Water Pollution
Control Plant (Below)

Riverbank
State
Park

Ped
Bridge

PAGE 152

1619

W 140 St
600
3435   3420

500

1622

A. Philip
Randolph
Campus HS

Shepard
Hall

W 139 St
600
3419   3410

500

1600

CUNY
North Campus

Admi
Build

W 138 St
606
600
3410

500

Robe
Mars
Buildi

A

W 137 St   1 9 137 St
596
600
3361   City College

North
Academic
Center

CONVENT AV

W 136 St
600
3340
535

Montefiore
Sq

500

B

W 135 ST (Shona Bailey Pl)
600
500

Aaron
Davis
Hall

W 134 St
500

M A N H A T T A N V I L L E

TWELFTH AV

Riverside Dr

W 133 St
600

W 132 St
Fairway
600

Old B'Way

BROADWAY

AMSTERDAM AV

W 131 St
600

Manhattanville
Houses

Convent

CONVENT A

HENRY HUDSON PKWY

W 130 St
600

W 129 S

St Clair Pl

Old B'Way

Sheltering Arms Park

D

W 128 S

449

Hudson
River

C

12

Riverside Dr Viaduct

511

1 9 125 St

W 126 St

498

P

W 127

501

476

411

RDR West

RDR East

Riverside Dr

555
595

Tiemann Pl

549   195

(Dr Martin Luther King Jr Blvd)

Gen. Grant
Houses

Claremont Av

180

3167

La Salle St

Gen. Grant
Houses

407

Roosevel
Sq

PAGE 144

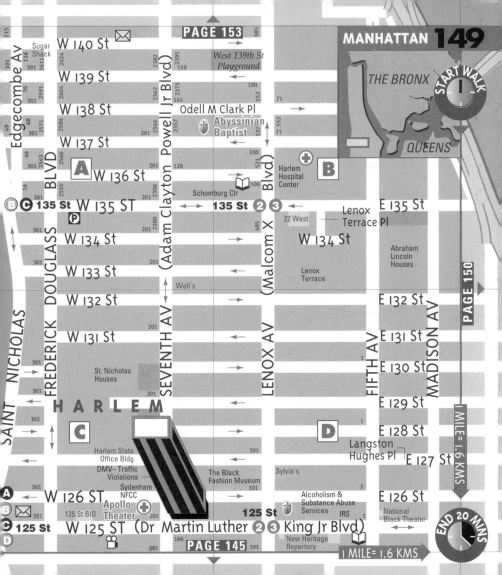

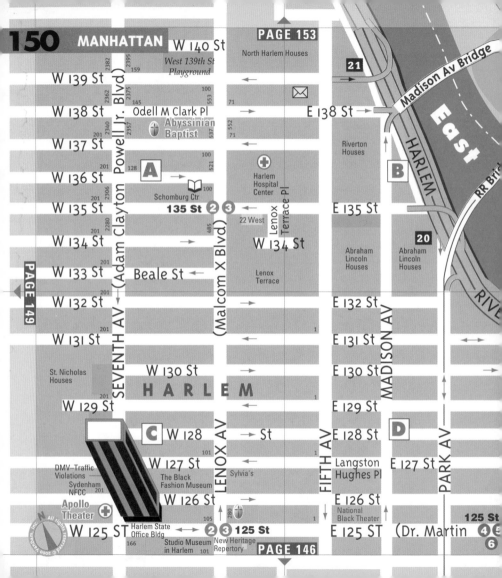

PAGE 153

North Harlem Houses

21

Madison Av Bridge

W 139 St   2382   2395   159
West 139th St
Playground

W 138 St   2362   2375   100   553   71   Odell M Clark Pl

E 138 St

Abyssinian
Baptist   2340   2357   201   537   552   71

W 137 St   201

A   128   2306   201   100   521

W 136 St

Schomburg Ctr   100

W 135 St   201   **135 St** ②③

Harlem
Hospital
Center

Riverton
Houses

B

E 135 St

W 134 St   201   2280   485   22 West   Lenox Terrace Pl

W 134 St

Lenox
Terrace

Abraham
Lincoln
Houses

20

Abraham
Lincoln
Houses

W 133 St   201   Beale St

W 132 St   201

E 132 St

E 135 St

W 131 St   201

E 131 St

St. Nicholas
Houses

H A R L E M

W 130 St

E 130 St

W 129 St   201

E 129 St

SEVENTH AV

(Adam Clayton Powell Jr. Blvd)

(Malcom X Blvd)

MADISON AV

C   W 128

LENOX AV

St

D

E 128 St

DMV – Traffic
Violations
Sydenham
NFCC   201

W 127 St   101

Sylvia's

Langston
Hughes Pl

E 127 St

PARK AV

FIFTH AV

The Black
Fashion Museum

**Apollo
Theater**

W 126 St

E 126 St

National
Black Theater

125 St

N   All rights reserved © 2000 VanDam, Inc.

W 125 ST   166   Harlem State
Office Bldg   105   280   ②③ **125 St**

Studio Museum
in Harlem   101   New Heritage
Repertory

E 125 ST   (Dr. Martin

④⑤
⑥

PAGE 146

PAGE 149

East

HARLEM

RR Bridge

RIVE

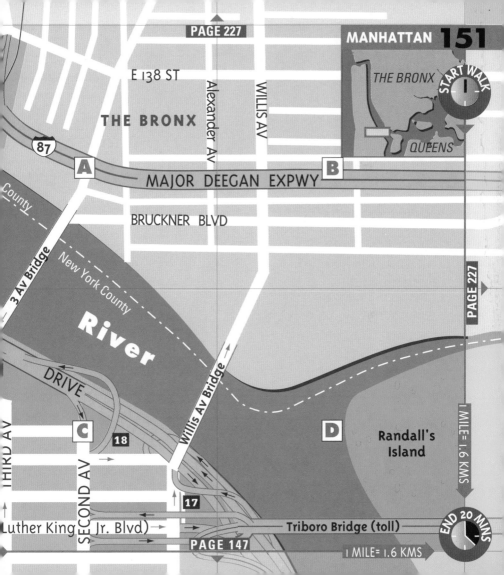

PAGE 227

MANHATTAN **151**

THE BRONX

START WALK

QUEENS

E 138 ST

WILLIS AV

Alexander Av

THE BRONX

87

A

B

MAJOR DEEGAN EXPWY

BRUCKNER BLVD

County

3 Av Bridge

New York County

PAGE 227

River

Willis Av Bridge

DRIVE

C

18

D

Randall's
Island

THIRD AV

SECOND AV

17

1 MILE= 1.6 KMS

END 20 MINS

Luther King Jr. Blvd)

Triboro Bridge (toll)

PAGE 147

1 MILE= 1.6 KMS

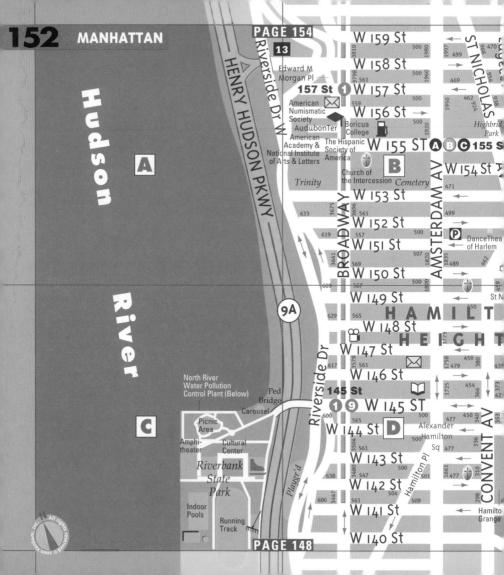

PAGE 154

13

Hudson

River

Henry Hudson Pkwy

Riverside Dr W

W 159 St
W 158 St
Edward M Morgan Pl
157 St ① W 157 St
American Numismatic Society
W 156 St
AudubonTer
Boricua College
American Academy & National Institute of Arts & Letters
The Hispanic Society of America
W 155 ST Ⓐ Ⓑ Ⓒ **155 S**
Trinity
Church of the Intercession
Cemetery
B
W 154 St
W 153 St
W 152 St
W 151 St
DanceThea of Harlem
P
W 150 St
St N
9A
W 149 St
H A M I L T
W 148 St
H E I G H
Riverside Dr
W 147 St
W 146 St
North River Water Pollution Control Plant (Below)
Ped Bridge
145 St
① ⑨ **W 145 ST**
Carousel
D
W 144 St
Alexander Hamilton Sq
Picnic Area
Amphi-theater
Cultural Center
Riverbank State Park
W 143 St
W 142 St
Playgr'd
Indoor Pools
Running Track
W 141 St
Hamilton Pl
Hamilto Grange
W 140 St

ST NICHOLAS
Highbrid Park
AMSTERDAM AV
CONVENT AV

PAGE 148

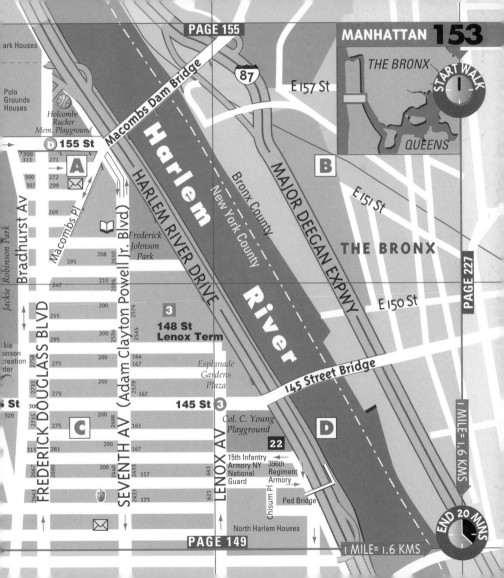

ark Houses

Polo
Grounds
Houses

*Holcombe
Rucker
Mem. Playground*

87

THE BRONX

E 157 St

START WALK
1

QUEENS

B

(D) 155 St

A

THE BRONX

E 151 St

Macombs Dam Bridge

HARLEM RIVER DRIVE

Harlem

MAJOR DEEGAN EXPWY

PAGE 227

(D)
300
313
271

300
307
272
299

269

Macombs Pl

*Frederick
Johnson
Park*

208
2610
2594

E 150 St

Bronx County
New York County

River

Jackie Robinson Park

295

247

210

200

2574

3

**148 St
Lenox Term**

Bradhurst Av

255

295

200

2556

2545

164
167

*Esplanade
Gardens
Plaza*

2758

275

200

2579

167

145 St **3**

FREDERICK DOUGLASS BLVD

2733

275

200

145 Street Bridge

Jackie
Robinson
Recreation
Center

S St

320

300

2715

275

161

*Col. C. Young
Playground*

D

SEVENTH AV (Adam Clayton Powell Jr. Blvd)

2498

200

167

22

2667
2690

281

315

200

157

2455

2440

*15th Infantry
Armory NY
National
Guard*

641

*396th
Regiment
Armory*

LENOX AV

2643

173

2433

621

Chisum Pl

Ped Bridge

END 20 MINS

North Harlem Houses

PAGE 149

I MILE= 1.6 KMS

I MILE= 1.6 KMS

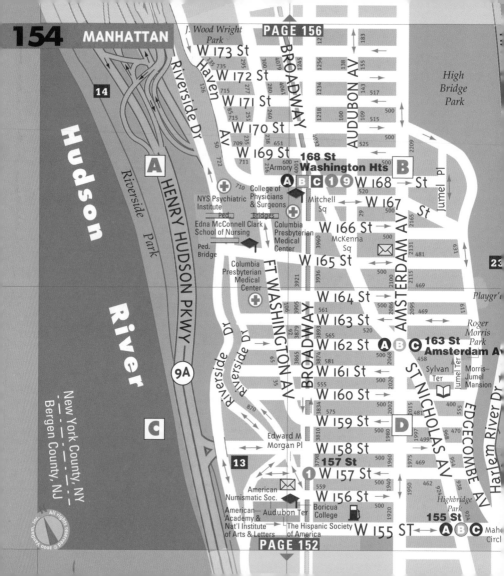

PAGE 156

14

J. Wood Wright Park

High Bridge Park

W 173 St
W 172 St
W 171 St
W 170 St
W 169 St

BROADWAY

AUDUBON AV

168 St
Washington Hts

A

Riverside Dr

Haven Av

168 St
Washington Hts
Armory

A B C 1 9 W 168 St

B

Jumel Pl

HENRY HUDSON PKWY

NYS Psychiatric Institute

College of Physicians & Surgeons

Mitchell Sq

W 167 St

Ped. Bridges

Edna McConnell Clark School of Nursing

Columbia Presbyterian Medical Center

W 166 St

McKenna Sq

Jumel St

23

Ped. Bridge

Columbia Presbyterian Medical Center

W 165 St

AMSTERDAM AV

Playgr'd

Riverside Park

FT WASHINGTON AV

W 164 St

Roger Morris Park

W 163 St

9A

W 162 St

A B C **163 St**
Amsterdam Av

Hudson River

Riverside Dr

W 161 St

ST NICHOLAS AV

Jumel Ter

Sylvan Ter

Morris–Jumel Mansion

BROADWAY

W 160 St

W 159 St

D

EDGECOMBE AV

Harlem River Dr

New York County, NY
Bergen County, NJ

C

Edward M Morgan Pl

W 158 St

13

157 St

1 W 157 St

W 156 St

American Numismatic Soc.

American Academy & Nat'l Institute of Arts & Letters

Audubon Ter

Boricua College

The Hispanic Society of America

Highbridge Park

155 St

W 155 ST A B C Mah... Circl...

PAGE 152

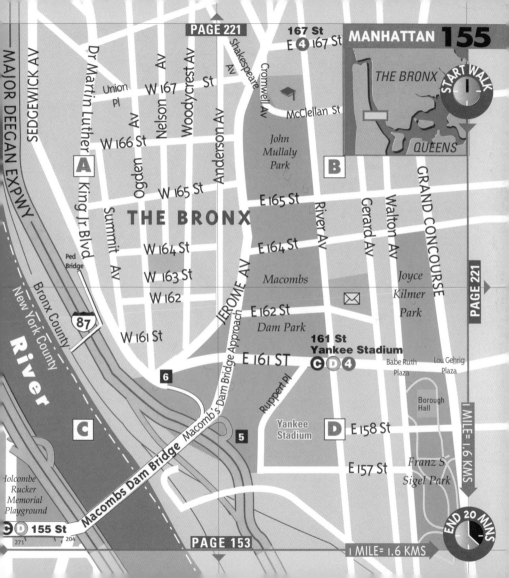

START WALK

THE BRONX

QUEENS

167 St
E **4** 167 St

McClellan St

John Mullaly Park

Dr Martin Luther King Jr Blvd

SEDGEWICK AV

MAJOR DEEGAN EXPWY

Union Pl

W 167 St

Nelson Av

Woodycrest Av

Anderson Av

Shakespeare Av

Cromwell Av

A

W 166 St

Ogden Av

THE BRONX

Summit Av

W 165 St

E 165 St

W 164 St

E 164 St

W 163 St

Macombs

JEROME AV

River Av

Gerard Av

Walton Av

GRAND CONCOURSE

B

W 162

E 162 St

Dam Park

Joyce Kilmer Park

Ped Bridge

New York County

Bronx County

87

W 161 St

6

C

161 St
Yankee Stadium
C D 4

E 161 ST

Ruppert Pl

Macomb's Dam Bridge Approach

Babe Ruth Plaza

Lou Gehrig Plaza

Borough Hall

5

Yankee Stadium

D E 158 St

E 157 St

Franz S Sigel Park

River

Holcombe Rucker Memorial Playground

Macombs Dam Bridge

C D 155 St

271 | 204

END 20 MINS

PAGE 221

1 MILE= 1.6 KMS

1 MILE= 1.6 KMS

PAGE 158

A 190 St

W 190 St

Gorman Memoria Park

BROADWAY

Bennett Av

Overlook

9A

HENRY HUDSON PKWY

RIVERSIDE DRIVE

Chittenden Av

Ter

W 186 St

Alex Rose Pl

B

W A

Pinehurst Av

W 185 St

River

Bennett Park

Riverside Dr

Fort Washington Park

Hudson

Cabrini

W 183 St

Magaw Pl

Col. R.

A 181 St

Plaza Lafayette

Blvd

FT

A

Bus Terminal

370 700

S Pinehurst Av

353

7

836

C Bridge **9** **I** **95** **1A**

D

WASHINGTON AV

A

George Washington

Haven

J. Wood Wright Park

135 735 295

126

Av

W 172 S

715 277

W 171 S

PAGE 159

THE BRONX

START WALK

QUEENS

190 St →
189 St ←
188 St ←
187 St ←
186 St

Wash Ter
185 St ←

A

N

G T O N

S

184 St →

Yeshiva Univ.

183 St ←

McNally Plaza

182 St ←

W 181 ST

High Bridge Park

HARLEM RIVER DRIVE

Laurel Hill Ter

Harlem

New York City

Bronx County

MAJOR DEEGAN EXPWY

B

W 174 St

Featherbed Ln

CROSS BRONX EXPWY

Washington Bridge

180 St →

179 St ←

178 St →

177 St ←

176 St ←

175 St ←

74 St ←

73 St ←

AUDUBON AV

AMSTERDAM AV

Pinehurst Pl

I

24

C

High Bridge Pedestrian

High Bridge Park

Alexander Hamilton Bridge

95

W 171

EDWARD L GRANT HWY

THE BRONX

D

W 169 St

SEDGWICK AV

87

River

END 20 MINS

PAGE 221

1 MILE= 1.6 KMS

1 MILE= 1.6 KMS

PAGE 155

80 240

200 215 223

186 215 525

138 155 183

143 517

500

PAGE 160

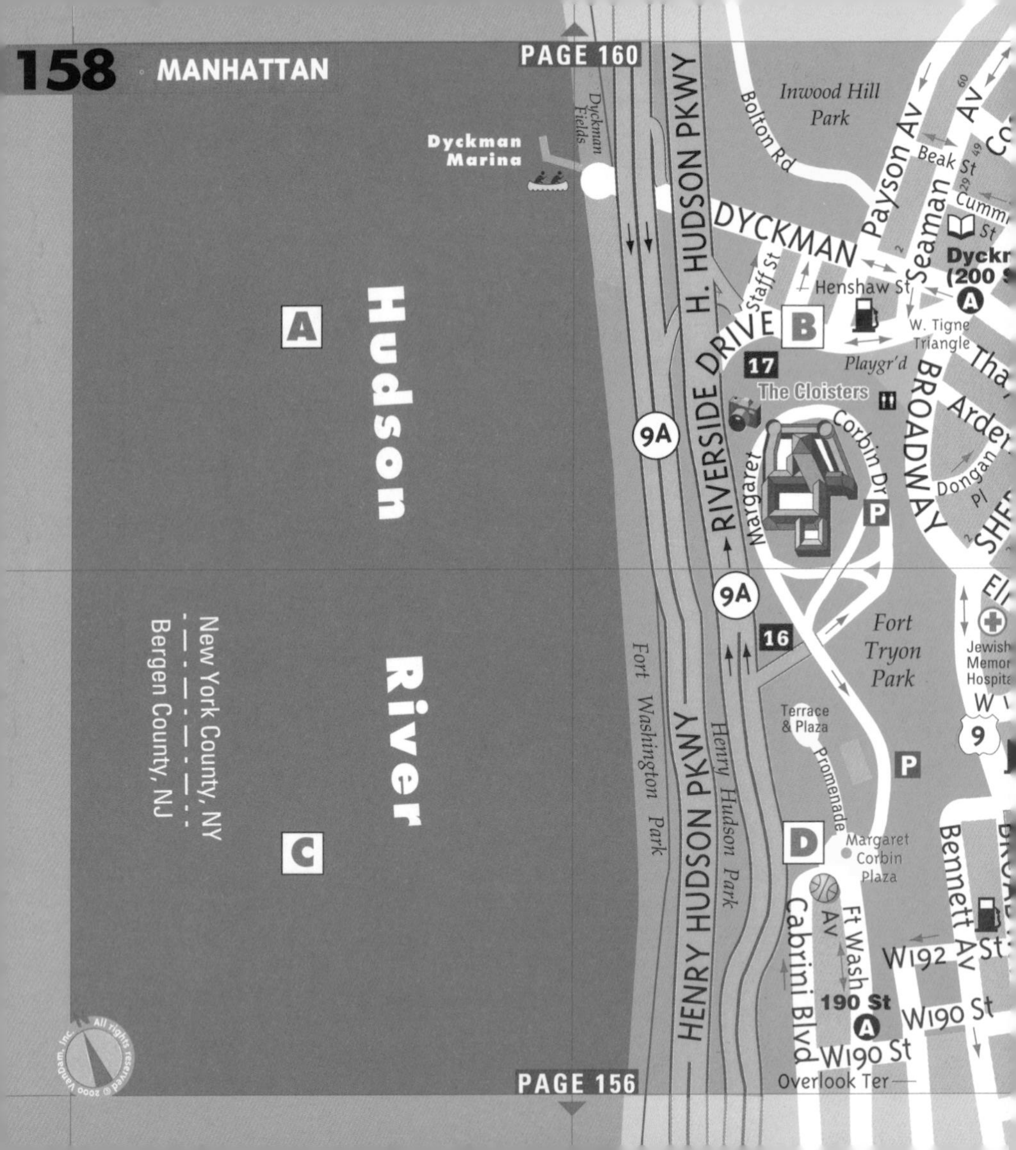

Inwood Hill Park

Bolton Rd

Dyckman Fields

Dyckman Marina

DYCKMAN

H. HUDSON PKWY

Payson Av

Beak St

AV

Seaman

Cummi St

Dyckr (200 S
Ⓐ

Staff St

Henshaw St

RIVERSIDE DRIVE

B

W. Tigne Triangle

Tha

17

Playgr'd

The Cloisters

9A

Margaret

Corbin Dr

BROADWAY

Arder

Dongan Pl

SHE

P

A

9A

16

Fort Tryon Park

Elr

Jewish Memor Hospita

Fort Washington Park

Terrace & Plaza

Promenade

P

9

W 1

New York County, NY
Bergen County, NJ

A

Hudson River

C

HENRY HUDSON PKWY

Henry Hudson Park

D

Margaret Corbin Plaza

Bennett Av

St

Ft Wash Av

Cabrini Blvd

W 192

W 190 St

190 St
Ⓐ

W 190 St

Overlook Ter

BINOAD

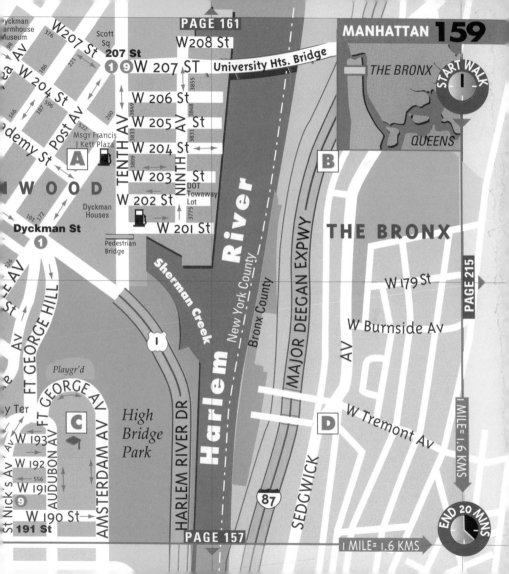

Dyckman
Farmhouse
Museum

W 207 St

Scott
Sq

W 208 St

207 St

① ⑨ W 207 ST

University Hts. Bridge

THE BRONX

START WALK

W 206 St

QUEENS

W 204 St

Post Av

TENTH AV

W 205 St

NINTH AV

St

Academy St

Msgr Francis
J Kett Plaza

A

W 204 St

W 203 St

DOT Towaway
Lot

W 202 St

Dyckman
Houses

Dyckman St

①

B

THE BRONX

Harlem River

New York County

Bronx County

MAJOR DEEGAN EXPWY

W 201 St

Pedestrian
Bridge

Sherman Creek

W 179 St

W Burnside Av

FT GEORGE HILL

FT GEORGE AV

Playgr'd

AV

HARLEM RIVER DR

Harlem

Fairview Ter

AUDUBON AV

C

W 193 St

W 192 St

AMSTERDAM AV

High
Bridge
Park

W Tremont Av

D

St Nick's Av

W 191 St

⑨

W 190 St

191 St

SEDGWICK

87

1 MILE= 1.6 KMS

END 20 MINS

1 MILE= 1.6 KMS

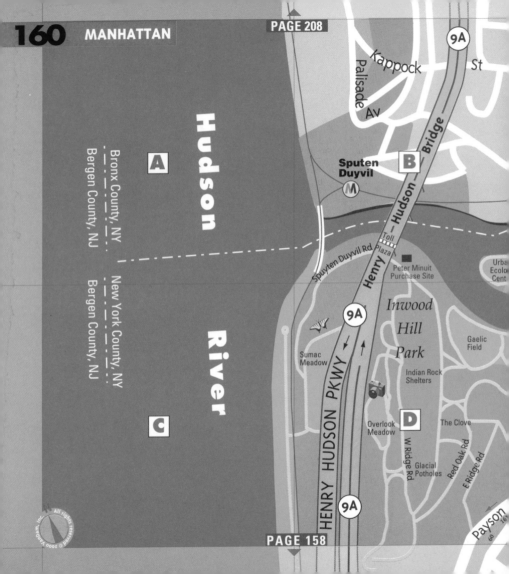

PAGE 208

9A

Kappock St

Palisade Av

Hudson

Sputen Duyvil
M

B

Hudson Bridge

Toll Plaza

Henry

Spuyten Duyvil Rd

■ Peter Minuit
Purchase Site

Urba
Ecolo
Cent

Bronx County, NY
Bergen County, NJ

A

New York County, NY
Bergen County, NJ

C

River

Inwood
Hill
Park

Gaelic
Field

9A

Sumac
Meadow

Indian Rock
Shelters

D

Overlook
Meadow

W Ridge Rd

The Clove

Glacial
Potholes

Red Oak Rd

E Ridge Rd

HENRY HUDSON PKWY

9A

Payson

PAGE 158

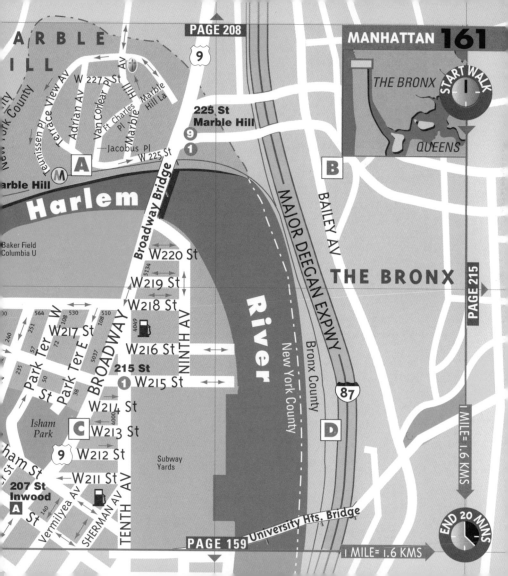

PAGE 208

MARBLE HILL

ARBLE
HILL

9

W 227 St

Adrian Av

Terrace View Av

Teunissen Av

New York County

Van Corlear Pl

Ft Charles Pl

Marble Hill Av

Marble Hill La

Jacobus Pl

225 St
Marble Hill

9
1

W 225 St

Marble Hill
M
A

MANHATTAN 161

THE BRONX

START WALK
1

QUEENS

Harlem

Broadway Bridge

B

Baker Field
Columbia U

MAJOR DEEGAN EXPWY

BAILEY AV

River

W220 St

W219 St

W218 St

THE BRONX

PAGE 215

W217 St

W216 St

NINTH AV

Park Ter W

Park Ter E

BROADWAY

215 St

1   W215 St

New York County

Bronx County

87

1 MILE= 1.6 KMS

W214 St

Isham
Park

C   W213 St

9   W212 St

D

Subway
Yards

W211 St

207 St
Inwood
A

Vermilyea Av

SHERMAN AV

TENTH AV

END 20 MINS

PAGE 159 University Hts. Bridge

1 MILE= 1.6 KMS

WESTCHESTER CO

P. 203

P. 205

P. 20

Pelham Park

Pelham Bay

P. 209

P. 211

21

Eastchester Bay

City Island

P. 215

P. 217

P.

THROGS NECK EXPWY E. TREMONT

Throgs Neck Bridge (toll)

P. 221

P. 223

P.

Bronx–Wh Bridge (to

George Washington Bridge (toll)

River

P. 227

P. 229

QUEENS

BRUCKNER EXPWY

Riker's Island

East River

Flushing Bay

MANHATTAN

Randall's Island

LaGuardia

Hudson River

Pelham Park

Eastchester Bay

City Island

E 241 ST

NEREID AV

E 233 ST

DYRE AV

BOSTON RD

NEW ENGLAND THWY

95

WHITE PLAINS RD

BRONX RIVER PKWY

BRONX BLVD

CITY ISLAND RD

CITY ISLAND AV

EASTCHESTER RD

E GUN HILL RD

W GUN HILL RD

MOSHOLU PKWY

WEBSTER AV

WHITE PLAINS RD

BOSTON RD

BRONX & PELHAM PKWY

WILLIAMSBRIDGE

BRONX RIVER PKWY

HUTCHINSON RIVER PKWY

BRUCKNER EXPWY

95

RIVERDALE

BROADWAY

MOSHOLU EXPWY

9

9A

87

HUDSON PKWY

MAJOR DEEGAN PKWY

9A

9

HENRY

BROADWAY

DYCKMAN ST

9A

9

87

W FORDHAM RD

E FORDHAM RD

UNIVERSITY AV

WEBSTER AV

CONCOURSE

3 AV

SOUTHERN BD

E TREMONT

MORRIS PARK

E TREMONT

CASTLE

WESTCHESTER

WHITE PLAINS

95

278

695

295

RIVER

HILL

PKWY

Throgs Neck Bridge (toll)

MAJOR

WEBSTER AV

JEROME

E BLVD

SHERIDAN EXPWY

AV

BRUCKNER EXPWY

895

SOUND VIEW AV

RD

278

678

E 167 ST

E 163 ST

HUNTS POINT AV

WESTCHESTER

BOSTON RD

AMSTERDAM AV

W 155 ST

W 145 ST

W 135 ST

BROADWAY

F. DOUGLASS BD

LENOX AV

5 AV

Harlem River

GRAND CONCOURSE

87

E 149 ST

WILLS AV

3 AV

E 138 ST

DEEGAN EXPWY

BRUCKNER BLVD

278

WILLIS AV

SOUTHERN BD

BRUCKNER

BRUCKNER EXPWY

COLLEGE POINT BLVD

14 AV

WHITESTONE EXPWY

3 AV

2 AV

st of the Bronx

ugh geographically part of the
mainland, the Bronx joins NYC's
er boroughs as a trendsetter in
ny areas of pop culture. Hip Hop
homeboys originated from here
ake the universe by rhyme.

onx Zoo/Int'l Wildlife
nservation Park

e of the world's best parks
greatest research institutions
h programs on five continents.
nx River Pkwy @ Fordham Rd,
-367-1010. **216A**

mmy's Bronx

the serious Mambo crowd
gargantuan disco-cum-
aurant is the G spot on
rsday nights. 281 W Fordham
d, 718-329-2000. **214B**

ave Hill

body in search of a robber
on mansion on the Hudson
uld do themselves the favor
visit. Yes, this is the Bronx.
W 252 St, 718-549-3200. **208A**

nkee Stadium

uably America's premier sports
nchise, the Bronx Bombers got their
rt in Manhattan as the Highlanders.
St & River Av, 718-760-6200. **221C**

NY Botanical Garden

A renowned leader in conservation
and, following its most recent
renovation, the most stunning
glass palace this side of Kew
Gardens, England. Its four
rainforest habitats alone are worth
the visit. 200 St @ Southern Blvd,
718-817-8705. **216A**

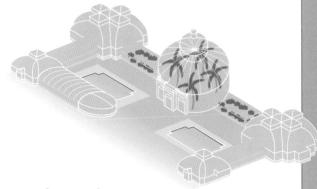

Le Refuge Bed &
Breakfast

Gourmands the world over flock to
Pierre Saint-Denis's eight-room sea
captain's house on Eastchester Bay.
Unique to the Bronx, there is
no better place for breakfast. Lunch,
however, should be enjoyed at Pierre's
restaurant, Le Refuge, on Manhattan's
Upper East Side. 620 City Island Av,
718-885-2478. **213B**

Enid A. Haupt Conservatory
restored in 1978 by
Edward Larrabee Barnes

Bronx Stats:
Population:
1.2 million

Area:
43 sq miles

Hudson River

Ferry

A

RIVERDALE AV

BROADWAY

B

RADFORD ST

VALENTINE LA

9

Delafield Pl | St Spence

Westchester County
Bronx County

College of
Mt St Vincent

W 263

W 262

Fieldston Rd

6300

Liebig Av

Delafield Av

Tyndall Av

400

C

W 261 St

750

M

**Mt St
Vincent**

6100

6000

D

550

RIVERDALE AV

W 260

400

Bronx County, NY
Bergen County, NJ

Judaica
Museum

Independence Av

✉

W 259

Palisade Av

Sigma
Pl

5900

Arlington Av

Netherland Av

5900

5600

N

5600

256 St

22

5600

PAGE 208

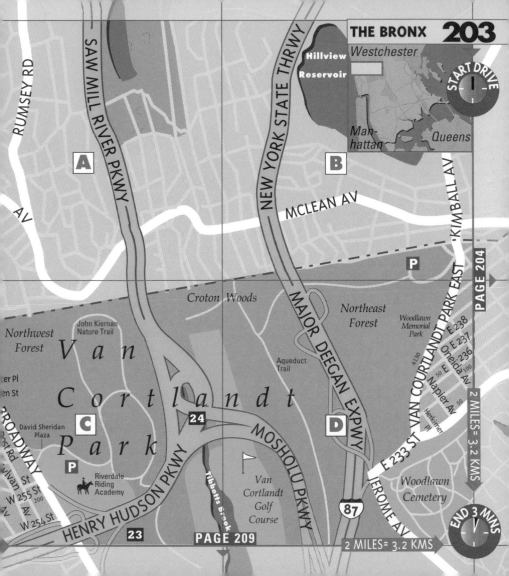

RUMSEY RD

SAW MILL RIVER PKWY

NEW YORK STATE THRWY

Hillview
Reservoir

Westchester

Man-
hattan

Queens

START DRIVE

A

B

MCLEAN AV

KIMBALL AV

AV

P

PAGE 204

Croton Woods

Northwest
Forest

John Kiernan
Nature Trail

Northeast
Forest

Woodlawn
Memorial Park

E 238

V a n

Aqueduct
Trail

E 237

Oneida AV

E 236

4130

50

E 100

er Pl
en St

VAN COURTLANDT PARK EAST

Napier AV

2 MILES= 3.2 KMS

C o r t l a n d t

David Sheridan
Plaza

C

24

MAJOR DEEGAN EXPWY

D

Herkimer
Pl

BROADWAY

P a r k

P

Riverdale
Riding
Academy

MOSHOLU PKWY

E 233 ST

ost Rd

an St

W 255 St

AV

200

Tibbetts Brook

Van
Cortlandt
Golf
Course

JEROME AV

Woodlawn
Cemetery

AZ

W 254 St

HENRY HUDSON PKWY

23

87

END 3 MINS

PAGE 209

2 MILES= 3.2 KMS

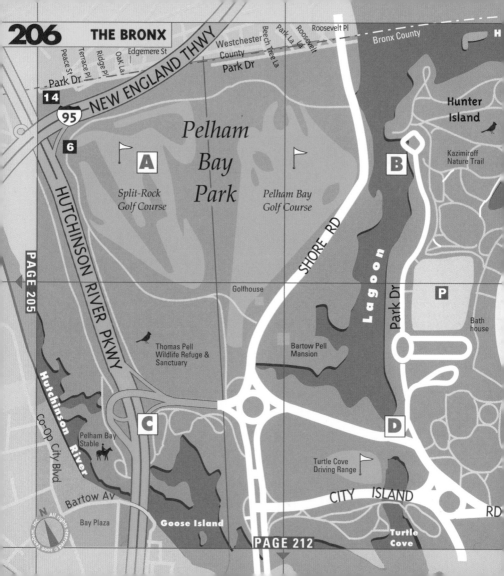

Westchester

Man-
hattan

Queens

Middle Reef

East
Nonations

South
Nonations

A

B

The Blauzes

Long Island Sound

Hart
Island

ham
y

Chimney Sweeps Islands

(Pelham Bay Park)

High
Island

Rat
Island

Green
Flats

C

D

Footbridge

Terrace St

King St

Bridge St

Sutherland St

Av 600

Kilroe St

Cross St

449

Beach

Minnieford Av

Bowne St

Kirby St

City
Island

Le-Refuge
Northwind
Undersea Institute

Ferry

City
Island Bridge

PAGE 213

2 MILES= 3.2 KMS

2 MILES= 3.2 KMS

START DRIVE

END 3 MINS

win
land

ntal

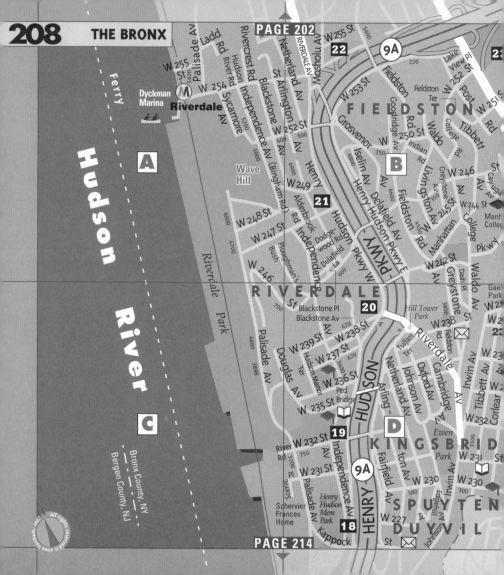

PAGE 202

22

9A

Lake View Pl

23

W 255 St

5400

220

Palisade Av

Ladd Rd

W 255 St

5400

Riverdale Av

Hudson River Rd

Rivercrest Rd

Netherland Av

RIVERDALE AV

HUDSON AV

W 253 St

Fieldston Rd

Fieldston Ter

W 252 St

Post Rd

W 251 St

FIELDSTON

Dyckman Marina

M

W 254 St

St Arlington Av

Blackstone Av

Independence Av

Sycamore Av

W 252 St

5200

500

600

Grosvenor Av

Goodridge Av

Waldo Av

College Rd

Tibbett Rd

Riverdale

A

Wave Hill

W 249 St

5000

Alderbrook Rd

Hudson Pkwy

Independence Av (Bingham Rd)

Henry

W 250 St

Iselin Av

Delafield Av

Livingston Av

Fieldston Rd

Indian Rd

250

Greystone Av

4600

W 246 St

215 St

W 244 St

St Cayuga Av

B

Manhattan College

21

4900

W 248 St

W 247 St

4800

4700

Ploughman's Bush

Dodgewood Rd

Delafield La

600

Henry Hudson Pkwy E

Manhattan College

4500

Manhattan Rd

W 212 St

Dash Pl

Greystone Av

Waldo Av

Gae Park

W 2

Riverdale Park

4600

W 246 St

Blackstone Pl

Blackstone Av

St

700

620

R I V E R D A L E

20

Hill Tower Park

3800

Fieldston Rd

W 238 St

W 2

23

Palisade Av

4600

3898

W 239 St

Douglas Av

Ter

Hudson Manor Ter

W 238 St

W 237 St

W 236 St

620

3600

Tulfan Ter

Riverdale Av

Arling

HUDSON

Netherland Av

Johnson Av

Oxford Av

Cambridge Av

Irwin Av

Tibbett Av

Corlear Av

W 23

W 2

W 23

Ped Bridge

W 235 St

D

Ewen Park

3100

K I N G S B R I D

River Rd

W 232 St

3100

750

Independence Av

19

Pl

W 231 St

Arling ton Av

Fairfield Av

Overhill Av

Irwin Av

Tibbett Av

W 231 St

W 230

W 230

580

300

9A

C

Bronx County, NY

Bergen County, NJ

Scenic

Schervier Frances Home

Palisade Av

Henry Hudson Mem Park

18

HENRY

Fairfield Av

Independence Av

Kappock St

Edgehill Av

Johnson Av

S P U Y T E N

W 227 St

D U Y V I L

PAGE 214

© 2000 VanDam, Inc. All rights reserved

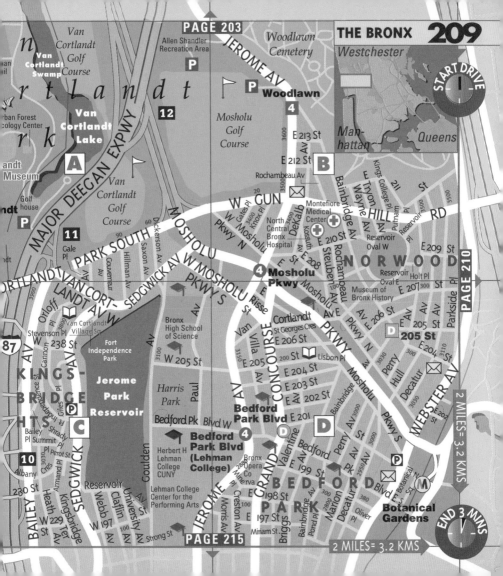

Van Cortlandt Golf Course

Van Cortlandt Swamp

rtlandt

Allen Shandler Recreation Area

JEROME AV

Woodlawn Cemetery

Westchester

Man-hattan

Queens

START DRIVE

n

an il

ban Forest cology Center

r k

Van Cortlandt Lake

12

Mosholu Golf Course

Woodlawn

4

andt Museum

A

Van Cortlandt Golf Course

E 213 St

E 212 St

B

ndt

Golf house

MAJOR DEEGAN EXPWY

Rochambeau Av

Kings College Pl

211 St

HILL RD

P

11

Gale Pl

PARK SOUTH

DICKERSON AV

MOSHOLU AV

W MOSHOLU

W GUN

W Mosholu Pkwy N

Gates Pl
Knoll Pl

20

DeKalb

North Central Bronx Hospital

Montefiore Medical Center

E 210 St

Kossuth

E 208
St

Bainbridge Av

Wayne Av

E Tryon Pl

Putnam Pl

Reservoir Oval W

E 209 St

N O R W O O D

PAGE 210

Dickerson Av

Saxon Av

Hillman Av

Gouverneur Av

Couverneur Av

SEDGWICK AV

W MOSHOLU PKWY S

Risse St

4

Mosholu Pkwy

E St

Steuben Av

Rochambeau Av

Mosholu AV

Reservoir Oval E

Holt Pl

Museum of Bronx History

E 207 St

300

E 206 St

E 205 St

Parkside Pl

87

W 238 St

Oloff Av

Stevenson Pl

Cannon

Bronx High School of Science

Van Cortlandt Village Sq

Fort Independence Park

AV

W 205 St

Van Villa Av

Cortlandt

St Georges Cres

E 206 St

200 St

Lisbon Pl

MOSHOLU PKWY N

Perry

Hull

Decatur

E 204

3110

E 205 St

WEBSTER AV

2 MILES = 3.2 KMS

CORTLANDT VAN CORT-LANDT AV

3900

Brince

Orloff

KINGS-

BRIDGE

HTS

10

Bailey Pl

Shrady Pl

Summit Pl

Perot St

Jerome Park Reservoir

Harris Park

Paul

Giles Pl

C

Bedford Pk Blvd W

Herbert H Lehman College CUNY

Bedford Park Blvd

E 201

Paul

E 205 St

E 204 St

E 203 St

E 202 St

Bedford Park Blvd

4

D

Valentine Av

CONCOURSE

GRAND

Bedford

Perry

Bainbridge Av

3000

AV

Mosholu

PKWY S

3000

Decatur

Perry

St

E 202 St

E 199 St

Botanical Sq

P

D

205 St

Albany

230 St

BAILEY

Heath

W 229 St

Kingsbridge Ter

SEDGWICK

Webb Av

Claflin Av

Reservoir

Golden

University AV

Morris Av

Minerva Pl

Lehman College Center for the Performing Arts

198 St

197 St

Miriam St

Strong St

JEROME

Creston Av

Briggs

Bainbridge

Pond Pl

B E D F O R D

P A R K

Bronx Opera Co

Valentine

Decatur

Marion

Oliver

Botanical Gardens

M

2950 AV

380

2800

Botanical Bl

E S

END 3 MINS

Woodlawn Cemetery

Woodlawn

4 JEROME AV

PAGE 204
PAGE 209

219 St ❷❺
E 219 St
E 218 St
Olinville Av
Willett Av
D'Onofrio Sq

WILLIAMS-BRIDGE

Oakley St

E 217 St
E 216 St   800   900   1000
E 215 St
E 214 St   900
Holland   3600
E 212 St
700   800   3600
Carlisle St
Tilden St
E 211 St   1000   3500

BRONX RIVER PKWY
WEBSTER AV
BRONX BLVD

E 213 St
Bainbridge
Rochambeau
Tryon
Wayne
HILL
Putnam Pl
Reservoir Pl

A

Kings College Pl
211 St

9

E 213 St   3600

E 211 St
E 212 St   3500

E 211 St
Duncomb Av
Magenta
Tilden St
Gun Hill Rd ❷❺

B
TE GUN HILL R
3300
3200
Duncan St
Paulding Av
Colden Av
Radcliff Av
Bronxwood Av

W GUN
North Central Bronx Hospital
De Kalb
Kossuth
E 210 St
E 208 St
Steuben Av
Rochambeau Av
E Mosholu
Van Cortlandt
Cres St Georges St
E 206

Montefiore Medical Center

N O R W O O D

Reservoir Oval E
Reservoir Oval E
Museum of Bronx History

E 209 St
Holt Pl
E 207 St   300
E 206 St
E 205 St
Parkside Av
Newell St

Williams-bridge **M**
3500   RD
3500

Wallace Av
Bartoldi St
N Chestnut St
S Oak Dr
800
N Oak Dr
S Oak Dr
800

Barker Av
Rosewood St
Burke Av ❷❺
Burke Av   3000
Lester St
Adee Av
IRS
Holland Av
Cruger Av
Barnes Av
Matthews Av

Burke Av

900
800
Bronxwood Av

WHITE
Amow Av
Britton St
Olinville Av
Allerton Av ❷❺

Arnow Av
2700
2600
800
Mace Av
PLAINS
BOSTON

Allerton Av

D

Lisbon Pl
E 205 St
E 204 St
E 203 St
E 202 St
E 201 St
200

205 St/Norwood
Perry
Hull
Decatur
E 204
3030
3110

3000   600   3900
Waring Av

C

Bedford Park Blvd **D**

Valentine
E 199 St
Bedford
Perry
E 198 St
Bainbridge
Pond Pl
Marion
Decatur Pl
Oliver Pl
380
300

MOSHOLU PKWY
Mosholu Pkwy N
Mosholu Pkwy S
DR THEODORE KAZMIROFF BLVD

WEBSTER AV
E 203

8A

BRONX PARK EAST

B r o n x

P a r k

Museum
Magnolia Dell

D
Beth Abraham Hospital

2600
2400
Barker Av
RD
700

Pelham Pkw

P **M** Botanical Sq **M**

Botanical Gardens
Rock Gardens
Main Conservatory

New York Botanical Garden

Snuff Mill
Rose Gardens

Thwaites Pl
Reiss Pl

Westchester

START DRIVE

Man-
hattan

Queens

**BAY
CHESTER**

I 95

Baychester

2800

1900

Sexton

EASTCHESTER

Kingsland Av

Tiemann Av

Hafeen
Park

Bruner Av

Wickham Av

Gunther Av

Ely Av

Seymour Givan

AV

3300

Mickle Av

Hammersley Av

3500

3600

3000

2900

orsa

3300

Av

Seymour G

sh Av 3300

Fox Ter
Deyo St

1400

on AV
xAv

Knapp St

Adee Av

Bartow Av

Arnow Av

Allerton Av

2700 AV

2880

3200

Bouck Av

3200

Av

Givan
Square

2000

2900

chester
ens Park

1200

Throop Av

Tenbroeck Av

Pearsall Av

Hering Av

A **Gun
Hill Rd**

Fenton

Schorr Pl

Bantam
Pl

Hawthorne
St

Fielding
St

Lodovick Av

Tiemann Av

Kingsland Av

Westervelt Av

Mickle Av

Woodhull Av

Wickham Av

Gunther Av

Lodovick Av

Delanoy Av

B

Bruner Av

1800

1900

Demeyer St

Vance St

Ely Av

9

8C

E GUN HILL RD

De Witt

Pl Sexton Pl

Morgan Av

Seymour Av

Fish Av

Young Av

Wilson Av

De Witt Pl

2800

2900

2700

2700

2600

2300

2200

Erskine
Pl

Pelham Bay
General
Hospital

PAGE 212

HUTCHINSON RIVER PKWY

Pelham Pkwy S

E 197 St

E 196 St

E 195 St

E 194 St

Hobart Av

2 MILES = 3.2 KMS

Stedman

1100

2500

Esplanade

North

PELHAM

and

PKWY

1500

2300

2200

Rhinelander Av

Stillwell Av

P

Wilkinson Av

Mulford Av

Mildred Pl

Hutchinson River

DGE
RD

Stell
Pl

2400

1100

1000

1200

1300

1400

Pelham
Pkwy

South

Van
Hoesen Av

Naragansett Av

Choctaw Pl

Pawnee Pl

Seminole

McDonald St

Seminole St

Bassett Av

1500

Jacobi
Medical
Center

**WEST-
CHESTER
HTS**

Hutchinson River Pkwy W

C

New York
Institution
for the
Blind Parkway

Esplanade

Lydig Av

2100

2100

2000

Yates Av

Hering Av

TenbroeckAv

Pritchard Pl

Lakewood Pl

Wilkinson
Av

D

Loomis
St

Hutchinson River Pkwy E

1700

1700

Laurie Av

Bronx
Psychiatric
Center

BRONX

Parkway

Woodmansten Pl

Tomlinson Av

Neill Av

Haight Av

Lurting Av

Hone Av

Paulding Av

Muliner Av

Matthews Av

WILLIAMSBRIDGE

2000

2000

1900

1800

Newport

Av

MORRIS PARK AV

1700

Albert Einstein
College of
Medicine

Ives St

Calvary
Hospital

Blondell Av

McAlpin Av

Chesbrough Av

St Raymond Av

Waters Pl

Waters Av

St Raymond

END 3 MINS

Barnes Av

5

Morris Park

1600

1550

RD

2 MILES= 3.2 KMS

PAGE 206

Turtle
Cove

Bay Plaza

Baychester Av

95

10

9
E GUN HILL RD

A

Hutchinson River Pkwy W

Hutchinson River

Hutchinson River Pkwy E

Einstein
Loop-N,S,E
Elgar Pl
Erdman Pl

Earhart La
Erskine Pl

Stillwell Av
Hunter Av

Boller Av

Palmer Av
Dietemet Av

PELHAM BRIDGE RD

B

Ely Av
1800   1900

Delanoy Av
Wickham Av
2400
Gunther Av
Bruner Av
Stillwell Av
3300

Lodovick Av
2300

Demeyer St
vance st

Erskine Pl

8C

8B

Pelham
Bay
Park

HUTCHINSON

8A

Pelham Bay
General
Hospital

SPI
EST

PAGE 211

WEST—
CHESTER
HTS

Bassett Av
1500

Wilkinson
Av

Loomis
St

Ives St
Calvary
Hospital

McAlpin Av

Hutchinson River Pkwy W

Cheesborough Av

St Raymond Av

RIVER
PKWY

C

Bronx
Psychiatric
Center

Waters Pl

Lee St

Waters Av

Pelham Pkwy S
Burr Av
Colonial Av
St Paul Av
E 197 St
Continental
2000
E 196 St
Hobart Av
E 195 St
E 194 St
Wilkinson

St Theresa

Mayflower Av

Pilgrim Av

Milford Av

Laurie Av

Libby Pl

WESTCHESTER

Schuyler Pl
Mildred Pl
P. L. Keane
Sq

Arnow Ln
Willow Ln
Sands Pl

Edison Av

Buhre

Av

6
Pelham
Bay Park

Bruckner

Mahan Av

Parkview

Bruckner Blvd

Buhre Av
6

Hobart Av
Crosby
1700

Jarvis Av

BRUCKNER
EXPWY

Issac Rice
Memorial
Stadium

MacDonough
Dwight Pl
Robertson Pl
Kenilworth Pl

Ampere Av

Watt Av
Ohm Av
1600

Stadium Av
1500

Library Av
Research Av

Bayview Av

Bay Shore Outlook

Griswold Av

Radio Dr

Lucerne

Spencer
3220

Randolph Pl

D

Country Club
Rd

Valhalla
Pl

Siegfried Pl
Lohengrin
Pl

Kearney Av

Cornell Pl

Reed Rd

Polo Pl
Agar Pl

Parsifal Pl

Rawlins Av
3270

7C

Roberts Av
2000

Daniel St
1600

Gillespie

Plymouth Av
1600

Hollywood Av
3000

Merry

Hobart Av

Coddington Av
1400

La Salle Av
1300

Wellman Av

Cornell
Pl

Middle-
town
Rd
6

Middletown Av

Roebling Av

Zulette Av

Ericson
Pl

95

7B

Waterbury Av
1300

Baisley Av

Ellsworth Av

Fairfax Av

Faim

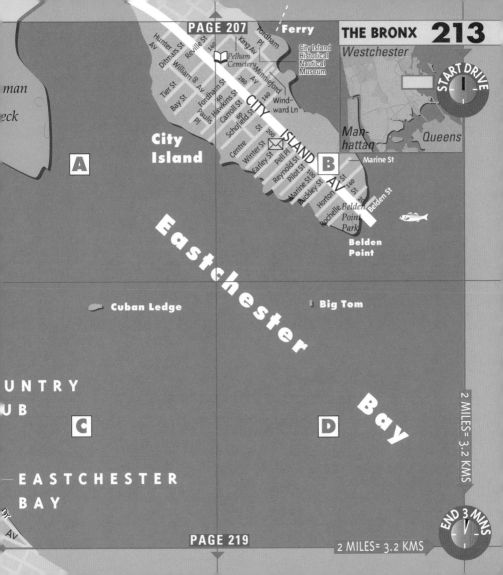

Ferry

Westchester

City Island
Historical
Nautical
Museum

Hunter Av

Ditmars St

William St

Tier St

Bay St

Reville St

King Av

Fordham Av

Minnieford Av

140

280

Wind-
ward Ln

Pelham
Cemetery

Fordham St

Hawkins St

Paulis Pl

Carroll St

60

Schofield St

50

Centre St

Winter St

Earley St

Pall Pl

Reynold St

Pilot St

Marine St

Buckley St

200

140

Horton St

140

20

Rochelle St

Belden
Point
Park

Belden St

**City
Island**

A

B

Marine St

Man-
hattan

Queens

START DRIVE

**Belden
Point**

E a s t c h e s t e r

Cuban Ledge

Big Tom

B a y

C

D

2 MILES= 3.2 KMS

**E A S T C H E S T E R
B A Y**

Av

2 MILES= 3.2 KMS

END 3 MINS

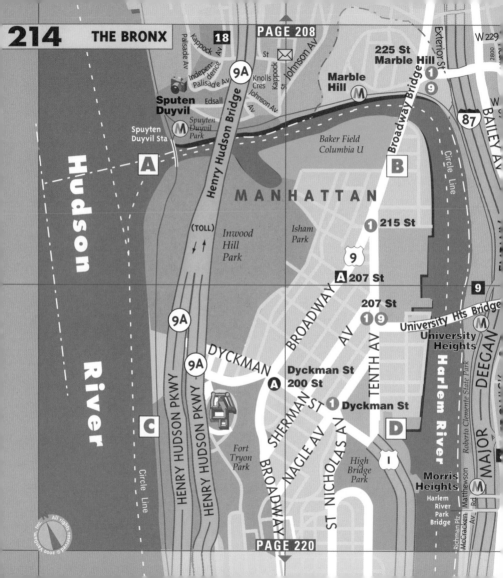

18

St

W 229

Kappock Av

Palisade Av

Independence Av

Knolls Cres

Johnson Av

Kappock St

Johnson Av

**225 St
Marble Hill** ①

⑨

Exterior St

2800

**Marble
Hill** Ⓜ

W

87

BAILEY AV

**Sputen
Duyvil**

Edsall

Palisade Av

Ⓜ *Spuyten
Duyvil
Park*

**Spuyten
Duyvil Sta**

Henry Hudson Bridge

Broadway Bridge

A

*Baker Field
Columbia U*

B

Circle Line

M A N H A T T A N

(TOLL)

↓↑

*Inwood
Hill
Park*

*Isham
Park*

① **215 St**

9

A **207 St**

9

207 St
① ⑨

University Hts Bridge Ⓜ

**University
Heights**

9A

BROADWAY

TENTH AV

DEEGAN

C

9A

DYCKMAN

Ⓐ **Dyckman St
200 St**

① **Dyckman St**

Roberto Clemente State Park

Harlem River

D

HENRY HUDSON PKWY

HENRY HUDSON PKWY

SHERMAN ST

NAGLE AV

BROADWAY

ST NICHOLAS AV

*Fort
Tryon
Park*

*High
Bridge
Park*

I

**Morris
Heights** Ⓜ

Circle Line

**Harlem
River
Park
Bridge**

Richman Plz

McCracken

Matthewson

MAJOR

Rd

© 2000 Maps.com, Inc. All rights reserved

Hudson

River

216 THE BRONX

PAGE 210

Pelham Pkwy

New York Botanical Garden

Main Conservatory

Snuff Mill

Rose Gardens

Fordham University

Bronx Park

Pine Grove

7W

Azalea Glen

E 191 St

E FORDHAM RD

E 189

E 188

Hoffman St

Lorillard Pl

Hughes St

Arthur Av

Belmont Av

Crotona Av

Beaumont Av

Cambreleng Av

A

Aviary Aquatic Bird House

Astor Court

Bronx Zoo

Int'l Wildlife

World of Birds

Conservation

Bronx Park E

B

Birchall Av

Mario's

Belmont Italian American Playhouse

E 186 St

Crescent Av

E 185 St

E 183 St

Grote St

Garden St

Northern Ponds

Wildfowl Marsh

Carter Giraffe Bldg

World of Darkness

Wild Asia

St Barnabas Hospital for Chronic Diseases

Adams Pl

E Grote St

182 St

Oak Tree Pl

Quary Rd

Prospect Av

Mapes Av

Crotona

Bronx Park South

Homaday Pl

Jungle World

Bronx Park Av

Bronx River

E 180 St

E 180 St

Lebanon St

Arthur Murphy Square

Clinton Av

E 181 St

E 180 St

E 179 St

Honeywell Av

Daly Av

Vyse Av

Bryant Av

E 179 St

Devoe Av

E 179 St

E 178 St

THIRD AV

Arthur Av

Lafontaine Av

Monterey Av

Oakland Pl

EAST E179 St

TREMONT

AV

Mohegan Av

Bronx Pkwy

E 178 St

West Farms Square

WEST

Morris Park Av

E 178 St

E 177 St

E 178 St

C

Elsmere Pl

Fairmount Pl

E Tremont Av
(West Farms Sq)

Wyatt St

D

FARMS

E TREMONT

E 176 St

E 175 St

95

Crotona Park N

E 175 St

Trafalgar Pl
Waterloo Pl
Vineyard Av
Mohegan Av
Marmion Av

Rodman Pl

CROSS BRONX

E 176 St

4A

4B

W Farms Rd

Bronx River

E 174 St

Stratford Av

Morrison Av

THIRD AV

3

E 173 St

Crotona Park

174 St

895

E 174 St

E 173 St

E 172

PAGE 222

PAGE 215

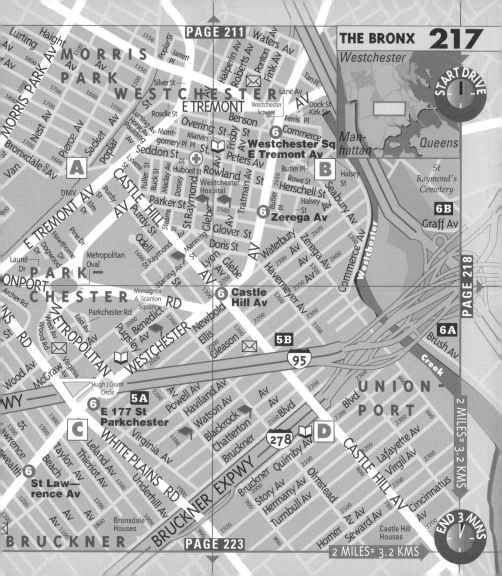

PAGE 212

7B

7A

Maitland Av

William Pl

Tran Pl

FORT

HUTCHINSON RIVER PKWY

Dock St
Kirk St
Ferris Pl

Commerce Av

Butler Pl
Halsey Pl

Rowe St
Herschell St
Halsey St

Waterbury
Newbold Av
Zerega Av
Ellis

Gleason

Powell Av
Haviland Av
Watson Av
Blackrock Av

95

278

Edwards Av
Latting Av
Ellison Av
Vreeland

Dudley Av
Hamington
Coddington

SCHUYLER RD

Balcom
Waterbury

Whittmore
Av

Commerce Av

Seabury Av

2400 Av

1100

UNION-

PORT

Quimby Av

Story Av

Hermany Av

2200

2300

2200

Olmstead

Lafayette Av

Homer Av

Seward Av

CASTLE HILL AV

Tumbull

Virgil Av

Havemeyer

Cincinnatus

Randall Av

2300

2300

2100

2200

700

800

2200

2200

2100

800

700

500

2300

2700

CASTLE

HILL

Jaimie
Towers

Castle Hill
Houses

Castle Hill Houses

La Salle Av

Paine St

Baisley St

Edison Av

1300

1400

Bradford Av

Mayflower Av

Puritan Av

2800

Av

St
Raymond's
Cemetery

Gifford
Av

6B

Graff Av

A

7C

Hadkin St

Meyers

Bruckner Blvd

95

Blvd Otis Av

Greene

Sommer
Pl

Scott
Pl

Sullivan Av

E TREMONT AV

Revere Av

Barkley

Brinsmade Av

Huntington Av

Balcom Av

1000

1000

900

1000

Hollywood Av

Logan Av

Lafayette

Calhoun Av

Quincy Av
Swinton Av

800

Dill

THROGS

NECK EXPWY

Throgs Neck

Phillip

700

900

800

700

6

B

SCHUYL

VILLE

Roosevelt Av
Lamport

700

500

500

500

400

Vincent Av
900

Clarence Av

Wilcox Av

Throgmorton Av 800

Ellsworth 700

Randall Av

CROSS BRONX

E 177 St

295

6A

678

Brush

Westchester

Creek

St
Raymond's
Cemetery

Randall Av

Buttrick
Av

Schley Av

Foote
Av

Wenner Av

Rohr Pl

Senger Pl

Jay Pl

Schley
Av

HUTCHINSON RIVER

Ferry Point
Park

Dewey Av

Sampson Av

Miles Av

Graff Av

Buttrick Av

Davis Av

Robinson Av

Hosmer Av

Emerson Av

D

Toll

P

PKWY

C

PAGE 217

PAGE 224

Westchester

Man-
hattan

Queens

START DRIVE

EDGEWATER
PARK

Long Island Sound

Locust
Point

4 Av
Sound View Dr
Center Av
3
1 St
Main Av
Stevens Av
St Av
9 St Av
Harding
Av
Av Edge
Dock
Miles Av
Av
Wissman Av
Reynolds Av
Prentiss Av
Meagher Av

Longstreet Av
Blair
A
B

Toll
Plaza

Chaffee Av
Hatting Pl
Clemmon Pl
Giegerich Av
E 177 St
Tierney Pl

Prentiss Av
Pennyfield Av

Reynolds
Longstreet Av

Mullan

295

3170

Throgs
Keamey Av
Ext
3000

Neck Blvd
Schurz Av

Hollywood
Wilton
2900
180

Pl

Chaffee Av
290
Clemmon Pl
330
Giegerich Pl
Tierney Pl

Oak Av
N Poplar Av
Holly
Av
N Mitchell

TS AV
Msgr
Halpin Pl

Catalpa Pl
Balsam Pl
Linder
Aster Pl
Pl

Sunset Tr
Plaza Pl
Acorn Pl
Beech Pl
Cedar Pl
Daisy Pl
Elm Pl
Fern Pl
Geranium Pl
Hazel Pl
Ivy Pl
Jasmine Pl

Dare Pl
Egert Pl
Fern Pl
Alan Pl
Bevy Pl
Casler Pl
Schurz
Ter

State University
of New York
Maritime College

THROGS NECK EXPWY

Magnolia Pl
Indian Ter

Sound View
Ter

C
D

East River

2 MILES = 3.2 KMS

Bronx County
Queens County

END 3 MINS

2 MILES= 3.2 KMS

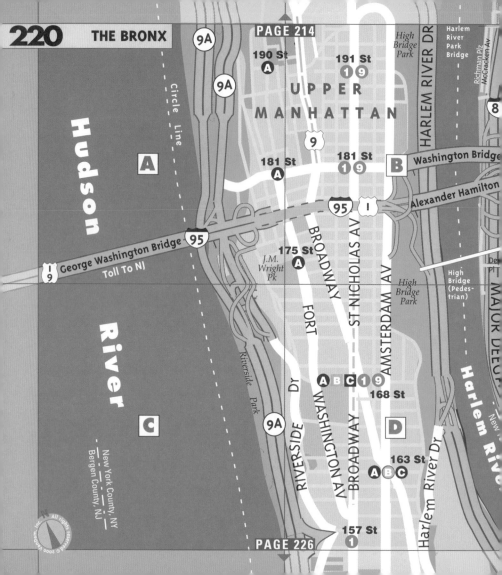

9A
9A

PAGE 214

190 St
A

191 St
1 9

U P P E R
M A N H A T T A N

9

High
Bridge
Park

HARLEM RIVER DR

Harlem
River
Park
Bridge

Richman Plz
McCracken Av

8

181 St
A

181 St
1 9

B Washington Bridge

Hudson

A

Circle Line

9

95 H Alexander Hamilton

95

George Washington Bridge
1 9
Toll To NJ

175 St
A

J.M.
Wright
Pk

BROADWAY

ST NICHOLAS AV

AMSTERDAM AV

High
Bridge
Park

High
Bridge
(Pedestrian)

De
Pl

MAJOR DEEG

River

Riverside Park

C

RIVERSIDE DR

FORT

WASHINGTON AV

BROADWAY

9A

A B C 1 9
168 St

D

Harlem River Dr

Harlem River

New York County, NY
Bergen County, NJ

A B C
163 St

157 St
1

PAGE 226

© 2000 Hagstrom, INC. All Rights Reserved

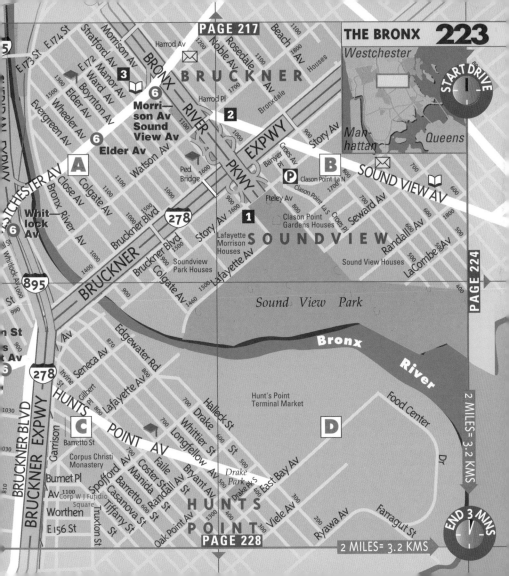

START DRIVE

Westchester

Manhattan

Queens

BRUCKNER

Harrod Av

Rosedale Av

Noble Av

Beach Av

Harrod Pl

Bronxdale

BRONX RIVER PKWY

EXPWY

Story Av

E 173 St

E 174 St

Stratford Av

Morrison Av

Manor Av

E 172

Ward Av

Boynton Av

Elder Av

Wheeler Av

Evergreen Av

Morrison Av
Sound View Av

Elder Av

Watson Av

Ped Bridge

Croes Av

Banyer Pl

Story Av

Clason Point La N

Clason Point La S

Fteley Av

Cross Pl

SOUND VIEW AV

WESTCHESTER AV

Colgate Av

Close Av

Bronx River Av

Bruckner Blvd

278

Story Av

Lafayette Av

Morrison Houses

Clason Point
Gardens Houses

Seward Av

Randall Av

LaCombe Av

Whitlock Av

BRUCKNER

Colgate Av

Bruckner Blvd

Soundview
Park Houses

Lafayette Av

SOUNDVIEW

Sound View Houses

895

Sound View Park

Bronx

River

Food Center Dr

Av

Edgewater Rd

Seneca Av

Lafayette Av

Hunt's Point
Terminal Market

278

Irvine St

Gilbert Pl

HUNTS

POINT

AV

Garrison

Barretto St

Halleck St

Drake St

Whittier St

Longfellow Av

Faile St

Bryant Av

East Bay Av

BRUCKNER BLVD

BRUCKNER EXPWY

Corpus Christi
Monastery

Burnet Pl

Corp W J Fufidio
Square

Worthen

E 156 St

Spofford Av

Coster St

Barretto St

Manida St

Randall Av

Casanova St

Tiffany St

Oak Point Av

Truxton St

Drake Park

Drake St S

Viele Av

Ryawa Av

Farragut St

HUNTS

POINT

PAGE 228

PAGE 224

2 MILES = 3.2 KMS

END 3 MINS

2 MILES= 3.2 KMS

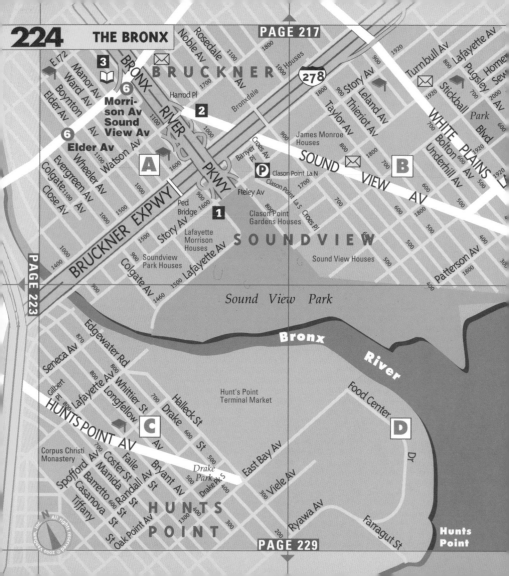

PAGE 217

PAGE 223

PAGE 229

BRUCKNER

SOUND VIEW AV

SOUNDVIEW

Sound View Park

Bronx

River

HUNTS POINT AV

HUNTS POINT

Hunts Point

E 172

Manor Av
Ward Av
Boynton Av
Elder Av

Noble Av
Rosedale Av

BRONX RIVER PKWY

Harrod Pl

Bronxdale

Houses

278

Story Av
Leland Av
Thieriot Av
Taylor Av

Turnbull Av
Lafayette Av
Pugsley Av
Home Sew

Stickball Park Blvd

WHITE PLAINS

Bolton Av
Underhill Av

Morrison Av
Sound View Av

Elder Av

Wheeler Av
Evergreen Av
Colgate Av
Close Av

Watson Av

A

Cross Av
Banyer Pl

James Monroe Houses

B

BRUCKNER EXPWY

Story Av

Ped Bridge

1

Lafayette Morrison Houses

Soundview Park Houses

Colgate Av

Lafayette Av

P

Clason Point La N

Clason Point La S

Fteley Av

Cross Pl

Clason Point Gardens Houses

Sound View Houses

Patterson Av

Seneca Av

Edgewater Rd

Gilbert Pl
Lafayette Av
Longfellow Av
Whittier St
Drake St
Halleck St

Hunt's Point Terminal Market

Food Center Dr

D

C

Corpus Christi Monastery

Spofford Av
Coster St
Faile St
Manida St
Barretto St
Randall Av
Bryant Av
Casanova St
Tiffany St
Oak Point Av

Drake Park

Drake St S

East Bay Av

Viele Av

Ryawa Av

Farragut St

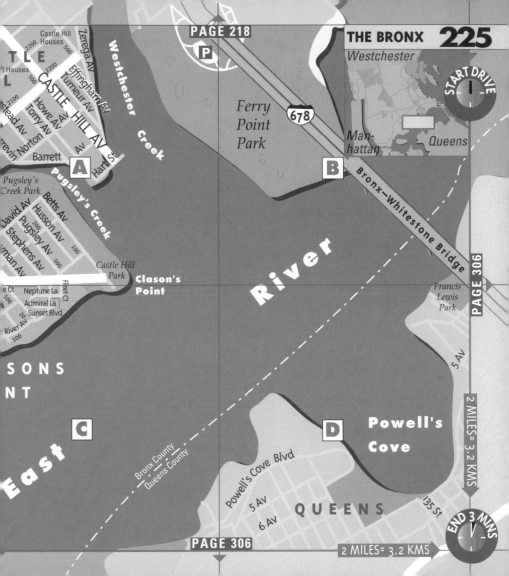

Westchester

START DRIVE

Ferry
Point
Park

678

Man-
hattan

Queens

Castle Hill
Houses 2200 500

Zerega Av

Effingham Av

Tumeur Av

Westchester Creek

l Houses 2200

CASTLE HILL AV

Howe Av

Torry Av

2100

stead Av

revin Norton Av

Barrett

Hart St

A

CASTLE
HIL
TLE
L

Pugsley's
Creek Park

Betts Av

David Av Husson Av

Pugsley Av 200

Stephens Av 100

rman Av

Pugsley's Creek

B

Bronx-Whitestone Bridge

PAGE 306

Francis
Lewis
Park

5 Av

Castle Hill
Park

Clason's
Point

e Ct

Neptune La

Admiral La

Sunset Blvd

River Av

100

Fleet Ct

River

SONS
NT

East C

Bronx County
Queens County

D

Powell's
Cove

Powell's Cove Blvd

5 Av

6 Av

QUEENS

135 St

2 MILES= 3.2 KMS

END 3 MINS

2 MILES= 3.2 KMS

PAGE 221

5

E 157 St

River Av

E 153 St

Bronx
Terminal
Market

87

E 151

Cromwell Av

E 15

① 157 St

155 St Ⓐ Ⓑ Ⓒ

W 155 ST

155 St Ⓓ Macombs Dam Bridge

Harlem

HARLEM R. DRIVE

9A

Ⓐ

ST NICHOLAS AV

EDGECOMBE AV

Jackie Robinson Park

FREDERICK DOUGLASS BLVD

Bronx County
New York County

Ⓑ

148 St ③

145 St Ⓐ Ⓒ
Ⓑ Ⓓ

W 145 ST

145 St ③

145 St Bridge

Ho
Co
Co

E 15

145 St
① ⑨

CONVENT AV

Hudson River

Riverbank
State
Park

River

Madison

UPPER
MANHATTAN

137 St
① ⑨

HENRY HUDSON PKWY

RIVERSIDE DR

135 St
Ⓑ Ⓒ

W 135 ST

Ⓒ

BROADWAY

AMSTERDAM AV

Ⓓ

SEVENTH AV

LENOX AV

FIFTH AV

PARK AV

PAGE 144

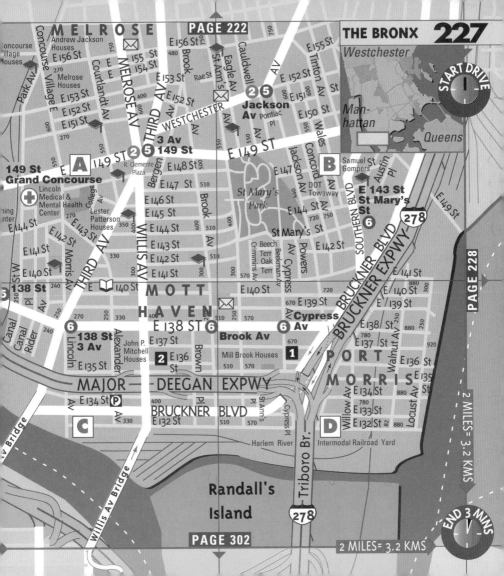

MELROSE

Andrew Jackson Houses

Concourse Village Houses

E 156 St

155 St

154 St

E 153 St

E 152 St

E 151 St

Park Av

Concourse Village E

Courtlandt Av

MELROSE AV

THIRD AV

WESTCHESTER AV

Brook

E 156 St

E 153 St

E 152 St

St Ann's AV

Eagle Av

Cauldwell AV

Rae St

E 155 St

Tinton Av

Wales AV

E 152 Av

E 151 St

E 150 St

Westchester

Manhattan

Queens

START DRIVE

Jackson Av

2 5

Jackson Av

Pontiac Pl

3 Av

149 St

2 5

149 St

R. Clemente Plaza

Bergen

E 148 St

E 147 St

E 146 St

E 145 St

E 144 St

E 143 St

E 142 St

E 141 St

Brook AV

College AV

WILLIS AV

THIRD AV

Morris AV

Lester Patterson Houses

149 St
A Grand Concourse

Lincoln Medical & Mental Health Center

E 144 St

E 143 St

E 142 St

E 141 St

E 140 St

138 St

St W

Morris AV

Canal Pl

Canal

Canal

Rider

Alexander

6

138 St
3 Av

John P. Mitchell Houses

E 137 St

2 E 136 St

E 135 St

E 134 St

Lincoln AV

Alexander

MAJOR — DEEGAN EXPWY

P

E 134 St

C

BRUCKNER BLVD

E 132 St

St Ann's

Brown

Pl

E 149 ST

St Mary's Park

DOT Towaway

E 147

E 144 St

St Mary's

E 142 St

Beech Terr

Oak Terr

Crimmins AV

Beekman AV

Powers

Cypress

6

B

Samuel St

Gompers

E 143 St
St Mary's St

Austin Pl

Concord AV

Jackson AV

Southern BLVD

E 149 St

E 141 St

E 140 St

E 139 St

Cypress AV

Cypress Av

6

Brook Av

Mill Brook Houses

MOTT

HAVEN

E 138 ST

6

E 140 St

670

670

1

BRUCKNER BLVD

BRUCKNER EXPWY

E 138 St

E 137 St

E 136 St

E 135 St

E 134 St

E 133 St

E 132 St

Walnut AV

Willow AV

Locust AV

PORT

MORRIS

D

Harlem River

Cypress Pl

St Ann's

Cypress Br

Triboro Br

Intermodal Railroad Yard

Randall's Island

278

278

END 3 MINS

PAGE 228

PAGE 223

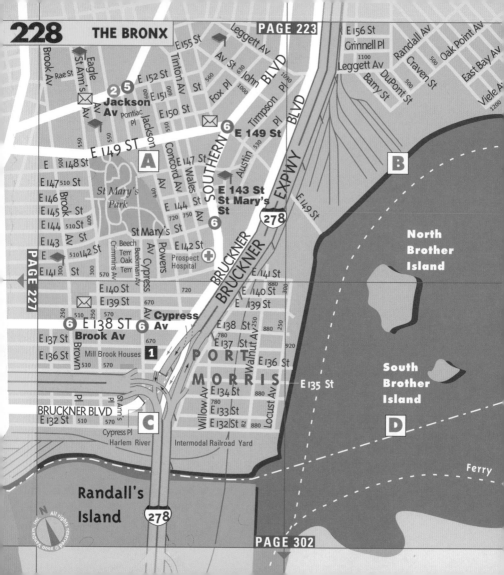

Brook Av
Rae Ave
Eagle Av
St Ann's
E 155 St
Leggett Av
E 156 St
Grinnell Pl
Leggett Av
1100
Randall Av
Craven St
Oak Point Av
East Bay Av
Viele Av

E 152 St
Tinton Av
Av St
John
30
560
BLVD
Barry St
DuPont St
500
1000

Jackson Av
Pontiac Pl
Jackson
E 151 St
E 150 St
Fox Pl
Timpson Pl
1060

SOUTHERN BLVD
E 149 St

EXPWY BLVD

E 149 ST

E 148 St
005
E 147 St 510 St
E 146 St
E 145 St
E 144 St 510 St
E 143 St
E 142 St

St Mary's Park

Concord Av
Wales Av

E 147 St
E 143 St
St Mary's St
St Mary's

E 144 St
720 750

Austin Pl
530

E 149 St

278
BRUCKNER
EXPWY

B

North Brother Island

Brook St
Beech Ter
Oak Ter
Beekman Ter
Crimmins Av

Powers
E 142 St
Prospect Hospital

Cypress Av

BRUCKNER

E 141 St
300

E 141 St

E 140 St
E 139 St
E 138 ST
Brook Av
E 137 St
E 136 St

Cypress Av
Brown

Mill Brook Houses
570
510
670
570

Cypress Av

E 140 St
300
E 139 St
E 138 St
E 137 St
250
780
920
E 136 St

Walnut Av
880
250

P O R T
M O R R I S
E 135 St

South Brother Island

D

BRUCKNER BLVD
E 132 St
510
570

St Ann's Pl
Pl
C

Cypress Pl
Harlem River

Intermodal Railroad Yard

E 134 St
E 133 St
E 132 St
82
880

Willow Av
780
880
Locust Av

Randall's Island

278

Ferry

PAGE 227
PAGE 302

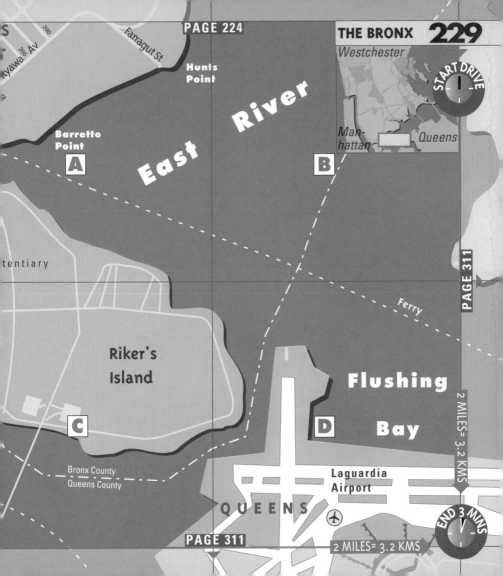

Westchester

START DRIVE

Man-
hattan

Queens

Farragut St

Hunts
Point

Barretto
Point

A

East River

B

tentiary

Riker's
Island

C

Bronx County
Queens County

D

Flushing

Bay

Ferry

2 MILES= 3.2 KMS

Laguardia
Airport

QUEENS

END 3 MINS

2 MILES= 3.2 KMS

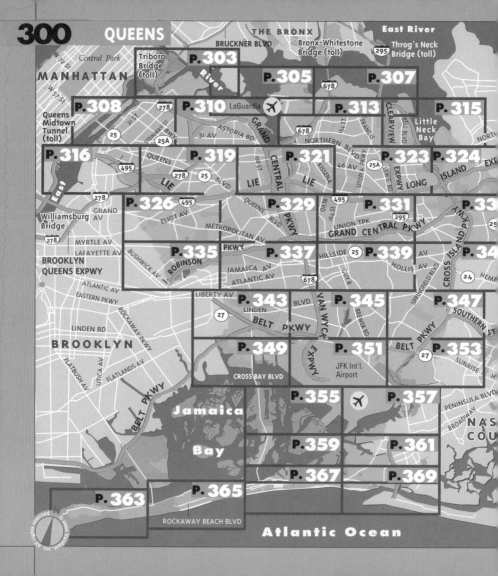

Best of Queens

onglomeration of towns, villages,
topian real estate developments
most diverse community on earth.
75 languages are spoken in NYC's
st borough. Among its 1.9 million
nts are the largest populations
eks outside Athens, Dominicans
le Santo Domingo, and Colombians
le Bogotá. Its cultural attractions
orld renowned.

erican Museum of the
ving Image

of TV, film, digital imaging
ology, and pop-art rejoice in
olendid resource. Its "Behind
enes" is a hands-on, interactive
en for would-be image makers.
t-see on the culture map of NYC.
35 Av (36 St), Astoria,
4-0077. **309C**

er's Edge

acular views of Manhattan
ement the elegant setting and
did seafood. 44th Dr ⮚ East River,
2-0033. **308C**

aica Bay Wildlife Refuge

s-in-the-know treasure these vast
vetlands and uplands to see over
fferent species of birds. The annual
mas count is a NYC ritual.
3:30AM-5PM. Cross Bay Blvd ⮚
channel. 718-318-4300. **358B**

Flushing Meadows–Corona Park

Created for the 1939 World's Fair,
this park is a celebration of city
impressario Bob Moses's vision
of the city beautiful. It is also
the center of culture in Queens.
Is it possible that Walt Disney was
inspired by the 1965 World's Fair
in creating a permanent one at
Walt Disney World? **320D**

Queens Museum of Art

In addition to its excellent art and
photography exhibits, the museum
showcases "The Panorama of NYC,"
the world's largest architectural
scale model. A revelation for anyone
fascinated by how the map becomes
the model. 718-592-5555. **320D**

NY Hall of Science

Over 150 interactive exhibits
covering light, color and quantum
physics make this **the** hands-on
science and technology center of NYC.
718-699-0005. **320B**

Shea Stadium

This arena is filled with history—
from bringing the National League
back to the city to winning the
World Series in '69. 126th St ⮚
Roosevelt Av. 718-507-8499.
320B

Queens Stats:
Population:
1.9 million

Area:
112.1 sq miles

THE US OPEN IS AN ANNUAL RITE

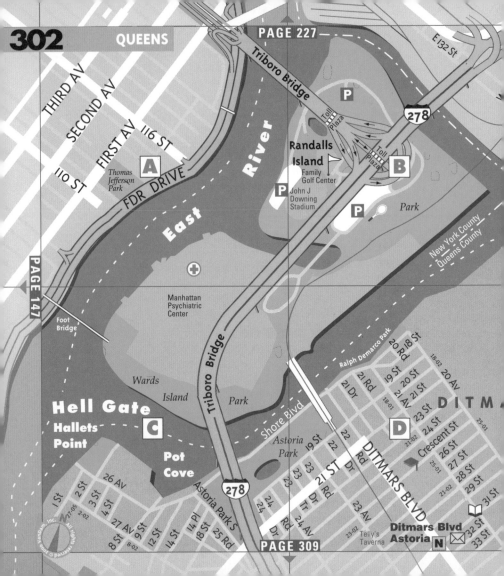

THIRD AV

SECOND AV

FIRST AV

116 ST

110 ST

Thomas Jefferson Park

A

FDR DRIVE

Triboro Bridge

E 132 St

P

278

Toll Plaza

Randalls Island

Family Golf Center

Toll Plaza

B

P

John J Downing Stadium

P

Park

East River

New York County
Queens County

Manhattan Psychiatric Center

Foot Bridge

Triboro Bridge

Wards Island

Park

Hell Gate

Hallets Point

C

Ralph Demarco Park

20 Rd

18 St

19 St

20 St

21 St

20 AV

18-02

21 Dr

21 Rd

21 AV

18-01

23 St

DITMAR

Shore Blvd

22

22 Rd

24 St

Crescent St

26 St

25-01

D

21-02

25-01

Pot Cove

26 AV

1 St

2 St

3 St

4

Astoria Park S

Astoria Park

19 St

22

21 ST

22 Rd

27 St

28 St

29 St

21-02

25-01

31 St

27 AV

9 St

12 St

14 St

14 PI

18 St

25 Rd

23

23

24

24 Dr

23 Tr

24

21 Rd

23 Dr

23 Rd

24 AV

23 AV

DITMARS BLVD

23-02

Telly's Taverna

Ditmars Blvd Astoria

N

32 St

33 St

8 St

8-02

278

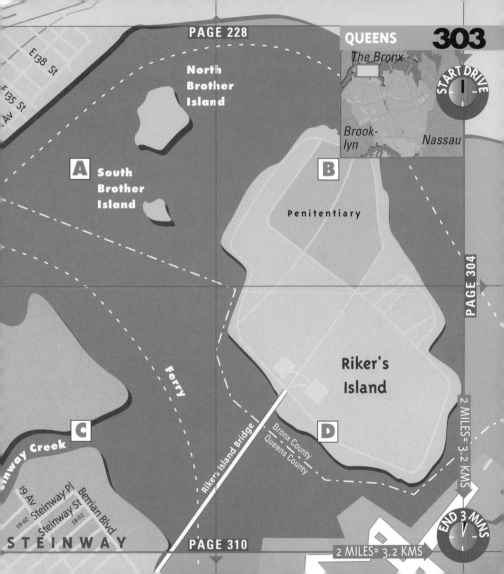

The Bronx

START DRIVE
I

Brook-
lyn

Nassau

E 138 St

E 135 St
Av

North
Brother
Island

A South
Brother
Island

B

Penitentiary

PAGE 304

Ferry

Riker's
Island

D

2 MILES = 3.2 KMS

C
nway Creek

Riker's Island Bridge

Bronx County
Queens County

19 Av
Steinway Pl
Steinway St
Berrian Blvd
19:02
18:02

S T E I N W A Y

2 MILES = 3.2 KMS

END 3 MINS

PAGE 229

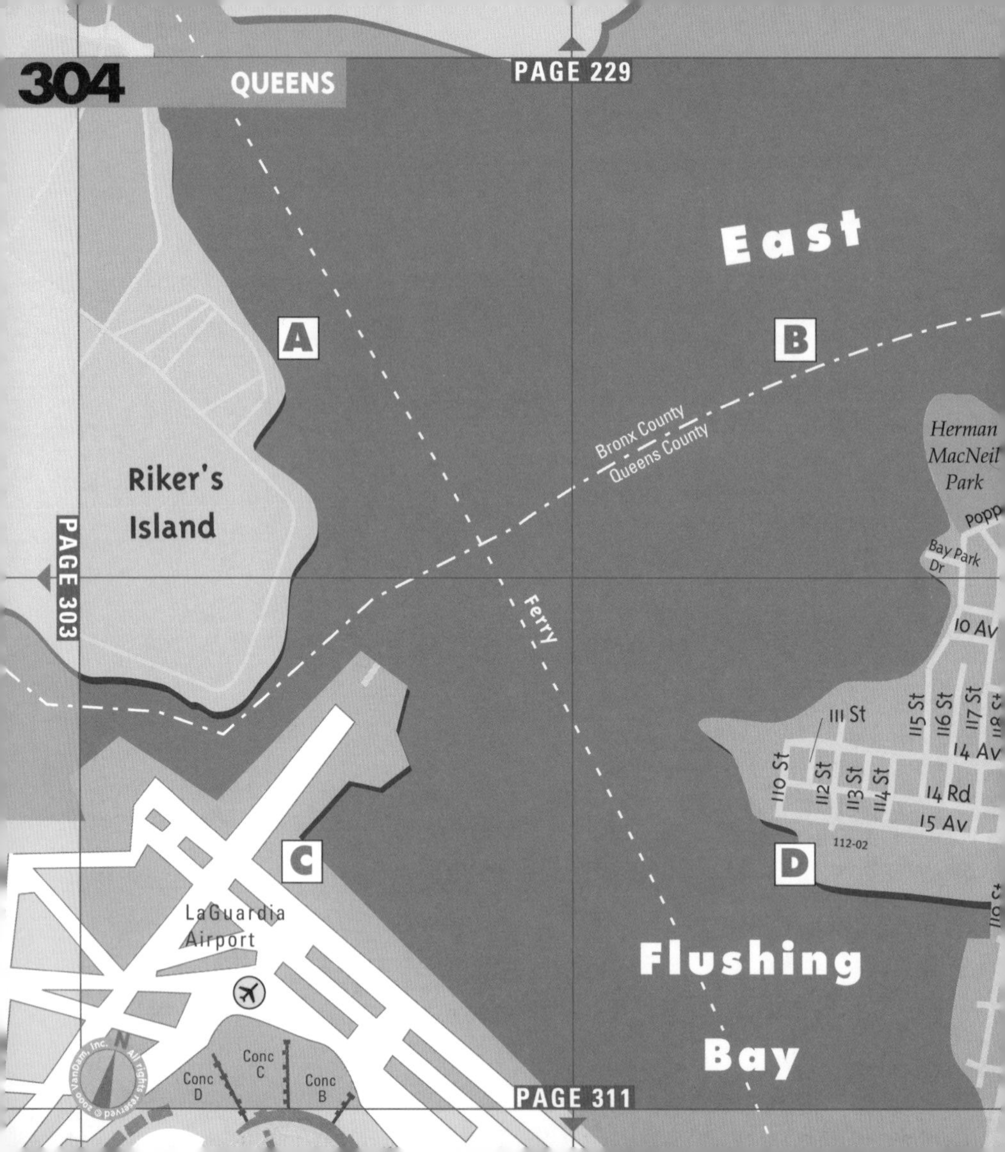

PAGE 303

East

A

B

Riker's
Island

Bronx County
Queens County

Ferry

*Herman
MacNeil
Park*

Popp

*Bay Park
Dr*

10 Av

111 St

110 St
112 St
113 St
114 St
115 St
116 St
117 St

14 Av

14 Rd

15 Av

112-02

C

LaGuardia
Airport

✈

Conc
D

Conc
C

Conc
B

D

Flushing

Bay

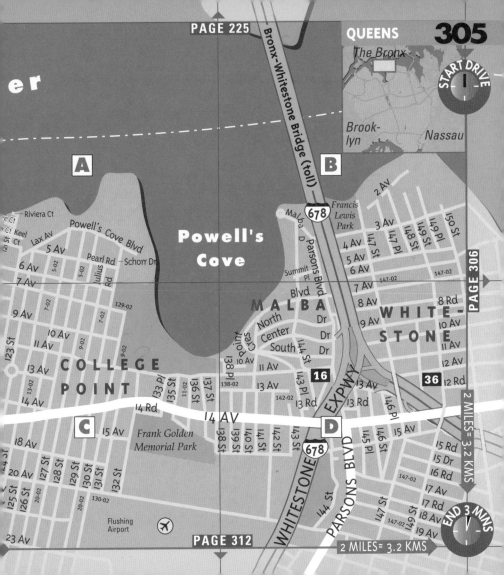

Bronx-Whitestone Bridge (toll)

The Bronx

START DRIVE

Brook-lyn   Nassau

A

B

2 AV

Riviera Ct

e Ct

Ct Keel

Ct

Lax Av

Powell's Cove Blvd

5 Av

Pearl Rd — Schorr Dr

6 Av

Julius Rd

7 Av

Malba Dr

678

Francis Lewis Park

3 Av

147 St

147 Pl

148 St

149 St

149 Pl

150 St

4 Av

5 Av

6 Av

Parsons Blvd

Summit Pl

Blvd

7 Av

147-02

147-02

Powell's Cove

129-02

7-02

7-02

M A L B A

8 Av

8 Rd

9 Av

W H I T E -

S T O N E

10 Av

11 Av

PAGE 306

9 Av

10 Av

11 Av

123 St

9-02

9-02

North Center South

Dr

Dr

Dr

12 Av

12 Av

C O L L E G E

P O I N T

13 Av

13-02

Point Cres

10 Av

114 St

143 St

11 Av

16

13 Av

12 Rd

36

138 Pl

138-02

142-02

14 Av

133 Pl

135 St

136 St

137 St

11-02

12-02

13 Av

13 Rd

13 Rd

146 Pl

14 Rd

14 AV

D

C

15 Av

Frank Golden Memorial Park

138 St

139 St

140 St

141 St

142 St

143 St

144 St

678

15 Av

146 Pl

145 Pl

15 Rd

15 Dr

16 Rd

18 Av

127 St

128 St

129 St

130 St

131 St

132 St

144 Av

20 Av

125 St

126 St

20-02

20-02

130-02

147-02

17 Av

17 Rd

18 Av

147 St

155 St

149 St

147-02

WHITESTONE

PARSONS BLVD

END 3 MINS

19 Av

Flushing Airport

23 Av

2 MILES = 3.2 KMS

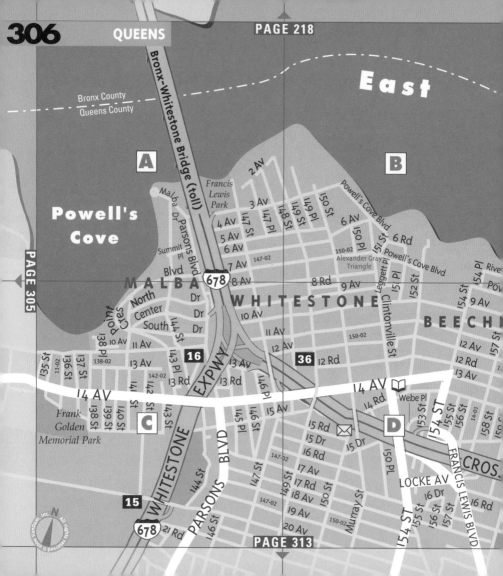

Bronx-Whitestone Bridge (toll)

Bronx County
Queens County

East

A

B

Francis Lewis Park

Powell's Cove

Malba Dr

Parsons Blvd

Summit Pl

Blvd

678

M A L B A

2 AV

3 AV
4 AV
5 AV
6 AV
7 AV
8 AV

147 St
147 St
148 St
149 Pl
149 St
150 St

147-02

Powell's Cove Blvd

6 AV

150 Pl
151 St

6 Rd

Powell's Cove Blvd

150-02
Alexander Gray Triangle

149-02 St
151 St
152 St

154 St
154 St

Rive
Pow
9 AV

W H I T E S T O N E

North
Center
Dr
South
Dr
Dr

8 Rd

9 AV

Clintonville St

B E E C H

Point Cres

138 Pl
10 AV
11 AV

144 St

10 AV
11 AV

12 AV
13 AV
13 Rd

142-02

143 St

141

142 St

135 St
137 St
136 St

120-11

138-02

138 St
139 St
140 St

10 AV
11 AV

12 AV
13 AV

13 Rd

16

EXPWY

13 AV
13 Rd

146 Pl
145 St
15 AV

12 AV

150-02

12 Rd

36

12 Rd

12 AV
12 Rd
13 AV

14 AV

14 AV

14 AV
14 Rd

Webe Pl

153 St

154 ST
155 St
156 St

14-01

158 St

C

Frank Golden Memorial Park

143 St

144 St

PARSONS BLVD

WHITESTONE

15 Rd
15 Dr
16 Rd

147-02

15 AV
145 St
146 Pl

15 Dr

✉

D

150 PL

FRANCIS LEWIS BLVD

CROS

15

678

21 Rd

146 St

141

147-02

17 AV
17 Rd
18 AV
19 AV
20 AV

149 St
150 St

Murray St

147-02

150-02

LOCKE AV

16 Dr

16 Rd

154 ST
155 St
156 St
157 St

PAGE 313

PAGE 305

N

The Bronx

START DRIVE

Brook-lyn

Nassau

River

295

State University
of New York
Maritime College

Throgs Neck Bridge (toll)

A

B

**Willets
Point**

Fort
Totten

Ordnance Rd

North
Loop

Shore Rd

Whistler Av

Walter
Reed Rd

Sylvester La

Abbot

Chapel Rd

Weaver Av

Willets St

Bayside Av

Willets St

Murray Av

Story Av

Pratt Av

Shore Rd

**Little
Bay**

Totten Av

Westaway Rd

Gen R W Berry
Dr

Sgt Beers Av

Sgt Beers Av

Totten Av

162-02

Blvd

166 St

Burton St

9-01

Totten St

Utopia PKWY

9-01

St

162-02

Burton St

165 St

14 Rd

Totten St

Burton St

C

33

Little Bay Park

D

32

ND

15 Dr

WILLETS POINT PKWY

UTOPIA PKWY

BLVD

15 Rd

200 St

201 St

202 St

34

295

PKWY

Clearview
Park

Emily Rd

Robin La

Estates La

Darren Dr

Melissa Ct

Lori Dr

Brian
Cres

Michael Ct

Estates Dr

Jordan Dr

Bonnie La

Diane Pl

208 Pl

Robert Rd

14 Av

15 Av

209 St

15 Av

212 St

215 St

Water Edge
Dr

216 St

215 St

Michael Pl

BELL BLVD

2 MILES= 3.2 KMS

2 MILES= 3.2 KMS

END 3 MINS

PAGE 131

PAGE 131

PAGE 316

E 75 St
E 65 St
THIRD AV
SECOND AV
FIRST AV
E 72 ST
E 60 St
E 57 ST
E 59 St
YORK AV

FDR DRIVE

Coler Memorial Hospital

New York County
Queens County

Ha
Co

Isamu Noguchi Garden Museum

33 Rd

Rainey Park

West Channel

River Rd

NY Hospital Cornell Medical Center

Rockefeller University Hospital

A

B

P

Roosevelt Is. Bridge

13
12-02

9 St
10 St
11 St
12 St

Ravenswood

Correction Hospital

60 St Heliport

Main St

Roosevelt Island

S

Roosevelt Island Tramway

Queensboro Bridge

East Channel

BLVD

VERNON

36 Av
37 Av
38 Av
39 Av
30 St

21 ST

Hous

West Rd
East Rd

Queens Bridge Park

Queensbridge

8-01
8-01

40 Av
41 Av

13 St

21 St (Queensbridge)

S

LO
CI

Goldwater Memorial Hospital

City Hospital

C

25

41 Av

Houses

22 St
23 St
24 St

Crescent St
27 St
28 St
29 Rd
29 St

D

38-02

N

Fila Sports Club

Water's Edge

9 St
10 St
11 St

43 Rd
43 Av

43-02

Plaza

Queens Plaza

41-02
41-02

Club Broadway

Queensboro Plaza

7

Roosevelt Island

44 Av
44 Rd
44 Dr
45 Av
45 Rd

11-01

43-02

42

Rd

N

Queensboro Plaza

E F

Queens Plaza

46 Av
46 Rd
47 Av

E F

23 St (Ely Av)

Hunter St

N

G R

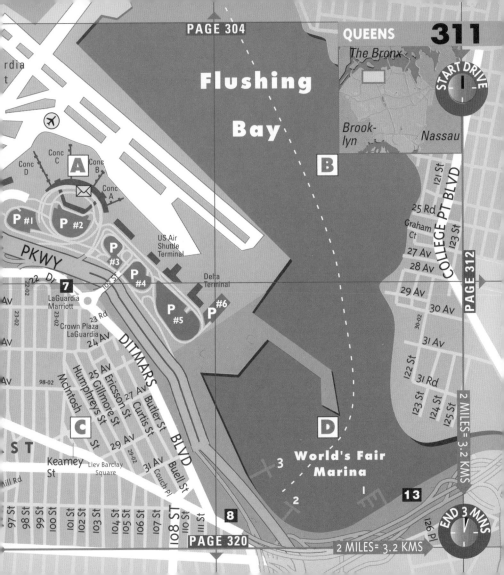

The Bronx

Brook-lyn

Nassau

START DRIVE

Flushing

Bay

rdia
t

Conc C

Conc D

A

Conc B

Conc A

B

P #1

P #2

121 St

25 Rd

Graham Ct

123 St

27 Av

US Air Shuttle Terminal

P #3

28 Av

COLLEGE PT BLVD

PKWY

22 Dr

22-02

7

P #4

Delta Terminal

29 Av

30 Av

PAGE 312

LaGuardia Marriott

23-02

23-02

23 Rd

P #5

P #6

30-02

31 Av

122 St

Crown Plaza LaGuardia

24 AV

DITMARS

31 Rd

123 St

124 St

125 St

25 AV

Ericsson St

Gillmore St

Humphreys St

Curtis St

Butler St

27 Av

McIntosh St

98-02

C

29 Av

29-02

BLVD

Buell St

D

2 MILES= 3.2 KMS

Keamey St

Liev Barclay Square

31 Av

Couch Pl

3

World's Fair Marina

13

97 St

98 St

99 St

100 St

101 St

102 St

103 St

104 St

105 St

106 St

107 St

110 St

111 St

108 St

8

2

I

126 Pl

END 3 MINS

S T

Av

23-02

Av

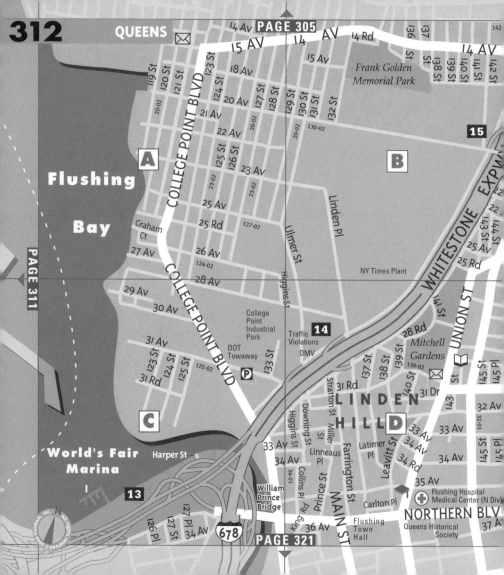

START DRIVE

The Bronx

Brook-
lyn

Nassau

2 MILES = 3.2 KMS

Rd

146 Pl

146 St

145 St

145 Pl

36

14 AV

CROSS

14 St

14 Rd

CLINTONVILLE

ISLAND

150 PL

Webe Pl

153 St

154 ST

155 St

156 St

157 St

14-01

14-01

157-02

12 Rd

13 Av

160 St

14 Av

158 St

159 St

Cryder's La

161 St

162 St

163 St

15 Av

15 Rd

15 Dr

15 Dr

16 Rd

147-02

17 Av

17 Rd

18 Av

19 Av

147-02

20 Av

20 Rd

21 Av

22 Av

23 Av

24 Av

A

150-02

147 St

149 St

150 St

147-02

Murray St

LOCKE AV

16 Dr

155 St

156 St

157 St

18 Av

16 Rd

16 Av

16-01

PKWY

B

Clintonville St

Larry Muss
Memorial
Square

WILLETS POINT BLVD

Clearview
Gardens

166-02

163-02

163-02

163-02

166-02

166-02

17 Av

19 Av

21 Av

200 St

201 St

202 St

17-02

20-02

21-02

Clearview Park

UTOPIA PKWY

154 ST

LLETS POINT BLVD

148 St

Memorial
Field
of Flushing

150-02

Murray La

24 Rd

25 Av

25 Dr

26 Av

27 Av

28 Av

29 Av

157 St

157-02

157-02

157-02

160 St

22-02

163 St

163-02

FRANCIS

166 St

166-02

169-02

169-02

169 St

22 Av

23 Av

24 Av

24 Rd

26 Av

27 Av

28 Av

LEWIS

203 St

28-02

28-02

C

P. R. Bayer
Square

150 St

149 Pl

Murray La

Murray St

152 St

153 St

155 St

156 St

29 AV

Bowne
Park

33 Rd

158 St

159 St

BAYSIDE LA

D

161 St

162 St

164 St

165 St

29-01

29 Av

29-01

168 St

167 St

33 Av

Henry T
Triangle

170 St

171 St

172 St

29-01

LEWIS

BLVD

30 Av

32
Rd

200 St

Jordan St

32 Av

29 Av

END 3 MINS

MURRAY

HILL

35 Av

38 Av

25A

33-01

33-01

33-01

2 MILES= 3.2 KMS

2 MILES= 3.2 KMS

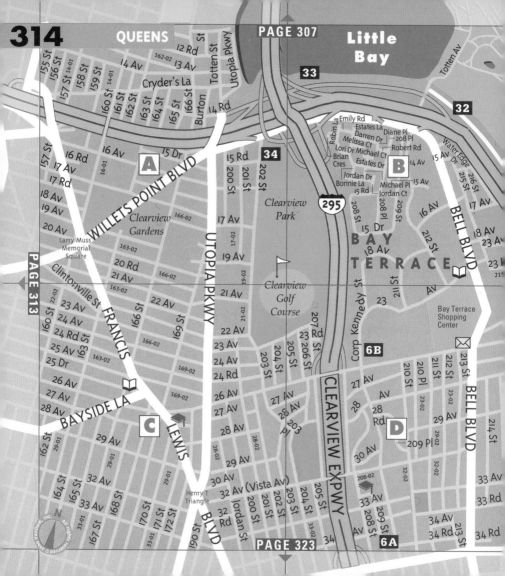

QUEENS

PAGE 307

Little Bay

12 Rd

162-02 13 Av

14 Av

Cryder's La

33

32

14 Rd

Emily Rd

Estates La

Robin La

Darren Dr Diane Pl 208 Pl

Melissa Ct Robert Rd

Lori Dr Michael Ct

Brian Cres

Estates Dr 14 Av 15 Dr

Water Edge Dr

15 Dr

15 Rd

34

Jordan Dr Michael Pl 15 Av

Bonnie La Jordan Ct

15 Rd 208 Pl

16 Av

15 Dr

15 Rd

Clearview Park

295

BAY

TERRACE

18 Av

23 Av

23

212 St

BELL BLVD

17 Av

18 Av

23 Av

16 Av 16 Rd

16-01

157 St 17 Av

17 Rd

18 Av

19 Av

20 Av

A

15 Dr

15 Rd

200 St 201 St 202 St

17 Av

17-02

19 Av

Clearview Gardens 166-02

Larry Muss Memorial Square

163-02

20 Rd

21 Av 166-02

163-02

B

Corp Kennedy St

23

211 St

Bay Terrace Shopping Center

PAGE 313

Clintonville St

FRANCIS

22-02 23 Av

191 St 24 Av

24 Rd St

163 St 25 Av

25 Dr

26 Av

27 Av

28 Av

166 St

169 St

22 Av

22-02

21-02

19-02

21 Av

22 Av

23 Av

24 Av

24 Rd

26 Av

27 Av

166-02

169-02

169-02

163-02

UTOPIA PKWY

203 St

204 St 205 St 206 St

207 St

23 Rd

23 Av

6B

27 Av

28

28 Av

28 Rd

209 Pl

D

210 Pl 211 St 212 St 213 St

210 St

23-02

29 Av

23-02

29-02 29-02

214 St

BELL BLVD

BAYSIDE LA

162 St 29-01

29 Av

29-01

32 Av

33 Av

29-01

C

LEWIS

28-02

28-02

29 Av

30 Av

32 Av (Vista Av)

Henry T Triangle

164 St 165 St

168 St

170 St 171 St 172 St

167 St

33-01

33-01

190 St

Jordan St

200 St 201 St

32 Rd

202 St 203 St

28 Av

203 Pl

204 St 205 St

33-02

CLEARVIEW EXPWY

30 Av

208-02

33 Av

34 Av

208 St

6A

34 Av 34 Rd

209 St

213 St

32-02

32-02

33 Av

33 Rd

34 Rd

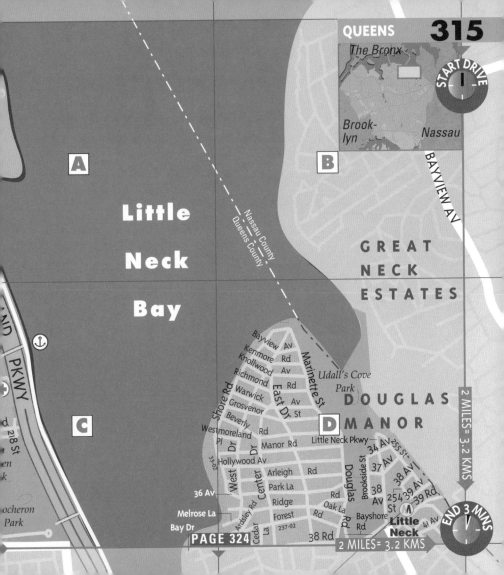

The Bronx

Brook-lyn

Nassau

START DRIVE

A

B

BAYVIEW AV

Little

Neck

Bay

Nassau County
Queens County

G R E A T

N E C K

E S T A T E S

Bayview Av
Kenmore Rd
Knollwood Av
Richmond Rd
Warwick Av
Grosvenor St
Beverly Rd
Westmoreland Pl

Shore Rd

East Dr

Marinette St

Udall's Cove Park

D O U G L A S

D **M A N O R**

Little Neck Pkwy

34 Av

255 St

C

West Dr

33-02

Manor Rd

Hollywood Av

Arleigh Park La

Ridge Rd

Forest Rd

Center Dr

Brookside St

Douglas Rd

37 Av

38 Av

38 Av

254 St

39 Av

39 Rd

Oak La

Bayshore Rd

Little Neck

41 Av

PKWY

218 St

en k

36 Av

Melrose La

Bay Dr

Ardsley Rd

Cedar La

237-02

38 Rd

PAGE 324

ocheron Park

2 MILES= 3.2 KMS

2 MILES= 3.2 KMS

2 MILES= 3.2 KMS

END 3 MINS

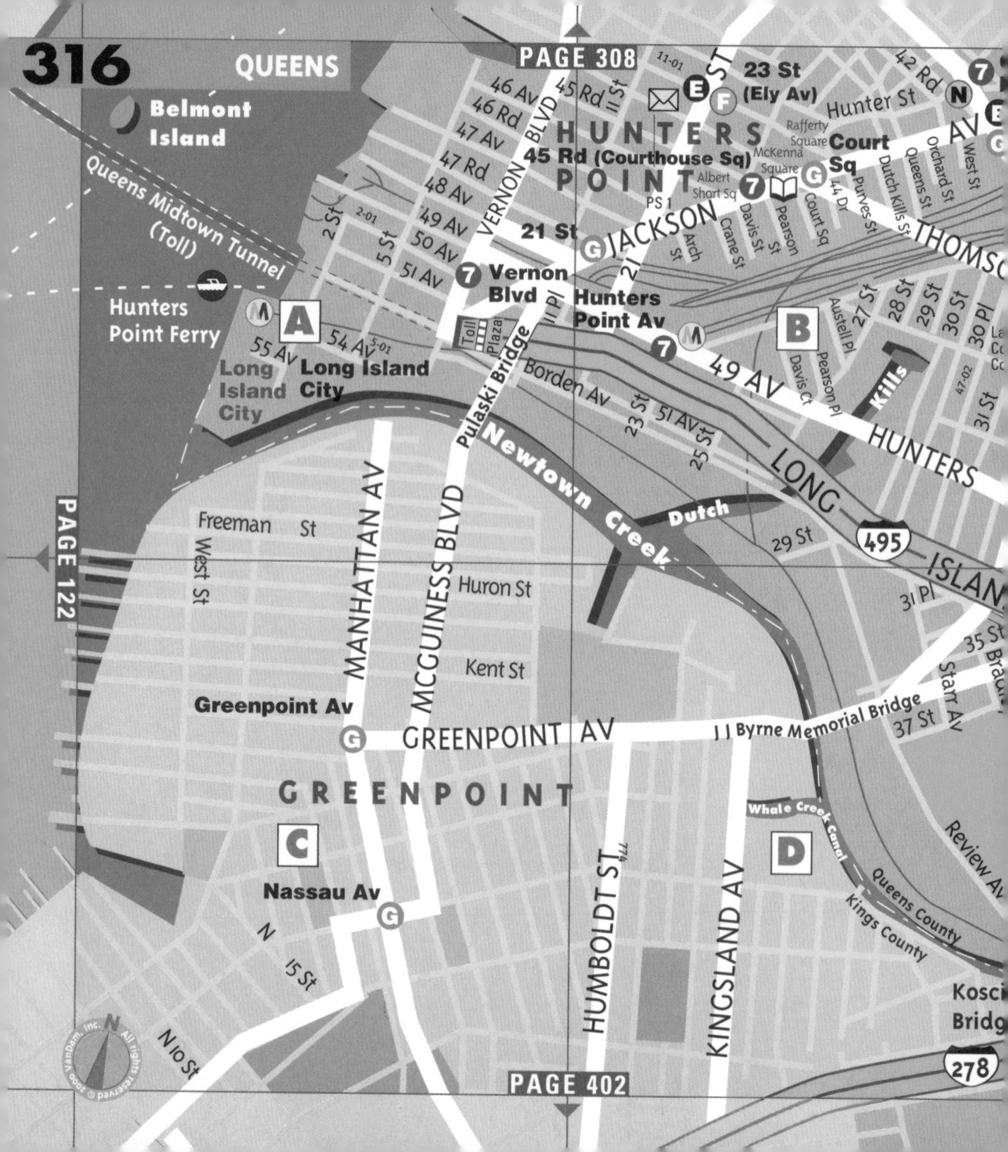

316

Belmont Island

Queens Midtown Tunnel (Toll)

Hunters Point Ferry

A

Long Island City

Long Island City

Long Island City

55 Av

54 Av

2 St

2-01

5 St

5-01

PAGE 308

11-01

E

F

23 St (Ely Av)

46 Av

46 Rd

47 Av

47 Rd

48 Av

49 Av

50 Av

51 Av

VERNON BLVD

45 Rd II St

45 Rd (Courthouse Sq)

HUNTERS POINT

Albert Short Sq

PS 1

21 St

G JACKSON AV

7 **Vernon Blvd**

Hunters Point Av

Rafferty Square

McKenna Square

Hunter St

Court Sq

Arch

Crane St

Davis St

Pearson

Court Sq

Purves St

L I Dr

Dutch Kills St

Queens St

Orchard St

THOMSON AV

N

E

42 Rd

7

West St

27 St

28 St

29 St

30 St

31 St

Austell Pl

47-02

Pearson Pl

Davis Ct

49 AV

B

LONG

HUNTERS

Kills

Le

Co

31 St

7

M

Toll Plaza

Pulaski Bridge

Borden Av

23 St

51 AV St

25 St

Newtown Creek

Dutch

29 St

495

ISLAN

31 Pl

35 St

Braden

PAGE 122

Freeman St

West St

MANHATTAN AV

MCGUINESS BLVD

Huron St

Kent St

Greenpoint Av

G GREENPOINT AV

J J Byrne Memorial Bridge

37 St

Starr Av

Review

G R E E N P O I N T

HUMBOLDT ST

KINGSLAND AV

Whale Creek Canal

D

C

Nassau Av

G

N 15 St

N 10 St

Queens County

Kings County

Kosci Bridg

PAGE 402

278

VanDam, Inc. all rights reserved

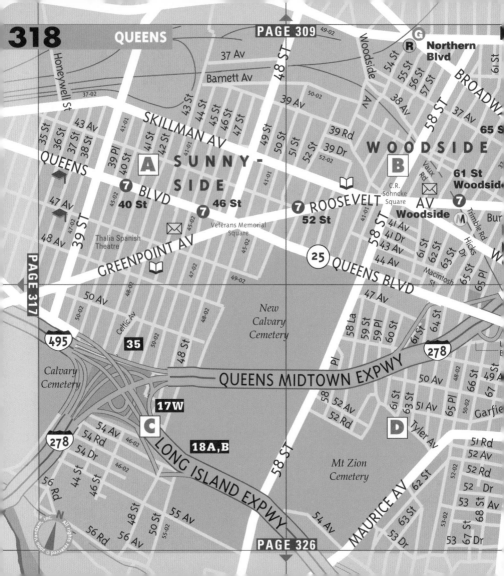

NORTHERN BLVD

71 St 72 St 73 St 74 St 75 St 76 St 77 St 80 St 81 St 82 St 83 St 84 St 85 St 86 St 87 St 88 St 90 St 91 St 92 St 93 St

34-02

25A Ⓟ

34 Av

The Bronx

START DRIVE

JACKSON

34-02

Brooklyn

Nassau

HEIGHTS

35 Av

Leverich St 70-02 Rd

37 Av

A ✉

37 Av

B

37 AV

Jackson Diner 37-02

37 Rd

74 St Broadway

82 St Jackson Hts

90 St Elmhurst Av

Junction Blvd

38 Av

37

E F 7 ROOSEVELT AV 7

Warren St

40 Rd

7

G R Jackson Hts Roosevelt Av

Baxter Av Forley Av

Benham St Aske St 40 Dr

97 Pl Spruce St 40 Rd

41 Av 41-02

Elmhurst Hospital Center

Pettit Pl

Gleane St

Denman St

41 Av

Case St

41 Rd

BAXTER AV

Ketcham St

Britton Av

Whitney

Elbertson St

42 Av

43 Av

National St 98 Pl

JUNCTION

44 Av

PAGE 320

AV

✉

Layton Vietor Av

ELMHURST AV

Hampton St Lamont

Ithaca St

43 Av

43 Av 43-02

44 Av

Judge St

Ketcham Pl

45 AV

Elmhurst Av R G

Whitney Av Macnish

Claremont Ter

48 Av 92 St 93 St

Corona Av

Alstyne Av

CORONA

46 Av

BROADWAY

Corona Av

50 Av

96 St 97 St 97 Pl 98 St

47 Av

Albion Av 76-02

Barnwell Av

88 St

91 Pl 91 St

Christie Av

Kneeland St Jacobus St

Cornish

Dongan

Corona Av

O'Connell

51 AV

BLVD

94 St

Ireland St

Poyer Av

St James

87 St

52 St

Henry Av 73 Pl

C

Hillyer St Gorsline St Manilla St

Simonson St Van Kleek St

Goldsmith St

Van Loon St

90 St

Grand Av Newtown

53 Av

D

Av

54

51 Rd 51 Dr

Kneeland Av

Codwise Pl

Reeder St

Justice Av

55 Av

AV

ELMHURST

55-02

Calamus Av

Calamus Cr

Elks Rd

Ankener Av

Haspel St

Van Horn St

R Seabury St

90-02

56 Av

57 Av

58 Av

IRS Lefrak City

52 Rd 52 Dr 52 Ct

GRAND AV

82 St 83 St 84 St 84-02

54 55 St

25

St Johns Hospital

Woodhaven Blvd

✉

59 Av

20

73 St 74 St

Weimar St

Hoffman Dr

R G

60 Av

END 3 MINS

2 MILES = 3.2 KMS

2 MILES = 3.2 KMS

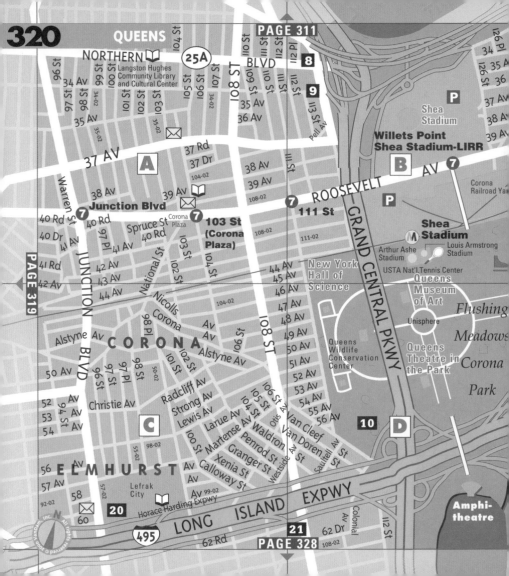

QUEENS

NORTHERN

Langston Hughes
Community Library
and Cultural Center

25A

PAGE 311

BLVD

8

9

101 St

96 St
66 St
86 St
34 St
34-02

101 St
102 St
103 St
35-02

108 St

110 St
109 St
110 St
111 St
112 St

113 St

Pell Av

34 Av

35 Av

36 Av

35 Av

A

37 AV

37 Rd
37 Dr
104-02

37 Dr

38 Av

38 Av
Junction Blvd

39 Av

Corona
Plaza

7

39 Av

7

**103 St
(Corona
Plaza)**

38 Av

39 Av

108-02

111 St

ROOSEVELT

7

AV

7

111 St

GRAND CENTRAL PKWY

Shea
Stadium

P

34
35 St
36

37 Av

38 Av

39 Av

126 Pl

126 St

**Willets Point
Shea Stadium-LIRR**

B

Corona
Railroad Yard

**Shea
Stadium**

Arthur Ashe
Stadium

Louis Armstrong
Stadium

USTA Nat'l.Tennis Center

P

Warren St

40 Rd
40 Dr

40 Rd

41 Av

97 St

41 Av

Spruce St
40 Rd

103 St

102 St

104 St

41 Rd

42 Av

JUNCTION

42 Av

National St

43 Av

44 Av

44 AV
45 AV
46 AV

47 AV

48 AV

**New York
Hall of
Science**

M

Queens
Museum
of Art

Flushing

Meadows

Unisphere

PAGE
319

C O R O N A

Nicolls

Corona

Av
Av

98 Pl

102 St

106 St

49 AV

50 AV

51 AV

Alstyne Av

Alstyne Av

BLVD

50 Av

96 St

97 St

98 St

101 St

50-02

52 AV

53 AV

54 AV

55 AV

Queens
Wildlife
Conservation
Center

Queens
Theatre in
the Park

Corona

Park

52 Av
53 Av
54 Av

94 St

Christie Av

Radcliff Av

Strong Av

Lewis Av

C

98-02

55-02

100 St

104 St

105 St

106 St

Larue Av

Martense Av

Waldron St

Penrod St

Granger St

Xenia St

Calloway St

Ohio

Van Cleef

Van Doren

Westside

Saultell St

56 AV

10

D

*Amphi-
theatre*

56 Av
57 Av

58

92-02

E L M H U R S T Av

Lefrak
City

57-02

99-02

20

60

Horace Harding Expwy

495

LONG ISLAND EXPWY

62 Rd

21

PAGE 328

62 Dr

108-02

Colonial

Av

112 St

QUEENS

PAGE 313

PAGE 321

PAGE 330

Roosevelt Av
Barton Av
41 Av
41 Av
Barclay Av
Murray Hill
146-02
SANFORD AV
Ash Av
Beech Av
Cherry Av
Delaware Av
Elm Av
45 Av
Hawthome Av
Hollywood Av
Jasmine Av
Kalmia Av
Laburnum Av

Depot Rd
Station Rd
Elmere Sturley Square
CROCHERON AV
Broadway
AUBURNDALE
37 Av
Auburnda
193-02
41 Av
42 Av
43 Rd
44 Av
45 Av
45 Rd
45 Dr
46 Av
46 Rd
47 Av

NORTHERN BLVD

UTOPIA PKWY
FRANCIS
Jordan St
34
34-02
Captain Mannheimer Circle
25A

157 St
158 St
159 St
160 St
161 St
35-01
163 St
164 St
165 St
166 St
157 St
158 St
159 St
160 St
161 St

162 ST

163 St
164 St
165 St
166 St
167 St
168 St
169 St
170 St
171 St
171 Pl
172 St

167 St
168 St
169 St
170 St
33-01
171 St
172 St
190 St
191 St
192 St

189 St
190 St
191 St
192 St
193 St
42-02
194 St
195 St
196 St

A
B
C
D

PARSONS BLVD

155 St
159 St
160 St
161 St
156 St
43 Av
43-02
45 Av
45-02
157 St
158 St

Smart St
Bowne Av
Burling St
Oak St
Poplar Av
Quince St
Rose AV
143-01

46 AV

Flushing Cemetery

Kissena Lake

Kissena Park

Bicycle Track

163 St
163 Pl
160-02

164 ST

Pidgeon Meadow
165 St
166 St
167 St
168 St
169 St
Lithonia Av
166
167
168
169
170 Pl
171
Metcalf Av
Underhill Av

Kissena Park Golf Course

Auburndale
Ashby Av
Bagley Av
Courtney Av
Effington Av
Fairchild Av
Gladwin Av
Underhill Av

Fresh Meadow
UTOPIA PKWY
175 Pl
184 St
185 St
50 Av
186 St
187 St
188 St
189 St
190 St
192 St
193St
195t

HOLLIS COURT BLVD

Underhill Av
Peck Av
53-02
56-02

157 St
158 St
159 St
160 St
161 St
162 St

BOOTH MEMORIAL AV

PAGE 315

Regatta Pl

38 Dr
38 Dy
39 AV
39 Rd
233 St
40 AV
231 St

233 Pl West Dr
Hillcrest Av
38 Dr
Cherry St
40 AV
41 AV

Willow Dr Willow Av Depew Av Depew Av
235 St
240 St

Douglaston 41 AV
42 AV

D O U G L A S T O N
43 AV 43 AV
242 St
243 St
247 St
248 St

DOUGLASTON PKWY
44 AV Cary Pl
242 St

38 Av
37 Av
223 St
41 Av
41 Rd
42 Av
222 St
220 St
221 St

38 Av
217 St
218 St
219 St
220 St
215 Pl
215 St
216 St
38-02
39 Av
40 Av
214 Pl

A

B

Golden Bear

31

25A

NORTH

**L I T T L E
N E C K**

Alameda Av
Rushmore
234 St
241 St
Hanford St
245 St
244 St
247 St
Ca
Va

Alley Pond
Environmental
Center

Alley
Pond
Park

Barrows Ct
243 St
51
Redfield St
241 St

Carolina Rd
Maryland Rd
51

NORTHERN BLVD

217 St
218 St
216 St
215 Pl
215 St
220 Pl
220 St
46 Av

42 Av
214 Pl
43 Av

PAGE 323

**Oakland
Lake**

47 Av

47 Rd
217-02

Dermody
Square

48 AV
49 Av
50 Av
51 AV

SPRINGFIELD

Enfield
Pl

Birmington Pkwy
Garland Dr
Kenilworth Dr

**Queensborough
Community
College**

Horatio Av
49 Rd Dr
Hoxie
228
229 St
230
56 St
231 St

232 St 231 St
East Hampton Blvd
50 Av
53 Av

CROSS ISLAND PKWY

240 Pl

52 Av
53 Av St
241 St
240 St

31

30N

53 Av
54 Av

C

56 AV
56-02
56-02

213 St
214 St
215 St
217 St
218 St
219 St
58-02

29

59 Av

56 Rd
57 AV
57 AV
225 St
226 St
223 St
224 St

Cloverdale Blvd
57 Av
57 Rd 230-02
58 Av
58 Rd

56 Rd
231 St
56 Av

EXPWY

DOUGLASTON PKWY

D

30

65 Av
66 AV
67 Av
68 Av
69 Av
70 AV
242 St

Horace Harding Expwy

LONG ISLAND

W Alley Rd

30S

495

BELL BLVD

212 St

BLVD

219-02

64 Av
64-02
224 St
65 Av
Cloverdale Blvd
228 St
229 St
230 St
231 St
232 St
233 St
67 Av

PAGE 332

**Decadon
Pond**

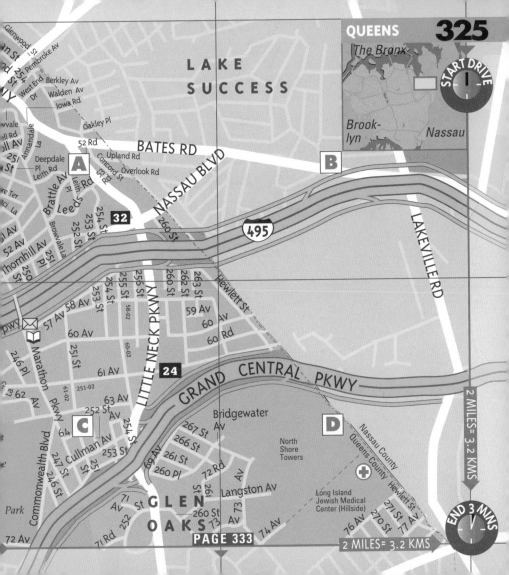

START DRIVE

The Bronx

Brook-lyn

Nassau

LAKE
SUCCESS

A

B

C

D

32

24

Glenwood St
an St 254
nd St
Pembroke Av
West End
Dr
Berkley Av
Walden Av
Iowa Rd
Oakley Pl
52 Rd
Upland Rd
Concord St
Overlook Rd
BATES RD
NASSAU BLVD

I-495

LAKEVILLE RD

wvale
ell Rd.
oll St
251
St
Annandale
Deepdale
Pl
Leith Rd
re Ter
nci La
Brattle Av
Leith Pl
Leith Rd
Leeds
254 St
253 St
252 St
Browvale La

52 Av
Thornhill Av
250
Pl

260 St

256 St
255 St
254 St
253 St

256 St
260 St

263 St
262 St
260 St

Hewlett St

58-02

pwy

246 Pl

Marathon
Pkwy

57 Av 58 Av
60 Av
251 St
61 Av
251-02
61-02
63 Av
252 St
Av
254 St
59 Av
59 Av
60 Av
60 Rd

64
Av
62
Av

LITTLE NECK PKWY

GRAND CENTRAL PKWY

Commonwealth Blvd
247 St
246 St

Cullman Av
253 St
251
St

252 St

267 St
266 St
261 St
260 Pl
69 Av
261
St

Bridgewater
Av

North
Shore
Towers

Nassau County
Queens County
Hewlett St

Long Island
Jewish Medical
Center (Hillside)

271 St
270 St
77 Av

76 Av

Park
72 Av
71 Rd
71
Av
252
St
260 St
73
Av
73 Av
74 St
Langston Av

GLEN
OAKS

PAGE 333

END 3 MINS

2 MILES = 3.2 KMS

2 MILES = 3.2 KMS

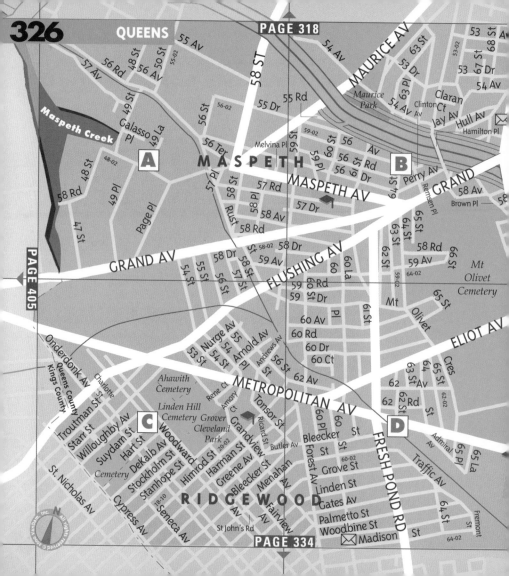

Woodhaven
St Johns Hospital **Blvd**
Hoffman Dr Rd

The Bronx

Brook-lyn Nassau

START DRIVE

72 Pl 52 Dr
73 St 52 Ct
Elks Rd
Ankener Av
Weimar St
84 St
83 St
80 St 54 Av 82 St
79 St
74 St
84 Av 55 Rd 85 St
55 Av
56 Av 57 Av
57 Av

Van Horn St
55-02

57 Av
73 Pl 73 St
57 Av

Horace Harding Expwy

LONG ISLAND EXPWY

495

A Horace Harding Expwy
58 Av
60 Av
85 St 61 Rd
60 Rd
60 Dr

B Austin St
62-02
Wetherole Dr
63 Dr Booth St
63
64 Rd
25

58 Rd
75 St 76 St
58-02

B

63-02

REGO

CALDWELL AV

ELIOT AV

82 St
81 St
80 St
79 St
78 St 62 Av
77 St
77 Pl
61-02
61 Dr
82 Pl
62-02

62 Rd
62 Dr Alderton St
63 Av Haring St
Bourton St
Carlton St
Fitchett St

PARK

65 Rd

PAGE 328

60-02
72 St
71 St
70 St
69 La

Juniper Blvd N
71-02
61-02
62-02

Everton St Fitchett
Dana Ct
Fleet Ct

Dieterle
Boelsen Cres
Asquith Cres
Cromwell

Juniper Valley
Park

Cowles Ct
64 Rd
Goldington Ct

Ellwell
65 DR Cres
Cres
Cres
65 Av

Av
2 Rd
Dr
62
63 Av
70 St
71 St 72 St
Juniper

Juniper Blvd S
75 St 76 St
74 St 75 Pl
Pleasant View St
Penelope Av

Furmanville Av
82 St
Furmanville Av
65 Rd

WOODHAVEN BLVD

Fleet St
66-02

65 DR Cres

66 Av
66 Rd
67 Av
67 Rd
67 Dr
68 Rd

C MIDDLE
66 Rd VILLAGE
66 Dr
71-02
65 Dr
Valley Rd
66 Dr
73 Pl Gray St

80 ST

D
St.
John's
Cemetery

2 MILES = 3.2 KMS

etropolitan Av
Cemetery

67 Rd
67 Dr
68 Av
68 Rd
69 Av
75 St
78 St
78-02
79-02

METROPOLITAN AV

COOPER AV

Trotting Course La
Polo Pl

END 3 MINS

2 MILES= 3.2 KMS

19

R G

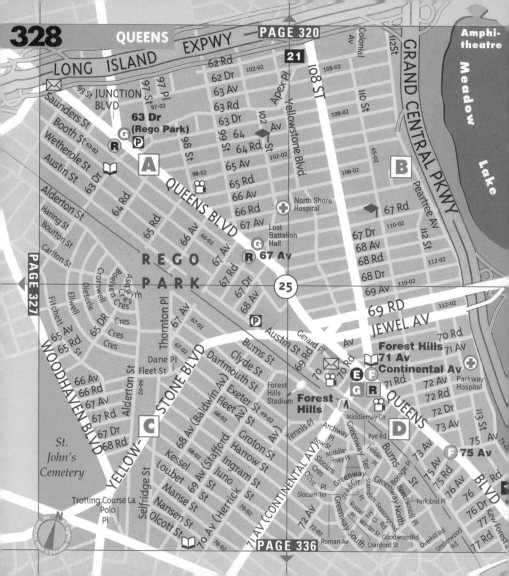

PAGE 320
PAGE 327
PAGE 336

LONG ISLAND EXPWY
QUEENS EXPWY

21

Amphi-theatre

Meadow Lake

GRAND CENTRAL PKWY

Colonial Av
112 St
108-02
110 St
108 St
Apex Pl
Yellowstone Blvd
102 Av

62 Rd
62 Dr
63 Av
63 Rd
63 Dr
99 St
64 Av
64 Rd
65 Av
65 Rd
66 Av
66 Rd
67 Av

102-02
98 St
98-02
102-02

A

63 Dr
(Rego Park)

93 St
JUNCTION BLVD
97-02
97 St
97 Pl

Saunders St
Booth St 63-02
Wetherole St
Austin St
63 Dr

G
R
P

QUEENS BLVD

65 Rd
66 Av
66-02
67 Av

North Shore Hospital

B

Peartree Av
65-02
112 St
110-02
112-02

67 Rd
67 Dr
68 Av
68 Rd
68 Dr
69 Av

Lost Battalion Hall

G
R 67 Av

Alderton St
Haring St
Bourton St
Carlton St

R E G O
P A R K

64 Rd
65 Rd

Cromwell
Boelsen Cres
Aswith Cres
Dieterle
Cres
Cres
Cres

Thornton Pl
67 Av
67-02
67 Rd
67 Dr
67 St
68 St

25

69 RD
112-02

JEWEL AV

70 Rd
71 Av

Forest Hills
71 Av

PAGE 327

Ellwell
Fitchett
65 Av
65 DR
65 Rd
65 St

Dane Pl
Fleet St
70-02
Alderton St

P

Austin St
69 St
70 St

Gerard Pl

R

Continental Av

Parkway Hospital

Burns St
Clyde St
Dartmouth St
Exeter St 69-02
Fleet St
68-02

Forest Hills Stadium

Forest Hills

M

E F
G R
71 Rd

72 Av
72 Rd
72 Dr
73 Av

113 St
75 Av 75-02

C

St. John's Cemetery

66 Av
66 Rd
67 Av
67 Rd
67 Dr
68 Rd

WOODHAVEN BLVD
YELLOW-STONE BLVD

Selfridge St
68 Av (Baldwin Av)
68-02
68 Av (Stafford Av)
Kessel St
66 St
Loubet St
66 St
Manse St
Nansen St
Olcott St
70 Av (Herrick Av)

Baldwin Av
Harrow St
Groton St
Ingram St
Juno St
70-02

D

Middlemay Cir
Bye Rd
Archway
Bow St
Middle-may Pl
Slocum Cres
Olive Pl
Slocum Ter

Greenway Ter
Greenway North
Greenway Cir
Greenway South

72 Av
72-02
Roman Av
Cranford St

Burns St
73 Av
Postage Pl
Standish Rd
72 Rd
Russel Rd
Winter St
Seasongood Rd
GoodwoodRd

Beechknoll Pl
Holder Pl
75 Av
75 Rd
Park End Pl

F 75 Av

76 Av
76 Rd
76 Dr

Overhill Rd
Underwood Rd

Kew Forest
77 Av
77 St

Trotting Course La
Polo Pl

PAGE 336

The Bronx

START DRIVE

Brooklyn

Nassau

23

63 Rd
63 Av
64 Av
64 Rd
137 St
146 Pl
148 Pl
149 Pl

Reeves Av

495

153-02
154 St
155 St
156 St

MAIN ST

Queens College CUNY

CUNY Law

Golden Center for the Performing Arts

64 Av
65 Av

Gravett Rd

Melbourne Av

Louis Armstrong Archives

A

68 Av
68 Rd

141 St

152 St

B

Pomonok Housing

160 St

Electchester

162

65-02
165 St
166 St

164 St

68 Dr
138 St
139 St
140 St
69 Av
69 Rd

36 St

KISSENA BLVD

Parsons Blvd

Houses

161 St

161-02

69 Av
167 St

11

JEWEL AV

153 St

156-02

156 St

Jewel Av

PAGE 330

147-02

70 Av
70 Rd
71 Av
71 Rd
72 Av

137 St
136 St

141 St

Vleigh Pl

147 St

Dana Garden

P

✉

71-02

71 Av

71-02

EXPWY

Park Dr E

72 Cres
72 Rd

139 St

141-02

72 Rd
72 Dr
73 Av
75 Av

150-02

Aguilar Av

K E W

G A R D E N S

H I L L S

160-02
162-02

73 Av
75 Av
75 Rd

76 Av

73 Ter

73-02

136 St

75 Rd
76 Av

141 Pl

75 Rd
✉
76 Av
76 Rd

160-02

164-02

76-02

678

C

77 Av

141 St

77 Av
77 Rd
78 Av
78 Rd

150 St

153 St

PARSONS BLVD

160 St

162 St

St Joseph's Hospital

D

10

77-02
138 St

78 Av
78 Rd
78 Dr

Vleigh Pl

141-02

150-02

153 St

UNION TPK

2 MILES = 3.2 KMS

14

15

MAIN ST

79 Av

146 St

149 St

152 St

154 St

159 St

160 St
161 St

162 St

164 Pl
165 St
166 St
167 St

81-02

81 Av

END 3 MINS

Charter Rd

150 St

Goethals Av

2 MILES = 3.2 KMS

BOOTH MEMORIAL AV

Peck Av

59-02
159 St
160 St
161 St
162 St
163 St
166 St
167 St
168 St
169 St
170 St
175 Pl
PKWY
56-02
184 St
185 St
58 Av
192 St
58-02

St Mary's Cemetery

59 Av
174
Social
Security

Horace Harding Expwy

156 St
157 St
64-02
156 St
157 St
64-04

24

160 St
162

A

Pomonok
Housing

Electchester
Houses

161 St
161-02

495

LONG   ISLAND   EXPWY

Edgar G Holmes
188-02
Oval

25
64 Av
64-02

B

F R E S H

65 Av
65-02

M E A D O

Horace Harding Expwy

65 Av
165 St
166 St
167 St
67 Av
168 St
169 St
170 St
171 St
172 St
173 St
174
175 St
Fresh Meadow La
UTOPIA
183 St
186 La

67-02
67-02

68 Av

67 Av
67-02

71 Us

164 St
69 Av
69-02

Jewel Av

69-02

69 Av
69-02

188-02

156-02

P

71 Av

71-02

K E W
160-02   162-02
73 Av
75 Av

73 AV

73-02

188 St
187 St
186 St
185 St

G A R D E N S

75 Rd

73-02

H I L L S

76 Av

71-02
73-02
74 Av
73-02
178 St
179 St
180 St
181 St
182 St
183 St
184 St
185 St
186 St
187 St

160-02
164-02

76-02

77 Rd

160 St
162 St

76-02
175 St
176 St
177 St
75-02

C

80 Rd

182-02

D

Kent St

Haddon St
Chevy Chase St

UNION TPK

80 Dr

Rd

Troo
Pew

St Joseph's
Hospital

Tryon

Kildare
Pl

Tudor Rd
Dumfries Pl

Surrey Pl
Aberdeen
Midland Pkwy

Rd

154 St

159 St
160 St
161 St
162 St
164 Pl
165 St
166 St
167 St
168 St
169 St

81 Av
170 St

St. Johns
University

Radnor Rd

Avon Rd

Goethals Av

Edgerton Rd

Doncaster
Pl

Queens
Hospital
Center

82 Rd

17

PAGE 329
PARSONS BLVD

27 28

26

The Bronx

Brook-lyn

Nassau

START DRIVE

198 St
197 St
58-02

65 Cres Av

LEWIS

FRANCIS

BLVD

A

4

295

3

Cunningham
Park

67 Av
67-02

69 Av

69-02

73-02

199 St
198 St
197 St
196 Pl
195 St

P

2

Cunningham
Park

P

20A,B

C

1

**HOLLIS-
WOOD**

64-02

OAKLAND
GARDENS

67 Av

67-02

69-02

69 Av

213-02

Windsor

67 Av

CLEARVIEW

HOLLIS HILLS TER

EXPWY

73 AV

Park

75 Av

Richland Av

208 St

209 St
210 St
211 St
212 St
213 St
214 St
215 St

82 Av
82-02

85 Av
85-02

86 AV

GRAND

CENTRAL

85 Rd

PKWY

217 St
218 St

BELL BLVD

68 Av
Bell Park
Gardens

69 Av

217-02

74 Av

220 St

SPRINGFIELD

75 Av

220-02

HOLLIS

HILLS

Apartments

Peck Av

Stewart Rd

UNION TPK

217 St

218 St

86 Av

76 Av
76 Rd
77 Av

Kingsbury Av

220 Pl
220 St
221 St
222 St
223 St

P

HARTLAND AV

S Peck Av
219 St

Ter

SPENCER AV

Sawyer Av

HILLSIDE AV

73
Rd

75 Av

BLVD

P

PAGE 332

2 MILES = 3.2 KMS

D

22

Whitehall

212 St
208-02

21

213 St
212 Pl
214 St
213 St
89 Av
215 St
216 St
217 St
218 Pl
218 St

END 3 MINS

2 MILES = 3.2 KMS

85 Rd
Laughlin
Nero Av
Como Av
Sandus
Pinto Av
Keno Av
Narengo St
Romeo Ct
Epsom St
Sutro St
Dunton St
86 Rd
208 St
Course Rd

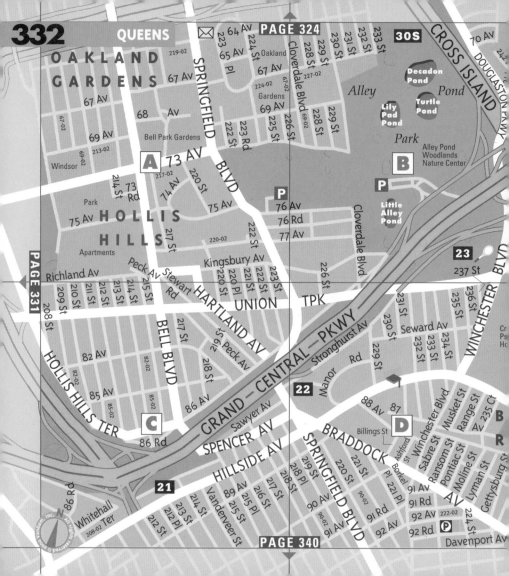

START DRIVE
1

The Bronx

Brook-lyn

Nassau

A

B

C

D

4

5

COOPER AV

69 Av
Cook Av
69 Rd
75 St
78 St
79 St
79-02
70 Av
76 St
69 Dr
71 Av
E.R. Miller Square
Edsall Av
71 Av
77 Av
77-02
77 Av
84-02
73 St
78 Av
76 St
78 St
77 Rd
78 St
75 St
74 St
73 Pl

Aubrey Av
Doran Av
Rutledge Av
83 St
84 St
METROPOLITAN AV
90-01
73 Av
74 Av
75 Av
76 Av
77 Av
88-02
79 Av
88-01

G L E N D A L E

78 Rd
79 St
79 Pl
79 La
81 St
82 St
83 St
84 St
85 St
86 St
87 St

Margaret Pl

Trotting Course La

WOODHAVEN BLVD

UNION TPK

81 Av
81 Rd
82 Av

82 Rd
83 Av

76-02

Mt Lebanon Cemetery

88 Pl
88 La
89 St
83 Dr

Victory Field

MYRTLE AV

Freedom Dr

Forest Park Golf Course

98 St

ON PKWY

Park Lane South

85 Rd
85 Dr
85
85 Rd
85 Dr
86
86 Rd
Dexter Ct
75 St
76 St
77 St
78 St
79 St
80 St
Forest Pkwy
Forest Av

85 St
86 St
87 St
88 St
90 St
85-02

85 Av
85 Rd
86 Av
85-02

85 Av
85 Rd
86 Av

WOODHAVEN

96 St
98 St
101 St
101 St

85 Av
85 Rd

86 Rd
86 Dr

85 St
86 Rd

85 St Forest Pkwy

Woodhaven Blvd

104 St

75 St
C **J Z**

87 Av
87 Rd
88 Av
88 Rd

87 Av
80 St
J **JAMAICA AV**

87 Av
87 Rd
88 Av
88 Rd

D **J Z**

89 Av
90 Av
74 Pl
90 Rd

89 Av
90-02

88 Rd

92 St
89-02

94-02
89-02

95 St
94 St
96 St
97 St

87 Av
88 Av
89 Av
90 Av

W O O D H A V E N

91 Av
92 Av
93 Av

ELDERT LA
EUCLID AV
ETNA AV
CA AV
ST

BLVD
91-02

END 3 MINS

2 MILES = 3.2 KMS

PAGE 336

Goethals Av
Village Rd

Queens
Hospital
Center

The Bronx

START DRIVE

Brooklyn   Nassau

GRAND CENTRAL PKWY

78

14   **15**

126 St 82 St
Bldg 82 Av
82 Av
Hoover Av
82 Dr
83 Av

QUEENS

VAN

135 St
134 St

141 St

MAIN ST

Coolidge Av

Daniels St

Lander St

Smedley St

84 Av
84 Rd

16

84 Av
84 Rd

159 St

8

Maple
Grove
Cemetery

Talbot St

Gardens

Briarwood
Van Wyck
Blvd

A

WYCK

BLVD

E **F**

Rd 86 Rd

127 St
126 St
125 St
134 St
135 St
136 St

87 St

7

Pershing Cres

Burden Cres

139 St

85 Rd
85 Dr
86 Av
86 Rd
87 Av
87 Rd
87 Dr

144 St

148 St
147 St

85 Av

150 St
151 St
152 St

85 Dr

86 Av

87 Av 150-02
87 Rd 150-02

B

85 Av

85-02

Normal Rd

Glenn Av
86 Av
86
Cres

86
Rd

164 ST

165 St
166 St

Gothic Dr

Park Cres

Highland Av

Clinton Pl
Clinton Ter

87 Rd

HILLSIDE AV

Queens Borough
Public Library

PAGE 338

Sutphin
Blvd

F

144-02

F

Parsons
Blvd

88 Av

JAMAICA

89 Av

163 St
162 St

164 St
165 St

METROPOLITAN AV

JAMAICA AV
Rd

88 Rd

130 St
131 St
132 St

133 St

89 Av

E

Jamaica
Van Wyck

EXPWY

88 Av
88 Rd

89 Av
90 Av

138 St
139 St
138 Pl

143 St

145 St

144 Pl

146 St

148 St

149 St

150 St

147 Pl

Supreme &
Surrogate
Court

Mary
Immaculate

Kings
Park

Lowe
Ct

Burdette

Rufus King Av
P.S.153

90 Rd

Family
Court

Grace St

161 St

160 St

King Av

Grace
Ceme-
tery

Jamaica
Arts Center

92 Rd

C

E **F**

Jamaica
Hospital

127 St
129 St
130 St
128 St

90 Av
91 Av
92 Av

127-02

134 St

6   Archer Av

Jamaica

King Manor
Museum

Sutphin Blvd
E J Z Archer Av

M

94 Av

95 Av

158 St

Beaver Rd

157 St

York
College

E J Z

**Jamaica
Center**

Twombly Pl

GUY R. BREWER BLVD

Union Hall

2 MILES = 3.2 KMS

93 Rd

Av

5

125 St
126 St
127 St
129 St
130 St
131 St
132 St

134 St
133 St

101 AV

678

131 St
138 St
143 St

Cresskill Pl

Sanders Pl

Brisbin St

Allendale St

Liverpool St

Waltham St

102 AV

97 Av

Liverpool St

Waltham St

D

Guinzberg Rd

105 Av
106 Av

107 AV

149 St
148 St
147 Pl

150

LIBERTY
BLVD

Tuckerton St

156 Pl

156 St

SOUTH RD

157 St

160 St

159 St

107-02

Union Hall St

END 3 MINS

2 MILES = 3.2 KMS

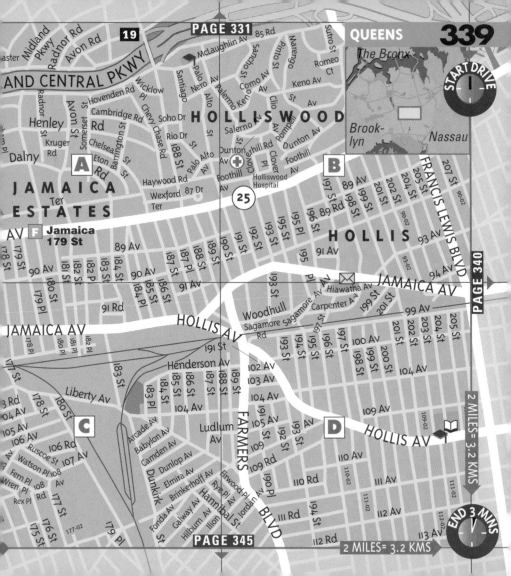

PAGE 332

QUEENS VILLAGE

SPRINGFIELD BLVD

Winchester Blvd

Pompeii Rd

Dunton Av

Foothill Av

25

HILLSIDE AV

208-02

Hollis

89 Av

243 St

214 St

Vanderveer St

215 St

215 Pl

216 St

217 St

218 Pl

218 St

219 St

91 Rd

92 Av

92 Rd

221 St

204 St

202 Av

88 Rd

212 St

210 Pl

211 Rd

89 Court

90 Ct

89 Rd St

90 Av

91 Av

92 Av

92 Rd

93 Rd

94 Av

94 Rd

94 Dr

219

92-02

A

207 St

208 St

209 St

210 St

90-02

Blvd

211 Pl

92-02

93 Av

214 Pl

93 Rd

94 AV

B

Amboy La

89 Av

197 Av

199 St

201 St

202 St

204 St

205 St

89 Rd St

198 St

196 St

91 Av

HOLLIS

90-02

93 Rd

93-02

94 Av

94-02

94 Rd

93-02

93-02

94-02

Queens Village M

97

Hiawatha Av

Carpenter Av

199 St

201 St

JAMAICA AV

Soca Paradise

209 St

98 Av

99

Sigourney Av

218 St

99 Av

100 Av

101 Av

196 St 26-02

197 St

196 St

100 Av

99 AV

200 St

201 St

202 St

203 St

204 St

205 St

205 Pl

207 St

208 St

Bellaire Pl

209 St

99-02

211 Pl

212 St

213 St

99 Av

102 Av

104 Av

104 AV

215 St

216 St

217 St

103 Av

103 Av

217 Pl

105 Av

220 St

HEMP

198 St

199 St

104 Av

100-02

104-02

210 St

211 St

104 Rd

212 Pl

214 St

106 Av

215-02

217 Pl La

104 Av

10

106 Av

107 Av

108 Av

195 St

109 Av

FRANCIS LEWIS BLVD

109-02

109-02

HOLLIS AV

214 St

215 St

216 St

217 St

217 Pl St

Robard La

Monterey

219 St

220 St

221 St

BLVD

109 Av

110 Av

109

110 A

C

Bardwell Av

Colfax

209 Pl

212 St

213 St

110 Av

110 Rd

111 Rd

Witthoff St

110 Av

111 Rd

222 St

223 St

110 AV

111 Av

112 Av

110 Av

110 Rd

110-02

111 Av

111-02

111 Rd

112 Av

113 Av

112 Rd

111-02

112-02

113-02

111 Rd

111 Rd

112 Av

112 Rd

113 Av

114 Av

113-02

112 Av

112 Rd

D

Convent

SPRINGFIELD

194 St

109-02

113-02

209 St

210 St

211 St

Nashville Blvd

Delevan St

219-02

221-02

221-02

113 Av

Murdock Av

113 Dr

219-02

225-02

Murdock Av

ST ALBANS

PAGE 347

PAGE 339

PAGE 333

87 Dr

87 Rd

88 Dr

89 Av

90 Av

91 Av

88 Rd

250 St

Common-wealth Blvd

247 St

245 St

246 St

247 St

251 St

88 Dr

JERICHO TPK

Queens County
Nassau County

BRADDOCK AV

Gettysburg St

225 St

239 St

240 St

241 St

242 St

241 St

242 St

244 St

240 St

JAMAICA AV

27

A

B

Bellerose
Ⓜ

The Bronx

START DRIVE

Brook-lyn

Nassau

TULIP AV

**FLORAL
PARK**

26D

CROSS ISLAND PKWY

Belmont Race
Track

PLAINFIELD AV

D

26B,C

C

24

HEMPSTEAD TPK

ELMONT

ELMONT RD

26A

2 MILES = 3.2 KMS

2 MILES= 3.2 KMS

END 3 MINS

The Bronx

START DRIVE

Brook-
lyn

Nassau

95 Av
114 Av
113 Av
112 St

117 St
118 St
95-02
116 St
101 Av

LEFFERTS BLVD

97-02
120 St
121 St
102 Av
102 Rd

101-02
123 St
124 St
125 St
126 St
127 St

101 Av
130 St
131 St
132 St
133 St

101-02
103-02

4

103 Av
103-02
103 Rd

LIBERTY AV

A A **Lefferts Blvd**

103 Rd

105 Av

St
(nwood Av)

A

107 Av

Van Sicklen St

134 St

B

135 St

107
Rd

Lakewood Av

109 Rd
Glassboro Av

678

139-02

142 St

107 Av
107-02

107-02

107-02

Hawtree Creek Rd

107-02

109-02

111-02

109 Av

109-02

109-02

111-02

109-02

111 Av
111-02

PAGE 344

141 St
140 St
139 St

Dr Charles
Andrews
Memorial Park

115-02

LINDEN   BLVD

115 Av
115-02

Lincoln St

115-02

116-02

115-02

116 Av

116-02

VAN WYCK EXPWY

Aqueduct
Race
Track

Sutter Av

ROCKAWAY BLVD

Foch   Blvd

C

133 Av

133 Av

Hawtree Creek Rd

121-02

117 Rd

D

120 Av

135 Av

117 St
118 St

S O U T H

Gotham Rd
Cedric Rd

123 Av

114 St
114 Pl
115 St
116 St

120 St
121 St
122 St
122 Pl

O Z O N E

P A R K

133-02

123 St
124 St
125 St
126 St
127 St
128 St

129 St
130 St

2

Alwick
Rd

131 St
132 St
133 St
134 St

135 St
135 Pl

149 Av
149 Av
150 Av
150-02

LEFFERTS   **BLVD**

149 Av

131 Av

130-02
131-02

END 3 MINS

2 MILES= 3.2 KMS

2 MILES= 3.2 KMS

The Bronx

Brook-lyn

Nassau

START DRIVE

173 St
174 St
175 St
176 St
110-02
171 PI
Sayres Av
177 St
178 PI
178 St
179 St
112 PI
180 St
111-02
Mangin Av
Keeseville Av
Lewiston Av
113 Av
113 Rd
114 Rd
114 Dr
112-02

111 Rd
Adelaide Rd
113 St
176 St
175 PI
Murdock Av
111-02
Ovid PI
Dormans Rd
Rome Dr
Quencer Rd
Dr Mexico St
Sullivan St
114 Rd

St Albans Memorial Park
113 Av

Marne PI

Tioga
Newburg St
Suffolk Dr
Turin Dr
Dunkirk St

LINDEN BLVD

A

115 Av
174 St
173 St
172 St
114 Av
175 St

St Albans

M

B

LINDEN BLVD

197 St
198 St
199 St
196 St
117 Rd
118 Av
118 Rd
119 Av
194 St
195 St
193 St

167 St
168 St
169 St
170 St
116 Av
171 St
116-02
Blvd
116 Av
166 St
165 St

St. Albans Veterans Adm. Exit Care Center

Roy Wilkins Southern Queens Park

Montauk Blvd
Lovingham PI
Foch St
118 St
Everitt

FARMERS BLVD

189 St
190 St
191 St
192 St
120 Av
193 St
194 St
195 St
196 St
197 St
119-02
120-02

170-02

MERRICK BLVD

Baisley Blvd

119 Rd
119 Dr
119 Rd
178 St
179 St
180 St
Riverton St

120 Rd
121 Av
122 Av
191 St
192 St
Lucas St
Benton St
Grayson St
Milburn St
Nashville

Blvd
193 St

Marsden St
Bedell St
118 Av
118 Rd
119 Av
Ring PI
Victoria Dr
Amelia Av
Merrill St
Brocher Rd
124 Av
Roe Rd
Sunbury Rd
Troutville Rd
Irwin
Ursina Rd
Leslie Rd
Selover Rd
Anderson Rd
St Zoller Rd
Sidway PI
Mars
Montauk St
Veterans Square

victoria
119 Rd
170 St
171 St
172 St
120-02
125 Av
126 Av
127 Av

Smith St
166 St
120 Av
168 St
Bedell St
172 St

C
P

127 Av
128 Av
129 Av

130 Av

Rochdale Village

130 Av
Garrett St
133 Av

178 St
176 PI
130 Rd
131 Av
132 Av
133 Av
133 Rd
134
Mathewson Ct
Denis St
Benner Ct
Crandall St
135 Av
Cheney St
136 Av
134 Av
135 Av
136
Belknap St
E Gate Plaza
137 Av

D

Williamson Av
Nellis St
Pineville
Defoe St
Ridgedale St

Nepton St
La St
Adair St
132 Rd
133 Rd
218-02

Eveleth
179 St

SPRINGFIELD BLVD

217 St
136 St
136 Rd
137 Av
219
220 St
134 Rd
216 St
219-02

Locust Manor
M

END 3 MINS

PAGE 346

2 MILES= 3.2 KMS

2 MILES= 3.2 KMS

FRANCIS LEWIS BLVD

207 St
208 St
209 St
115-02 St
Campus Magnet
116 Rd

Nashville Blvd
217 St
218 St
219 St
220 St
221 St
115 Rd
222 St
223 St
224 St
225 St
226 St
227 St
228 St
229 St
230 St
231 St

113 Dr
114 Av
114 Rd
227-02
114 Dr
114 Ter

115 AV
115-02
116 Av
116-02

The Bronx
Brook-lyn
Nassau

START DRIVE
1

205 St
117 Rd
116-02

A
118 Av
118 Av

119 Av
118-02

120 Av
119-02

121 Av
120-02

CAMBRIA

HEIGHTS

Blvd

Montefiore Cemetery

226-02

Francis Lewis

117 St
218 St
219 St

3 St
224 St
225 St
226 St
227 St
228 St
229 St
230 St
232 St
233 St
234 St
235 St
236 St
237 St

Francis Lewis Blvd

130 Av

131-02

120-02
121 Av
125 Av
126 Av
128 Av
128 Rd
128 Dr
129 Av

232 St
233 St
234 St
235 St

236 St
237 St
238 St

128-02

119-02

118-02

116-02

CROSS ISLAND PKWY

Queens County
Nassau County

B

DUTCH BROADWAY

25B

ELMONT RD

LINDEN BLVD

SOUTHERN ST PKWY

25A

D

BELT PKWY

128 Av
128 Rd
128 Dr
129 Av
243 St
129 Rd
130 Av

C

2 MILES = 3.2 KMS

END 3 MINS

2 MILES = 3.2 KMS

348

PAGE 342

17S

17

Tahoe St
Raleigh Av
Hawtree St
Huron St
66 Pl

**Aqueduct
North
Conduit Av**

Ⓐ

153 Av
80 St
82-02
84-02
St
St
79 St
81 St
82 St
83 St
153-02
155
84 St
88
89 St
Av
155 St
86 St

155 Av

153-02
155-02
81-02

156 Av
90-02
156-02

77 St
156-02
156-02
92 St
91 St

157 Av

Killarney St
Jahn St
Huron St
Bridgeton St
Cohancy St
98 St

94 St
95 St
96 St

Race Track Rd

Ⓐ

Ⓑ

157 Av
101 St
102 St

BELT PKWY

83 St
84 St
85 St
86 St
87 St
88 St
89 St
90 St

97 St
98 St
99 St
100 St

158 Av
158 Av

158-02

158-02

Coleman
Square

103 Rd

Ⓐ

**Howar
JFK Ai**

78 St
79 St
80 St
81 St
82 St

158 Av

159 Av

159 Av

159 Rd

159-02

✉

159-02
159-02

H O W A R D

160 Av

160 Av

103 St

B E A C H

160-02

159-02
160-02
164-02

C R O S S

161 Av

161 Av

Russel St

81-02

162-01
162-01

162 Av

162-01

162-02

B A Y

162 Av

**Ped
Bridge**

1 St
Rau Ct
Davenport Ct

162 Av
162 Av
163 Av

162-02
163-02

163 Av

163-02

B L V D

163 Av

163 Dr

Ⓓ

164 Av

164 Rd
164 Dr

164-02
162-02
163-02

164 Av

164-02

Shellbank

Ⓒ

164 Av

164 Av

165 Av

**F M Charles
Memorial
Park**

Hawtree

**Hamilton
Beach
Park**

165 Av

Basin

**Spring Creek
Park**

Queens County
Kings County

PAGE 419

Basin

Grassy Bay

✉

**Congressman Joseph
Addabo Bridge**

PAGE 433

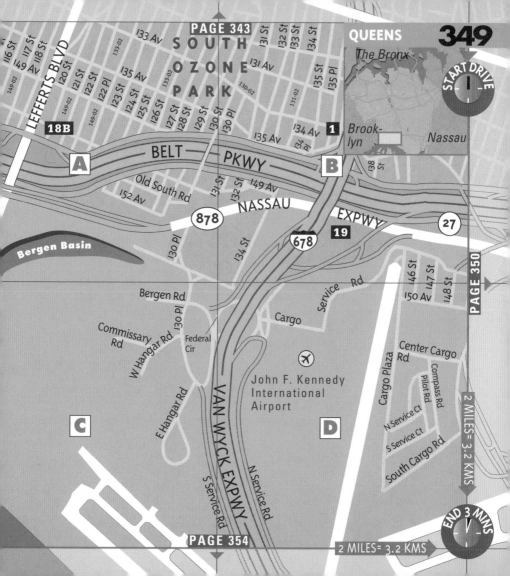

350

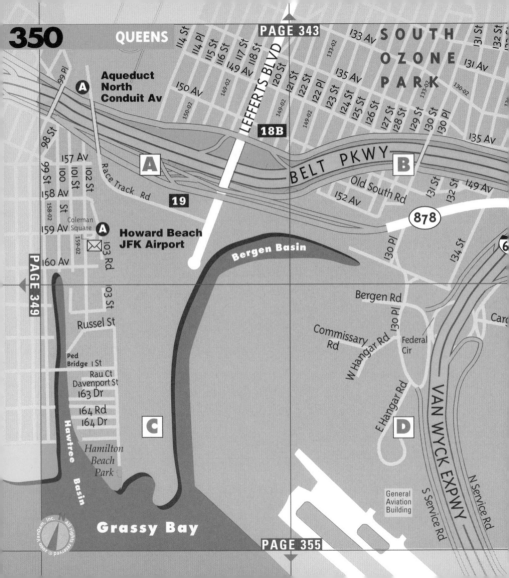

A Aqueduct
North
Conduit Av

PAGE 343

S O U T H

O Z O N E

P A R K

114 St
114 Pl
115 St
116 St
117 St
118 St
149 Av
120 St
120 St
127 St
122 St
122 Pl
123 St
124 St
125 St
126 St
127 St
128 St
129 St
130 St
130 Pl
131 St
132 St
131 Av
131 Av
130-02
133 Av
133-02
133 Av
135 Av
135 Av

150 AV

150-02

149-02

149-02

149-02

18B

135 Av

99 Pl

98 St

157 Av

99 St

100

101 St

102 St

158 Av

158-02 St

159 Av

Coleman
Square

159-02

A

A 103 Rd

Howard Beach
JFK Airport

160 Av

A

Race Track Rd

19

BELT PKWY

Old South Rd

152 Av

B

131 St
132 St
149 Av

130 Pl

878

134 St

6

PAGE 349

103 St

Russel St

Ped
Bridge 1 St

Rau Ct
Davenport St
163 Dr

164 Rd
164 Dr

Hawtree Basin

Bergen Basin

C

Hamilton
Beach
Park

Grassy Bay

Bergen Rd

Commissary
Rd

W Hangar Rd

130 Pl

Federal
Cir

E Hangar Rd

D

VAN WYCK EXPWY

S Service Rd

N Service Rd

Cargo

General
Aviation
Building

PAGE 355

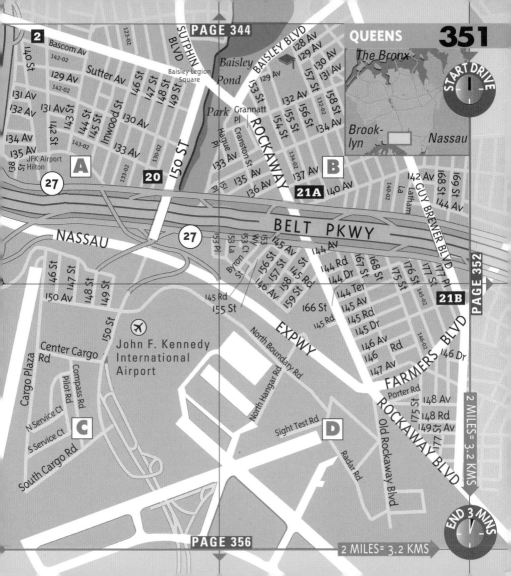

2

START DRIVE
1

The Bronx

Brooklyn

Nassau

140 St
Bascom Av
142-02

Sutter Av

129 Av
142-02

146 St
147 St
148 St
149 St

131 Av
132 Av
131 Av
143 St
144 St
145 St
142 St
143-02

Inwood St

130 Av

133 Av

134 Av
135 Av
JFK Airport Hilton
138

27

A

20

150 ST

123-02

SUTPHIN BLVD

Baisley Legion Square

Baisley Pond Park

Grannatt Pl

Hague Pl

Cranston St

133 Av

135 Av

136 Av

BAISLEY BLVD
128 Av
129 Av
130 Av
131 Av

129 Av

153 St

132 Av
156 St
155 St
154 St

157 St
158 St
132-02

134 Av

137 Av

140 Av

ROCKAWAY

B

21A

142 Av
144 Av

168 St
169 St

GUY BREWER BLVD

Latham La

140-02

NASSAU

27

153 Wy
153
153 Ct
53 La
Byron St
153 Pl

145 Av

144 Av

156 St
157 St
158 St
145 St
159 St

145 Rd
146 Av

BELT PKWY

144 Rd
144 Dr

167 St
168 St

144 Ter

144 Av
145 Av
145 Rd
145 Dr

176 St
175 St
177 St
145-02

21B

146 St
147 St
148 St
149 St

150 Av

145 Rd
155 St

166 St
145 Rd

146 Av
Rd
146
147 Av

146 Dr
146-02

FARMERS BLVD

EXPWY

North Boundary Rd

North Hangar Rd

Center Cargo Rd

150 St

John F. Kennedy International Airport

Cargo Plaza

Compass Rd
Pilot Rd

N Service Ct

S Service Ct

C

South Cargo Rd

Sight Test Rd

D

Radar Rd

Porter Rd
175 St
177 St

148 Av
148 Rd
149 Av

Old Rockaway Blvd

ROCKAWAY BLVD

2 MILES = 3.2 KMS

END 3 MINS

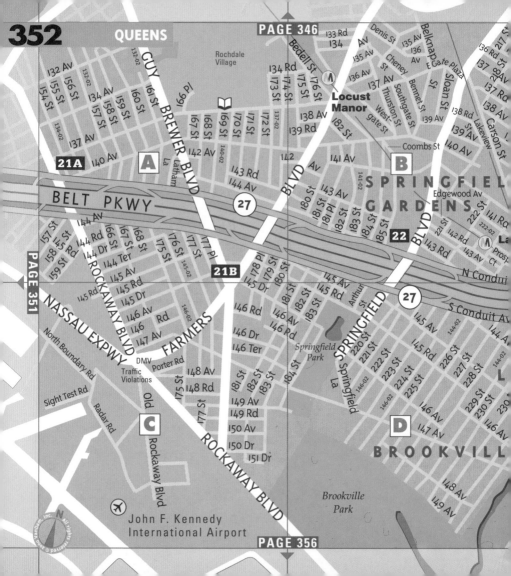

352 QUEENS

Rochdale Village

133 Rd
134
Denis St
135 Av
136 Av
Belknap St
E Gate Plaza
136 Rd
137 Av
137 Rd
138 Rd
138 St

Cheney St
Bennet St
Sloan St
Lakeview St
Carson St

132 Av
156 St
155 St
154 St
132-02
134 St
159 St
158 St
157 St
160 St
161 St
166 Pl
134-02
137 Av
140 Av

GUY BREWER BLVD

134 Rd
173 St
174 St
175 St
176 St
137-02
138 Av
139 Rd
182 St

135 Av
136 Av
137 Av
Thurston St
Southgate St
West- gate St
Westgate St
139 Av

Locust Manor

167 St
168 St
169 St
170 St
171 St
172 St
140-02
142 Av

La
Latham

143 Rd
144 Av
(27)

142 Av

141 Av

Coombs St
140 Av

Edgewood Av

A

21A

B

SPRINGFIELD GARDENS

141-02
222 St
221 St
142 Rd
143 Rd
143 Av

BLVD
180 St
181 St
181 Pl
182 St
183 St
184 St
85 St

143 Av

22

142 Rd
221 St
222-02

La
Prosp
Ct

BELT PKWY

144 Av
157 St
158 St
145 Rd
159 St

144 Av
144 Rd
166 St
167 St
168 St
144 Dr
144 Ter
145 Av
145 Rd
145 Dr

176 St
177 St
175 St
145-02
177 Pl

21B

178 Pl
179 St
180 St
145 Dr
145 Av

145 Av
145 Rd

N Condui
S Conduit Av

(27)

146 Av
146
146 Av
147 Av

Rd
146-02

ROCKAWAY BLVD

FARMERS

146 Rd
146 Av
146 Rd

181 St
182 St
183 St

Arthur

145 Av
145 Rd

144-02
144 A

146 Dr
146 Ter

Springfield Park

SPRINGFIELD

220 St
221 St
222 St
223 St
224 St
225 St
146-02

226 St
227 St
228 St
229 St
230 St

L

NASSAU EXPWY

North Boundary Rd

DMV
Traffic Violations

Porter Rd

148 Av
148 Rd

181 St
182 St
183 St
184 St
175 St

149 Av
149 Rd

150 Av

Springfield La

146 Av
146 Av
147 Av

230

C

D

BROOKVIL

Sight Test Rd

Radar Rd

Old Rockaway Blvd

150 Dr
151 Dr

148 Av

149 Av

ROCKAWAY BLVD

Brookville Park

✈ John F. Kennedy International Airport

PAGE 351

START DRIVE

The Bronx

Brook-lyn — Nassau

MERRICK BLVD

131-02
226 St
227 St
228 St
229 St
230 St
Lewis Blvd
232 St
233 St
234 St
235 St
236 St
237 St

129 Av
130 Av

PKWY

129 Rd
130 Av

St

135-02
135 Av
Francis

133 Av

131-02

24B

243 St
242 St
131 St Rd
131 St
242 St

130
131

132 Av
132 Rd

137-02
137 Av

133 Av

A

135-02

133 Rd
134

B

VALLEY
STREAM

138 Av
137-02

133 Rd
133 Dr
134 Av

24A

W MERRICK RD

9 Av
138-02
230 Pl
Francis Lewis Blvd
234 Pl
137-02
135-02

BELT

241 St
242 St
243 St
244 St
135-02
135-02
245 St
135 Av
135 Rd
136 Av

41 Av
139-02
138-02

Brookville Blvd
137-02
Francis

138 Av
136 Rd
137 Av
246 St
137 Rd

St

23

Rosedale

140 Av
245 St
246 St
SUNRISE
249 St
27
HWY

23B
141 Av
142 Av
143 Av
Weller Av
Caney
Rd 243-02
Memphis Av
247 St
248 St
249 St
250 St
Lewis Blvd

250 St
Caney La

D

Green Acres
Shopping
Center

Pond

C

241 St
243 St
Newhall
144 Av
145 Av
Mayda Rd
Caney La
253 St
254 St

255 St
256 St

HOOK CREEK

46 Av
245 St
249 St
Edgewood St
147
148 Av
253 Pl
Weller La
255 St
257 St
258 St
259 St
144 Av
145 Av
Frankton
145

St

BLVD

Queens County
Nassau County

2 MILES= 3.2 KMS

END 3 MINS

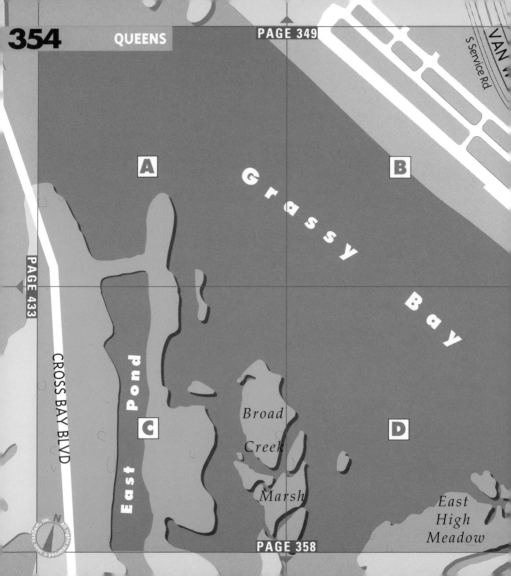

PAGE 349

S Service Rd

VAN W

A

B

G r a s s y

B a y

PAGE 433

CROSS BAY BLVD

E a s t   P o n d

C

D

Broad
Creek

Marsh

East
High
Meadow

PAGE 358

N

Brook-
lyn

Nassau

START DRIVE

Terminal 8:
American
Airlines
(International)

Terminal 7:
British Airways

Terminal 9:
American
Airlines
(Domestic)

Terminal 6:
TWA
(International)

678

A

#3

B

Terminal 1:
Air France,
Japan Airlines,
Korean Air, Lufthansa

P #2

#1

Terminal 5:
TWA
(Domestic)

Terminal 2:
Delta Airlines

Terminal 4:
International
Arrivals Building

Terminal 3:
Delta Airlines

PAGE 356

2 MILES= 3.2 KMS

John F. Kennedy
International Airport

C

D

END 3 MINS

2 MILES= 3.2 KMS

PAGE 351

Brookville Park

Bog Cr

Terminal 6:
TWA
(International)

Terminal 5:
TWA
(Domestic)

A

B

ROCKAWAY BLV

Thurston Bas

PAGE 355

John F. Kennedy
International Airport

C

D

N

PAGE 360

Head of Bay

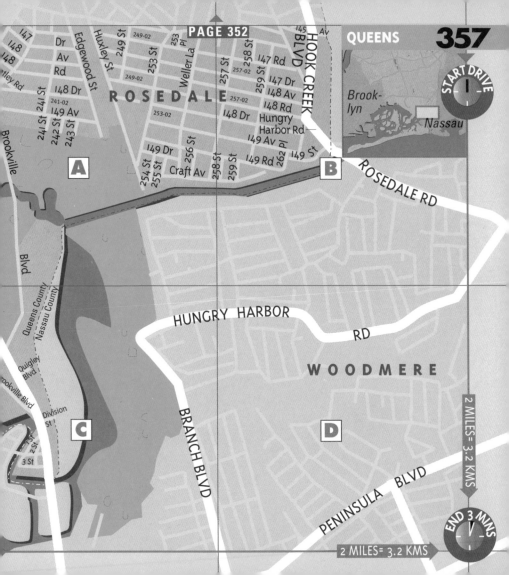

147
148
148
...tley Rd
Dr
Av
Rd
Edgewood St
Huxley St
249 St
249-02
253
253 Pl
253 St
Weller La
257 St
257-02
258 St
145 Av
HOOK CREEK BLVD
147 Rd
147 Dr
148 Av
148 Rd
259 St
R O S E D A L E
257-02
148 Dr
Hungry
Harbor Rd
149 Av Pl
149 St
149 Av
149-02
241 St
241 St
242 St
243 St
241-02
253-02
149 Dr
254 St
255 St
256 St
Craft Av
258 St
259 St
149 Rd
262 Pl
149 St

Brookville

A

B

ROSEDALE RD

Blvd

Queens County
Nassau County

Quigley Blvd

rookville Blvd

Division St

2 St
3 St

C

HUNGRY HARBOR

RD

W O O D M E R E

BRANCH BLVD

D

PENINSULA BLVD

Brook-lyn

Nassau

START DRIVE

END 3 MINS

2 MILES= 3.2 KMS

2 MILES= 3.2 KMS

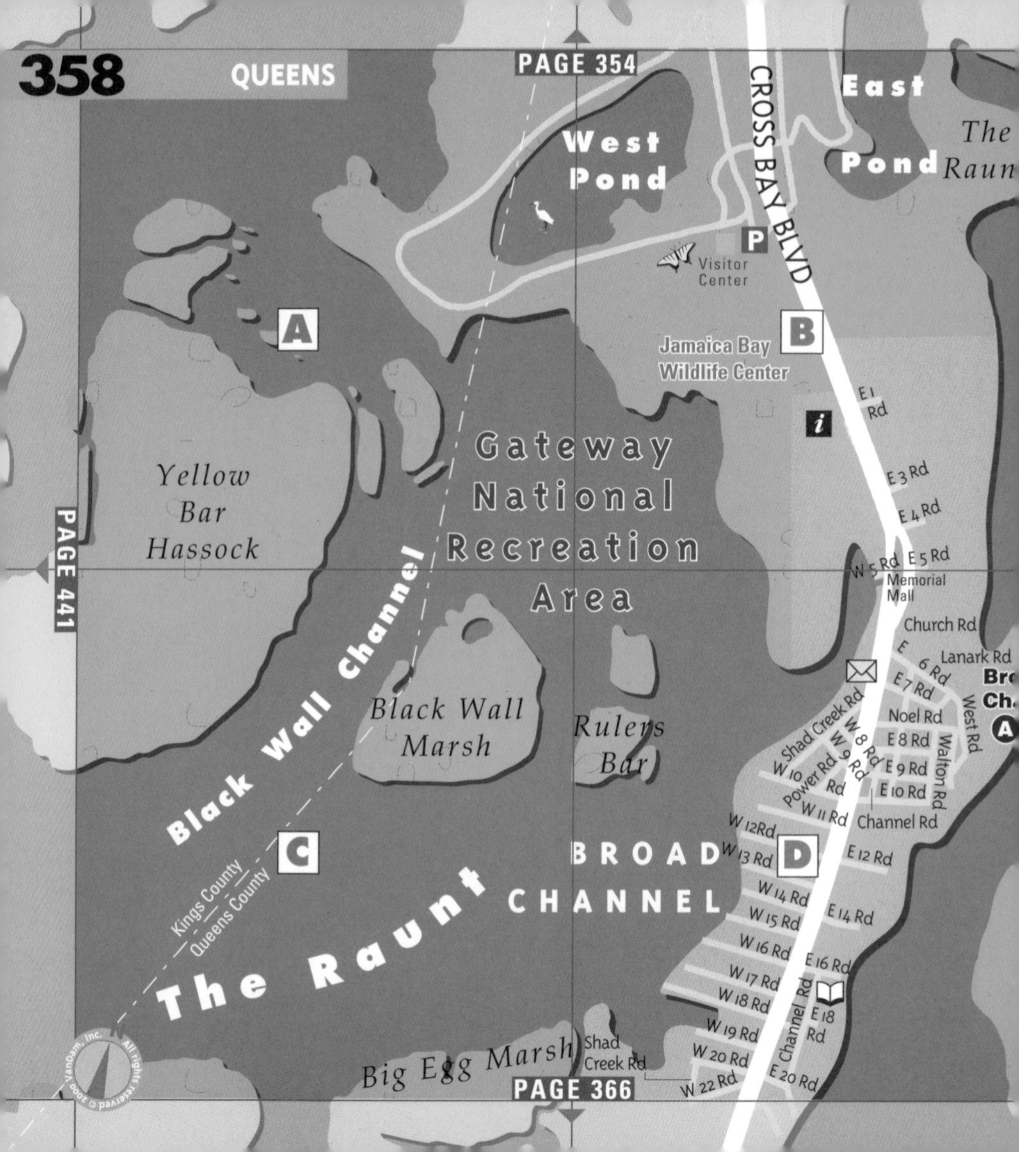

PAGE 354

CROSS BAY BLVD

East

The
Pond Raun

West
Pond

P

Visitor
Center

Jamaica Bay
Wildlife Center

B

i

E 1
Rd

E 3 Rd

E 4 Rd

Gateway
National
Recreation
Area

W 5 Rd E 5 Rd

Memorial
Mall

Church Rd

A

E 6 Rd

Lanark Rd

Yellow
Bar
Hassock

E 7 Rd

Bro
Ch.

Shad Creek Rd

Noel Rd

West Rd

A

Black Wall Channel

W 8 Rd

W 10 Rd

E 8 Rd

Power Rd

W 9 Rd

E 9 Rd

Walton Rd

Black Wall
Marsh

Rulers
Bar

W 11 Rd

E 10 Rd

W 12 Rd

Channel Rd

C

W 13 Rd

E 12 Rd

D

BROAD

W 14 Rd

CHANNEL

W 15 Rd

Kings County
Queens County

W 16 Rd

E 14 Rd

The Raunt

W 17 Rd

E 16 Rd

W 18 Rd

E 18
Rd

Channel Rd

W 19 Rd

Big Egg Marsh Shad
Creek Rd

W 20 Rd

E 20 Rd

W 22 Rd

PAGE 366

PAGE 441

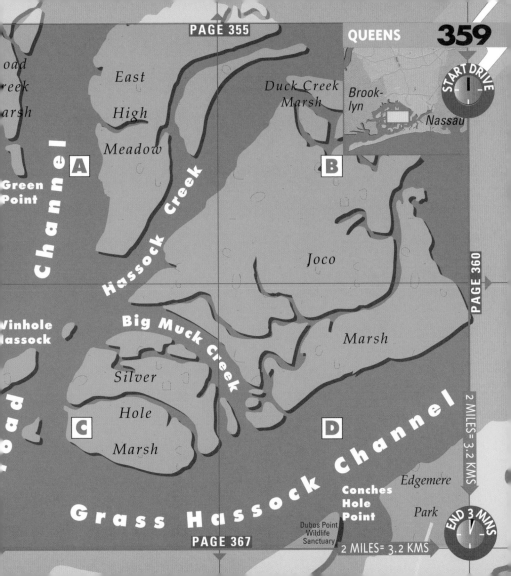

START DRIVE

Duck Creek Marsh

Brook-lyn

Nassau

oad

reek

arsh

East

High

Meadow

A

Green Point

Channel

Hassock Creek

B

Joco

PAGE 360

Winhole Hassock

Big Muck Creek

Silver

Hole

Marsh

C

Marsh

D

oad

2 MILES = 3.2 KMS

Conches Hole Point

Edgemere

Park

END 3 MINS

Grass Hassock Channel

Dubos Point Wildlife Sanctuary

2 MILES = 3.2 KMS

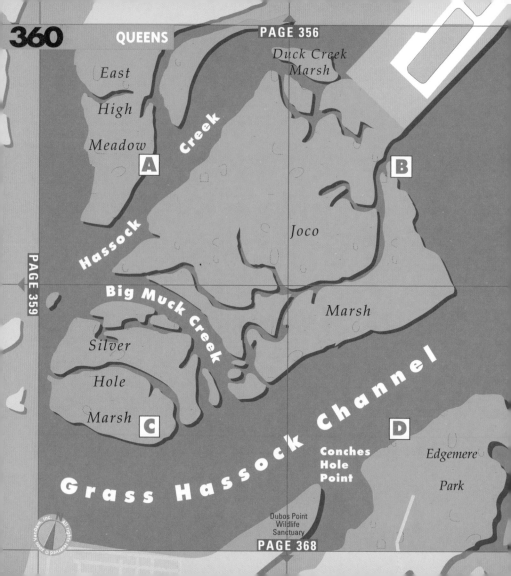

QUEENS

PAGE 356

Duck Creek
Marsh

East

High

Meadow

Hassock Creek

A

B

PAGE 359

Joco

Hassock

Big Muck Creek

Marsh

Silver

Hole

Marsh

C

Grass Hassock Channel

D

**Conches
Hole
Point**

Edgemere

Park

Dubos Point
Wildlife
Sanctuary

PAGE 368

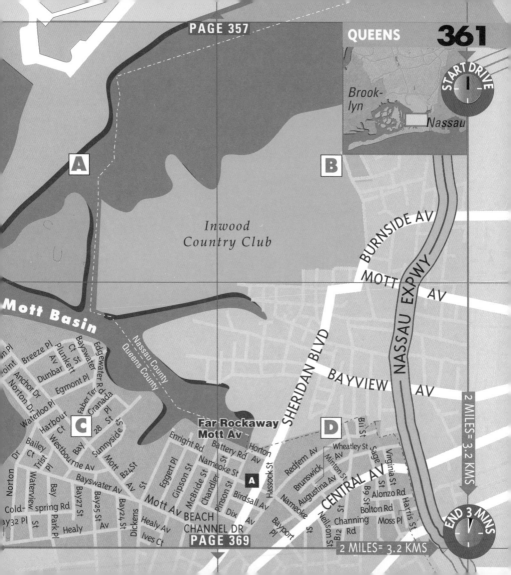

START DRIVE

Brooklyn

Nassau

A

B

Inwood Country Club

BURNSIDE AV

MOTT

AV

NASSAU EXPWY

Mott Basin

SHERIDAN BLVD

BAYVIEW

AV

2 MILES = 3.2 KMS

Point Pl

Breeze Pl

Plunkett

Bayswater

Ct St

Av

Dunbar

Edgewater Rd

Anchor Dr

Egmont Pl

Faber Ter

Norton Dr

Waterloo Pl

Oranada

Nassau County

Queens County

Harbour

Ct

28 Pl

St

C

Bailey

Bay

Sunnyside

Far Rockaway

Mott Av

D

Bil St

Westbourne Av

Mott

St

B2 St

Enright Rd

Battery Rd

Horton

Redfern Av

Wheatley St

Sage

Virginia St

Trist

Pl

Bayswater Av

Av

Namoke St

Av

Nimton St

St

Norton

Dr

Eggert Pl

Gipson St

Chandler

Nameoke

Augustina Av

CENTRAL AV

Alonzo Rd

Ct

Waterview

Bay

McBride St

Pinson St

Birdsall Av

Brunswick

B9 St

Harris St

Cold-

Bay27 St

Bay25 St

Dix

A

Hassock St

Bolton Rd

ay32 Pl

St

Park Pl

Dickens

Healy Av

St

Bayport

Neilson St

Bl2

Channing

Moss Pl

Healy

Ives Ct

Mott Av

BEACH CHANNEL DR

Pl

Rd

PAGE 369

END 3 MINS

2 MILES = 3.2 KMS

A

Palmer Dr

Clinton Wk
Bath Wk
Bay Ter
Bay Dr
Bayway Wk
Bayview Wk

B218 St
B216 St
12

Deauville Wk

B

Bayside
Chapel
Wk

ROCKAWAY POINT BLVD

Seabreeze
Wk

Hillcrest Wk
Point Breezy
Av

B209
St

B208 St
Ocean Av

9

5 Av

Utica Wk
Tioga Wk
Suffolk Wk
Roosvelt Wk
Queens Wk
Pelham Wk
Olive Wk
Newport Wk
Marion Wk
Lincoln Wk
Killdare Wk
Jamaica Wk
Irving Wk
Hudson Wk
Gotham Wk
Fulton Wk
Ocean Wk
Atlantic Wk
Essex Wk
Devon Wk
Chester Wk
Brant Wk
Arc

Oceanside Av

7 A

B220 Av
B221 Av

B224 St

Breezy Point Blvd

Breezy Point Blvd

B219 St
B217 St
B216 St
B215 St
B211 St

**BREEZY
POINT**

C

D

Rockaway
Point

Atlan

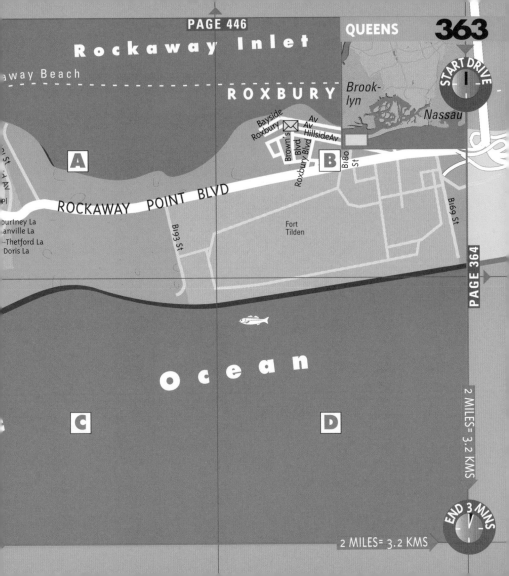

Rockaway Inlet

away Beach

ROXBURY

QUEENS

Brook-lyn

Nassau

START DRIVE

Bayside
Roxbury

Av
Av
HillsideAv

Brown's

A

Roxbury Blvd
Roxbury Blvd

B

B180 St

ROCKAWAY POINT BLVD

B193 St

B169 St

urtney La
anville La
Thetford La
Doris La

Fort
Tilden

Ocean

C

D

2 MILES= 3.2 KMS

END 3 MINS

2 MILES= 3.2 KMS

PAGE 439

PAGE 363

Floyd
Bennett
Field

FLATBUSH AV

Aviation Rd

Dead Horse Bay
Natural Area

Toll
Plaza

A

U.S. Navy

Kings County
Queens County

B

R o c k a w a y   I n l e t

Marine Parkway Bridge

136-0

Cron

145-01

142-01

502

B39 St

B40 St

B43 St

B44 St

B45 St

63

Ne

Riis Av

Gil Hodges
Memorial
Bridge

402

N E P O N S I T

302

Neponsit Av

302

P

Jacob Riis
Park

202

402

U.S. Coast
Guard

ROCKAWAY BEACH

Nepsonsit
Health Care
Center

D

Fort
Tilden

B169 St

C

BOARDWALK

B49 St

B48 St

B47 St

B46 St

B45 St

Brook-
lyn

Nassau

START DRIVE

Beach Channel

126

A

Marine Park
120-01

BEACH CHANNEL DR

502

B

Beach 105 St

A S

Bl04 St

Seaside Av

502

Bl31 St

Bl30 St

Bl29 St

Bl28 St

Bl27 St

Wainwright Ct

Bl07 St

R O C K A W A Y   P A R K

Rockaway Water
Pollution Control Plant

Seaside
Rockaway
Houses

502

Bl32 St

**Rockaway Park
Beach 116 St**

A S

402

202

113-01

Bl09 St

Bl08 St

Bl06 St

105-01

Bl05 St

B E L L

Bl26 St

Bl25 St

202

Memorial Cir

Bl20 St

Bl19 St

Bl18 St

Bl17 St

Bl16 St

Bl15 St

Bl14 St

Bl11 St

Shore Front

Pkwy

Bl02 La

H A R B O R

Bl24 St

Bl23 St

Bl22 St

Bl21 St

BOARDWALK

202

Ocean
Rockaway Park

Promenade

Beach

C

A t l a n t i c   O c e a n

D

PAGE 366

2 MILES = 3.2 KMS

END 3 MINS

2 MILES= 3.2 KMS

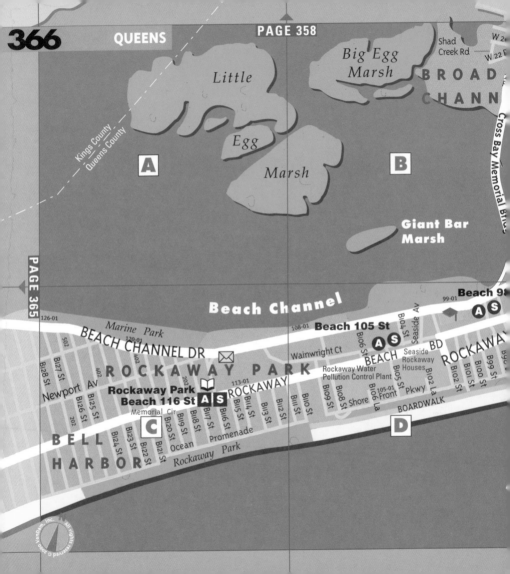

QUEENS

PAGE 358

Shad
Creek Rd

W 2

W 22

*Big Egg
Marsh*

BROAD

CHANN

Little

Cross Bay Memorial Brid

Kings County

Queens County

Egg

A

Marsh

B

**Giant Bar
Marsh**

**PAGE
365**

Beach 9

99-01

A **S**

Beach Channel

126-01

Marine   Park

108-01

Beach 105 St

502

120-01

BEACH CHANNEL DR ✉

A **S**

402

Wainwright Ct

BEACH

Seaside Av

Bl06 St

Bl04 St

Seaside
Rockaway
Houses

ROCKAWA

ROCKAWAY   PARK

Rockaway Water
Pollution Control Plant

Bl09 St

Bl08 St

Bl06 La

105-01
Front Pkwy

Bl03 St

Bl02 St

Bl01 St

Bl00 St

B99 St

B9

402

ROCKAWAY

Shore

BEACH

Bl27 St

Bl28 St

Newport Av

Bl26 St

Bl25 St

202

**Rockaway Park
Beach 116 St** 📖 **A** **S**

Memorial Cir

113-01

Bl14 St

Bl13 St

Bl11 St

Bl12 St

Bl05 La

BD

BOARDWALK

D

Bl24 St

Bl23 St

Bl22 St

Bl21 St

Bl20 St

Bl19 St

Bl18 St

Bl17 St

Bl16 St

Bl15 St

C

BELL

Ocean

Rockaway Park

HARBOR

Promenade

nel Rd

merest Rd
Brunt Rd

**Brant
Point**

Barbadoes Dr
Bayfield Av
De Costa Av
Hillmeyer Av
Almeda Av
Burchell Av
Elizabeth Av
Thursby Av
Hessler Av
Gouverneur Av

Brook-
lyn

Nassau

Burchell Rd
Elizabeth
Rd

Elizabeth Av
Edgemere
Houses

65-01

101

101

501

105

400

A

St Cloud Rd
Scheer St
Amstel Blvd

Barbadoes Dr

Vernam Basin

72-01

72-01

Crugers Rd

69-01

B

Parvine
Av

A R V E R N E

Arverne
Houses

B58 St

B57 St

B56 St

Barbadoes Dr

Barbadoes Basin

Rockaway
Industrial
Park

BEACH

B84 St
B86 St
B87 St
B89 St
B88 St

Beach 67 St
A

DR

Beach 60 St
A

Arverne Blvd

B83 St
B82 St

FRWY

Finnard Av

63-01

ROCKAWAY FRWY

PAGE 368

Java Pl

CHANNEL

B76 St
B75 St

Gull Ct

OCKAWAY

Hammel Houses
81-01

B80 St
B79 St

202
202

Swan Rd
Story Rd

Larkin Av

Seafoam Ct

B56 Pl

BLVD

Holland Av

and Av
B92 St
B91 St
B90 St

84-01

B81 St

B77 St

B74 St
B73 St
B72 St
B71 St
B70 St
B69 St
B68 St
B67 St
B66 St
B65 St
B64 St
B63 St
B62 St
B61 St
B60 St
B59 St

BOARDWALK

Rockaway Beach

C

D

A t l a n t i c   **O** c e a n

END 3 MINS

2 MILES = 3.2 KMS

2 MILES = 3.2 KMS

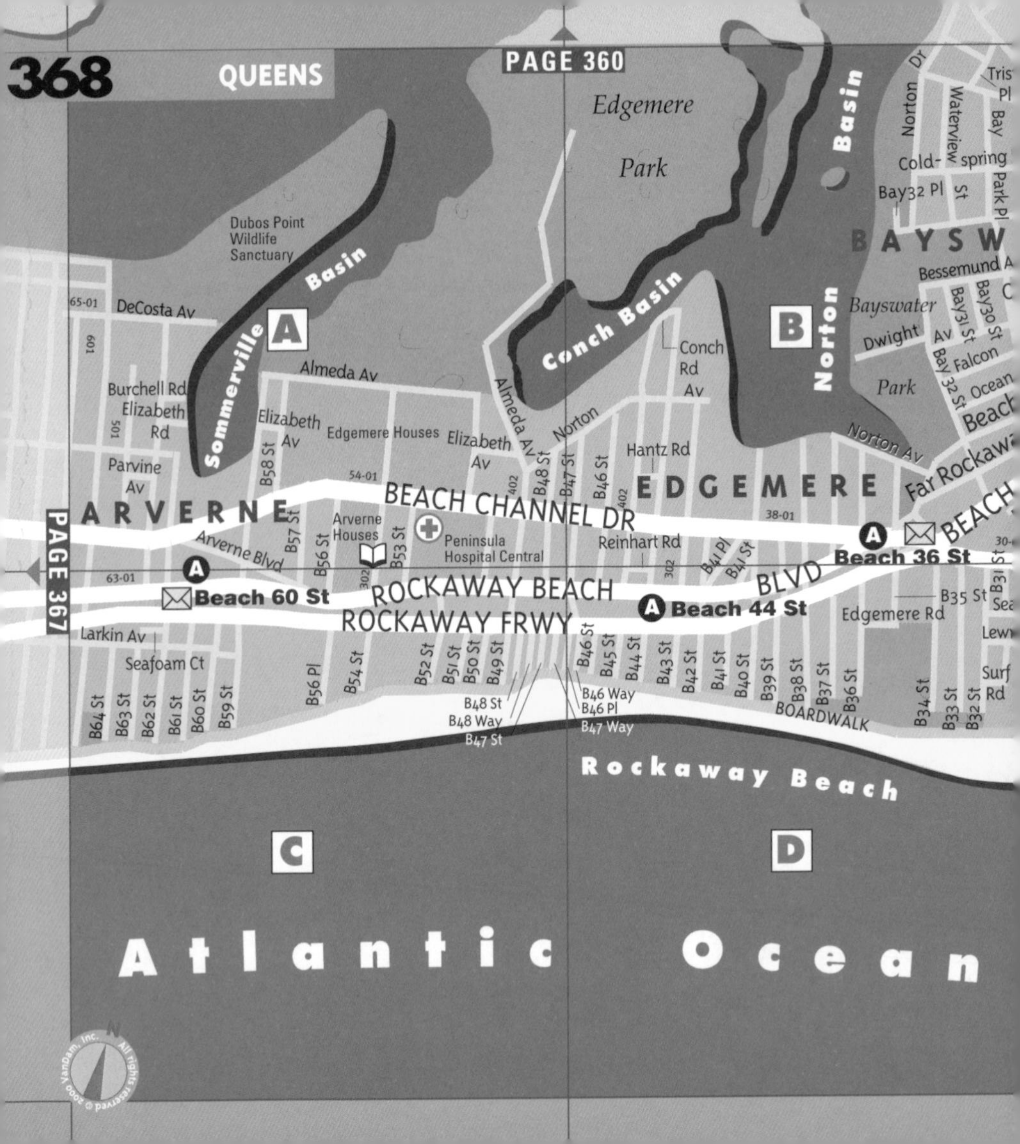

PAGE 360

PAGE 367

Edgemere Park

Edgemere Basin

B A Y S W

Dubos Point Wildlife Sanctuary

Sommerville Basin

Conch Basin

Bayswater Park

A

B

Norton Dr

Tris Pl

Norton St

Waterview St

Bay Park Pl

Cold-spring

Bay32 Pl

Bessemund Av

Bay30 St

Dwight Av

Bay31 St

Bay 32 St

Falcon

Ocean

Beach

65-01 DeCosta Av

601

Burchell Rd

Elizabeth Rd

501

Parvine Av

Almeda Av

Elizabeth Av

Edgemere Houses

Elizabeth Av

Almeda Av

Norton Av

Conch Rd Av

54-01

Hantz Rd

Far Rockaw

Norton Av

E D G E M E R E **BEACH**

A R V E R N E

BEACH CHANNEL DR

402

B48 St

B47 St

B46 St

Arverne Blvd

Arverne Houses

63-01

302

Peninsula Hospital Central

Reinhart Rd

38-01

B41 Pl

B41 St

A ✉ **Beach 36 St**

30-0

B31 St

Sea

B57 St

B56 St

B53 St

A ✉ **Beach 60 St**

ROCKAWAY BEACH

ROCKAWAY FRWY

A **Beach 44 St**

BLVD

B35 St

Edgemere Rd

Lew

Larkin Av

Seafoam Ct

B64 St

B63 St

B62 St

B61 St

B60 St

B59 St

B56 Pl

B54 St

B52 St

B51 St

B50 St

B49 St

B46 St

B45 St

B44 St

B43 St

B42 St

B41 St

B40 St

B39 St

B38 St

B37 St

B36 St

B34 St

B33 St

B32 St

Surf Rd

B48 St

B48 Way

B47 St

B46 Way

B46 Pl

B47 Way

BOARDWALK

C

D

R o c k a w a y   B e a c h

A t l a n t i c   O c e a n

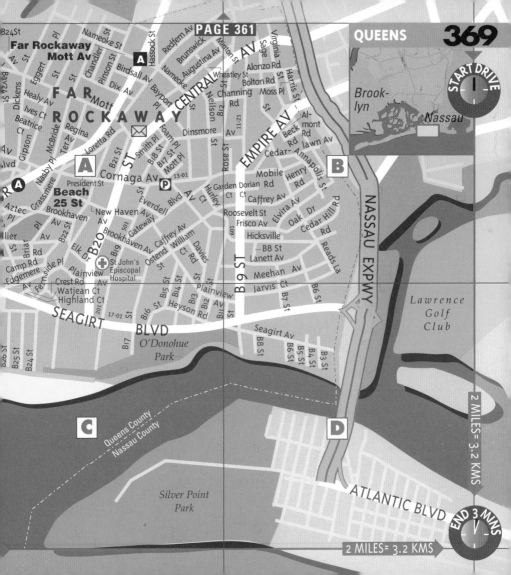

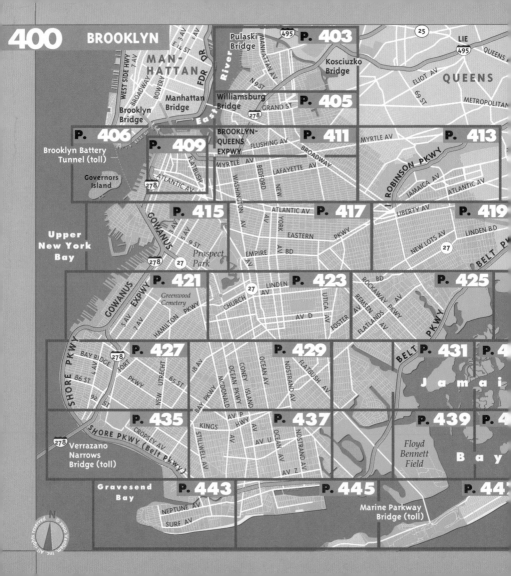

ooklyn's Best

oklyn, NYC's most populous rough, is a metropolis in own right, and home to 2.3 lion people. It has been a tural Mecca, shipping ›ital, ocean front resort, the gateway to America. e could fit four Manhattans ‹ its 81.8 sq es of land. e out of every Americans ls from at would be the country's rth largest city if it wasn't "the mistake": the annexation New York City in 1898.

Brooklyn Museum of Art

The museum's permanent collection includes paintings and sculpture by Rodin, Modigliani, Degas, Monet, Chagall, Gauguin, Sargent, Bierstadt, plus one of the foremost collections of Egyptian art. 200 Eastern Pkwy, 718-638-5000. **416A**

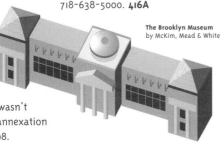

The Brooklyn Museum by McKim, Mead & White

ver Café

s haute dining barge boasts most fabulous views of nhattan and competes with best food palaces anywhere. erve. 1 Water St, 718-522-5200. ›A

tanic Garden

acres of flora plus the gest public rose and bonsai lections in the country. ‹ Washington Av, ‹622-4433. **416C**

BAM

The loadstar of the avant-garde performing arts scene is an annual rite and de rigueur for New Yorkers in the mix. The careers of composer Philip Glass, multimedia artist Laurie Anderson and choreographers Mark Morris and Bill T. Jones were launched here under the auspices of BAM's Next Wave Festival and visionary impressario, Harvey Lichtenstein. Brooklyn Academy of Music 30 Lafayette St, 718-636-4100. **407D**

Peter Luger

Candle-lit antebellum atmosphere, and the best steaks around. Cash only. Reservations are essential. 178 Broadway at Driggs Av, 718-387-7400. **404A**

Prospect Park

America's leading landscape architects, Olmsted & Vaux, designed this urban oasis. The arch, by John Duncan, was built in honor of the Union Army in 1870. Flatbush Av & Plaza Street. **416B**

Grand Army Arch

PAGE 308

Midtown Tunnel

Pulaski
Bridge

Long

Newtown C

HU

LONG

River

Queens County
Kings County

New York County
Kings County

A

B

Ash St
St 40
Box
Commercial St 100
Clay St 150
Dupont St
230 Eagle St 170
60 Freeman St 190
Green St 190
70 Huron St 190
70 India St 170
40 Java St 190
60 Kent St 190

Paidge Av

MANHATTAN AV

BLVD

McGUINNESS

Provost St

Kingsla

GREENPOINT

Jewel St

St

Av

Moultrie St

West St
180
FRANKLIN ST

Greenpoint Av
Milton 90 St 150

Noble St

G Greenpoint
Av

Calyer

Diamond St

110

780

Greenpiont Piers

A

B

GREENPOINT

Oak St
Calyer St 120

Quay St

Lorimer St

Guernsey St

809

Leonard St

230

McGUINNESS BLVD

Eckford St

88

Norman Av

Newel St

HUMBOLDT ST

Bushwick Inlet

East

Circle Line

PAGE 119

P Meserole
St

Clifford Pl

Gem St

Banker St

Dobbin St

N 15 St

Wythe Av

N 14 St

N 13 St

N 12 St

Nassau Av

G Nassau Av

Driggs Av

Broome St

Engert
Av

McG
Blvd

Graham Av

Newton St

C

D

KENT AV

83

53

N 11 St

N 10 St

N 9 St 110

N 8 St 110

Galapagos

7 St

N 6 St 110

Planet
Thailand

Berry St

120

BEDFORD AV

Driggs Av

McCarren
Park

Bayard St

430

148

N 5 St 110

River St

N 4 St 90

N 3 St 90

Oznot's
Dish

170 210

T Raymond
Nutley Sq

10

110

Metropolitan 90

N 1 St 90

**NORTH
SIDE**

N 9 ST

260

Union Av

20

Mt Carmel
Sq

40

BROOKLYN - QU

33

160
370

Grand St

L Bedford
Av

Roebling

240

260

110

150

PAGE 404

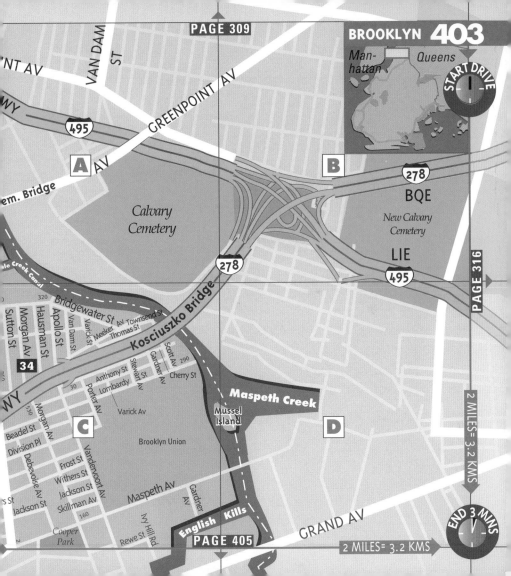

Man-hattan   Queens

START DRIVE

A

B

$\boxed{495}$

GREENPOINT AV

VAN DAM ST

NT AV

WY

em. Bridge

Calvary Cemetery

$\boxed{278}$

BQE

New Calvary Cemetery

LIE

$\boxed{495}$

PAGE 316

$\boxed{278}$

le Creek Canal

320

Bridgewater St

Van Dam St

Varick St

Meeker AV Townsend St

Thomas St

Kosciuszko Bridge

Morgan Av

Hausman St

Apollo St

Sutton St

34

WY

530

Anthony St

Porter Av

Lombardy

Stewart St

Gardner Av

Scott Av

290

Cherry St

Varick Av

Maspeth Creek

Mussel Island

C

30

Morgan Av

Beadel St

Division Pl

Debevoise Av

Frost St

Vandervoort Av

Withers St

Jackson St

Skillman Av

Brooklyn Union

D

rs St

Jackson St

Maspeth Av

Gardner Av

160

Cooper Park

Ivy Hill Rd

Rewe St

English Kills

GRAND AV

END 3 MINS

2 MILES= 3.2 KMS

2 MILES= 3.2 KMS

PAGE 405

Man-hattan   Queens

START DRIVE
1

KINGSLAND ST
Debevoise St
Morgan Av St
St
Vandervoort Av
St

Brooklyn Union

Maspeth Av

Gardner Av

English Kills

Cooper Park
Sharon St
Calhoun St
Rewe St
Orient Av
Olive St
Catharine St
Dickinson St
Ivy Hill Rd

160

1010

A METROPOLITAN   AV   **B**

Linden Hill Cemetery

Grand St

GRAND ST

BUSHWICK

Stagg St

Maujer St
Ten Eyck St
Meadow St
Waterbury St

Morgan Av

Ten Eyck St
Meadow St
Stagg St
Scott Av

Scholes
Meserole St

230 Randolph
Seneca Av

Onderdonk Av

1220

590

610

Gardner Av
Stewart Av
Varick Av

Cypress Av

PAGE 326

Bushwick Terminal
Johnson Av 320
410   410

L Bushwick Pl

Boerum St
McKibben St
White St
Seigel St
Moore St
Varet St
Cook St 160

Ingraham St
Harrison St
Grattan
Porter Av
Pl

Morgan Av **L**
Bogart St

Vander-Voort Pl

Thames St
Rock St

Jefferson St **L**

Troutman St
Irving Av
Starr St

Willoughby Av
Suydam St

St. Nicholas Av
440
Kings County
Queens County

270

DeKalb Av **L** ✉

1000

Hart St
DeKalb
Stockholm St
Stanhope St

Wyckoff Hts.
Medical Ctr. ✚

190

FLUSHING AV

George St
Melrose St
Jefferson St
Wilson Av

Knickerbocker Av
Bushwick Park

310
150
90
1490

Himrod St
Harman St
Greene
Bleecker St

Wyckoff Av

230
260
310

C

Bushwick Houses
Debevoise St

Montieth St
Forrest
Garden St
Beaver St
Noll

Starwix St

Central Av

D

E A S T

W I L L I A M S B U R G

2 MILES = 3.2 KMS

90
320
490
150
320
250
390
240
250
1130

170
130
710
120

BUSHWICK AV

Ellery St
Park St
Locust St
Belvidere St
Arion Pl
Melrose
Jefferson St

Troutman
St
Av

Charles Pl

Cedar St

M
Central Av

MYRTLE AV

1325

130
1250
1290

M **Knicker-bocker Av** **P**

END 3 MINS
1

Lewis Av
Stockton St
Sumner Housing
1110

210
250
190
210
200

240
160
1250
190
240
230

2 MILES= 3.2 KMS

PAGE 104

WALL ST

FDR DRIVE

Barge

Liberty & Ellis
Island Ferries

Battery
Park

FULTO

FERRY

A

Governors
Island
Ferry

B

2

East River

Broo
Hei
Prome

3

Staten
Island
Ferry

4

5

BROOKLYN

HEIGHTS

6

New York County

Kings County

Furman St

Carder Rd

Castle
Williams

**Governors
Island**

Fort Jay

COLUMBIA

7

27

Long Island
College Hospital

278

Wheeler Av

Hay Rd

Early Bird Rd

STREET

8

9A

Warren St

Baltic St

Columbia St

60

Craig Rd N

Gresham Rd

Division Rd

WATER

C

FRONT

Kane St

Irving St

Tiffany Pl

Emright Rd

Craig Rd S

Yankee
Pier

Brooklyn
Battery
Tunnel
(Toll)

9B

D

Sedgwick St

Degraw St

Ferry Pl

Van Brunt St

50

Sackett St

Hicks St

BQE

490

Cheever Pl

HENRY

Tango
Pier

Lima
Pier

Buttermilk Channel

10

Union St

President St

Carroll St

Hamilton Av

Summit St

P

150

22

BROOKLYN

PAGE 404

WILLIAMSBURG

Taylor St
Wilson St
Ross St
Rodney St
Hooper St
Hewes St
Marcy Av
Lynch St
Middleton
Lorr

Williamsburg St E
Penn St
Rutledge St
Heyward St
Lee Av
110
220

Navy Yard Basin

N A V Y
Y A R D

Brooklyn
Navy Yard
Industrial Park

Com. J
Barry
Park

A

U.S. Naval
Station

278

31

B

Kent St
Classon Av
Kent Av
Skillman St
Spencer St
Walworth St
Wartoff Pl

Wallabout s

FLUSHING AV
PARK AV

Cumberland St
N Oxford St
N Portland Av
N Elliott Pl
40
140
190
10
20
60
10

280

Williamsburg Bridge
Hooper St

Little Nassau St
Park Av
Taaffe Pl
Kent Av
Franklin Av

350
410
90
50
790
760
110
820
90
60

MYRTLE AV

Sandford St

Cumberland
Hospital

St Edwards St

Walt
Whitman
Houses

Aubum Pl

F O R T
G R E E N E

MYRTLE AV

Emerson Pl
Steuben St
Grand Av
Ryerson St
Hall St
Waverly Av
Clinton Av
Vanderbilt Av
Clermont Av
Adelphi St

107
110
90
120
210
280
380

Willoughby Av

Pratt Institute

210
160
910

BEDFORD AV

Spencer
Ct

910
540

C
L
H
I

University
Towers
Housing

Kings View
Housing

De Kalb Av

L.I.
University

Fort
Greene
Park

Washington Park

160
230

**Brooklyn Hospital
Center, Downtown**

DE KALB AV

St Joseph's
College

St Josephs
College

240
330

The
Quadrangles

Steuben
St

Lafayette
Gardens

G

150
190
1060

B
N

G

Ashland
Rockwell Pl

Hudson Av

Ft Greene Pl
St Felix St

S PORTLAND

310

BAM Harvey Theatre,
UrbanGlass
Fulton St

C

360
10

Clifton Pl

Classon Av

170

Greene Av

G

G

Clinton Av
Washington Av

250

370

D

Temple
Sq

BAM
Café
Brooklyn
Academy of Music

100

G

C
Lafayette Av

C

CARLTON AV
Cumberland St
S Oxford St

850
410
450
10
40

Cambridge Pl
St James Pl
Grand Av
Downing St
Irving Pl
Classon Av
Franklin Av
Claver Pl

30
90
170
30
10
170
70
130
240
80
290
90
250

2 **3** **D** Hanson Pl
4 **5** **Q** **M**
Atlantic Center

St Elliott Pl

WASHINGTON AV

A **C**
Clinton Av
Washington Av

FULTON ST

Atlantic Av

440

PAGE 416

PAGE 407

N

Manhattan   Queens

START DRIVE

Lindsay Park Houses

Moore St   Moore St **PAGE 405**

Varet St   Varet St

Cook St   Cook St

90

160

430

AV

FLUSHING AV

Wilson Av   150

George St   320

Melrose St   250

Jefferson St

Central Av

70

Montieth St   Forrest St   Starwix St

Bushwick Houses

Debevoise St

Flushing Av J M

10

Woodhull Medical Center A

180

Whipple St

Thornton St

Av   Delmonico Pl

20   160

760

Jr Pl

Tompkins Houses

90

940

210   1010

Sumner Housing

Garden St   Beaver St   Noll

Sumner Pl   Fayette St   Ellery St   Park St   Locust St   Belvidere St   Arion Pl   Melrose

Stockton St

Jefferson

BUSHWICK

Charles Pl

Troutman

130   110

St

AV

130   110

St

B **MYRTLE AV** M **Central Av**

BUSHWICK

130   1250

1110

Myrtle Av J M Z

Ditmars St   Willoughby   Suydam   Hart   Lawton St   Dodworth St   DeKalb St   Kosciuszko St

310

40

240

Vernon Av

Willoughby Av   760

310

Hart St

130   310   90

220

310

AV

270

Evergreen Av

10

Menahan St

Grove St

10

10   930

450

50

1050

1060

Eleanor Roosevelt Housing

Kosciuszko St J

Kossuth Pl

Lafayette Av

Van Buren St

Greene   Goodwin Pl

70

1160

PAGE 412

Pulaski St

870

DE KALB AV

Kosciuszko St

330

790

LAFAYETTE   AV

Van Buren St

ber Von ng Park ompkins) P

Greene Av

260

Tompkins Av

Lexington

Quincy St

Gates Av

Monroe St

310

390

850

310

410

930

850

470

130

10

Brevoort Housing

890

60

1010

BROADWAY

Patchen Av

790

770

890

710

1110

20

Z

J

P 1030

Gates St

840

2 MILES= 3.2 KMS

END 3 MINS

N

680

410   500

420

480

370

430

540

Throop Av

Madison St

Putnam Av

Jefferson Av

Hancock St

Halsey St

750

240

730

490

600

280

680

Marcus Garvey Blvd

Lewis Av

200   630

170

630

C

530

540   540

350

410

Stuyvesant

Av

240

BEDFORD

STUYVESANT

Macon St

630

600

660

610

590

D

120

730

680

180

570

McDonough St

Decatur St   470

PAGE 417

320

320

MALCOLM X BLVD

890

790

910

80

Ralph Av

810

910

Howard Av

1060

20

910

610

520

390

2 MILES= 3.2 KMS

PAGE 326

FRESH POND RD

E A S T

W I L L I A M S B U R G

Knickerbocker Av

Stanhope St

Himrod St

Harman St

Greene Av

Bleecker St

Wyckoff Av

1490
410
230
260
310
340
370

1490

120
1325
210
1290

Wilson Av

M Knicker–bocker Av

A **P**

130
160
1250
240
230

B U S H W I C K

Menahan St

Grove St

Linden St

Central Av

Woodbine St

Madison St

Putnam Av

Cornelia St

Jefferson Av

Hancock St

Weirfield St

Halsey St

Eldert St

Covert St

Schaefer St

Decatur St

1310
350
180
430
1390
240
610

Gates Av

Palmetto St

320
460

M

L Myrtle Av

MYRTLE AV

M Wyckoff Av

Ridgewood Pl

1490
370
430
1390

1390

B

1380
470
1330

L Halsey St

740
310
270
260
1320
810

Irving
Square

Goodwin Pl

30
70
1160
1110
10
930

20
20

Z
J

1030

J

Gates St

890
80
910

20

1060

910

C

Halsey St

130
810
610
520
390
290
220

Ralph Av

Howard Av

Saratoga Av

Hopkinson Av

Saratoga Sq
Park

750

670

590

470

510

Chauncey St

Marion St

Evergreen Av

130
550
1120
1110

140
126
120
620

530

1120

BROADWAY

BUSHWICK AV

970
1110
1040
1000
990
10
970

J

Chauncey St

Z
J

Moffat St

Chauncey St

L Wilson Av

COOPER ST

Pilling St

Granite St

Furman Av

Aberdeen St

Stone Av

DeSales Pl

Vandeveer St
Cooke Ct

Cemetery
of the
Evergreens

D

1

**Bushwick Av
Aberdeen St**

CYPR

JACKIE RO

Vermo

Crosby Av

Miller

Pl

2

N

PAGE 411

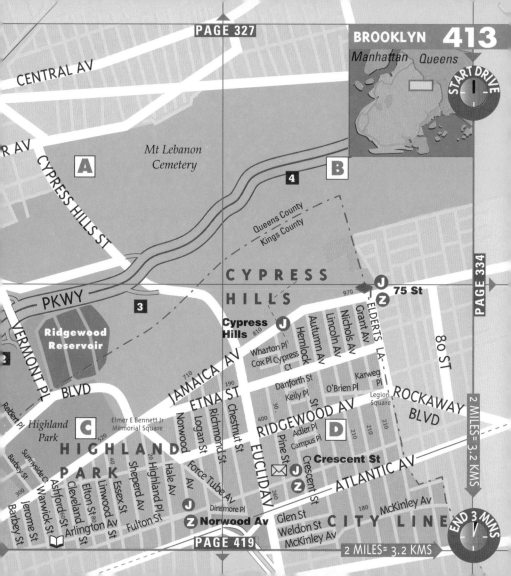

Manhattan   Queens

START DRIVE
1

CENTRAL AV

R AV

A

Mt Lebanon
Cemetery

B

4

CYPRESS HILLS ST

Queens County
Kings County

CYPRESS

HILLS

PKWY

3

PAGE 334

J
Z
75 St

970

VERMONT PL

Ridgewood
Reservoir

Cypress
Hills
810
J

ELDERTS LA

80 ST

BLVD

Grant Av
Nichols Av
Lincoln Av
Autumn Av
Hemlock

Wharton Pl
Cox Pl Cypress
Ct

710

JAMAICA AV

190

ETNA ST

Danforth St
Keily Pl

Karweg
Pl

O'Brien Pl

Legion
Square

ROCKAWAY

BLVD

Robert Pl

Highland
Park

C

Elmer E Bennett Jr
Memorial Square

Norwood

Logan St

Richmond St

Chestnut St

30

400

RIDGEWOOD AV

210 210 210

D

2 MILES= 3.2 KMS

HIGHLAND

Barbey St

Sunnyside Ct

Ashford St

Highland Pl

40

20

Hale Av

Force Tube Av

Adler Pl
Pine St
Campus Pl

EUCLID AV

Crescent St
260

Crescent St

PARK

300

Jerome St

Warwick St

Cleveland
Elton St
Linwood Av

80

Essex St

Sheperd Av

Av

J

Dinsmore Pl

☒
J
Z

ATLANTIC AV

180

McKinley Av

Barbey St

Arlington Av

Fulton St

Z Norwood Av

Glen St
Weldon St
McKinley Av

CITY   LINE

END 3 MINS

📖

2 MILES= 3.2 KMS

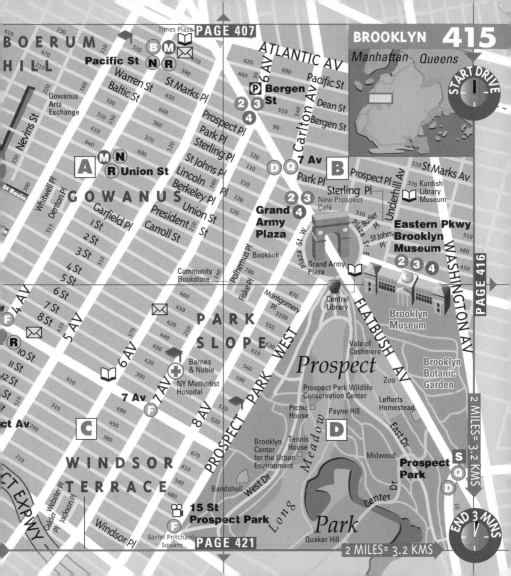

PAGE 410
PAGE 415
PAGE 422

PROSPECT HEIGHTS

CROWN HEIGHTS

RUGBY

Prospect Park

ATLANTIC AV

FULTON ST

Franklin Av

Nostrand Av

Hancock St
Halsey St
Macon St
MacDonough St
Decatur St

Lefferts Pl
Spencer Pl
Brevoort Pl

Herkimer St
Herkimer Pl
Herkimer Ct

Billie Holiday Theatre

Kingston Park

Pacific St
Dean St
Bergen St
St Marks Av
Prospect Pl
Park Pl Pl
Lincoln Pl

Kurdish Library Museum

Eastern Pkwy
Brooklyn Museum

Botanic Garden
Union St
Franklin Av

President St
Carroll St
Crown St
Montgomery St

Medgar Evers College

Sullivan Pl

Sterling St

EMPIRE BLVD

Prospect Park

Lincoln Rd

Mike's International

Beekman Pl

Brooklyn Museum

Prospect Park

Brooklyn Botanic Garden

Zoo
Lefferts Homestead

Boathouse

EASTERN PKWY

Nostrand Av

Union St
President St
Carroll St
Crown St
Montgomery St

Sterling St
Lefferts Av
E New York Av
Maple St
Midwood St
Rutland Rd
Fenimore St

The Brooklyn Childrens Museum

Brower Park

Pacific St
Dean St
Bergen St
St Marks Av
Prospect Pl
Park Pl
Sterling Pl
St Johns Pl
Lincoln Pl

Kingston Av
Hampton Av

Grant Sq

Claver Pl
Bedford Av
Grand Av
Classon Av
Washington Av
Bedford Av
Nostrand Av
New York Av
Rogers Av
Flatbush Av
Ocean Av

A C S
A C
M
A C

2 3
2 3
4 5
3
2 5
2 5
S
D Q
S

B
A
C
D
W
V
R

King

Revere Pl
Virginia Pl
Balfour Pl
Lamont Ct
Tampa Ct
Palm Ct
Miami Ct

Manhattan Queens

START DRIVE
1

MALCOLM X BLVD

Lewis Av
320
380
250
470
320
230

Bainbridge St

Av
Fulton Chauncey St
Park

Chauncey St
Ralph Av 290
Marion St 220
Brevoort Sumpter St
Housing

Saratoga Av

Marion St
830

Ralph Av 30
McDougal
1840 1930

er St
Jewell
McKoy La 80
Hattie–
Jones Ct

Utica Av
Harmony
Park
400

A C FULTON ST A C ✉

O C E A N   H I L L
1130

and
Center

ATLANTIC AV

A

Hunterfly Pl
Suydam Pl
60
1850

Kane Pl
Columbus Pl
360

Prescott Pl
Bancroft Pl
320

Dewey Pl
Louis Pl

Roosevelt Pl

2080 270

B

1610 80

1760

Kingsborough Housing

2020

Hopkinson Av

Rockaway Av

W E E K S V I L L E
1720

St Johns
Park
1130 120 P
1338

144

Ralph Av

Howard Av

Saratoga Av

2184

1350

1590

1750

1610

1564

PKWY

YORK AV

P

Howard
Housing

1280

St Mary's
Hospital ✚
175
1430
1710

1410 1470

Schenectady Av

Rochester Av

Buffalo Av

PAGE 418

1310
1380 1430
1590

B R O W N S V I L L E

1010
1670 310
641

TERN PKWY 3 4 Utica Av
1320

1651
783 Ford St
1003

Lincoln
Terrace
Park

Portal St
Union St

EASTERN

1250

EAST

1330

NEW

Pitkin Av

Grafton Av
Legion St
Tapscott St
Union St

KINGS

Saratoga Av
Strauss St
Herzl St

Amboy St

Bristol St
Chester St

Thatford St
Rockaway Av

135

Sutter Av

500 250

540

C

E 98 St
E 96 St
E 95 St
E 94 St
E 93 St
E 92 St

Ralph Av

1990
170
170
610
200
260

PIRE BLVD
880

E 91 St

Rutland
1012 Rd

93

Sutter Av
Rutland Rd 3

E A S T   F L A T B U S H

120
180

Blake Av

Dumont Av

Hopkinson Av

641

Blake
Square
81

D

94

2110

Livonia Av

Kingsbrook
Jewish
Medical
Center ✚

E 49 St
E 46 St
E 45 St

Rutland
105
117

Winthrop St

ROCK–

AWAY PKWY

1075 Av

310

Saratoga
Av

240

Howard
Gardens

2110

Riverdale Av

430

N

GE

UTICA AV

REMSEN AV

Clarkson

267

Lenox
Rd

Howard Av

350

40
840

Newport St

2190 40

870

END 3 MINS

2 MILES = 3.2 KMS

2 MILES = 3.2 KMS

PAGE 412

Sumpter St
MacDougal St
Hull Av
Rockaway Av
FULTON
Herkimer St
Radde Pl
Marconi Pl
Gunther Pl
ATLANTIC

Broadway 310
Eastern Pkwy
Somers St
A C ST
Monaco Pl
Sherlock Pl
Pleasant Pl

BUSHWICK AV
B'WAY
Cooke Ct
Stewart St
Conway St
Fanchon Pl
B R O A D W A Y
EXT
Truxton St
JCT
Williams Pl
Jewell Square
Sackman St
Jardine Pl
Havens Pl

Sunnyside Av
Miller Av
Marginal St E
JAMAICA AV
Arlington Av
Fulton St
Van Siclen Av

A C **Broadway**
East New York
J **Alabama Av**
ATLANTIC AV
LIBERTY AV

M L
Atlantic Av
A C
Liberty Av
B
Glenmore Av

EASTERN PKWY
EAST NEW YORK AV
P
Howard Housing
Mother Gaston Blvd
1880
Van Sinderen Av

Pitkin Av
Herzl St
Amboy St
Bristol St
Chester St
Thatford Av
Osborn St
Watkins St
Christopher Av
Sackman St
Powell St
Junius St
Sneaker Av

Sutter Av
Blake Av
C **3**
Rockaway Av
Dumont Av
Livonia Av
Saratoga Av
Strauss St
Hopkinson Av
B R O W N S V I L L E
Newport St
Riverdale Av
Watkins St
Osborn St
Thatford Av
Sackman St
Christopher Av
Lott Av

Brownsville Brooklyn Heritage House Housing
Dyke
Housing
SJ Tilden Houses

L **Sutter Av**
3 **Junius St**
L **Livonia Av**
L **New Lots Av**

GRANVILLE PAYNE AV
Sheffield Av
Georgia Av
Alabama Av
Williams Av
Hinsdale St

East NY Neighborhood Family Care Center

A C
Van Siclen Av
Pitkin Av
Barbey St
Schenck Av
Jerome St

Van Siclen Av
Miller Av
Bradford St
Wyona St
New Jersey Av
Vermont St

Linton Park
3 **Pennsylvania Av**
3 **Van Si Av**
D
N E W
L O T S
NEW LOTS AV
PENNSYLVANIA AV
Sheffield Av
Alabama Av
Van Siclen Av
Miller Av
Bradford St
Wyona St
New Jersey Av
Vermont St
LINDEN

E A
Bla
Hendrix St

PAGE 424

PAGE 417

© 2004 MAPQUEST, Inc. All rights reserved

Gowanus

Bay

A

Bush Terminal Docks

35 St

39 St   36 St

Marginal St

7
6
5

B

37 St

39 St

40 St

44 St

250

250

Ferry   57 St

250

52 St

250

GOWANUS EXPWY

N **R**

47

48 St

49 St

50 St

51 St

4

5400

74

Lutheran
Medical
Center

3

2

I

1 AV

2 AV

250

58 St

250

250

3 AV

4 AV

N **R** **53 St**

53 St

54 St

55 St

56 St

57 St

5 AV

540

540

440

6 AV

D

IA

C

245

1

250

SHORE PKWY

65 St

Shore Rd

Owls
Head
Park

Sedgwick Pl

Bergen Pl

67 St

Wakeman Pl

N **R**

59 St

59 St

60 St

61 St

440

62 St

63 St

64 St

550

540

640

640

278

P

68 St

P

Manhattan   Queens

START DRIVE
I

25 St
M N R
24 St
25 St
26 St
27 St
23 St
20 St
21 St
22 St
6 AV
7 AV
8 AV
270
220
330
320

P
200
28 St
29 St
30 St
31 St
32 St
33 St
200
820

36 St
M R
35 St
36 St
36 St
28 ST
5 ST
6 AV
7 AV
37 St
A

Greenwood
Cemetery

B

Terrace Pl
Seeley St
Vanderbilt St

MCDONALD AV

Greenwood Av
Fort Hamilton Pkwy
F
PAGE 422

CATON AV

Sunset Park
6 AV
640
7 AV
8 AV
9 AV
UTRECHT AV
B
M **9 Av**
Hefferman Square

E 4 St
E 3 St
E 2 St
Albemarle Rd
310
310
CHURCH AV

S E T
K
750
740
830
830
940
1050
1050
HAMILTON
PKWY
Mirna St
I2 AV
Tehama St
Chester Av
Clara St
Micieli Pl
Bills Pl
Louisa St
Story St
37 St
36 St
3301
112

2 MILES = 3.2 KMS

760
750
830
860
C
Maimonides Medical Center
Alben Memorial Square
B M
K E N S I N G T O N
Fort Hamilton Pkwy
1260
D
38 St
39 St
40 St
41 St
1470
1440
F
Church Av
Av C
110
Dahill Rd

I0 AV
II AV
FORT
9 AV
950
830
Ocean Palace
B M
50 St
PAGE 427
I2 AV
I3 AV
14 AV
42 St
43 St
44 St
45 St
46 St
47 St
1250
1250
1250
1120
1150
I5 AV
1440
1449

END 3 MINS
V

Fenimore St
Hawthorne St
Winthrop St
inthrop St

Kings
County
Hospital

Kingsboro
Psychiatric
Center

Kingsbrook
Jewish
Medical
Center

Health Science
Center SUNY
Downstate

27

Raleigh Pl
Fairview Pl

A LINDEN BLVD **B**

5500

Ralph Av

E 31 St
E 32 St
E 34 St
E 35 St

Brooklyn Av

CHURCH AV

E 37 St
E 38 St
E 39 St
E 40 St

Albany Av

E 42 St
E 43 St

Troy Av

E 45 St
E 46 St

Schenectady Av

E 48 St
E 49 St

E 51 St
E 52 St
E 53 St
E 54 St
E 55 St

E 58 St
E 59 St

UTICA AV

Snyder Av

P

NEW YORK AV

1050
340
420
1000

*Holy Cross
Cemetery*

Tilden Av

1020
550 550 510
460

Beverly Rd

KINGS HWY

E 56 St

5701

E 57 St

442

PAGE 424

Beverley Rd

2 5

1540
180 180

3620

1170

CLARENDON RD

1160

F A R R A G U T

E 29 St

1720
350
1260

3620

AV D

Jodie Ct

Whitty
La

D

Newkirk
Av
2 5

C

Newkirk Av

Victor Rd

Brooklyn Av

3000

E 37 St
670
630

E 38 St
E 39 St

Albany Av
670 640

E 40 St

E 42 St
E 43 St

590 610

Foster Av

1320

Troy Av
E 45 St
E 46 St

790

880

1350

1340

830

870

Foster Av

554
561

Farragut Pl

Brooklyn Rd

*Paerdegat
Park*

3310

Farragut Rd

Harwood Pl

END 3 MINS

2 MILES= 3.2 KMS

PAGE 418

PAGE 423

PAGE 431

Willmohr St
Hopkinson Av
Lott Av
Amboy St
Chester St
Rockaway Av
Thatford Av
Osborn St
Watkins St
Sackman St
Hegeman Av
Malta
460
870
450
570
610
890
850
250
670
640
620
710
LINDEN BLV
Herzl St
Bristol St
Hegeman
St
De Witt Av
Will Pl
Anna Ct
429
970
10
2310
1020
Church Av
9401
447
Brookdale
Hospital
27
E 105 Wk
Bank St
Stanley Av
Williams Av
Breukelen
Housing
1154
Abraham Miller
Square
Brookdale Plaza
E 105 St
Av
10300
E 108 St
LINDEN
BLVD
1080
Rockaway
E 101 St
E 100 Av
E 105 St
710
563
Av A
E 92 St
E 91 St
Av B
E 96 St
E 95 St
E 94 St
E 93 St
730
Turnbull
10300
E 106
8802
E 89 St
E 88 St
E 87 St
Ditmas
Av
690
740
750
770
710
10300
Coventry Rd
E 86 St
690
Av D
Av D
Nolans La
970
9400
P
970
E 104
Dorset St
Branton St
Ralph
Ames La
Krier Pl
980
Rockaway Pkwy
Canarsie
E 103 St
E 102 St
E 101 St
E 100 St
E 99 St
Pieter Claesen
Wyckoff House
Museum
Brooklyn
Terminal
Market
Farragut Rd
Smiths La
Glenwood Rd
1020
L
Trucklemans La
E 98 St
Tiemans La
Chase Ct
Preston Ct
Bedell La
970
Conklin Av
FLATLANDS AV
Hoyt La
La
FOSTER AV
510
510
510
Bayview Pl
School La
Durland
1238
Skidmore
Av J
E 95 St
E 94 St
Holmes La
E 96 St
510
Varkens Hook
Rd
E 89 St
E 88 St
E 87 St
E 86 St
E 85 St
E 84 St
E 83 St
910
Church La
Av K
E 93 St
E 92 St
E 91 St
Pl
CANAR
E 59 St
E 82 St
E 81 St
E 80 St
E 79 St
E 78 St
E 77 St
E 76 St
510
910
910
910
Canarsie
Cemetery
REMSEN AV
Stillwells
Av L
Av M
Rost Pl
Kaufman Pl
Av N

A B C D L

N

Manhattan Queens

START DRIVE

70

Wortman Av
270
Cozine Av
Schenck Av
Flatlands Av
Vortman Houses
Linden
Houses
Vandalia Av
1020
SPRING CREEK

Erskine St
890
NYS Office
of Mental Retardation and
Developmental Disabilities
1180

Vermont St

AV

Ardsley Loop
A
AV
Van Siclen Av
Bethel Loop
Schenck Av
Walker St
Elton St
Seaview Av
Seaview Loop
B

Dale Pl
Vandalia
20
1270
Delmar Loop
1260
Croton Loop
Elmira Loop
Schroeders Av
STARRETT
CITY
Twin Pines Dr
650
1420
Freeport Loop
1440
Geneva Loop
Seaview Av
11320
Spring Creek

Park

(no access)

PAGE 348

1490
Homell Loop

F5 St
F6 St
F7 St
F8 St
F9 St
F10 St
870
Border Av
14
D

10310
C
1410
Seaview Av
1530
1410

North Channel

2 MILES = 3.2 KMS

Bayview
Houses

Fresh Creek Basin

BELT PKWY

Elders
Point
Marsh

END 3 MINS

2 MILES= 3.2 KMS

PAGE 420

Upper
New York
Bay

Old Glory
Look Out

Upper New York Bay

Owls
Head
Park

A

B Bay Ridge Av

C

D

BAY
RIDGE

BAY RIDGE PKWY

77 St

86 St

FORT

HAMILTON

Shore Rd Dr

Leif Ericsson Park

67 ST

Senator St

68 St Senator St

Ovington Av

72 St
73 St
74 St

76 St
77 St
78 St
79 St
80 St
81 St
82 St
83 St
84 St
85 St
87 St
88 St
89 St
91 St

24 Hr
Rite-Aid

Comfort Inn,
Brooklyn

Monastery
Square

Colonial
Gardens

GOWANUS EXPWY

27

McDonald
Square

W E Coffey
Square

FORT HAMILTON PKWY

Dyker Pl

Battery Av
Parrott Pl

Gelston Av
Gatling Pl
Forest Pl

3 AV
4 AV
5 AV
6 AV
7 AV

Ridgecrest Ter
Perry Ter
Bay Cliff Ter
Madeline Ct

Narrows Av
Colonial Rd
Ridge Blvd

68 St
70 St
71 St
72 St
73 St
74 St
76 St
77 St
78 St
79 St
80 St
81 St
82 St
83 St
84 St
85 St
87 St
88 St
89 St
90 St
91 St
92 St
93 St
94 St
95 St
96 St

SHORE PKWY

Mackay Pl

Harbor View Ter
Colonial Ct
Harbor La
Westerly La

Shore Ct
Shore Ct

Colonial Rd
Oliver St
Ridge

Bliss Ter
Louise Ter

Owls Head Ct

Sedgwick Pl
Bergen Pl
Wakeman Pl

Senator St
Bay Ridge Pl
Ridge Ct
Bennett Ct
Vista Pl

Leif Ericsson Dr
(Leif Ericsson Dr)

Hamilton Wk
Lafayette Wk

92 St
93 St
94 St
95 St
96 St

PAGE 434

Manhattan Queens

START DRIVE

8 Av

A

Fort
Hamilton Pkwy

FORT HAMILTON PKWY

Bocchino D
Memorial Plaza

49 St

50 St

50 St

51 St

52 St
53 St
54 St
55 St

55 St

B

56 St
57 St
58 St
59 St
60 St

62 St
63 St

Tabor Ct

New
Utrecht Av

64 St

62 St

65 ST
66 St
67 St
Ovington Av
70 St
Bay Ridge Av
71 St
72 St
73 St
74 St

Regina
Opera

RIDGE PKWY

C

KER

IGHTS

76 St
77 St
78 St
79 St
80 St
81 St
82 St
83 St

NEW UTRECHT AV

71 St

Duryea Ct

Ovington Ct

D

Wallaston Ct
Cameron Ct

NEW UTRECHT

68 St

18 Av

17 AV
16 AV
15 Av
14 Av
13 Av
12 Av
11 AV
10 Av
9 Av
8 Av

END 3 MINS

2 MILES= 3.2 KMS

2 MILES= 3.2 KMS

PAGE 423

PAGE 429

PAGE 438

Paerdegat Av S
Troy Pl
Glendale Ct
Glenwood Rd
Av H
E 81 St
E 80 St
E 79 St
E 78 St
E 77 St
E 76 St
E 71 St
E 84 St
E 83 St
E 82 St
910
910
910
Av J
Av K
Paerdegat Av N
South Shore Plaza
Paerdegat 1 St
Paerdegat 2 St
Pdgt 3 St
Pdgt 4 St
Pdgt 5 St
Pdgt 6 St
Pdgt 7 St
Pdgt 8 St
Paerdegat Av N
B

KINGS HWY
Troy Av
E 45 St
E 46 St
E 48 St
Schenectady Av
E 49 St
A
E 42 St
E 43 St
Albany Av
E 51 St
E 52 St
E 53 St
E 54 St
E 55 St
E 56 St
E 57 St
E 58 St
E 59 St
Av I
Av J
990
940
800
880
860
1710
980
980
1710
1710

FLATLANDS
FLATLANDS AV
Ryder Sq
1170
1160
Av K
Bergen Av
E 73 St
E 72 St
Av L
RALPH AV
M
Av
Av
Peri La
Bergen Ct
Royce Pl
Royce St
GEORGETO

Paerdega

E 40 St
E 41 St
Lott Pl
Harden St
Father Kehoe Sq
Baughman Pl
E 43 St
1940
2110
1530
Av L
1470
1430
1390
1340
1210
1250
1210
Av M
Charles W Boyce Square
Av N
Av N
Av T

Av P
Quentin Rd
Hendrickson St
Coleman St
Kimball St
Ryder St
E 38 St
Av R
E 37 St
Peter Trust Square
FLATBUSH AV
C
1650
1620
1570
1530
1430
1410
Av O
Fillmore Av
Av S
1810
1830
1790
1750
1620
1540
E 60 St
E 61 ST
E 59 St
E 58 St
E 57 St
E 56 St
Pearson St
D
Mill La
Veterans Av
Mill Av
E 63 St
E 65 St
E 64 St
E 66 St
E 67 St
E 68 St
Strickland Av
2010
2110
Ohio Wk
East Mill
Mayfair Dr N
AV U
E 69 St
E 70 St
E 71

1510
1610
1610
4210
1810

N
© 2005 Vanguard Inc. All rights

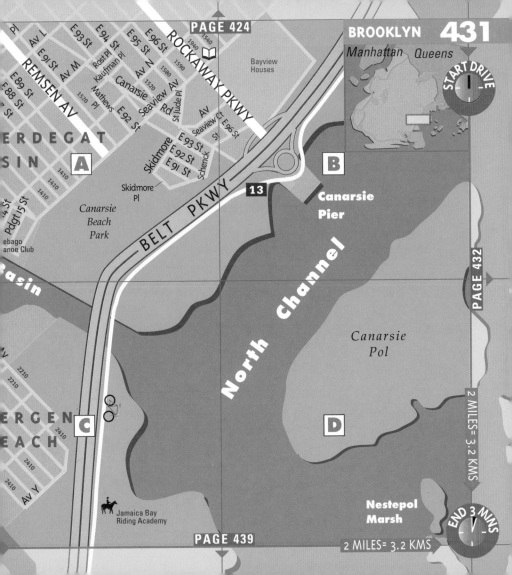

Manhattan Queens

START DRIVE

Pl
Av L
E 93 St
E 94 St
E 95 St
E 96 St
ROCKAWAY PKWY
1940
1540
Bayview
Houses

REMSEN AV
E 91 St
Av M
Rost Pl
Kaufman Pl
E 95 St
Av N
1590
1580

Canarsie
Mathews Pl
Seaview Av
Rd
St Jude Pl
1520

E 89 St
E 92 St
Av
Seaview Ct E 96 St
St

E 88 St

ERDEGAT
SIN

A

Skidmore
E 93 St
E 92 St
E 91 St
Schenck

1410

Skidmore
Pl

13

BELT PKWY

B

Canarsie
Pier

1410
1410

St
Pdgt 15 St

Canarsie
Beach
Park

ebago
anoe Club

North Channel

Canarsie
Pol

Basin

C

V
2210
2210

D

ERGEN
EACH

2410

2410

Av Y
2410

Jamaica Bay
Riding Academy

Nestepol
Marsh

END 3 MINS

2 MILES= 3.2 KMS

PAGE 432

2 MILES= 3.2 KMS

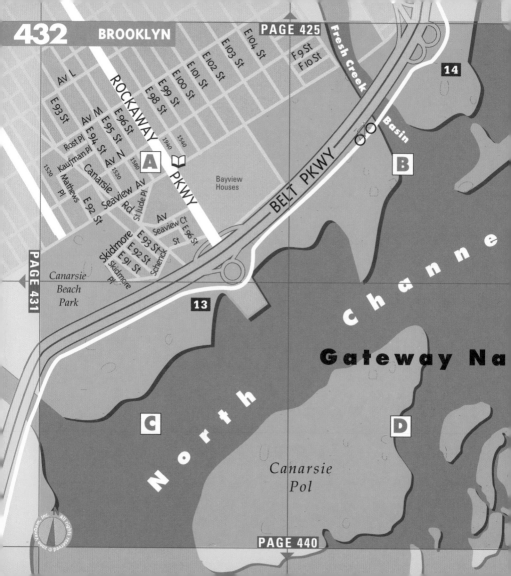

PAGE 425

Fresh Creek

14

Av L

E 93 St

ROCKAWAY

E 104 St

E 103 St

E 102 St

E 101 St

E 100 St

E 99 St

E 98 St

F 9 St
F 10 St

Av M

E 96 St

E 95 St

Rost Pl

E 94 St

Kaufman Pl

Av N

1540

1560

1520

1520

1540

A

PKWY

Mathews Pl

E 92 St

Canarsie

Seaview Av

Rd

St Jude Pl

Bayview
Houses

Basin

B

BELT PKWY

Av

Seaview Ct

Skidmore

E 93 St

E 92 St

E 91 St

Schenck

Seaview Ct

E 96 St

St

Skidmore

Pl

*Canarsie
Beach
Park*

PAGE 431

13

C h a n n e

C

N o r t h

Gateway Na

D

*Canarsie
Pol*

PAGE 440

© 2000 MICHELIN Inc. All rights reserved

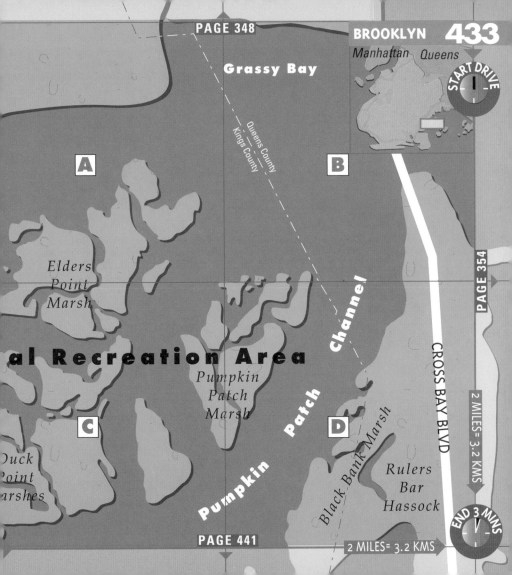

Grassy Bay

Manhattan   Queens

START DRIVE

Queens County
Kings County

A

B

*Elders
Point
Marsh*

Channel

al Recreation Area

*Pumpkin
Patch
Marsh*

Pumpkin Patch

C

D

Black Bank Marsh

*Duck
Point
arshes*

*Rulers
Bar
Hassock*

CROSS BAY BLVD

PAGE 354

2 MILES= 3.2 KMS

END 3 MINS

2 MILES= 3.2 KMS

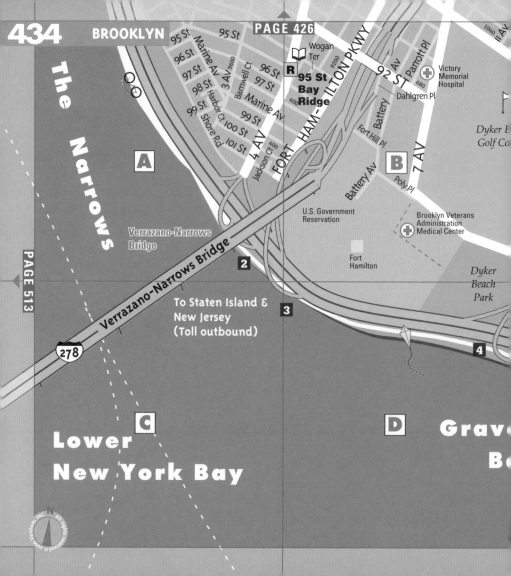

PAGE 426

PAGE 513

The Narrows

95 St
96 St
97 St
98 St
99 St
Marine Av
3 AV 9600
Barnwell Ct
Harbor Ct
Shore Rd
95 St
96 St
97 St
Marine Av
99 St
100 St
101 St
Jackson Ct
4 AV
4 AV 400

Wogan Ter

R
95 St Bay Ridge

FORT HAM-ILTON PKWY

9200

92 ST

Parrott Pl

680

Victory Memorial Hospital

Dahlgren Pl

1040 AV

92 AV

Battery

Fort Hill Pl

7 AV

Dyker B Golf Co

A

B

Battery Av

Poly Pl

Verrazano-Narrows Bridge

U.S. Government Reservation

Brooklyn Veterans Administration Medical Center

2

Fort Hamilton

Verrazano-Narrows Bridge

Dyker Beach Park

To Staten Island & New Jersey (Toll outbound)

3

278

4

C

D

Grave

B

Lower New York Bay

N

© 2000 geonova inc. All rights reserved

Manhattan Queens

START DRIVE
I

83 St
81 St
82 St
84 St
85 St
13 Av

B E N S O N H U R S T

1440

1670

72 St

73 St
1750

74 St

BAY RIDGE PKWY

1750

76 St

77 St

78 St

79 St

80 St

NEW UTRECHT AV

18 AV

86 ST

15 Av

16 Av

17 Av

A

50

1570

1670

1670

1670

1760

79 St

B
M

B

1910

B

Benson Av

Bay 7 St
Bay 8 St
Bay 10 St
Bay 11 St
Bay 13 St
Bay 14 St

8740

8752

8691

8610

Bath Av

16 St

17 St

Rutherford Pl

215

403

CROPSEY AV

ndence

17 Ct

Shore

B A T H

B E A C H

ELT   PKWY

ZO

C

d

19 La

Rd

20 Dr

20 La

1460

21 Dr 21 La

Bensonhurst Park

19 Av

20 Av

1910

1920

2

2

8610

Bay 19 St

Bay

Bay

Bay 20 St

Bay

22 St

23 St

Benson Av

8630

2

Bay 25 St

Bay 26 St

Bay 28 St

Bay 29 St

8710

20 Av

B
M

21 St

2

2160

2530

2140

BAY PKWY

2210

2240

2240

2230

2230

B
M

Bay Pkwy

23 Av

24 Av

2410

25 Av

D

Benson St

Bay 31 St

Bay 32 St

8880

Bath Av

Bay 34

Bay 35

8620

8630

Bay 37 St

Bay 38 St

Bay 40 St

Shore Rd

24 Av

2 MILES= 3.2 KMS

END 3 MINS

5

PAGE 430

PAGE 437

PAGE 446

MARINE PARK

MILL ISLAND

Marine Park Nature Trail

Marine Park Golf Course

Mill Creek

Gerritsen Creek

Marine

White Island

GERRITSEN BEACH

Park

Marine Park

Pratt-White Field

Sheepshead

Bay

Houses

Kings Plaza Shopping Center

Streets and labels:

Quentin Rd, E 34 St, E 33 St, E 32 St, E 31 St, Marine Pkwy, Madison Pl, Burnett St, Stuart St, AV R, Coleman St, Kimball St, Ryder St, Hendrickson St, Fillmore, E 38 St, E 37 St, E 36 St, E 35 St, AV S, AV T, AV U, AV V, E 56 St, E 55 St, E 54 St, E 53 Pl, E 52 St, Hendrickson, Strickland, Mill Av, National Dr, E 57 Pl, 57 Dr, E 63 St, E 64 St, E 65 St, E 66 St, E 60 Pl, E 59 Pl, AV Z, Whitma-Ark-, Whitney Av, Flatbush Av, Gerritsen Av, Knapp St, Brigham St, Bragg St, Batchelder St, Ford St, Coyle St, Brown St, Haring St, AV T, AV V, AV W, AV X, AV Y, Plumb 2 St, Plumb 1 St, Aster Ct, Bevy Ct, Celeste Ct, Bijou Ct, Dictum Ct, Ebony Ct, Fane Ct, Garland Ct, Allen Ct, Channel Av, Devon Av, Everett Av, Fane Ct, Garland Ct, Hazel Ct, Ira Ct, Joval Ct, Florence Av, Cotham Av

A B C D

P P P

N

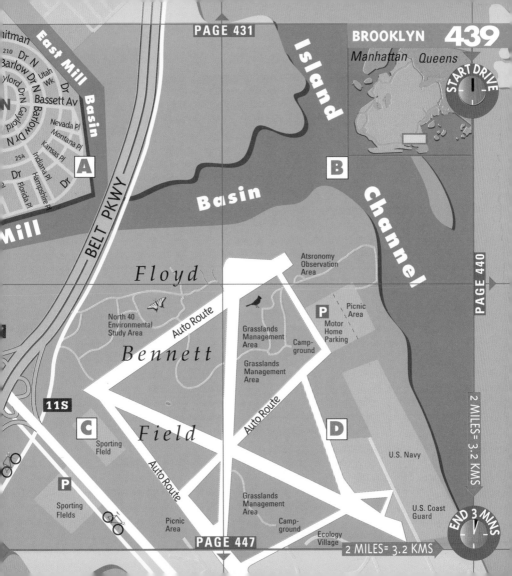

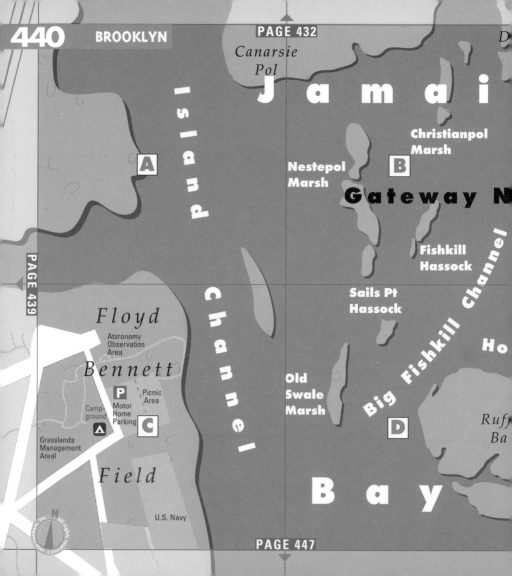

PAGE 432

Canarsie Pol

D

J a m a i

c a

Island

A

Christianpol
Marsh

Nestepol
Marsh

B

Gateway N

Fishkill
Hassock

Channel

Sails Pt
Hassock

PAGE 439

Floyd

Atsronomy
Observation
Area

Bennett

P Picnic
Area

Camp-
ground

Motor
Home
Parking

C

Grasslands
Management
Areal

Field

U.S. Navy

Big Fishkill Channel

Ho

Old
Swale
Marsh

D

Ruf
Ba

B a y

N

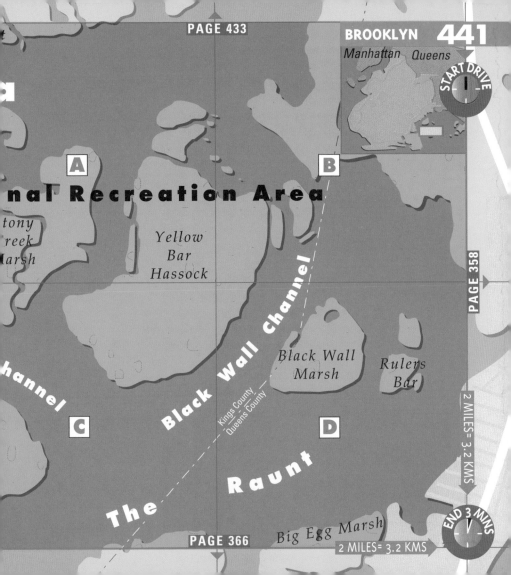

Manhattan   Queens

START DRIVE

A

B

nal Recreation Area

tony
reek
Iarsh

Yellow
Bar
Hassock

Black Wall Channel

Black Wall
Marsh

Rulers
Bar

hannel

Kings County
Queens County

C

D

2 MILES= 3.2 KMS

The   Raunt

END 3 MINS

Big Egg Marsh

2 MILES= 3.2 KMS

Gravesend

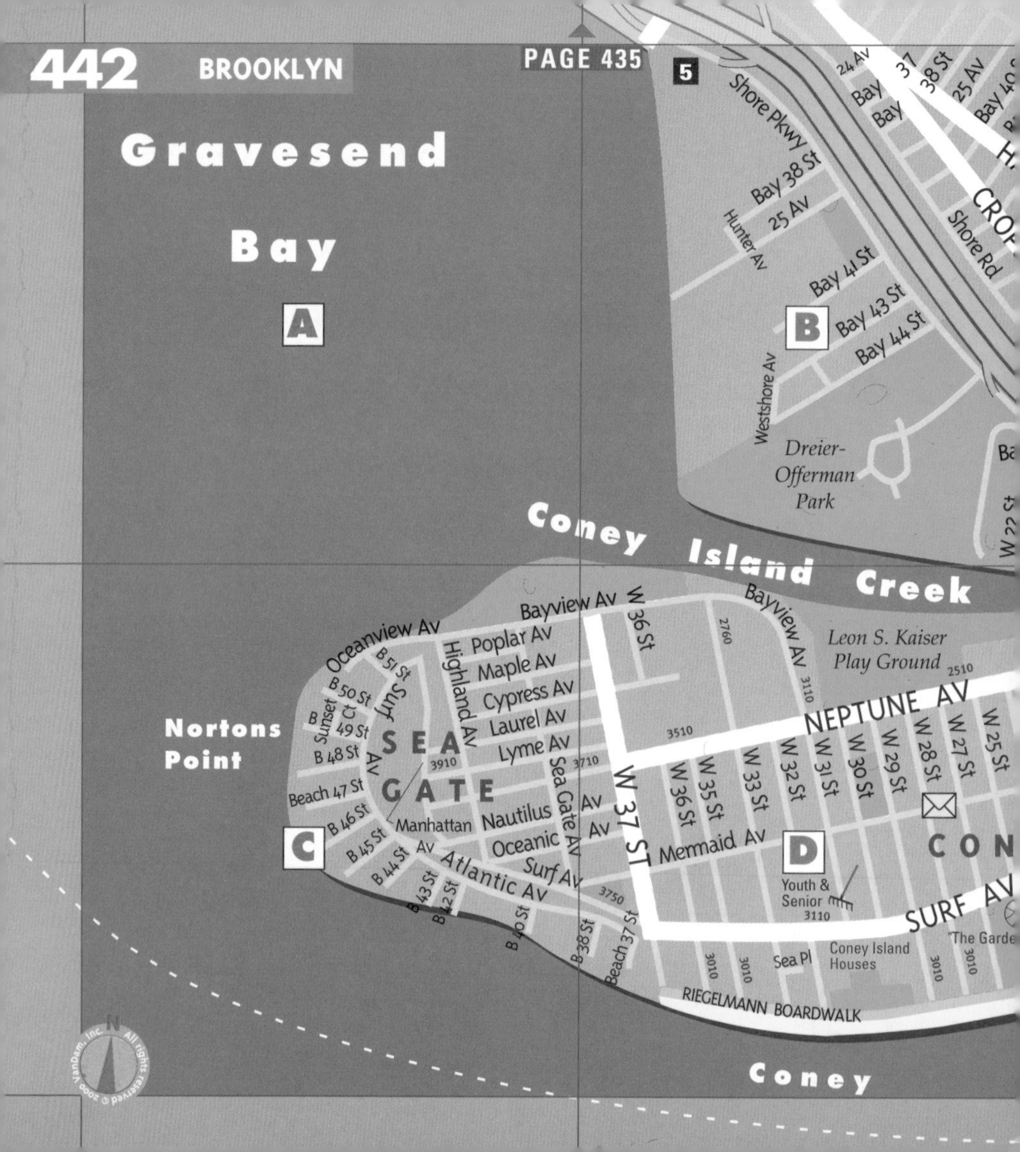

Bay

A

Shore Pkwy

24 Av
37
38 St
25 Av
Bay 40
Bay
Bay

Bay 38 St

25 Av

Hunter Av

Bay 41 St

Bay 43 St

B

Bay 44 St

Westshore Av

CRO

Shore Rd

Ba

W 22

Dreier-
Offerman
Park

Coney Island Creek

Oceanview Av

Bayview Av

W 36 St

Bayview Av

Leon S. Kaiser
Play Ground 2510

B 51 St

Poplar Av

Surf

Highland Av

Maple Av

2760

B 50 St

Cypress Av

3110

Sunset Ct

Laurel Av

NEPTUNE AV

W 25 St

**Nortons
Point**

B 49 St

Lyme Av

3510

W 28 St

W 27 St

B 48 St

S E A

3910

Sea Gate Av

3710

W 35 St

W 33 St

W 31 St

W 30 St

W 29 St

Beach 47 St

G A T E

Manhattan

Nautilus Av

W 36 St

W 32 St

B 46 St

Oceanic Av

Atlantic Av

Surf Av

W 37 ST

Mermaid Av

D

C O N

B 45 St

B 44 St

Youth &
Senior

3110

SURF AV

'The Garde

B 43 St

B 42 St

B 40 St

B 38 St

Beach 45 St

3750

3010

3010

C

Sea Pl

Coney Island
Houses

3010

3010

RIEGELMANN BOARDWALK

Coney

Manhattan Queens

START DRIVE 1

STILLWELL AV

N 86 St

Av W

Av X
40

B Bay 50 St

Av X

28 Av

Bay 49 St

Bay 50 St

110

W 16 St
W 17 St
Av Z St

W 13 St

A

Boynton Pl

Lake St

440

Southgate Ct

Av X

F

W 3rd St
W 2 St
W 1 St

Bouck Ct

360

SHELL RD

Cobek Ct
Dank Ct
580

AV Z

Atwater Ct

Bokee Ct

Colby Ct

Shore Rd

2400
2410

Ocean Ct
Parkway Ct

2410

Manhattan Ct

2510

Brighton Ct

2510

750

Murdock Ct
Nixon Ct

7N

B

Ocean Pkwy

Guider

CONEY ISLAND

Blake Ct

Lawn Ct
Av

B 10 Ct
B 10 Path
B 10 Ter
B 10 La

BELT PKWY

Shore Rd

Canal Av

Hart Pl

STILLWELL AV

W 15 St

5 St

W 17 St
W 16 St
W 19 St
W 20 St

2730

Shore Rd

W 6 St

F Neptune Av

West Av

Shore Pkwy

7S

Br 3 Rd
Br 3 Rd

Banner Av

Br 4 Rd

Br 4 Ter

370

OCEAN PKWY

NEPTUNE AV

B 2 Wk
B 3
Wk
B 4
Wk
B 5
Wk
B 7 Wk

Oceanview

B 8 St

B 10 Av
B 11 St

PAGE 444

Sheepshead Bay Rd

W 12 St

W 8 St

2810

DMV

W 5 St
W 3 St
W 2 Pl
W 2 St

Brighton Av

Seabreeze Av

BRIGHTON BEACH

Brighton 1 St

2800

W 8 St
NY Aquarium

P

810

D F
550

1910

Stillwell Av
Coney Island

B D
F N

Bowery St

Coney Island
USA

New York
Aquarium

Ocean Pkwy

Seaside

SURF AV

LAND

C

Schweickerts Wk

Kensington Wk

Henderson Wk

Jones Wk

W 10 St
W 8 St

3020

3020

BOARDWALK

WEST

W J Hennessy
Square

B 1 Wk
B 2 St
B 3 St
B 4 St

Brighton 1 St

B 1 Rd

Brightwater Ct

Seabreeze Wk

B 5 St
B 6 St

3081

BRIGHTON BEACH AV

D Q

Brighton
Beach

BOARDWALK EAST

Brighton Beach

D

Steeplechase
Pier

Island Beach

END 3 MINS

2 MILES= 3.2 KMS

2 MILES = 3.2 KMS

PAGE 437

PAGE 443

SHEEPSHEAD BAY

BRIGHTON BEACH

MANHA...

Av X

Bouck Ct
W 3 St
W 2 St
W 1 St

510
Av X
Desmond Ct
Desmond Ct
Dunne Ct
Dunne Ct
Hubbard St
Av Y
Gerald Ct
Kathleen Pl

Ocean Av
2410
Parkway Ct

E 18 St
E 17 St
E 16 St
E 15 St
E 13 St
E 12 St
E 11 St

OCEAN AV

E 19 St
2449
Homecrest

Bedford Av
Mansfield Pl
Delamere Pl
E 21 St
E 23

SHELL RD

AV Z

Atwater Ct
Bokee Ct
Colby Ct

360
2410

Manhattan Ct
Cobek Ct
Dank Ct
2510
2510

Brighton
Murdock Ct
580
Nixon Ct

750
Coney
Island
Hospital

8

Manor Ct
Montauk St

Sheepshead
Bay

2543
William Ct
Gilmore Ct

Sheepshead

2610

D Q Bay

Jerome Av
2660
Dooley
Poole

SHORE PKW

EMMON

7N

A

7S
West Av
2730
370

Br 3 Rd
Br 3 Rd
Br 4 Rd
Br 4 Ter
Banner Av

NEPTUNE AV

B 2 Wk
B 3 Wk
B 4 Wk
B 5 Wk
B 7 Wk
B 8 St

Guider
AV

Blake Ct
Lawn Ct
Shore Pkwy
2770

B 9 St
B 10 Ct
B 10 Path
B 10 Ter
B 10 La
Av

B 11 St
B 12 St
B 13 St
B 14 St

Cass Pl

SHORE BLVD

WEST END AV

110
500
Shore Blvd
Shore

B Foot
Bridge
10 9 8 7

MANHA

Neptune Av

Oceanview

Oceanview

Hampton Av
Beaumont
Amherst
Coleridge
Dover St
Exeter St
Ocean Av
Falmouth St

ORIENTAL BLV

BRIGHTON BEACH

Sheepshead Bay

W 5 St
W 3 St
W 2 Pl
W 2 St
W 1 St
2800
Seabreeze Av
Brighton Av

OCEAN PKWY
Beach Rd

Brighton 1 St

B 1 Wk
B 1 Pl
B 3 St
B 4 St
B 5 St
B 6 St
Brighton Beach Av
Ter

Seacoast Av

Brighton Beach
Av

Gerald H
Chambers
Sq
Corbin Pl
260
260
260
4220
ESPLANADE

BRIGHTON BEACH AV

D Q

Brighton
Beach

Ocean Pkwy
Seaside
W J Hennesy
Square
Beach Wk
B 1 Rd
Brightwater Ct
Seabreeze Wk

D

Brightwater Av

BOARDWALK EAST

550
SURF AV

New York
Aquarium

Park

C

BOARDWALK

Brighton Beach

D

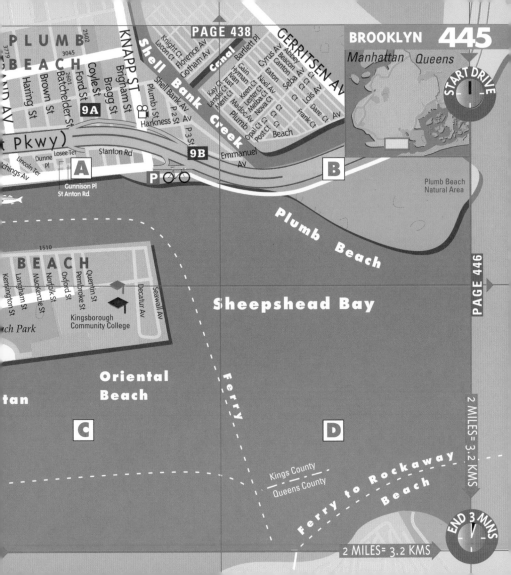

PLUMB
BEACH
2502
3779
3045
ISLAND AV

KNAPP ST

Shell Bank Av

Coyle St
Brigham St
Bragg St
Ford St
Batchelder St
Haring St
Brown St
2601

9A

Knight Ct
Florence Av
Gotham Av
Lacon Ct

Canal

Bartlett Pl

GERRITSEN AV

Cyrus Av
Cain
Hyman
Lamsis Ct
Ivan
Merit Ct
Keen Ct
Lester Ct
Madoc Av
Melba Ct
Opal Ct
Nova Ct
Post Ct
Kay Ct
Abbey
Beacon
Canton
Eaton
Noel Av
Lois Ct
Dare Ct
Frank Ct
Seba Ct

Manhattan   Queens

START DRIVE

(Belt Pkwy)

Dunne Pl
Lincoln Ter
Hitchings Av
Losee Ter

Plumb St
Shell Bank Av
P 2 St
P 3 St
Harkness Av

Stanton Rd

A

Gunnison Pl
St Anton Rd

9B

Emmanuel Av

B

P

Plumb Beach
Natural Area

Plumb Beach

BEACH
1510
Langham St
Kensington St
MacKenzie St
Norfolk St
Oxford St
Pembroke St
Quentin St

Beach Park

Kingsborough
Community College

Decatur Av
Seawall Av

Sheepshead Bay

Oriental
Beach

tan

C

Ferry

D

PAGE 446

Kings County
Queens County

Ferry to Rockaway Beach

2 MILES= 3.2 KMS

END 3 MINS

2 MILES= 3.2 KMS

BROOKLYN

PAGE 438

Brigham St

Shell Bank Creek

Shell Bank Av

Plumb 1 St

P 2 St

P 3 St

Harkness Av

Kay Ct

Ivan Ct

Landis Ct

Just Ct

Merit Ct

Cyrus Av

Keen Ct

Lester Ct

Madoc Av

Melba Ct

Opal Ct

Noel Av

Nova Ct

Abbey Av

Beacon Av

Canton Ct

Eaton Ct

Lois Av

Dare Ct

Frank Ct

Post Ct

Plumb

Beach

Seba Ct

9B

Emmanuel Av

Plumb Beach Channel

BELT PKWY

P

Ⓞ Ⓞ A

B

Plumb Beach
Natural Area

**Dead
Horse
Bay**

Barre
Isla
Mari

P

Dead Horse Inlet

Plumb Beach

PAGE 445

Decatur Av

Seawall Av

Kingsborough
Community
College

**Oriental
Beach**

Ferry

C

D

Ferry t

R o

Kings County
Queens County

N

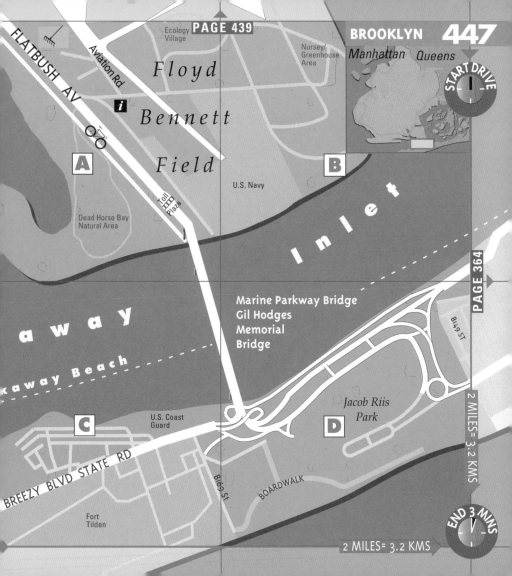

aten Island's Best

en praised as the most tranquil
d verdant of New York City's five
roughs, Staten Island is rich in its
ysical beauty. While spiritually
re connected to NJ, its residents
ve the best of both worlds, not the
st of which is the Wu-Wear Store,
me to Wu-Tan Clan, one of the
ttiest and mega-selling hip-hop
oups in the world—a place of
grimage for suburban youth
ound the world.

aug Harbor

e cultural heart of the island is
mposed of 28 historic buildings
Victorian, Beaux Arts and Greek
vival styles. The jazz, classical and
p concerts are legendary as is
e historical tour on weekends.
o Richmond Terrace @ Tysen St,
8-448-2500. **506B**

'u-Wear Store

parents can attest, this is Mecca
their teenage offspring who
nk this experience above a visit to
e Statue of Liberty. 61 Victory Blvd
Bay Street, 718-720-9043
aily 11-7, closed Sunday). **507A**

The Greenbelt

At 2,500 acres easily the city's
largest park, with landscapes so
varied one can forsake the
Hamptons for these shaded wood-
lands, wetlands and hiking trails.
Nearby Prall's Island sports the
largest egret and heron rookery
on the East Coast. 200 Nevada Av,
718-667-2165. **517C**

Staten Island Ferry

Spectacular views of the
Downtown Manhattan skyline
make this a must-do for visitors.
507B

Verrazano-Narrows Bridge

The world's largest suspension
bridge has become virtually
synonymous with the NY Marathon
when 30,000 runners funnel through.
513D

SI Institute of Arts & Sciences

Designed by Peter Eisenman
Architects and slated for a 2002
opening, this is bound to be
the most dramatic new
structure in NY Harbor.
507B

SI Stats:
Population:
378,977

Area:
60.2 sq miles

SI Institute of Arts & Sciences
by Eisenman Architects

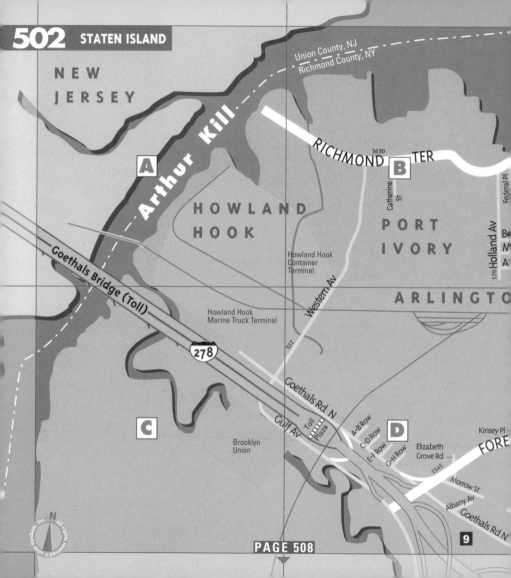

NEW

JERSEY

Union County, NJ
Richmond County, NY

A

RICHMOND TER

3630

B

Catherine St

HOWLAND

HOOK

PORT

IVORY

170 Holland Av

Federal Pl

B
M
A

Howland Hook
Container
Terminal

Western Av

ARLINGTO

Goethals Bridge (Toll)

Howland Hook
Marine Truck Terminal

322

278

Goethals Rd N

Toll
Plaza

A-B Row

C-D Row

E-F Row

G-H Row

D

Kinsey Pl

FORE

Gulf Av

C

Brooklyn
Union

Elizabeth
Grove Rd

1545

Morrow St

Albany Av

Goethals Rd N

N

2000 VanDam Inc. All rights reserved

9

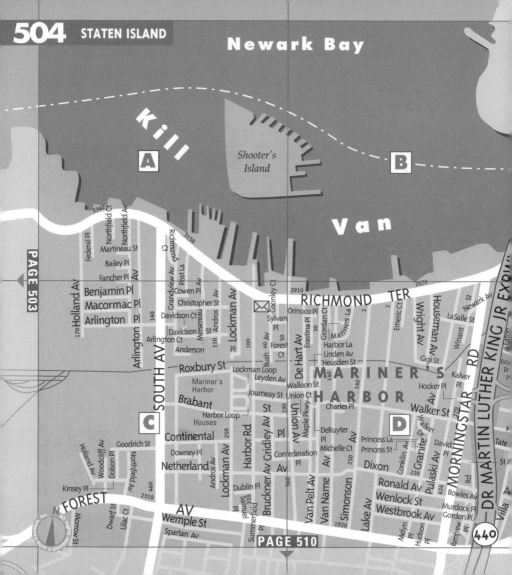

Newark Bay

Kill

A

Shooter's Island

B

Van

PAGE 503

3340

Federal Pl
Northfield Ct
Northfield Av
Martineau St
Bailey Pl
Fancher Pl

Richmond Ct
3150
Post La
Grandview Av
Cowen Pl
Christopher St
Davidson Ct
Davidson Ct

Lockman Av
Andros Av
Mersereau Av

Coonley Ct
2910

RICHMOND TER

2670

Houseman Av
Wright Av
Emeric St
Winant
LaSalle St
Newark Av Expwy

170 Holland Av
Benjamin Pl
Macormac Pl
Arlington Pl
140

Orinoco Pl
Sylvan Pl
50
40 Forest Ct
De Hart Av
Erastina Pl
30
Giordan Pl
Mariners La
2
Harbor La
Linden Av
Heusden St

Gigi St

Arlington
Arlington Ct
Anderson

Bush St
110
Lockman Pl
100

Lockman Loop
Leyden Av
Walloon St
Joumeay St
Union Ct

M A R I N E R ' S
140
H A R B O R

Kalver Pl
Hooker Pl

SOUTH AV

Roxbury St

Mariner's
Harbor
Brabant

Harbor Loop
Houses

190 Union Av
Maple Pkwy
Charles Pl

Walker St
270
Walker Dr

C

Goodrich St
Downey Pl
Netherland

Continental
250

Harbor Rd
Gridley Av
Bruckner Av

St
Pl
Confederation
Av

DeRuyter Pl
Michelle Ct
250
Princess La
Princess St

Granite Av
Conklin Av
220

David Pl
Pulaski Pl
424

D

MORNINGSTAR RD

Holly Av
Woodcliff Av
Dolson Pl
Northfield Av
460
2310

Kinsey Pl
Dwarf St
Lilac Ct

FOREST
Morrow St

Andros Av
Lockman Av
Dublin La
360

Summerfield
3100 James Pl

AV
Wemple St
Spartan Av

1920

Van Pelt Av
Van Name Av
Simonson Av
Lake Av

Dixon
Ronald Av
Wenlock St
Westbrook Av

Melyn Pl
Hudson Pl

Bowles Av
Murdock Pl
Gordon Pl
Renfrew Pl

DR MARTIN LUTHER KING JR EXPWY

Tate Av
St A
Villa

440

PAGE 510

NEW JERSEY

Kull

NJ

START DRIVE

Ferry

son County, NJ
nond County, NY

A

B

North St

RICHMOND TER

1410

Howard Ct
Harrison Pl

Davis Ct

50

Harrison Pl

60 N Elm St

Bement Ct

Fraser Park

Gales La

Ferry St
2060

North St

1660

Van St

40

Edwin Markham Gardens

Barrett La

2260

Larkin St

Church St

Ann St

Bennett St

10

50

Fountain Cemetery

Tompkins

Woodruff

Wayne St

150

Henderson Av

180

Grove Av

Av

Staten Island Cemetery

Chappell St

Wayne St

Trinity Pl

100

Campbell Av

WEST

Slaight St

Maple St

110

Vreeland St

1850

Cottage Pl

Dongan St

Taylor St

Barker St

BRIGHTON

Harrison 60 Av

Park Av

New Bond St

Rector St

De Groot Pl

Taylor Ct

Alaska St

Market St

Doe Pl

Castleton 1610 Av

220

210

91

1480

Wygant Pl

250

1300

1210

100

1040

270

Britton St
South St

290

300

310 Oakland Av

Treadwell

Anderson Av

Simonson

CASTLETON AV

State St
West St
460

340

Bement Av

Sharpe

Faber

Albion Pl

Post Av

30

Washington

Catherine Ct

Hurst St

White Pl

190

200

Roe St

Caroline St

Noble St

90

Seneca St

Sheffield St

360

Av

970

Homestead Av

Heberton Av

Cary Av

600

510

130

Hatfield

nton

Palmer Pl

PORT

30 Pl

Rainbow Av

Post St

Dubois St

Olive St

Cornell Av

Greenleaf Av

270

Delafield Av

620

BROADWAY

470

690

ckford Av

en Av

C RICHMOND

Decker

Holbermt Ct

Marion St

Raymond

Disosway

D

850

Myrtle Av

FOREST

Lorer Pl

Morrison Av

Catherine St

Lexington Av

Kramer Pl

Derby Ct

Bache St

Floyd St

Brooks

Arcadia Pl

220

Allen Ct

Ludwig St

AV

E Raleigh Av

LaGrange

Montell St

155

Dryden St

Haughwout Av

Pl

790

Clove Lake Pl

Purcell St

Ford Pl

Lynmhaven Pl

Harvest Av

Lloyd

580

Bosworth St

Rabb Pl

ange Av

Beekman St

Cornell St

Sharrett Pl

Newkirk St

Delafield Av

1160

2

1050

W Raleigh Av

Berwin La

Hardin Av

690

Colonial Law

Blaine Ct

aman Pl

Barrett Av

Hamlin Pl

Ordell Av

1280

Zachary Ct

Green Ct

Arthur Ct

Dore Ct

Brooks Lake

Brooks Pond Pl

JEWETT

Veltman Av

Mundy Pl

PAGE 511

2 MILES= 3.2 KMS

END 3 MINS

PAGE 506

2 MILES= 3.2 KMS

NEW JERSEY

Kill Van Kull

Hudson County, NJ
Richmond County, NY

Ferry

A

B

North St

RICHMOND TER

Pelton Pl
Delafield
Delafield Pl
Elizabeth
Arlington
Ct
Howard
Ct
Davis
Ct
Harrison Pl

Bard
Av
Amelia
Ct
Livingston
Wales Pl
Kissel
Linden St
Donald St

Snug Harbor Rd

Walker
Park

The John A
Noble Collection
Norwood Art Lab

Staten Island
Botanical
Gardens

Staten Island
Children's Museum

Sailors
Snug Harbor
Cultural Center

Gordon Pl

1126

800

Van Buren St
Tysen St
Clinton Av
Cassidy

Grace
Ct

Clinton
Ct

LIVINGSTON

Fountain
Cemetery

Staten Island
Cemetery

Trinity
Pl

Dongan
St

Taylor
St

Taylor Ct

White
Pl

Edwin
Markham
Gardens

Wayne St

N Burgher

Elm St

Bement Ct
Stebbins Av
Curtis Ct

Walnut St

Henderson Av
Alban St
Moody Pl

Henderson Ct
Rokeby St

Devon Pl
Lois Pl

Caldera Av
Prospect Av

Snug
Harbor
Cemetery

WEST NEW

Campbell Av

BRIGHTON

Market St
Doe Pl

N St Austin's Pl
Austin's
St
Pl
S St Austin's Pl

Springhill
Av

St Vincents
Hospital &
Medical Center

Allison
Ausable Av
Penbroke Av

Conyngham Av

Park

CASTLETON AV

Joe
Holzka

State St
West St

Britton St
South St

Pelton
Av

Civil
Court

Bard
Av
Hoyt Av

Valencia Av

Abby
Pl

Hunter
Pl

Elwood Pl

Randall Av

BROADWAY

Elizabeth St
Caroline St
Noble
Pl

Seneca St

Bement
Av

Sheffield St

Oakland
Av
Regan Av

DeKay St
N Mada
Delafield Av

Kissel Av
Walbrooke Av

Gregg

Hart
Pl

Oakwood
Blvd

Revere St

CLOVE RD

Delafield Av

Myrtle Av

Arcadia Pl

Allen Ct
Ludwig St
Clove Lake Pl
Purcell St

Morrison
E Raleigh Av
Harvest Av

Green St

Baker Pl
Welles Ct

FOREST AV

Pelton Av
Davis Av
Oakland Av

Lawrence Av

Hart Av

Dana St
Metropolitan

Huron
Parsons
Pl
Norma Pl
Crosshill St

Sharon Av

City Blvd

Edstone Dr

Oakwood Av
Lakewood Rd

Park Ct

Rose Ct

University Pl
Lake Park Rd

Silver
Res

Colonial
Blaine Pl

Bosworth St
Nutly
Mathews Av

Birch Av
Thames Av

Silver Ct
Shawnee St

Griswold St

Silver

PAGE 505

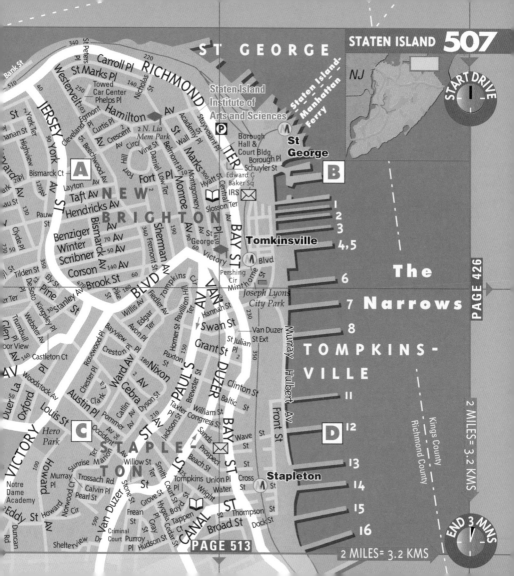

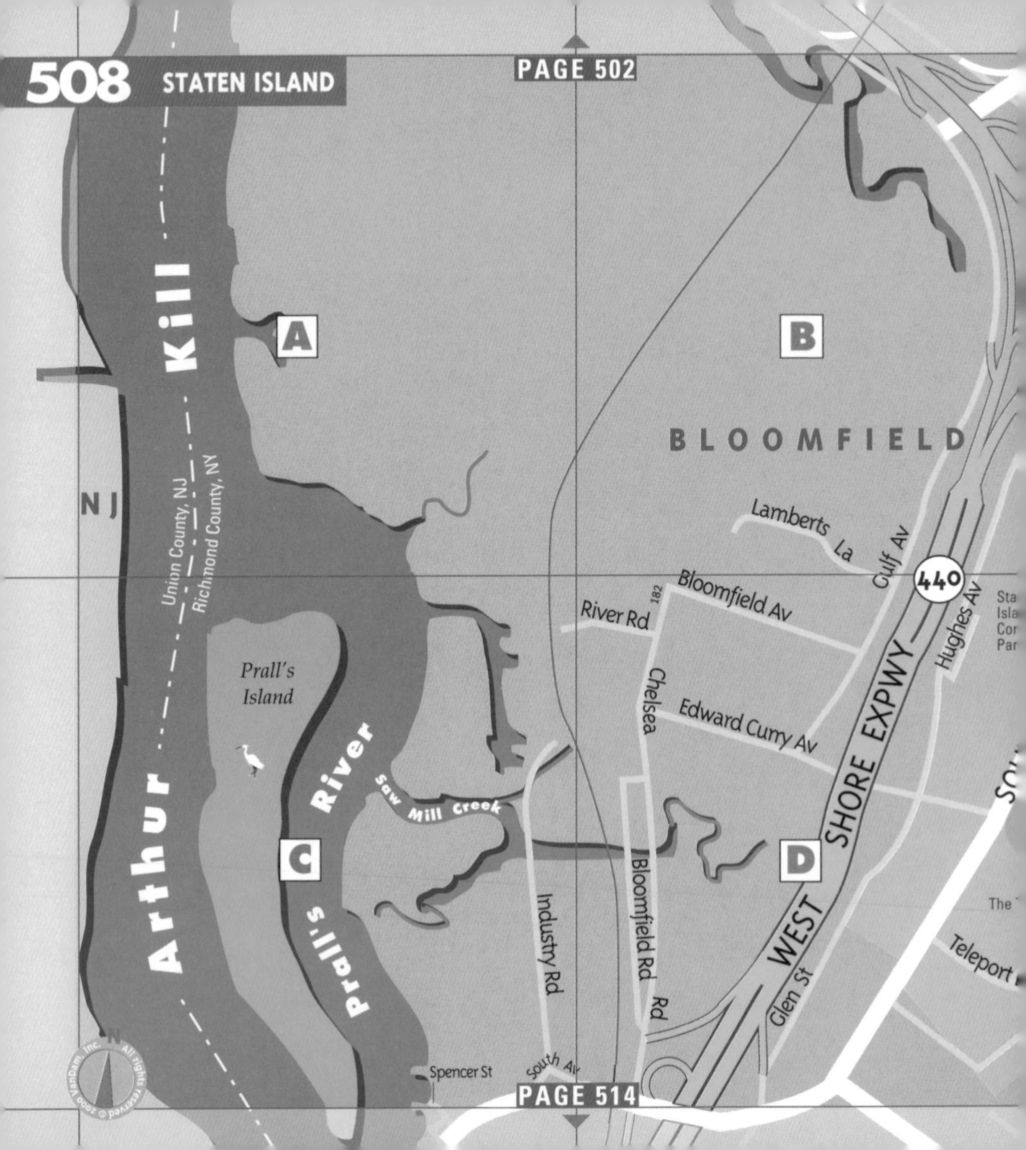

PAGE 502

A

B

BLOOMFIELD

N J

Union County, NJ
Richmond County, NY

Lamberts La

Gulf Av

440

Sta
Isla
Cor
Par

River Rd

Bloomfield Av

182

Hughes Av

*Prall's
Island*

Chelsea

Edward Curry Av

Prall's River

Saw Mill Creek

C

WEST SHORE EXPWY

So

D

The

Teleport

Arthur Kill

Industry Rd

Bloomfield Rd Rd

Glen St

Spencer St

South Av

PAGE 514

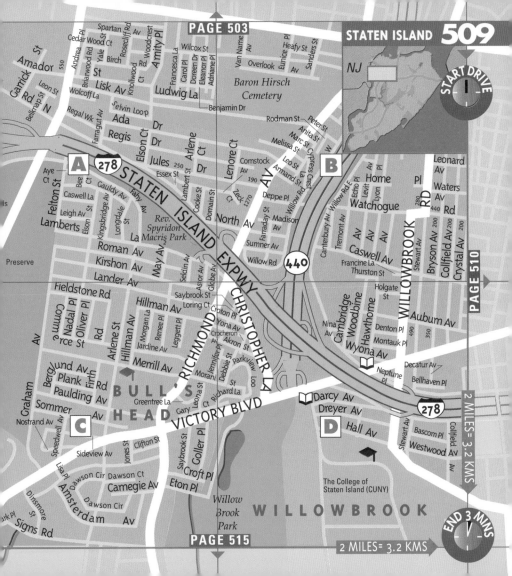

PAGE 509

Knollwood Ct
Amity Pl
Wilcox St
Francesca La
Carol Pl
Doreen Dr
Eleanor Pl
Adriane Pl
Heafy St
Eunice St
Monsey Pl
N Tremont
Melym
Smith Pl
Egbert Sq
Pontiac St
Amprior St
360
1580
Burns Av
Eldridge
Clark St
St Anthony
FOREST
AV
Marianne St
No

Lisk Av
Ludwig La
Overlook Av
Holiday Dr
Vedder Av
James Ct
1040
Rieglemann St
Galloway Av
College
530
Bidwell Av
350

Selvin Loop
Ada Dr
Baron Hirsch Cemetery
Benjamin Dr
Rodman St
Holiday Way
Lynn Ct
Tiger Ct
Houston St
Houston La
Willowbrook
Ct
2
Maine Av
Garrison Av
Hagedom Av

Regis Dr
Elson Ct
Jules 250
Arlene Ct
Essex St
Lambert St
Lenore Ct
190
Peter St
Anita St
Marc St
Melissa St
Leo St
Armand St
Jaffe St
Devens St
ELM
PARK
Lathrop
Av
Leonard
Av
160
WESTERL
Springfield
Av
140

A
Deppe Pl
Comstock Av
Madison
Teck 370
Cooke St
Domain St
North Av
Sumner Av
Willow Rd
Faraday St
Eagle Rd
Echo Pl
Levit Pl
Lyon St
Home
Watchogue
Av
Tuttle St
Waters
280
440 Rd
Muller Av
Glascoe Av
Columbus Av
Wooley Av
Livenmoore Av
Dickie Av
240
Bidwell
Demorest
Neal Dow Av
St John
B
Av

Rev. Spyridon Macris Park
Roman Av
May Av
Kirshon Av
Seldin Av
Astor Av
Globe Av
Caswell Av
Tremont Av
Canterbury Av
Francine La
Thurston St
Willow Rd
WILLOWBROOK
RD
Stewart Av
Bryson Av
Collfield Av
200
200
Crystal Av
Dora St
Wade St
Earl Av
Ruth St
Delmore St
Harvey Av
Marble Av
Seward Av
Avon La
Iowa Av

Lander Av
Hillman Av
Hillman Av
Morgan La
Renee Av
Jardine Av
Merrill Av
Saybrook St
Loring Ct
Staten Island Hotel
Croton Pl
Yona St
Crocheron St
Akron St
Leggett St
Jennifer St
Debbie St
Morani St
CHRISTOPHER LA
RICHMOND
Cambridge Av
Woodbine Av
Hawthorne
Holgate St
Nina Av
Denton Pl
Montauk Av
Wyona Av
Auburn Av
490
350
130
Fillat St
Gurdon St
Wilbur Pl
O'Connor Av
St Paul's Seminary
VICTORY BLVD
Crafton
Woodward
N Gannon
Wooley
Martin
Caro St
Bass St
Ardmore
Sheraden
Ingram
Camel Av
Warwick
Av

278
Neptune
Decatur Av
Bellhaven Pl

Greentree La
Park view Loo
Richards La
Gary
Leona St
C
Darcy Av
Dreyer Av
Hall Av
Jones St
Clifton St
Saybrook St
Croft Pl
Goller Pl
Eton Pl
Dawson Ct
Camegie Av
Bascom Pl
Collfield Av
Stewart Av
Westwood
D
Sunrise Hill Park
S Gannon Av
650
Av
Ash Pl
Av
Av
Dawson St
Warwick Av
President St
Harris Av
Sunset Av
Taft Ct
Bri

Willow Brook Park
The College of Staten Island (CUNY)
WILLOWBROOK RD
960
Rd
Uxbridge St
Boone St

W I L L O W B R O O K

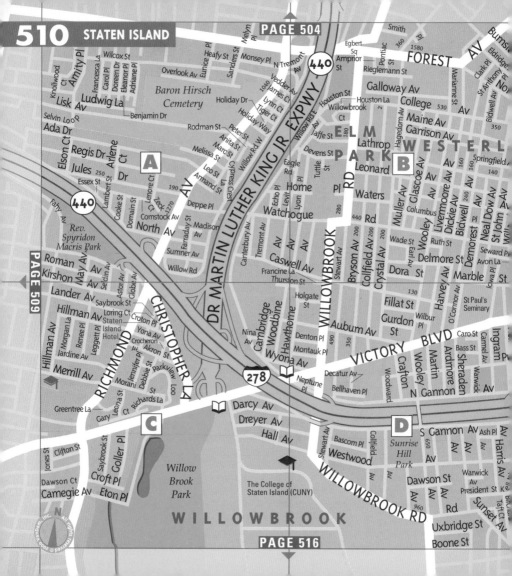

NJ

START DRIVE

Egbert Av

Curtis Av
Alpine Ct

Ravenhurst Av

Brooks Pond Pl

Brooks Lake

Brookside Av

Staten Island Zoological Society

Glenwood Pl

Coughlan Av

Dallas St

Hartford Av

Douglas Av

Tyler Av

710

Benedict Av

Colorado St
69

Greenleaf Av

MANOR

Delaware Pl

Martling Av

Richmond Pond

St Peters Cemetery

Starr Av

Clove Way

sley Av

New York Pl

Alabama Av

Carolina Av

Miller St

Maryland Pl

Slosson Av

240

100

190

Elmira Av

Meminan Av

New York State Armory

Clove Lakes Park

Virginia Av

Constant Av

Drake Av

Av Ct

180

A

60

Fairview Av

Clove

Fox Hunt Ct

Waldron Av

Glenwood Av

ber

argaretta Ct

120

Joan Pl

S Utter Av

Smith Av

260

Rice Av

260

Potter Av

140

B

Lake

CLOVE RD

Dudley Av

wyer

odwin

70

110

Goodell St

Lakeland Rd

420

Royal Oak Rd

Niagara St

Genesee St

Schoharie Av

rowell

120

Westcott Blvd

S Greenleaf Av

Sturges St

Knox Pl

Renick Av

Ontario Av

Cayuga Av

Seneca Av

Kemball Av

Chandler Av

70

Governor Rd

Sanford Pl

Cypress Av

Logan Av

Oswego Av

Coale Av

Raymond Av

Dongan Av

Beechwood Pl

Hodges Av

Ellsworth Pl

Brenton

1610

Walters St

Albert St

Dobbs Av

Northern

tz Pl

Windsor Rd

Marx

Aynar

Bristol Av

Cattaraugus Av

PAGE 512

ETON

Josephine St

Lester St

Henning St

Little

Otsego Av

Clove Rd

Tioga St

ERS

Mountain View

Gansevoort

Clermont

Quinlan

Garden St

Elvin St

Penn St

Sommers La

Todt Hill Rd

Windsor Ct

278

Perry

Cemetery

Gower St

Reon Av

110

Alexandra Pl

STATEN ISLAND EXPWY

Lortel Av

Milford Dr

Ocean Ter

Willem La

C

Schmidts St

Todt Hill Rd

La

Lightner Av

Melhom Rd

College of Staten Island (Sunnyside Campus)

Milford Av

Staten Island Blvd

704

Waldo Pl

Motley Av

Athena Av

Deere Park

150

150

Av

Pl

MANOR

Poland St

Fine Blvd

270

350

P

260

Franklin Pl

Area Pl

Andes Pl

Valleyview Av

D

Dresden Pl

Butterworth Av

Louise La

De Noble La

Deerpark Pl

Mohn Pl

Beebe St

170

170 Ct

Av

520

Suffolk Av

Graves St

Livingston Av

Roosevelt Ct

Norwalk Av

Townley Av

Portsmouth Av

1440

Coverly Av

Wellbrook Av

Holden Blvd

Duke Pl

Tillman St

Elmhurst Av

Tiber

230

OCEAN

TER

Queen St

Fanning St

Gower St

Melba St

Lincoln Av

Croak Av

Woodhaven Av

Vermont Ct

Harold St

Bolivar St

Wooddale Av

Merrick Av

Oceanview La
Basket Willow Swamp
—Shady Pl

END 3 MINS

2 MILES = 3.2 KMS

2 MILES = 3.2 KMS

Staten Island Zoological Society

St Peters Cemetery

Douglas Av
Tyler Av
710
Hartford Av
Whitewood Av
Shawnee St
Sunset Hill Dr
Herkimer St
Griswold Ct
Parkview Pl
Croton Av
Berwick Pl
Starr Av
Bard Av
Irma Pl
Bard Pl
Oxholm Av

Clove Way
Greenway Dr
Putters Ct
Fairway La

Clove Lakes Park

Royal Oak Rd
2

Clove  **A**

Lake

Silver Lake Golf Course

Marine Cemetery

Silver Mount Cemetery

Silver Lake Cemetery
Woodland Cemetery

Stratford Av

720
Theresa Pl
Grymes Hill Rd
Bertha
Rd
Greta Pl
300
Duncan Pl
Ada Pl
Howard
Shelterview
Hillcrest
G R Y M E S
H I L L
Arlo Rd
St John's University
Oakland Ter
Ba
Center Av
Yo

Chesire Pl
Beverly Av
Melrose Av
Waldron Av
Fox Hunt Ct
Lily Hunt Ct
Glenwood Av
Dudley Av
1030
2

Highland Av
Rugby Av
Grand Av
Alpine Av
Van Cortland Av
Seth Ct
500
Ridge Ct
750
Howard
B   A
Nesmythe Ter
Cedarcliff Rd
Signal Hill
Claire Hill
Woodside Av
Ramsey Pl
Pl
Hillside Av
890
Me

VICTORY BLVD

CLOVE RD

Niagara St
Genesee St
Renwick Av
Cypress Av
Schoharie St
DeKalb St
Seneca St
Ontario Av
Cayuga St
Oswego Av
Elm Pl
Sunnyside Ter
Foote Av
Martha St
Oneida Av

Rugby Av
Campus Rd

Wagner College

Ridgefield Av
Cunard Av
Cedar Ter
Cunard Pl
Wandel Av
Pleasant Valley Av
Hamilt
Cornell
Pl
Longview
Ma

Little Clove Rd
Walters St
St Marx
Albert St
Aymar St
Bristol Av
Northern
Dobbs Pl
Cattaraugus St
Otsego Av
Brenton Pl
Windsor Ct

Tioga St
Clove

Howa

Inwood Av
Starlight Rd
Longview
Holsman Rd
Wetmore Rd
Concord Pl
Starbuck
Longview
Av
Pierce
Dekalb St

Narrows Rd N

S T A T E N   I S L A N D

278

Lortel Av
Lightner Av
Motley Av
Melhom Rd
Athena St
Valleyview Pl
Townley Av

Milford Dr

College of Staten Island (Sunnyside Campus)

C

Deere Park

Ocean Ter
Witten Pl
Milford Av
Staten Island Blvd

Endor Av
Hewitt Av
Silver Beech Rd
Twin Oak Rd Dr
Diana's Trail
Emerson Dr
Seven Gables Rd
Douglas Rd
Overlook Dr
Douglas Rd

Milden Av
Longfellow Av
Emerson Av

Butterworth Av
Deerpark Pl
Mohn Pl
Beebe St
Portsmouth Av

Dresden Pl
Tiber Pl
Elmhurst Av
De Noble La
Louise La
230
1440
OCEAN
Woodhaven Av
Woodale Av
Merrick Av

Coverly Av

Oceanview La
Basket Willow Swamp
Shady Pl

Carlton Pl
Emerson Ct

E M E R S O N
H I L L
Edgar Pl
Lyman Pl
Wilson Ter
Madigan Pl
Spring St
Ridge Rd
Medford
Eltinge St
Hunter St

Roosevelt St
Ralph Pl
Marie Pl
60
Wilson Ter

D
Rhine Av
Baltic Av
Oder Av
TARGEE
CLOVE
Britton
Hanover
Neckar

R I C H M O N D
Meadow Av
Wilson Ter
Hay St
Alan Loop
Doctor's Hospital of Staten Island
Venice Av
Rome Av
Stonesgate L
Pamela
Gateway Dr
Stanwich
Gile

C O N C O R

Grasmere Ⓜ

© 2005 Hagstrom Map Company Inc. all rights
N

START DRIVE
I

NJ

ROSE-
BANK

17
18
Clifton
19
20
21
22 23
24
25

B

CLIFTON

Bayley Seton
Hospital

Stapleton
Housing

Adele Ct
Quinn St
Tompkins St
Harrison St
Brownell St
St

Oad St

ill St
Coursen Pl
Dix Pl
Pleasant Ct
Susan Ct
Thelma Ct
Park Hill Av
Park Hill Ter
Park Hill Ct
Pine Pl
Norwood Av
Talbot Pl
Errington Av
AV
Townsend
Greenfield Av
Camden St
Greenfield Av
Edgewater St
AV

Kings County
Richmond County

The
Narrows

Austen
House
Park

Alice
Austen
House

St
Coursen
Pl
ILT AV
Fairway Av
Park Hill Av
Park Hill Ct
Hill Ct
Park Hill Dr

A
TOMPKINS
Willow
Chestnut
AV
Lynhurst Av
Anderson St
Langere
Dixon St
Ormond Pl
Sylvaton Ter
Church La
Sylva
Pl
Wiman
AV
St

Sylvaton Ter
300

Park
Nunley Ct
Sky Dr
Skyline Stage
Rodeo La
Studio Loop
Garibaldi Meucci
Museum
White Plains Av
Shaughnessy La
Smith St
St Mary's AV
Butler
Kaltenmaier
Tilson Pl
BLVD
BAY ST
Rosebank
Pl
Abbott St
Andrease St

Hill
Long Pond La
Theatre
Studio Loop
Skyline
Virginia Av
Oak St
Fletcher St
Amity
Clifton AV
Vermont Av
Maryland Av
Keeley St
New
Scarboro
Cliff Ct

Scenic La
Skyline
FOX
Reynolds St
Fox Hill
260
Vaughn Av
Wingham St
White St
210
Anchor Pl
Cliff St
Nautilus Ct
Nautilus St

Eibs
Pond
HILLS
Bell
Tone La
Virginia Av
Colton St
Donley
Reynolds St
400
Ter 240
Thompson Pl
Deal Ct
Clayton St
Hope Av
Evelyn Pl
Bang
30
Nautilus St
Harbor View Pl N
Harbor View Pl E

ILA
Kansas Av
Rockwell
AV
Dayna Dr
Belair
James
290
Cabot
700
Home Av
High
RD
Summer St
Harbor View Pl S
Shore Acres Rd
Lake Dr
Sea Gate Dr
Harbor
Wadsworth
Av

s Rd N
St John's Av
Mendelssohn St
Beethoven St
Schubert St
Wagner St
Rubenstein St
Strauss St
North Dr
Hillcrest St
Hillbrook Ct
Hillridge Ct
Wadsworth Ter
Meyer La
Egbert Av
High
Lyman Av
61
Arthur Von Briessen Park

C
Narrows Rd S
278
FINGERBOARD
Brown Pl
Fillmore Pl
Harvey St
Lincoln Pl
SCHOOL
Wadsworth Av
RD
D
Dennis
Toricelli Sr St
US Coast
Guard

Brady's
Park
Grasmere Dr
Legion Pl
Joseph La
Claradon La
Dogwood La
SHORE
ACRES

Brady's
Pond
Manonville
Olga
Pl
Overlook
Ter
Rd
Hillbrook Dr
Cleveland Al
Vista Pl
Columbia
Chicago
Garson
Av
Garfield
Av

view
Delphine Ter
Windemere
Overlook Ter
HYLAN BLVD
Piedmont
Pouch Ter
Pouch
Cleveland Pl

Verrazano Narrows Bridge

Toll
Plaza

Richmond

Fort
Tompkins

END 3 MINS

PAGE 432
2 MILES = 3.2 KMS

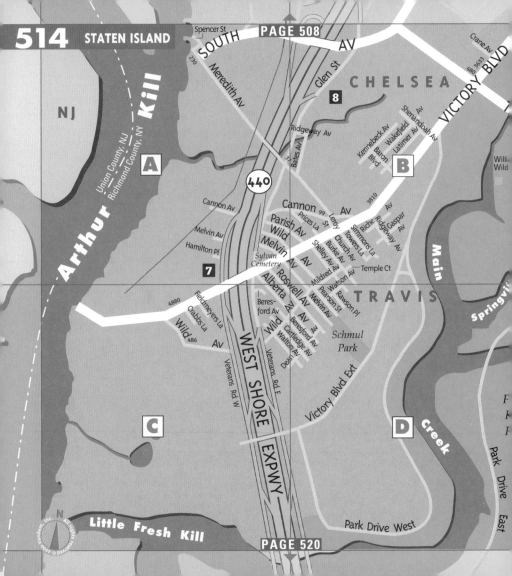

NJ

PAGE 508

Spencer St

SOUTH AV

230

Meredith Av

Glen St

CHELSEA

Crane Av

480 3433

VICTORY BLVD

Union County, NJ
Richmond County, NY

Arthur Kill

A

Ridgeway Av

Bates Av

8

Kennebeck Av
Wakefield
Baron
Blvd
Shenandoah Av
Latimer Av
Av

371

B

440

Cannon Av

Cannon Av

99
Prices La
Leroy
St

3810

Riche Av
Ridgeway Av
Gaspar Av

Parish Av
Wild

Melvin Av

Hamilton Pl

Sylvan
Cemetery

Simmons La
Church St
Towers La
Burke Av

Williι
Wild

Melvin Av

Shelley Av
Watson Av

Temple Ct

7

Alberta Av

Roswell Av

Mildred Av
Pearson St
Melvin Av

Rawson Pl

T R A V I S

Main

4880

Fieldmeyers La

Beresford Av

Schmul
Park

Springvi

Crabbs La

Wild
486 Av

Beresford Av
Av
Cartledge Av
Walton Av
Dease

WEST SHORE EXPWY

Veterans Rd W

Veterans Rd E

Victory Blvd Ext

C

D

Creek

Park Drive
East

Pk

N
© 2000 Hagstrom Map Co., Inc. All rights reserved

Little Fresh Kill

Park Drive West

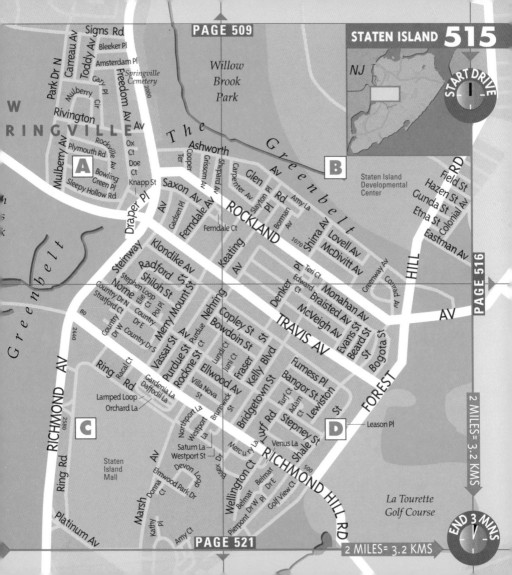

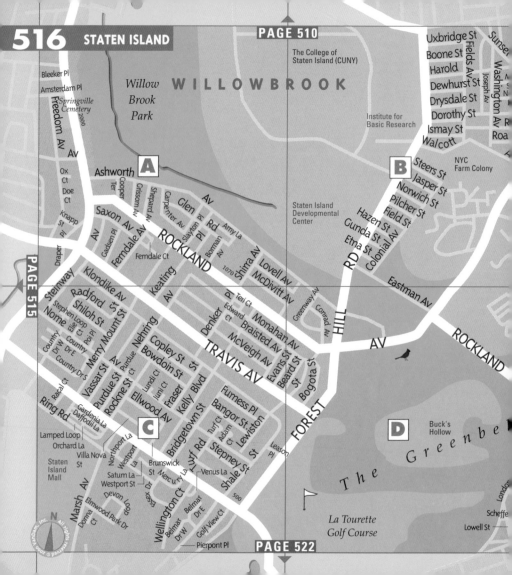

PAGE 510

The College of
Staten Island (CUNY)

Uxbridge St
Boone St
Harold
Dewhurst St
Drysdale St
Dorothy St
Ismay St
Walcott

Sunse...
Washington Av
Roa...
Joseph Av
Fields Av

WILLOWBROOK

Willow
Brook
Park

Institute for
Basic Research

NYC
Farm Colony

A

B

Ashworth

Bleeker Pl
Amsterdam Pl
Springville
Cemetery
2000
Freedom Av
Av

Ox
Ct
Doe
Ct
Knapp
Pl

Saxon Av
Av

Cooper
Ter
Grissom St
Shepard Av
Carpenter Av
Slayton
Glen Rd
Pl
Amy La
Borman
1070
Shirra Av
Lovell Av
McDivitt Av

Staten Island
Developmental
Center

Steers St
Jasper St
Norwich St
Pilcher St
Field St
Hazen St
Gunda St
Colonial Av
Etna St

Eastman Av

Ferndale Av
Gadsen Pl

Ferndale Ct

ROCKLAND

Keating

Teri Ct

Monahan Av
Braisted Av
Edward
Ct

Greenway Av
Conrad St

HILL
RD

AV

ROCKLAND

Draper

Steinway
Klondike Av
Radford St
Shiloh St
Nome
Stephen Loop
Ellie Ct
Pol Pl
Country
Dr W Dr E
Country Dr S
Country

Merry Mount St

Vassar St
Purdue St
Rockne St
Purdue
Ellwood Av

Denker
Copley St
Nehring
Bowdoin St
Lundi Ct
Juni Ct

McVeigh Av
Beard St
Evans St

TRAVIS AV

Bogota St

FOREST

D

Buck's
Hollow

The Greenbe...

Rafal Ct
Ring Rd

Gardenia La
Daffodil La
Lamped Loop
Orchard La
Staten
Island
Mall

Villa Nova
St

Marsh
Av
Dorma
Ct
Elmwood Park Dr
Devon Loop
Wellington Ct
Belmar Dr W
Belmar Dr E
Golf View Ct

C

Northport La
Westport
Satum La
Westport St

Brunswick
St
Mercury La
Essex
Dr

Fraser
Kelly Blvd
Bridgetown St
Turf Rd
Adam
Venus La
Stepney St
Shale St
500
Lewiston

Bangor St
Furness Pl
Turf La
Leason
Pl

The
La Tourette
Golf Course

London...
Scheffe...
Lowell St

Pierpont Pl

PAGE 522

N
©2004 Langenscheidt Publishers, Inc. All rights reserved

PAGE 515

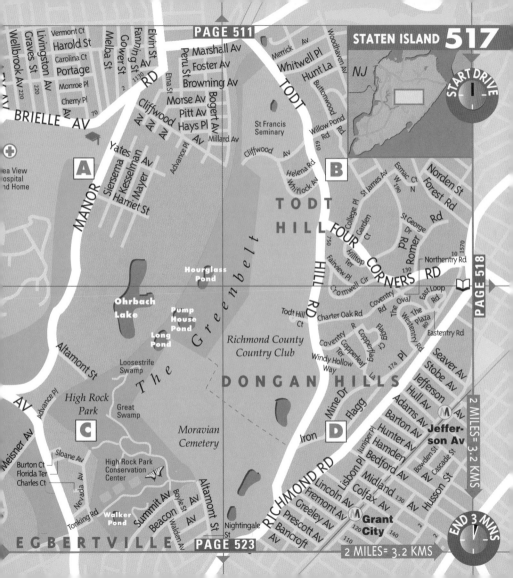

NJ

START DRIVE

Wellbrook Av 220
Graves St
Livingston Av
Harold St
Vermont Ct
Carolina Ct
Portage
Monroe Pl
Cherry Pl
220
70
Melba St
Gower St
2
Fanning St Av
Elvin St
Peru St
Etna St
1130

BRIELLE AV

Marshall Av
Foster Av
Browning Av
Morse Av
Pitt Av
Hays Pl
Millard Av
Cliffwood Av
Cliffwood Av
Bogert Av
Advance Pl

Yates Av
Siersema Av
Keselman Av
Mayer Av
Harriet St

A

Merrick Av
Whitwell Pl
Hunt La
Woodhaven Av
Buttonwood Rd
Willow Pond Rd
610

St Francis
Seminary

Helena Rd
Whitlock Av

B

TODT

ea View
ospital
nd Home

+

MANOR RD

**T O D T
H I L L F O U R C O R N E R S R D**

College Pl
St James Av
Esmac Ct N
Norden St
Forest Rd
Garden Ct
St George Dr
Romer Rd
750
Hilltop Ter
Fairview Pl
Cromwell Cir
130
Northentry Rd
10 1570

East Loop Rd

HILL RD

Coventry Rd
The Oval
The Plaza
Westerly Rd
Eastentry Rd

80

PAGE 518

Todt Hill Ct
Charter Oak Rd

Coventry Ter
Copperflag
Copperleaf La
Flagg Ct
174
Windy Hollow Way

**Hourglass
Pond**

**Ohrbach
Lake**

**Pump
House
Pond**

**Long
Pond**

The Greenbelt

Altamont St

Loosestrife
Swamp

Great
Swamp

*Richmond County
Country Club*

D O N G A N H I L L S

Mine Dr
Flagg
Iron

Seaver Av
Stobe Av
Jefferson Av
Hull Av
Adams Av
Barton Av
Hunter Av
Hamden Av
Bedford Av
Juniper Pl
Bowden Av
Cascade St
Husson St

**Jeffer-
son Av**

M

D

C

**High Rock
Park**

*Moravian
Cemetery*

Meisner Av
Burton Ct
Florida Ter
Charles Ct
Advance Pl
Sloane Av
Nevada Av
Tonking Rd

**High Rock Park
Conservation
Center**

Boyle St
Beacon Av
Walden Av
Summit Av
Altamont St
Nightingale St

**Walker
Pond**

Lincoln Av
Fremont Av
Greeley Av
Prescott Av
Bancroft Av
Lisbon Pl
Colfax Av
Midland Av
Husson St
130
2
110 120 140

**Grant
City**

M

RICHMOND RD

END 3 MINS

2 MILES = 3.2 KMS

2 MILES= 3.2 KMS

Basket Willow Swamp **PAGE 512**

Medford Rd
Rome Av
Columbus Av
W FINGERBOARD
Scranton St
N Railroad Av
Glendale Av
Tacoma St
Providence St
Urbana St
Daws
Pl
ON
Rd

Merrick Av
Whitwell Pl
Hunt La
Highpoint Rd
Westminster Rd
Annfield
Shady Pl
Forest La
Francis Pl
Keune
Duncan St
Sparkill Av
St
Mason St
Meadow Av
Holly St
Hunton St

TODT
Callan Av
Benedict Rd
Buttonwood
Palace Ct
Ridge Loop
Ridge
Concord La
Vista Av
Golf
Mountainside Rd
Hasbrouck St
Midway
Upton
St

Hillview La
Elaine Ct
Old Farmers La
Ress La
Noble Ct
Woodale Av
Glendale Av
Alderwood
Greenport
Dellwood Rd
Whitaker Pl
Mark St

St Francis
Seminary
Willow Pond Rd
Circle Rd
Hillview Pl
Chapin Av
Rochelle St
Dutchess Av
Overlook Av
Savin Ct
Albright St
Wilson St
Durges St
Old Town

Cliffwood
AV
Gorge Rd
Dalemere
Delaware St
Newberry Av
Bank St
Comelia St
Railroad AV
Devine St
Reid
Dumont
Av

A
Cornwall AV
Esmac Ct N
Norden St
Forest Rd
Burgher
Atlantic
Raritan
Delaware
Johnson St
Bear St
Remsen St
Mimna St
Bath Av
Cooper Av
Benton

Helena Rd
Whitlock Av
Redmond St
St James Pl
College Pl
W 599
B
Alter
Plattsburg St
Perine Ct
Cromwell
Garetson
Evergreen Av

TODT
HILL
FOUR
Garden
Ct
Hilltop Ter
Fairview Pl
St George Dr
Romer Rd
Northentry Rd
Cromwell
Garetson
N Railroad Av
Hancock St
Henry Pl
Perine

Todt Hill
Ct
Charter Oaks Rd
Coventry
The Oval
East Loop Rd
Liberty
Buel
Dongan
SEA
**Dongan
Hills**
Laconia Av

Richmond
County
Country Club
CORNERS
RD
The Plaza
Eastentry Rd
Hancock
Hills Av
VIEW
Magnolia Av
Simpson St

DONGAN
Coventry Copperfield
Ter
Windy Hollow
Way
Flagg Ct
Copperflag La
Seaver Av
Stobe
Jefferson
Zoe
Cletus
Naughton Av
Seaver Av
Vera
Joyce
HYLAN BLVD
State
Unive
(Nort

HILLS
Iron Mine Dr
C
Flagg
Hull
Adams Av
Barton Av
Hunter
Juniper Pl
Bowden St
Cascade St
Husson St
**Jefferson
Av**
Vera
Joyce
D
Naughton Av
Nugent Av

RICHMOND RD
Lisbon Pl
Hamden
Bedford Av
Midland Av
Bermuda Pl
Filbert Av
Rowan Av
Stobe Av
Jefferson
SLATER BLVD

Lincoln Av
Fremont Av
Greeley Av
Prescott Av
Colfax Av
**Grant
City**
Haven Av
Meadow
Laconia Av
Adams Av

NJ

START DRIVE

ASMERE

Vista Pl
Piedmont Av
Pouch Ter
Columbia Av
Chicago Al
Knauth Pl
Lands Av

Normalee Rd
Allendale Rd
Beverly Rd
Briarcliff Rd
Radcliff Rd
Roderick Av
Chicago Av

RD ARROCHAR

Cameron Pond

BLVD
STEUBEN ST
Norway
Mallory
Kramer St
970
130
Pickersgill Av 200
Major Av
MacFarland Av
McClean Av
Linwood Av
Hickory Av
Jerome Av
Bionia Av
Pershing St
Diaz St.
Humbert St

Hastings St
120
LILY POND
Duer Av
Tompkins Av
60
60
Florida Av
Waterford Ct
Galesville Ct
Palisade St
Guilford St
Railroad Av
Conger St
Jackson Av
Windom Av
Ocean AV

Cedar Av
Wallace St
Mills Av
Austin Av
Remer Av
Jackson
Linda Av
Drury La

SAND LA
Arthur Av
Plave St
270
Cambria St

A
Lamport
Kensington Av
140
550
Oberlin Av
Av
2

Lid Av
Cameron Av
Scott Av
Appleby Av
Nugent Av
Foch AV
Olympia Blvd
BLVD
250
240

Vulcan Av
Winfield St
Quintard St
Lava St
Patterson Av
St

Robin Rd
Doty Av
B

South Beach Park

Olympia Blvd
Andrews
McLaughlin
Pearsall
Balfour St
Gony St
South
Orlando St
Agnes Pl
Reynaud St

Av
St
St

Lansing St

Wills Pl
Tuscany Ct

South Beach

Lower

New

York

Bay

Quincy
Oceanside Av
St
St
380

Wentworth Av

BOARDWALK
FRANKLIN D. ROOSEVELT

SOUTH
BEACH

FATHER CAPODANNO BLVD

C

South Beach Psychiatric Center

780
Quincy AV
Oceanside AV

D

2 MILES= 3.2 KMS

Hoffman Island

END 3 MINS

2 MILES= 3.2 KMS

Park Drive West

440

Little Fresh Kill

Fresh

Kills

Island of
Meadow

Richmor

A

Great Fresh Kill

Park

NJ

Middlesex County, NJ
Richmond County, NY

B

*Fresh Kills
City Landfill*

Fresh

Kill Rd

WEST SHORE EXPWY

Kenilw

Service Rd W

Service Rd E

Muldoon Av

Bianca Ct

1380

Bi

KILL RD

Amanda Ct

Aspen

Cha

C

D

Ilyssa Way

Jamie

Knolls Way

La

ARTHUR KILL

GREEN-

Emily

La

Ilyssa

RIDGE

Way

Jay

Ilyssa

Ken

ROSSVILLE

440

4

1800

Kyle Ct

Chestnut Cir

N

START DRIVE

NJ

A

B

Park Drive

Fresh Kills Park

Ring Rd

Platinum Av

Yukon Av

Independence Hill

Av

Forest

Alaska Pl

2860

Staten Island Mall

Marsh Av

Windham

Kathy Pl

Loop

Amy Ct

Arielle La

Canon Dr

Gregory La

Stone

Pierpont Pl

Rd

Rumson Rd

Forest Hill Rd

Old Mill Rd

Historic Richmond Town

La Tourette Park

Revere La

Newale Av

Franklin La

180

Tanglewood Dr

RICHMOND AV

217

Vinton

Cicero Av

Glencoe St

Lacon St

Otho St

Mena St

Pemberton AV

420

Corbin Av

Troy St

Cromer St

Daleham St

Greaves

Elkhart

Miles

St

St

Fairfield

Gurley

Eric La

Hereford St

Islington St

KILL RD

500

Teakwood Ct

2 MILES = 3.2 KMS

C

D

Amadale Rd

End Pl

n St

n St

st

f St

hore St

Cheryl

Av

Gold

Pl

Av

Berry Av

Watkins Av

Dorval

Sunfield Av

Futurity Pl

Token St

Ladd Av

Alexandra Ct

850

Abbey Rd

Lennon Ct

Abingdon Ct

ARTHUR

Crossfield

RICHMOND PKWY

Gurley Av

Brandis Av

Eltingville Blvd

Bartlett Av

Opp Ct

Getz Av

Ridgewood Av

Cortelyou Av

Wainwright Av

Macon Av

Barlow Av

620

E Gurley

E Brandis Av

E Macon Av

Armstrong Av

Fenway Cir

Abingdon Av

Brookfield Av

Colon Av

351

E Reading Av

378

Doane Av

Leverett Av

Arkansas

Lexington La

Stieg Av

Elverton Av

Barlow Av

Jumel St

60

Kennington St

GIFFORDS LA

Linton Pl

END 3 MINS

2 MILES = 3.2 KMS

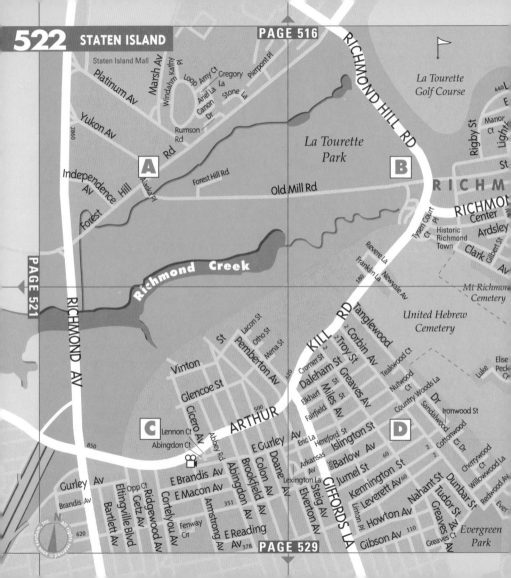

PAGE 516

PAGE 521

PAGE 529

Staten Island Mall

Platinum Av

Marsh Av

Windahm Pl Kathy Loop Amy Ct Gregory La

Yukon Av

Ariel La

Canon Dr Stone La

Pierpont Pl

RICHMOND HILL RD

La Tourette Golf Course

440L

E

Manor Ct

Lighth

Rumson Rd

Rigby St

St

Independence Av

Forest Hill Rd

Rd

Alaska Pl

A

La Tourette Park

B

RICHM

RICHMON Center

Ardsley

Forest

Old Mill Rd

Tysen Court Pl

Ct Pl

Historic Richmond Town

Clark Gilbert St

Av

Richmond Creek

Revere La

Franklin La

Newvale Av

180

Mt Richmon Cemetery

United Hebrew Cemetery

Elise Peck Ct

Luke

St

Lacon St

Otho St

Pemberton Av

Mena St

KILL RD

Tanglewood

Corbin Av

2

Troy St

Cromer St

Daleham St

Greaves Av

Teakwood Ct

Nutwood Ct

Vinton

520

Elkhart

Mill St

St

Country Woods La

Dr

Sandalwood

Ironwood St

Glencoe St

Fairfield

Cottonwood

Cherrywood Ct

500

ARTHUR

C

Lennon Ct

Cicero Av

Abbey Rd

E Gurley Av

Eric La

Hereford St

Islington St

D

Ct Dr

Willowood La

Redwood La

Abingdon Ct

850

Colon Av

Doane Av

Barlow Av

Nahant St

Dunbar St

Ever

Gurley Av

Opp Ct

Getz Av

E Brandis Av

E Macon Av

Ridgewood Av

Eltingville Blvd

Brookfield Av

Abingdon Av

Arkansas Av

Lexington La

Steig Av

Jumel St

Kennington St

Leverett Av 60

Tudor St

Greaves

Brandis Av

Bartlett Av

351

Cortelyou Av

Armstrong Av

Fenway Cir

E Reading Av 378

Elverton Av

GIFFORDS LA

Linton Pl

Howton Av

Gibson Av 110

Greaves Ct

Evergreen Park

620

60

2

Barlow Av

Linton Pl

2

60

NJ

EGBERTVILLE

Meisner Av
London Ct
Channel
View Ct
Terrace Ct
Eleanor St
Nugent St 70
Rd
50
Lawn Av
Nadine St
Summit Av
Beacon Av
Geldner Av
Sydney Av
Walnut St
Milburn St
Enfield Pl
Luigi Ct
Di Marco Pl
Luigi Pl
Walden Av
Foxholm St
St Stephens Pl
Nightingale
Otis Av
Locust Av
Cloister Pl
New Dorp
RD
2
3

New Dorp

Meisner Av
Aultman Av
Ascot Av
Rd
McCully Av
Boyle Av
Hitchcock
Call St
3310
Morley Av
RICHMOND
Ilion Pl
Grace Rd
Cubberly Av
Holly
Odin St
Rose Av
St
Ross
4

archais
Tibetan Art
ge

OWN
RD
A
Morton
St
Andrews St
Wilder St
Natick St
Pinewood Av
Park St
Barbara St
Maplewood Av
Tysens La
Altoona Av
Cranford Ct
Cranford Av
Joel Pl
Vincent St
Dalton
Ebony St
Belfast Av
Bishop St
Dorothea Pl
Dale Av
Oakley Pl
Prospect Pl
RD
New Dorp Plaza N
New Dorp Plaza S
7 St
Beach
Allison
Princeton
9 St
Sterling Av
Allison Av
Lindbergh Av

B

NEW
DORP

NEW

Bache Av
La
Coddington Av
Jacques Av
90
330
BLVD
250

DORP

NEW
DORP
BEACH

E Broadway
Mobile Av
Coverly Av
Shadow La
Wiley Pl
Amber St
Amber St
Wolverine St
Thomas St
Combs Av
Riedel Av
AMBOY
Arc Pl
Francine Ct
Belmont Pl
Cannon Blvd
Reno Av
Penn Av
Peter Av
8 St
9 St
Ella Pl
Isora Pl
Colgate Pl
Clawson St
Allison Av
Ebbitts Av
Ina St

RICHMOND
Wolverine St
Thomas St
Joyce Av
Rene Dr
Cedarview Av
Oakwood Hts
Clarence Pl
Windemere Av
Penn Av
Peter Av
O Thomas Pl
HYLAN
OAKWOOD
Ebbitts St
Ina St
Rd
Cuba Av
Titus Av
Isernia Av
Weed Av

Douglas
Frederick
Memorial
Park Cemetery
Chesterton Av
Cemetery
3290
Sheridan Ct
Emmet Av
Hajtstrom St
Savoy Av
Fairbanks Av
Acorn St
Tarring St
Leeds St
White Hall St
Windemere Av
Oak St
Elmira St
Flint St
Clawson Av
Pendale St
GUYON AV
Brook Av
Malden Pl
Primrose Av
Tysens La
Penn Av
Peter Av
Gerard P
Dugan Park
Eva Av
Roberts Dr
Manila Av
Milton Av
Agda Av

C

Benton Ct
N Railroad Av
S Railroad Av
Twombley Av
Spratt Av
O'Gorman Av
Hopkins Av
Hooper Av
Durant Av
Buffalo St
Tatro St
Peel Pl
Platt St
Malone Av
Montreal Av
Fairbanks Av
Chesterton Av
Currie Av
Emmet Av
Thollen Av
Block St
Champlain Av
Adelaide Av
Grayson St
Pendale Av
Emmet Av
Dugdale St
Medina St
Tarrytown Av
Falcon Av
Lynn St
Aviston Av
Amherst St
Isabella Av
Guyon Av
Riga St
Mill St
Old Mill Rd
Kissam Av
Foss Av
Promenade Av

D

Bay
Terrace

PAGE 518

Grant City

New Dorp

A

B

C

D

GRANT CITY

NEW DORP

NEW DORP BEACH

OAKWOOD

OAKWOOD BEACH

MIDLAND BEACH

New Dorp Beach

Cedar Grove Beach

Miller Field (Gateway National Recreation Area)

Great Kills Park

Gerard P Dugan Park

Colfax Av
Bedford Av
Midland Av
Bancroft Av
Greeley Av
Prescott Av
Grant Pl
Zeni Pl
Zwicky Av
BLVD
MIDLAND AV
Lincoln Av
Maplewood Pl
Boundary St
Samilac St
Rudyard St
Poultney St
Oldfield St
Mason St
Moreland St
Kiswick St
Greeley Av
Elm Tree Av
Olympia Blvd
Colony Av
Baden Pl
Patterson
FATHER CAPODANNO
Haven Av
Laconia Av
Stobe Av
Rowan Av
Filbert Av
Jefferson Av
Adams Av
Beachview Av
Idlease Av
Graham Blvd
Nugent Av
Grimsby St
Freebom St
Wahler Pl
Mapleton Av
Hempstead Av
Jay St

Otis Av
Allison Pl
Kruser St
Locust
N Railroad
Burbank
Steele Av
Bache Av
Jacques Av
New
Dorp La
St Railroad Av
Bryant Av
St Av
Edison Av
HYLAN
Coddington Av
Rose Av
Ross Av
Sterling Av
Beach Av
Allison Av
Lindbergh Av
Colgate Av
Cannon Blvd
Thomas Pl
Reno Av
Ebbitts St
Beacon
Celtic Pl
Ina St
Winham Av
Marine Way
Clayboard St
Tysens La
Penn Av
Peter Av
Falcon
Malden Pl
Primrose Pl
Isabella Av
Amherst St
Riga St
Lynn Guyon Av
Mill St
Old Mill Rd
Foss Av
Agda St
Mill Rd
Titus Av
Cuba Av
Weed Av
Manila Av
Isernia Av
Diaz Pl
Marila Av
Milton Av
Navesink Pl
Finley
Hett
Roma
Eva Av
Agda Av
Roberts Dr
Michelle La
Jennifer La
Dustan St
Neptune St
Waterside St
Seafoam St
Wavecrest St
Maple Ter
Topping St
Garibaldi Av
Cedar Grove Ct
Milbank Rd
Neutral Av
Cedar Grove Av
Great Kills Park
Great Kills

NEW DORP LA

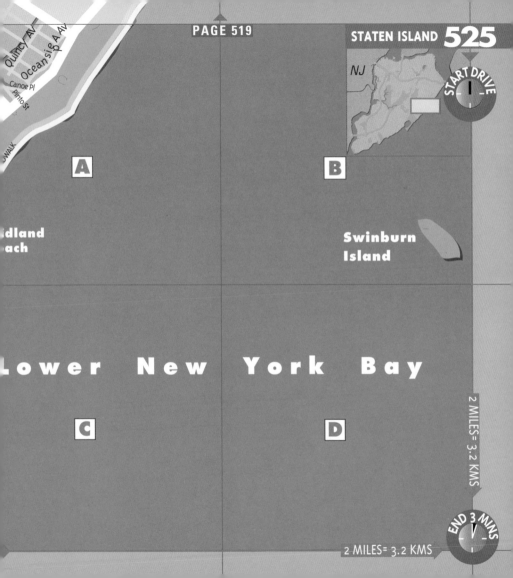

NJ

START DRIVE

Quincy Av

Oceanside A Av

Canoe Pl

Pinto St

WALK

A

B

dland
ach

**Swinburn
Island**

L o w e r   N e w   Y o r k   B a y

C

D

2 MILES= 3.2 KMS

END 3 MINS

2 MILES= 3.2 KMS

N J

Kill

Arthur

A

Middlesex County, NJ
Richmond County, NY

B

Old Bermuda
Inn

St Lukes Av

Zebra Pl

Veterans Rd W

Arthur Kill
Correctional
Facility

Chemical La

Majestic Av

EXPWY

Johnson St

Loop

Industrial

Shamrock Av

ARTHUR KILL

Grille Ct

Gericke
Farm

2700

RD

Veterans Rd

3

West
Av

Lucille A

WEST SHORE

Wirt La

Prince
La Candon

Malvine

Lorraine Loop

Cor

3980

Clay Pit Ponds

4100

Ellis Rd

Clay Pit Rd (Closed)

Clay Pit
Ponds
State Park
Preserve

Harris La

BLOOMINGDALE

Turner St

Crab Tree Av

Cemetery

Clay Pit Rd

C

D

Park
Preserve HQ

State Park

Gladwin
Av

Sharrotts Rd

Muriel St

Lundsten Av

Storer

Carlin St

Av

Neilsen Av

Clay Pit Ponds
State Park
Preserve

440

Spruce La

White Oak

Red Cedar La

Poplar La

Salamander Loop

Hemlock La

Sharrotts Rd

350

Winant Pl

Androvette St

Manley St

Kent St

Darnell La

Robin Ct

Pembrook Loop

k Loop

Mallare
La

WEST SHORE EXPWY

440

1800

1990

Crocker Ct

A

South Shore
Golf Course

Sussex
Green

R O S S V I L L E

Totten

Gunton Pl

Selkirk St

Pl

Barrow Pl

Mallow St

Rossville Av

Hemlock St

Alverson Av

Berne Pl

Helios Pl

Elks Pl

Latham Pl

Wieland Av

Lenevar Av

Spar Av
1270

Alverson Av

Gilroy St

Ramapo Av

Stafford Av

Sinclair Av

Sheldon Av

Rensselaer Av

Rathbun Av

Ramona Av

Lamont Av

Ionia Av

Edgegrove Av

C

Foster Rd

Vernon Av

Marcy Av

Kyle Ct
Dover
Carlyle Green
Green
Green
Forest
Cody Ct
Pratt Ct
Carlyle
Poets Cir
Lombard Ct
Princeton
Rally Ct
Bunnell Ct
Albert
Ashton
Mimosa La
Daffodil
Yucca Dr
Russel
Dogwood Dr
Geyser Dr
Avon Green
Rumba Pl
Myrna La
Ebey La
Hammock La
Stack Dr
Lisa La

ARDEN
HEIGHTS

Chestnut Cir
Birch La
Bunell
St
Barclay Cir
Beekman Cir
Nedra La
Cornell Av
Country La
La Tourton Green
Harmon
Regent
Cir
Maple
Ct
Sutton Pl
Hill Green
Valley
Crgen
Manchester Dr
Victoria Rd
Everton
La
Delmar
Av
Anaconda
Ballard Av

Hickory
Cir
Rolling
Rd
Tulip
Rd
Vespa Av
Jefferson Av
Canton Av
Holcomb Av
Everton Av
Belfield Av
Sperry Pl
Crown
Pl

Almond St
Ruxton Av

Vineland Av
Stafford Av
Sinclair Av
Sheldon Av
Rensselaer Av
Rathbun Av

B

WOODROW RD

Macon Av
Barlow Av
Waring
Av
Regina La
Swatara La
Carlton
Blvd
Evan Pl
Tyron
Av
Grantwood
Carlton Blvd

510

Heenan
Av

Sheldon
Av

Rensselaer Av

Rathbun Av

D

RICHMOND PKWY

Drumgoole Rd E

Drumgoole

Ionia
Belfield

Edgegrove Av

Detroit Av

Rosedale

Powell La

Shift Pl

Castor Pl

W Castor Pl

Cardiff

Boulder St

Coventry
Loop

Crown

Vineland

Nippon Av

Stafford Av

Sinclair

Sheldon Av

Rensselaer Av

Rathbun

Ramona

Lamont

Ionia Av

Edgegrove Av

Darlington Av

Dahlia St

Powell St

Walker Pl

Powell Pl

Ellsworth Av

Deserte Av
770

Ellsworth Av

Cemetery

Delmar Av

N Railroad St

S Railroad St

Downes

Bennett

Collyer Av

Buffington Av

Archwood Av

Albee Av

Tenafly

Ionia

Lexa Pl

PAGE 523

GIFFORDS

Howton Av
Tudor St
Dunbar St
Greaves Av
Exeter St
Greaves Av
Linton St
Gibson Av
Miles Av
Shafter Av
110
Greaves Pl
Dewey Pl
Woodcutters La
Nancy Dr
Evergreen Park
Ridge Av

Steig Av
Elverton Av
Doane Av
Colon Av
Woodland Av
160
Schley Av
Katan Av
260
Sampson Av
120
160
N Rhett Av

AMBOY RD
Benton Ct
S Railroad Av
Twombley Av
Spratt Av
Hopkins Av
Buffalo St
Currie Av
O'Gorman Av
80
Hooper Av
Durant Av
Thollen Av
Block St

Dewey Av
Katan Loop
Lamoka Av
Stem Ct
Greaves La
Old Amboy Rd

GREAT KILLS

Bay Terrace
Taunton St
Bay Ter
Bay Ter Ct
Kelvin Av
Justin Av
Thayer Pl
Ovis Pl
Baldwin Av

Grattan

Brookfield Av
Abingdon Av
Margaret St
Hardy Pl
St
Baltimore
110
2
Property St
Lindenwood Av
4090
Giffords Glen

A
Great Kills
Oak Ct
Stonecrest Ct
Clinton Rd
Adrienne Pl
Clovis Pl
Ramble
Rd
Dent Av

Redgrave Av
Bartow St
Ainsworth Av
Cranford St
Keegans La
Keats St
Trent St
Fieldway Av
Great Kills Rd
Highland Rd
Maybury Pl

B

HYLAN BLVD

3630

Gr
(Ga
Re

Nolan
St
Sherwood
Seeley La
Beth Pl
Pleasant St
Scarsdale St
Park Ter
Fontaine Pl
Belden St
Rustic Pl
Grandview
Hillside
100
Locust Pl
Midland Rd
Ocean Rd
Cleveland
Rustic Pl
Pl
Cottage Av
Greencroft Av
Maybury
Ter
Rd
Fairlawn Loop
Fairlawn Av
Mansion Av

Montyvale Pl
Highmount Rd
Hillcrest
Lindenwood
School St
Edgewood Rd
NELSON AV

Waterside Pl
N Ct
S Ct
McKee Av

PAGE 529

Oakdale St
Ramblewood Av
Acacia Av
Holly Av
Cloverdale Av
Elmwood Av
Armstrong
Robinson
Beach
Ocean View Pl
Eleanor Av
Monticello Ter
Durant Av
Nash Ct
Whitman Av
Melrose Pl
Florence St
Tarlee Pl
Mercer Pl
Hartford St
Cornish St

Bennington St
250
260
280
150
David
St
Driggs
Osbom
King
Pl
Lillian Pl
Russell St
Wiman Av
Sweetwater
Ackerman St
Morris Av
Fitzgerald St
Cindra Av
Beach La

C
William
Av
140
Thornycroft
Rd
Hillcrest
Winchester
Av
King St
107
Goodall St
Glover St
Heinz Av
Walnut Av
Groton St
Littlefield Av
A221
178
Harbour Ct
Byrd Pl
Highland La
Filipe La
Tennyson Dr
Point St

Great Kills Harbor **D**

P

Crookes Point

Great

PAGE 535

N

© 2003 Thomas Inc. All rights reserved

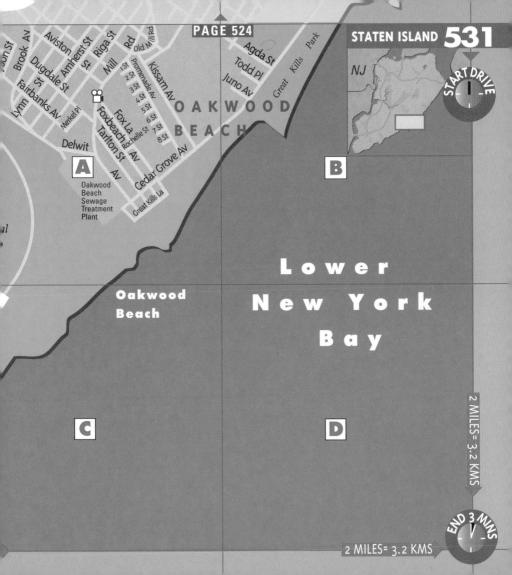

NJ

START DRIVE

Mason St
Brook Av
Aviston
Amherst St
Dugdale St
Riga St
Fairbanks Av
Mill
Rd
Old Mill Rd
Lynm
Merkel Pl
1 St
2 St
3 St
4 St
5 St
Kissam Av
Promenade Av
Delwit
Fox La
Foxbeach Av
Rochelle St
6 St
7 St
8 St
Tarlton St
Cedar Grove Av

Agda St
Todd Pl
Juno Av

Great Kills Park

O A K W O O D

B E A C H

A

Oakwood
Beach
Sewage
Treatment
Plant

Great Kills La

B

al

**Oakwood
Beach**

L o w e r

N e w Y o r k

B a y

C

D

2 MILES= 3.2 KMS

END 3 MINS

2 MILES= 3.2 KMS

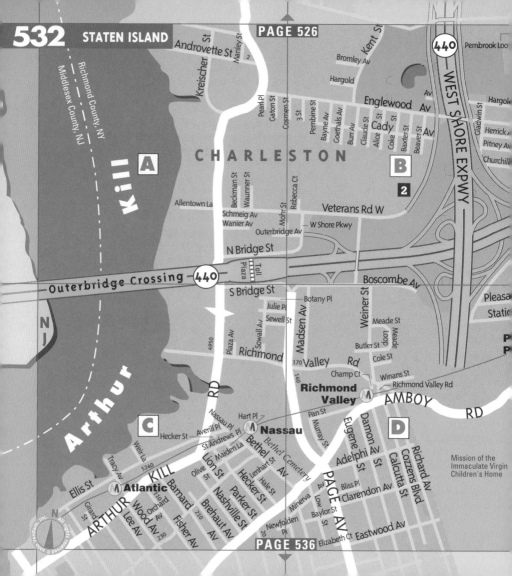

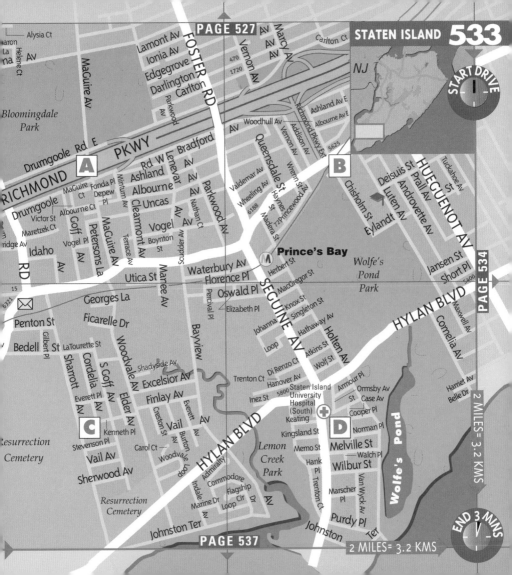

PAGE 529

PAGE 533

HUGUENOT
Ⓜ **Huguenot**

HUEGUENOT AV

ARDEN AV

Blue Heron
Pond Park

Wolfe's
Pond
Park

HYLAN BLVD

Arbutus Lake

Huguenot Beach

Wolfe's Pond

Atla

A

B

C

D

Lexa Pl
Collyer Av
Bland St
Ruggles St
Billious St
Philip Av
Community La
Edwin St
Poillon Av
Alvine Av
260
Kraft Pl
Edwin St
Sycamore St
Tallman St
Eylandt St
Sanborn St
Lipsett Av
130
Liss St
Oban St
Seidman Av
1305
WO

AMBOY
5440
Rose La
Eugene Pl
Sala Ct
Deisius St
Koch Blvd.
Jansen St
Harold Av
Lenzie St
Elm
Bath

Algonkin St
330
Stecher St
Rockport St
Christine Ct
Arbutus
Barclay
Weaver St
Holdridge
Shirley Av
Noel
Lenzie St
Luna Ct
Ravenna Ct
Bennet
Pl

Deisius St
Comely St
Tuckahoe Av
Kingdom Av
Denise Ct
Walsh St
Bertram Av
Eadie Av
Tyndale St
Kingham St
Peare Pl
Ryan Pl
Sand

Prall Av
Androvette Av
Luten AV
St
Colon AV
Louise St
Arbutus Way
Jansen Ct
Jansen St
Wendy Dr
Allegro St
Newton St
Dole St
Lipsett Av
Allen Pl
Leola Pl
HYLAN

Capellan St
Lotus Av
Rockport St
Leonard St
4895
Lynch St
Philip Av
Orangeburg Av
Petersburg Av
Poughkeepsie Av
51
Oceanview Av
Bayview Ter
Boardwalk Av

Jansen St
Short Pl
5600
Pierre Pl
Jarvis Av
Arbutus
Kenwood Av
Zephyr Av

HYLAN
Maxwell Av
Dixwell Av
12340
Swaim Av
Stecher Av
Edith
Arbutus Av
Nicolosi Loop Dr

Cornelia Av
Irving ton St
Veith Pl
Chester Av
Shore Av
Yeomalt Av
Trout Pl
Nicolosi

Harriet Av
Belle Dr

ndale
rd
st
BLVD
Seacrest Av
Oceanic Av
Av
Av
Prol Pl
4485
Wakefield Rd
Rd
Promenade
ale

Crookes Point

NJ

START DRIVE

A

B

O c e a n

c

C

D

2 MILES= 3.2 KMS

END 3 MINS

2 MILES= 3.2 KMS

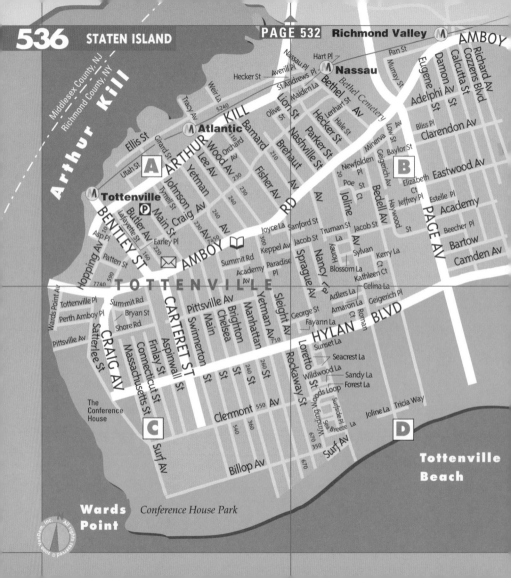

PAGE 532 Richmond Valley Ⓜ

AMBOY

Arthur Kill

Middlesex County, NJ
Richmond County, NY

ARTHUR KILL

Ⓜ Atlantic

Ⓜ Tottenville

Ⓟ

BENTLEY ST

A

B

Ⓜ Nassau

Hart Pl
Pan St
Nassau Pl
Averill Pl
Hecker St
St Andrews Pl
Maiden La
Bethel
Bethel Av
Bethel Cemetery
Murray St

Ellis St
Weir La
Tracy Av
5240
Girard St
Utah St

Hecker St
Olive St
Lion St
Nashville St
Lenhart St
Hale St
Parker St
Lenhart St

Bamard
Orchard
Wood Av
Lee Av
Yetman
Johnson
Craig Av
Main St
Tynell St
Lafayette St
Earley Pl
Butler Av
Asp Pl
Patten St
110
230
230
230
230
240
240
220
160

Brehaut Av
Fisher Av
FISHER RD
Joyce La
Keppel Av
Sanford St
Jacob St
Joline Av
AMBOY

Newfolden
Poe St
20
Joline
Bedell Av
Haywood
Geigerich Av
Minerva
Baylor St
Low St
Low Av
Eugene St
Adelphi Av

Bliss Pl
Clarendon Av

Elizabeth Ct
Eastwood Av
Jeffrey Pl
Estelle Pl
Academy
Beecher St
Bartow
Camden Av

Richard Av
Cozzens Blvd
Calcutta St
Damon St

PAGE AV

Truman St
Jacob St
La
Sylvan
Kerry La
Blossom La
Kathleen Ct
Adlers La
Celina La
Amaron La
Geigerich Pl
Roman
George St
Fayann La

Summit Rd
Academy
Paradise Pl
Sprague Av
Nancy La

TOTTENVILLE

Wards Point Av
Tottenville Pl
Perth Amboy Pl
Pittsville Av
Summit Rd
Bryan St
Shore Rd
Hopping Av
7740
5590
7450

Satterlee St
CRAIG AV

Pittsville Av
Swinnerton
Finlay St
Aspinwall St
Massachusetts St
Connecticut St
CARTERET ST
Brighton
Chelsea
Manhattan
Main
St
St
St
710
240 St
260 St
550
540
360
670
Yetman Av
Sleight Av

HYLAN BLVD

Sunset La
Seacrest La
Loretto St
Rockaway St
Wildwood La
Woods Loop
Sandy La
Forest La
Surfside Pl
Joline La
Tricia Way
Breeze La
Sea
350

C

D

The
Conference
House

Clemont Av

Surf Av

Billop Av

Surf Av

**Tottenville
Beach**

**Wards
Point**

Conference House Park

START DRIVE

I

NJ

Resurrection Cemetery

Everett Pl

Kenneth

Pl

Elder Av

S Goff

Stevenson Pl

Vail Av

Sherwood Av

Shamrott Av

Gaston St

Vail Av

Everett Av

Burton Av

Carol Ct

Woodvale Loop

Lindale

Woodvale Av

HYLAN BLVD

Bayview

Inez St

Lemon Creek Park

Admiralty

Commodore

Flagship

Marine Dr

Loop Cir

Resurrection Cemetery

6220

Johnston Ter

A

the
e Virgin
Home

B

Purdy Pl

Johnston Ter

Seguine
Point

MOUNT
LORETTO

**Prince's
Bay**

C

D

Bay

Raritan

2 MILES= 3.2 KMS

END 3 MINS

2 MILES= 3.2 KMS

Locating a street is easy. All streets in NYC are indexed alphabetically by borough. Each borough has a unique color bar for easy reference to its maps and indices as shown at right.

Each street is followed by a page number and a grid coordinate. In order to find West Broadway in Manhattan simply go to the Manhattan index starting on page 608. West Broadway....104 B. 104 represents the page number and "B" the grid coordinate.

INDICES 601

611 THE BRONX

NEIGHBORHOODS

608 MANHATTAN

INDEX

602 NEIGHBORHOODS

616 QUEENS

624 BROOKLYN

642 PHONE BOOK

630 STATEN ISLAND

604 SUBWAYS

Page
Grid

The Bronx
Baychester .....211 B
Bedford Park .209 D
Bruckner ....217 C
Castle Hill .....218 C
Co-Op City ....205 D
Country Club .212 D
Edgewater Pk 219 A
East Chester ..205 C
East Tremont ..215 B
Eastchester Bay ....
...............212 D
Fieldston ......208 B
Fordham ....215 A
High Bridge ...221 D
Hunts Point....223 C
Kingsbridge ..208 D
Kingsbridge Hts .....
...............209 D
Melrose ....221 C
Morris Hts ....221 A
Morris Park ...217 A
Morrisania ....221 B
Mott Haven ...227 C
Norwood ......209 B
Parkchester ...217 A
Port Morris....227 C
Riverdale ......208 B
Schuylerville ..218 B
Soundview .....223 B
Spencer Estates .....
...............212 D
Spuyten Duyvil 208 D
Throgs Neck ..218 D
Tremont ....215 D
Unionport .....217 D
University Hts 215 A
Van Nest ......216 B
Wakefield .....204 B
West Farms ...216 B
Westchester ...217 A
Westchester Hts .....
...............211 D
Williamsbridge204 D
Woodlawn ....204 C

Brooklyn
Bath Beach ...435 B
Bay Ridge .....426 A
Bedford
Stuyvesant ...411 C
Bensonhurst ..435 A
Bergen Beach 431 C
Boerum Hill ...407 C
Borough Park 428 A
Brighton Beach .....
..............443 D
Broadway Jct 418 A
Brooklyn Hts ..406 B
Brownsville ...417 B
Bushwick .....411 B
Canarsie .....424 D
Carroll Gardens ....
..............414 B
City Line .....413 D
Clinton Hill ...410 D
Cobble Hill ...407 C
Coney Island .442 D
Crown Hts ....417 A
Cypress Hills .413 D
Ditmas Park ..422 D
Downtown ....407 C
Dumbo ....407 A
Dyker Hts .....427 C
East Flatbush .417 D
East New York 419 C
East Williamsburg ...
..............405 D
Farragut ......423 C
Flatbush ......422 D
Flatlands .....429 B
Fort Greene ..407 B
Fort Hamilton .426 C
Fulton Ferry ..406 B
Georgetown ..430 D
Gerritsen Beach ....
..............438 D
Gowanus .....415 A
Gravesend ....436 B
Greenpoint ...402 D
Highland Park 413 C

Homecrest .....437 C
Kensington ....421 D
Manhattan Beach ..
..............445 A
Manhattan Terrace ..
..............437 A
Mapleton .....428 C
Marine Park ..438 A
MetroTech ....408 D
Midwood ......429 C
Mill Basin .....439 A
Mill Island ....438 B
Navy Yard ....404 C
New Lots .....418 C
New Utrecht .427 D
Northside .....402 C
Ocean Hill ...417 B
Ocean Parkway .....
..............436 B
Paerdegat Basin ....
..............431 A
Park Slope ....415 A
Plumb Beach ..445 A
Prospect Hts ..416 A
Prospect Lefferts
Gardens ....422 B
Prospect Park S .....
..............422 B
Red Hook .....414 A
Remsen Village .....
..............417 C
Rugby ....417 C
Seagate ....442 C
Sheepshead Bay ....
..............444 B
Southside .....404 A
Spring Creek .425 B
Starrett City ..425 A
Sunset Park ..421 C
Vinegar Hill ..407 A
Weeksville ....417 A
Williamsburg .404 C
Windsor Terrace ....
..............415 C
Wingate ....417 C

Manhattan
Alphabet City ..114 D
Battery Park City ....
..............102 A
Carnegie Hill .138 B
Chelsea ....117 C
Chinatown ....107 C
Civic Center ..104 B
Clinton ....124 D
Diamond District ....
..............125 D
DoMa ....102 B
East Midtown 122 B
East Village ...114 B
El Barrio ......146 D
Fashion District .....
..............117 A
Flatiron ....117 D
Flower Market ......
..............117 A
Fashion District .....
..............117 A
Garment District ....
..............121 D
Gold Coast ...130 D
Gramercy Park .....
..............118 D
Greenwich Village ..
..............113 A
Hamilton Hts .152 D
Harlem ....149 C
Inwood ....159 A
Kips Bay ......123 C
Koreatown ....121 D
Lincoln Square .....
..............128 D
Little India ...118 B
Little Italy ....107 A
Lower East Side .....
..............107 D
Manhattanville .....
..............148 B
Marble Hill ...161 A
Meatmarket ..112 A
Midtown East 126 D

Morningside Hts ....
..............144 B
Murray Hill ...122 C
NoHo ....110 A
Nolita ....107 A
Rockefeller Center ..
..............125 B
S SoHo ....106 B
SoHo ....106 B
S Village ......109 A
Spanish Harlem .....
..............146 B
Stuyvesant Town ....
..............119 C
Theater District ....
..............125 C
TriBeCa ......104 B
Turtle Bay ....127 A
Two Bridges ..107 C
Union Square ......
..............118 D
Upper West Side ....
.......132 B-140 D
Washington Hts .....
..............156 B
Wechee ....116 C
West Village ..112 D
World Financial
Center (WFC) ..104 C
World Trade
Center(WTC) ..104 D
Yorkville ......139 C

Queens
Arverne ....367 B
Astoria ....309 B
Auburndale ..322 D
Bay Terrace ..314 B
Bayside ....323 A
Bayswater ....368 B
Beechhurst ...306 D
Belle Harbor ..365 A
Bellerose ......332 D
Breezy Point ..362 D
Briarwood .....337 B

Broad Channel
Brookville
Cambria Hts
College Point
Corona
Ditmars
Douglas Mano
East Elmhurst.
Edgemere
Elmhurst
Far Rockaway
Flushing
Floral Park
Forest Hills
Fresh Meadow
Glen Oaks
Glendale
Hollis
Hollis Hills
Holliswood
Howard Beach
Hunters Point.
Jackson Hts
Jamaica
Jamaica Estate

Kew Gardens .

Kew Gardens ▶

Laurelton
Linden Hill
Little Neck
Long Island Cit

Malba
Maspeth
Middle Village

y Hill 313C	Grasmere 519A
sit 364D	Great Kills 530A
d Gardens	Greenridge 520D
.........331B	Grymes Hill 512B
Park.....342B	Howland Hook ....
s Village	.........502A
.........340B	Huguenot 534A
ark.....327B	Livingston 506B
ond Hill	Mariner's Harbor.....
.........336D	.........503C
wood 326C	Midland Beach ......
way Park	.........524B
.........365A	Mount Loretto ......
ale 357A	.........537A
y 363B	New Brighton 507A
aica 344B	New Dorp 523C
e Park .343D	New Dorp Beach..
field	.........523B
ns 352B	New Springville ....
ans 340C	.........515A
ay 303C	Oakwood 523D
side 317A	Oakwood Beach ....
stone 305C	.........524C
aven 335D	Park Hill 513C
ide 317B	Port Ivory 502B
	Port Richmond .....
n Island	.........505C
ale 529C	Prince's Bay ...537B
Hts 528B	Richmond 523C
on.........502B	Richmondtown......
ar 519A	.........522B
field 508B	Rosebank 513B
lead 508C	Rossville 520C
ton Corners ..	Shore Acres....513D
.........511C	South Beach ...519C
ston 532A	Stapleton 507C
a.........514B	Todt Hill 517B
.........513A	Tompkinsville...507D
rd 512D	Tottenville 536A
n Hills ..517D	Travis.........514D
ville 517C	West Brighton ......
ille 529A	.........505B
on Hill..512D	Westerleigh ...510B
ls 513C	Willowbrook ..508D
City 524A	Woodrow 527C

AIRPORTS & HELIPORTS

Floyd Bennet Field (CAN), BK 439C
LaGuardia (LGA), QS 311A
JFK International (JFK), QS 351C
Newark International (EWR) NJ 2
Teterboro (TEB), NJ 2
Wall St Heliport, MA 103C
30 St Heliport, MA 120C
34 St Heliport, MA 123D
60 St Heliport, MA 131D

BUS & TRAIN TERMINALS

Atlantic Terminal, BK 407D
George Washington Br, MA 156D
Grand Central Station, MA 122B
Penn Station, MA 121C
Port Authority, MA 121A
PATH WTC, MA 104D

FERRY TERMINALS

Governor's Island, MA 103C
Hunters Pt, QS 316B
Liberty & Ellis Island 102D
St George, SI 507B
South St Seaport, Pier 17, MA 103B
South Ferry, MA 103A
Staten Island,MA & SI 103C-507B
Wall St, Pier 11, MA 103B
Whitehall, Slip 5, MA 103C
World Financial Center, MA 104C
Yankee Stadium, BX 226B
E 34 St, MA 123C
E 90 St, MA 139D
W 38 St, Pier 78, MA 120A

TO FIND A BASIC

Simply turn to page and locate the basic in grids **A,B,C or D**.

MA = Manhattan
BX = The Bronx
BK = Brooklyn
QS = Queens
SI = Staten Island

TUNNELS & BRIDGES

Alexander Hamilton Br 157C-220B
Bayonne Br (toll) 505A
Broadway Br.........161A-214B
Bronx-Whitestone Br (toll) 225B-305B
Brooklyn Battery Tun (toll) 102D-406D
Brooklyn Br 105D-408B
City Island Br.........207C
Congressman J Addabo Br.........348D
Cross Bay Mem (toll).........366B
George Washington Br (toll) 156C
Goethals Br (toll) 502A
Harlem River Park Br 214D-220B
Henry Hudson Br (toll) 160B-214A
High Br (Ped.) 220B
Holland Tun (toll) 106A
J J Byrne Mem Br 316D-403A
Kosciuszko Br.........316D-403C
Lincoln Tun (toll).........120D
Macombs Dam Br 153A-226B
Madison Av Br 150B-226D
Manhattan Br 107D-408B
Marine Pkwy Br (toll) 364A-447A
Outerbridge Crossing Br (toll) 532C
Pulaski Br 316A-402B
Queens Midtown Tun (toll) 123C-316A
Queensboro Br (toll) 131C-308C
Roosevelt Island Br 308B
Throgs Neck Br (toll) 219D-307A
Triboro Br (toll) 147B-302C
University Hts Br 159B-214D
Verrazano Narrows Br (toll).....434A-513D
Washington Br 157A-220B
Whitestone Br (toll) 225B-305B
William Prince Br 312C
Williamsburg Br 111A-404A
Willis Av Br 151C-227C
3 Av Br 151A-227C
145 St Br 153D-226B

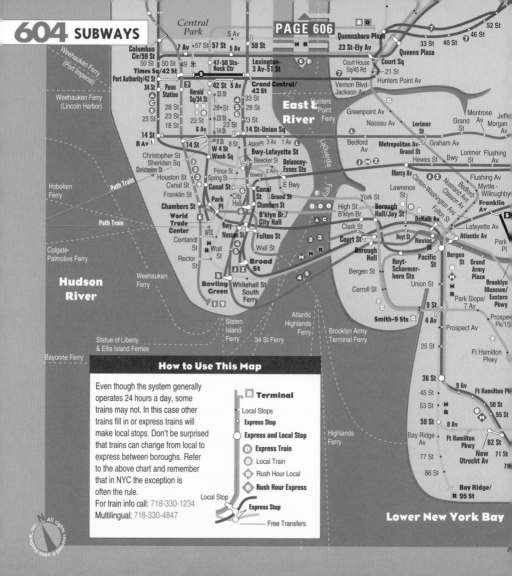

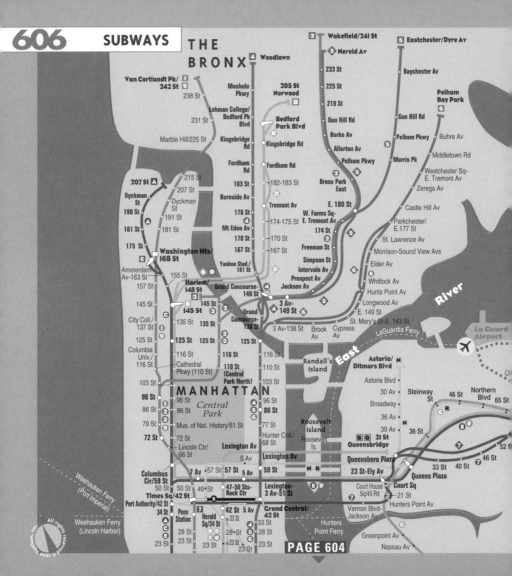

THE BRONX

Wakefield/241 St

Eastchester/Dyre Av

Nereid Av

Woodlawn

233 St

Baychester Av

Van Cortlandt Pk/ 242 St

238 St

Mosholu Pkwy

205 St Norwood

225 St

219 St

Pelham Bay Park

Lehman College/ Bedford Pk Blvd

Bedford Park Blvd

Gun Hill Rd

Gun Hill Rd

231 St

Burke Av

Pelham Pkwy

Buhre Av

Marble Hill/225 St

Kingsbridge Rd

Kingsbridge Rd

Allerton Av

Morris Pk

Middletown Rd

Fordham Rd

Fordham Rd

Pelham Pkwy

Westchester Sq- E. Tremont Av

207 St

215 St

183 St

182-183 St

Bronx Park East

Zerega Av

Dyckman St

207 St

Burnside Av

E. 180 St

Dyckman St

191 St

176 St

Tremont Av

174-175 St

W. Farms Sq- E. Tremont Av

Castle Hill Av

190 St

181 St

181 St

Mt Eden Av

174 St

Parkchester/ E.177 St

175 St

170 St

170 St

St. Lawrence Av

Washington Hts/ 168 St

167 St

167 St

Freeman St

Morrison-Sound View Avs

Amsterdam Av-163 St

Yankee Stad./ 161 St

Simpson St

Elder Av

155 St

Intervale Av

157 St

Harlem/ 148 St

Grand Concourse-149 St

Prospect Av Jackson Av

Whitlock Av

145 St

145 St

Hunts Point Av

145 St

3 Av- 149 St

Longwood Av

City Coll./ 137 St

135 St

135 St

Grand Concourse-138 St

E. 149 St

St. Mary's St-E. 143 St

125 St

125 St

3 Av-138 St

Brook Av

Cypress Av

LaGuardia Ferry

La Guard Airport

Columbia Univ./ 116 St

116 St

116 St

116 St

East

River

103 St

Cathedral Pkwy (110 St)

110 St (Central Park North)

110 St

Randall's Island

Astoria/ Ditmars Blvd

96 St

MANHATTAN

103 St

Astoria Blvd

Central Park

96 St

96 St

30 Av

Steinway St

46 St

Northern Blvd 65 St

86 St

86 St

86 St

Broadway

79 St

Mus. of Nat. History/81 St

77 St

Roosevelt Island

36 Av

36 St

72 St

72 St

Hunter Coll./ 68 St

Roosevelt Is.

39 Av

Lincoln Ctr/ 66 St

Lexington Av

21 St Queensbridge

Queensboro Plaza

33 St

40 St

46 St

52 St

Columbus Cir/59 St

7 Av

57 St

57 St

5 Av

59 St

23 St-Ely Av

Queens Plaza

Weehauken Ferry (Port Imperial)

50 St

50 St

49 St

47-50 Sts-Rock Ctr

Lexington-3 Av-51 St

Court House Sq/45 Rd

21 St

Court Sq

34 St

Times Sq/42 St

42 St

5 Av

Grand Central/ 42 St

Vernon Blvd-Jackson Av

Hunters Point Av

Port Authority/42 St

Weehauken Ferry (Lincoln Harbor)

Penn Station

Herald Sq/34 St

33 St

33 St

28 St

28 St

28 St

28 St

Hunters Point Ferry

Greenpoint Av

23 St

23 St

23 St

23 St

23 St

23 St

Nassau Av

PAGE 604

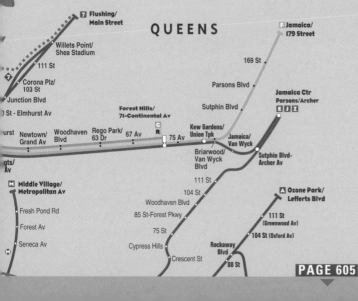

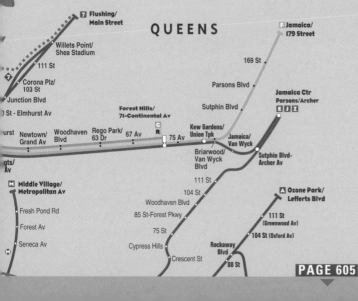

SUBWAYS 607

Express Trains	Local Trains	Rush Hour Trains
Here's how New Yorkers used to refer to the lines of their system		
2 3 4 5	**1 9** Skip-Stop Service in Upper Manhattan during rush hour **6 7**	**5** Brooklyn & The Bronx
A E Queens	**A** Brooklyn after 9 pm & weekends **C** **E** Manhattan **S**	**A** Rockaway
B Manhattan & Bklyn eves	**B** Brooklyn 36 St–Coney Island late nights **C**	**Manhattan 59 St - Bklyn 36 St**
D Manhattan	**D** Brooklyn & The Bronx	**Manhattan 59 St - 168 St**
	F Manhattan & Brooklyn	**Manh & Bronx Bklyn**
J Z Queens Myrtle-Marcy Av, Manhattan	**J** evenings **M**	**Queens 71 Av - Queens Plaza**
G No service after 9pm. Queens use B train, Brooklyn use D train.	**N** **R**	**N** Brooklyn
	S Shuttle	**N** Queens & Manhattan
	L Canarsie	

THE BRONX

QUEENS

MANHATTAN

QUEENS

7 Flushing/Main Street

F Jamaica/179 Street

Willets Point/Shea Stadium

111 St

169 St

Corona Plz/103 St

Parsons Blvd

Jamaica Ctr Parsons/Archer
E J Z

Junction Blvd

St - Elmhurst Av

Sutphin Blvd

Forest Hills/71-Continental Av

hurst Newtown/Grand Av Woodhaven Blvd Rego Park/63 Dr 67 Av **C R** 75 Av Kew Gardens/Union Tpk Jamaica/Van Wyck

gts/Av

Briarwood/Van Wyck Blvd

Sutphin Blvd-Archer Av

M Middle Village/Metropolitan Av

111 St

A Ozone Park/Lefferts Blvd

Fresh Pond Rd

104 St

Woodhaven Blvd

111 St [Greenwood Av]

Forest Av

85 St-Forest Pkwy

104 St [Oxford Av]

75 St

Seneca Av

Cypress Hills

Rockaway Blvd

Crescent St

88 St

PAGE 605

MANHATTAN
A Phillip Randolph
Sq..............145C
Abingdon Sq ..112B
Abraham A. Kazan
St 111A
Academy St ...159A
Adam Clayton
Powell Jr Bd ....
..........145A-153A
Adrian Av 161A
Albany St 102B
Alex Rose Pl...156B
Alexander
Hamilton Sq ..152D
Allen St............107B
Amsterdam Av ......
..........128D-159C
Ann St 105C
Academy St ...159A
Archbishop F J
Sheen Pl 122B
Arden St 158B
Asser Levy Pl..119A
Astor Pl 113B
Attorney St......111A
Audubon Av ....
............154B-159C
Audubon Ter ..152B
Av A-B.............114D
Av C 115C
Av D 115C
Av of The Americas
............106B-129D
Av of the Finest ....
............................105A
Broadway Ter 158D
Bank St............112D
Bankers Trust Plz...
............................104D
Barclay St 104D
Barrow St 108B
Baruch Dr........111A
Baruch Pl 111B
Battery Pl........102B
Baxter St 105A
Bayard St 107C
Beach St.........106C

Beak St............158B
Beaver St 102B
Bedford St 109A
Beekman Pl 127A
Beekman St 105C
Bennett Av 156B
Benson Pl........105A
Bethune St 112B
Bleecker St 109A
Bloomfield St ..112A
Bogardus Pl ...159C
Bond St............113D
Bowery 107A
Bradhurst Av ..153A
Bridge St 102D
Broad St 103A
Broadway...........
..........102B-161B
Broadway Al ..118B
Broadway Ter 159C
Broome St 106A
Cabrini Bd 156B
Canal St 106A-110D
Cannon St 111A
Carder Rd
(Governors Is) 406C
Cardinal Hayes Pl ..
............................105A
Cardinal Stepinac
Pl 120B
Carlisle St........102B
Carmine St 109A
Cathedral Pkwy 140A
Catherine La ...105A
Catherine Slip 105B
Catherine St....105B
Cedar St 102B
Central Park N 141A
Central Park S 129C
Central Park W......
..........129A-142C
Centre Market Pl ..
............................107A
Centre St 105A-110C
Chambers St ...104A
Charles La 112D
Charles St.......112D
Charlton St 109A

Chase Manhattan
Plz 103A
Chatham Sq 105B
Cherokee Pl ...135D
Cherry St 105B
Chisum Pl 153D
Chittenden Av 156B
Christopher St 108B
Chrystie St 107A
Church St 104B
Claremont Av ..144A
Clarkson St......108B
Cleveland Pl....109D
Cliff St 105C
Clinton St 110B
Coenties Al......103A
Coenties Slip ..103A
Col R Magaw Pl .....
............................156B
Collister St 106A
Columbia St 111A
Columbus Av ....
..........128D-140D
Columbus Cir ..129C
Commerce St...108B
Convent Av......148D
Convent Hill ...148D
Cooper Sq.......114C
Cooper St 158B
Cornelia St 113C
Cortlandt Al 106D
Cortlandt St 104D
Craig Rd N & S
(Governors Is) 406C
Crosby St 106B
Cumming St 158B
Dag Hammarskjold
Plz 127C
Delancey St.....110D
Depew Pl 126D
Desbrosses St 106A
Dey St 104D
Division Rd
(Governors Is) 406C
Division St 105D
Dr Martin Luther
King Jr Bd...........
..........146B-151C

Dominick St 106A
Donellon Sq ...152B
Dongan Pl........158B
Douglass Cir ...141A
Dover St 105D
Downing St 109A
Doyers St 105A
Duane St..........104B
Duarte Sq 109C
Duffy Sq 125C
Duke Ellington Bd ..
............................140A
Duke Ellington Cir ..
............................142B
Dutch St 105C
Dyckman St 158B
Dyer Av 120D
Early Bird Rd
(Governors Is) 406C
East Dr
(Roosevelt Is)..308C
East Dr ..130B-142A
E Broadway............
..........105B-111C
East End Av 135C
E Houston St ...114C
Edgar Allan Poe St
............................132B
Edgar St 102B
Edgecombe Av 149A
Edward M Morgan
Pl 152B
Eldridge St 107B
Elizabeth St 107A
Elk St 105A
Ellwood St 158D
Enright Rd
(Governors Is) 406C
Ericsson Pl......106A
Essex St 110B
Exchange Al.....102B
Exchange Pl.....102B
Exterior St 159B
Extra Pl 110A
Fairview Av 159C
Fashion Av 117A
Father Demo Sq......
............................113C

Father Fagan Sq. ....
............................109A
FDR Dr .. 103C-151C
Finn Sq 104B
Fletcher St 103A
Foley Sq 105A
Forsyth St 107B
Ft Charles Pl....161A
Ft George Av ..159C
Ft George Hill ..159C
Ft Washington Av ..
............................154C
Frankfort St 105C
Franklin Pl 106D
Franklin St 104B
Federal Plz 105A
Frederick Douglass
Bd 145C-153C
Freedom Pl......128A
Freeman Al......110A
Front St 103A
Ft George Av ..159C
Ft Washington Av ..
............................158D
Fulton St 104D
Galvin Av 120B
Gansevoort St 112A
Gateway Plz.....102A
Gay St 113A
Gold St 103A
Gouverneur La 103A
Gouverneur St 111C
Gouverneur Slip
W & E 111C
Gracie Sq 139D
Gracie Ter 135C
Gramercy Park
N & S 118D
Grand Army Plz 129D
Grand St 106B
Great Jones St 113D
Greeley Sq 121D
Greene St 106B
Greenwich Av 112B
Greenwich St ....
..........102B-112B
Gresham Rd
(Governors Is) 406C

Grove Ct ....
Grove St ....
Gulf Western P
H Howard Sq ..
Hamill Pl ....
Hamilton Pl.....
Hamilton Ter ...
Hancock Pl......
Hancock Sq ....
Hanover Sq ....
Hanover St ......
Harlem River D
............153A
Harrison St .....
Haven Av ....
Hay Rd
(Governors Is) ..
Henderson Pl...
Henry Hudson P
(9A) 128C-1
Henry J Brown
Bd ....
Henry St ....
Henshaw St ....
Herald Sq ....
Hester St ....
Hillside Av ......
Hogan Pl.........
Holy Rosary Sq
Horatio St ....
Howard St ....
Hubert St ....
Hudson Sq ......
Hudson St ....
............104B-1
Independence
Indian Rd ....
Irving Pl ....
Isham St ....
J.P. Ward St ....
Jackson Sq ....
Jackson St......
Jacobus Pl......
James St..........
James Madison
............1

St 112A
St 104B
rson St ...107B
ey St 109B
St 103A
s Al 110A
s St 113C
el Ter 154D
el Pl 154B
nare St 107A
au Sq 105A
St 109A
alle St 144B
yette St .....
.......105A-114C
yette Ct ...113B
uardia Pl ..109B
nt St 106A
ston Hughes
...................149D
el Hill Ter 157A
n Mem Sq103A
x Av145D-153D
x Ter 149B
ard St 104B
y St 108B
s St 111B
agton Av ....
.........118B-150D
ty Pl 104D
ty St 102B
oln Sq 128B
oln Plz 128D
oln Tunnel
unce 120D
enard St ...106B
West St ..102D
W 12 St ..112A
se Nevelson
...................103A
ow St 107B
Muñoz Marin
...................147C
Dougal Al 113A
Dougal St 109A
ombs Pl....153A
ison Av ....
.........118A-150B

Madison Sq Plz .....
...................118A
Madison Sq N 118A
Madison St....105B
Maher Cir 153A
Maiden La 103A
Main St (Roosevelt
Island) 308A
Mangin St 111B
Malcom X Bd ....
..........145D-153D
Manhattan Av ....
..........145D-153D
Marble Hill Av 161A
Marble Hill La 161A
Margaret Corbin Dr
...................158B
Margaret Corbin
Plz 158D
Market Slip ...107D
Market St 107D
Marketfield St 103A
McCarthy Sq ..113A
McKenna St ..154B
McNally Plz ...157A
Mercer St 106B
Mill La 103A
Milligan Pl ...113A
Minetta La 113C
Minetta St 109A
Mitchell Pl ...127C
Mitchell Sq....154B
Monroe St 105B
Mott St ..105A-114C
Msgr Francis J
Kett Plz 159A
Montefiore Sq 148B
Montgomery St111C
Moore St.......103C
Morningside Av 144B
Morningside Dr 144D
Morris St 102B
Morton St 108B
Mosco St 105A
Mott St 105A
Mt Carmel Sq..145D
Mt Morris Pk W ....
...................145B

Mulberry St ...105A
Murray St 104C
Museum Mile .....
.........133B-142B
N D Perlman Pl ...
...................119C
Nagle Av 159C
Nassau St.....103A
New St 102B
Norfolk St 110B
N Moore St ...104A
North End Av ..104C
Odell M Clark Pl ...
...................149A
Old B'way 148D
Old Slip 103A
Oliver St 105B
Orchard St ...107B
Overlook Ter ..156B
Paladino Av ...147B
Park Av ..122D-150D
Park Av South 118D
Park Pl 104D
Park Pl W 104A
Park Row 105C
Park Ter E & W ....
...................161C
Patchin Pl 113A
Payson Av 158B
Pearl St........102D
Peck Slip 105D
Pell St 105A
Penn Plz 121C
Peretz Sq 110B
Perry St........112D
Pershing Sq ..122B
Peter Cooper Rd ...
...................119A
Peter Minuit Plz ...
...................103C
Pike Slip 107D
Pike St 105A
Pine St 102B
Pinehurst Av ..156B
Pitt St 111A
Platt St 103A
Plz Lafayette ..156D
Pleasant Av ...147D

Police Plz 105A
Pomander Wk 136B
Post Av 159A
Prince St.......109A
Printing House Sq ..
...................105C
Queens Midtown
Tunnel Entrance ..
...................122D
Reade St 104B
Rector Pl......102A
Rector St 102B
Reinhold Niebuhr
Pl 144A
Renwick St....106A
Rev P Ladson Pl ...
...................146C
Ridge St 111A
River Rd (Roosevelt
Island) 308A
River Ter 104C
Riverside Drive ....
...........132C-158B
Riverside Dr E & W
...................144A
Riverside Dr ....
Viaduct 148C
Riverview Ter..131D
Rivington St ..110B
Robert F. Wagner
Sr. Pl 105B
Rockefeller Plz 125D
Roosevelt Sq ..148D
Rose St 105A
Rutgers St 107D
Rutherford Pl ..118D
Ryders Al 105C
St Clair Pl 148C
St James Pl ...105A
St Johns La ...106B
St Josephs La 106A
St Lukes Pl ...108B
St Mark's Pl ..114A
St Pauls Pl ...146D
St Nicholas Av ....
.........145A-157C
St Nicholas Pl 153A
St Nicholas Ter 149C

Samuel Dickstein
Plz 111C
Schiff Pkwy ...110D
Scott Sq 159A
Seaman Av 158B
Seminary Rd ..144B
Sheridan Sq ..113C
Sheriff St 115C
Sherman Av ...158B
Sherman St ...128B
Sheriff St 111A
Shinbone Al ...113D
Shona Bailey Pl ...
...................148B
Sickles St 158B
Sniffen Ct 122D
South End Av ..102A
South St 103A-111D
S Pinhurst St 156D
S William St ...103A
Spring St 106A
Spruce St 105C
Stable Ct 113D
Staff St 158B
Stanton St 110B
Staple St 104B
State St 102D
Stone St 103C
Straus Sq 107B
Stuyvesant Al 114A
Stuyvesant Sq 119C
Stuyvesant St 114A
Suffolk St 110B
Sullivan St ...109A
Sutton Pl 131C
Sutton Pl S ...127A
Sutton Sq 131D
Sylvan Pl......146B
Sylvan Ter 154D
Szold Pl........115A
Taras Shevchenko
Pl 114C
Terrace View Av ..
...................161A
Teunissen Pl ..161A
Thames St 102B
Thayer St 158B
Theater Row ..120B

Theatre Al 105C
Thomas St 104B
Thompson St ..106B
Times Sq 125C
Tiemann Pl 148C
Tompkins Sq...114B
Trans Manhattan
Expwy 156D
Trimble Pl 104B
Trinity Pl 102B
Trump Plz 131C
Tudor City Pl ..123A
Tunnel Entrance St
...................123A
Tunnel Exit St..122B
Union Sq E & N ....
...................118D
Union Sq W 118C
University Pl ..113B
University Plz..113D
Van Corlear Pl 161A
Vandam St 109A
Vanderbilt Av ..122B
Varick St 106A
Vermilyea Av ..158B
Verdi Sq 128B
Vesey St 104C
Vestry St 106A
Village Sq 113A
W Houston St 108B
W C Handy Pl 124B
W Tigne Triangle ..
...................158B
W Union Plz ..102D
Wadsworth Av156D
Wadsworth Ter 156B
Walker St 106B
Wall St 103A
Wanamaker Pl113B
Warren St 104A
Wash Pl 113D
Washington Sq
E & N 113D
Washington Sq
S & W 113C
Washington Mews
...................113B
Washington Sq 113C

Washington St 102B-112B	9 Av 116D-124B,161C	E 118-25 St 146B
Washington Ter157A	10 Av 116D-124B,161C	E 126-32 St 150D
Water St 103A	11 Av ...116B-124B	E 135 St..........150B
Watts St 106A	12 Av 116A-124B,148C	E 138 St..........150B
Waverly Pl 112B	65 St Transverse 130A	W 3 St.............113C
Weehawken St108B	79 St Transverse 133A	W 4 St.............112B
W Broadway ..104B	85 St Transverse 137C	W 8-9 St 113A
West End Av 128C-140A	97 St Transverse 137A	W 10-11 St 112D
W Houston St 108B		W 12-14 St 112A
West Side Hwy 102C-124A	E 1-2 St 110A	W 15-21 St 116D
West Dr..129C-141A	E 3 St.............114C	W 22-25 St 116B
West Rd (Roosevelt Is)..308A	E 4 St.............113D	W 26-29 St 116A
West St 102B	E 5-6 St 114C	W 30-36 St 120D
W Thames St..102A	E 7 St.............114A	W 37-38 St 120B
W Washington Pl.... ....113C	E 8 St.............113B	W 39-44 St 120A
Wheeler Rd (Governors Is) 406C	E 9-14 St 113B	W 45-49 St 124D
White St 106D	E 15-20 St 117D	W 50-57 St 124B
Whitehall St ...103C	E 21 St..........118C	W 58-64 St 128D
Willett St........111C	E 22-29 St 118A	W 65-72 St 128B
William St.......103A	E 30-36 St 121D	W 73-79 St 132C
Wooster St 106B	E 37-40 St 121B	W 80-86 St 132A
Worth Sq 117B	E 41-43 St 122A	W 87-91 St 136C
Worth St 104B	E 44-49 St 125D	W 92-99 St 136A
York Av ..131D-139D	E 50 St..........125B	W 100-103 St ...140C
York St.............106B	E 51 St..........126B	W 104-09 St ...140A
	E 52-57 St 126A	W 111-17 St ...145C
NUMBERED AV • PI • ST	E 58-64 St 130D	W 118-25 St ...145A
1 Av 110B-147A	E 65-72 St 130B	W 126-29 St ...148D
1 Pl..................102D	E 73-79 St 133D	W 130-32 St ...148C
2 Av 110A-151C	E 80-82 St 133B	W 133 St.........148A
2 Pl..................102B	E 83-86 St 134B	W 134 St.........148B
3 Av 114C-150D	E 87-91 St 137D	W 135-40 St ...148A
3 Pl..................102B	E 92-95 St 137B	W 141-49 St ...152D
4 Av 113B	E 96-99 St 138B	W 150-59 St ...152B
5 Av 113B-150B	E 100 St.........143C	W 160-64 St ...154D
6 Av 106B-129D	E 101-03 St ...141D	W 165-68 St ...154B
7 Av .....117C-130C 145C-153A	E 104-07 St ...141B	W 169-73 St ...154A
7 Av S 109A	E 108-10 St ...142B	W 174-80 St ...157C
8 Av 112B-125A	E 111-12 St ...146D	W 181-90 St ...157A
	E 113-14 St ...147C	W 191-93 St ...159C
	E 115-17 St ...146D	W 196 St.........158D
		W 201-07 St ...159A
		W 208 St.........159A
		W 211-18 St ...161C
		W 219-20 St ...161A
		W 225 St 161A
		W 227 St 161A

Arithmetic of The Avenues

To locate an address on an avenue in Manhattan without knowing cross street is quite simple. Just drop the last figure, divide by 2 and or subtract as listed below. The resulting number is the nearest cr street. This does not apply to Broadway below 8 St.

Avs A, B, C, D add 3	**Broadway**
1 & 2 Av add 3	754–858 subtract 29
3 Av add 10	858–958 subtract 25
4 Av add 8	> 100 St subtract 30
5 Av to 200 add 13	**Columbus Av** add 60
to 400 add 16	**Convent Av** add 127
to 600 add 18	**Central Park W** divide St
to 775 add 20	number by 10 & add
to 775 - 1286 drop last figure & subtract 18	**Edgecombe Av** add 134
to 1500 add 45	**Lenox Av** add 110
to 2000 add 24	**Lexington Av** add 22
Av of the Americas subtract 12	**Madison Av** add 26
7 Av add 12, > 110 St add 20	**Manhattan Av** add 100
8 Av add 10	**Park Av** add 35
9 Av add 13	**Pleasant Av** add 101
10 Av add 14	**Riverside Dr** divide house
Amsterdam Av add 60	number by 10 & add
Audubon Av add 165	up to 165 St
	West End Av add 60

East	Cross Streets	We

To find a crosstown street address and the avenues it is in between, follow the key.

Manhattanwide	Below 59th St	Above 59th Str
1–49 5–Madison Avs	**1–99** 5–6 Avs	**1–99** Central Pa W–Columbus A
50–99 Madison– Park Avs	**100–199** 6–7 Avs	**100–199** Columb
100–149 Park– Lexington Avs	**200–299** 7–8 Avs	**200–299** Amsterdam Av
149–199 Lex–3 Avs	**300–399** 8–9 Avs	**200–299**
200–299 3–2 Avs	**400–499** 9–10 Avs	Amsterdam–W End Av (WEA)
300–399 2–1 Avs	**500–599** 10–11 Avs	**300–399** West Av–Riverside D
400–499 1–York Avs (Av A below 14 St)		
500–599 Avs A–B		

...NX

...Griffin Pl....227A
...ot St 204A
...n Pl 219C
...ns Pl 215D
...ns St 216D
...e St...........219A
...e Av 210D
...iral La 225C
...Pl............212D
...Pl 219D
...ny Cres 209C
...tt Pl..........205D
...n Pl 215D
...brook Rd 208B
...ch St.........205D
...s St 223C
...ander Av....227C
...ton Av 210D
...thyst St 216B
...ere Av 212D
...ndson Av 205A
...erson Av ...221C
...ews Av N & S
............215C
...ony Av......215C
...a Pl...........216D
...educt Av E215C
...educt Av W .....
............215A
...er Rd 217C
...er St 217C
...gton Av....202D
...and Pl.......209C
...w Av 210D
...w Pl.........212D
...ur Av 215B
...ur Murphy Sq ..
............215D
...a Loop 205D
...r Pl..........219C
...r Av 210D
...in Pl.........227B
...t John 228A

Babe Ruth Plz 221C
Bailey Av.......209C
Bailey Pl........209C
Bainbridge Av 209B
Baisley Av 212D
Baker Av........216D
Balcom Av 218A
Baldwin St 204A
Balsam Pl......219C
Bantam Pl......211A
Banyer Pl......223B
Barker Av......210B
Barkley Av.....218B
Barn Hill Sq ..215A
Barnes Av......204D
Barrett Av......225A
Barretto St 223C
Barry Plz.......221B
Barry St 228B
Bartholdi St ...210B
Bartow Av......205D
Bassett Av 211D
Bassford Av....215B
Bathgate Av....215B
Bay Shore Av..212D
Bay St 213A
Baychester Av204B
Bayview Av 212D
Beach Av 217C
Beach St........207C
Beatty Plz......221B
Beaumont Av...215B
Beck St 222D
Bedford Pk Bd E
...............209D
Bedford Pk Bd W.
...............209C
Beech Pl........219C
Beech Ter.......227B
Beech Tree La .....
...............206A
Beekman Av ...227B
Belden St 213B
Bell Av...........205A

Bellamy Loop..205D
Belmont Av.....215B
Belmont St 221B
Benchley Pl ...205D
Benedict Av ...217C
Benson St.......217B
Bergen Av 217C
Bernard S. Deutch
Plz 221A
Betts Av 225A
Bevy Pl 219D
Billingsley Ter 214D
Birchall Av......216B
Bissel Av........204B
Bivona St 205C
Blackrock Av ..217D
Blackstone Av 208A
Blackstone Pl 208B
Blair Av..........219A
Blondell Av......211D
Bogart Av 216B
Boller Av.........205C
Bolton Av........224B
Bolton St........216B
Bonner Pl 221D
Boone Av 223A
Boscobel Pl ...221A
Boston Rd ....
............210D-224B
Botanical Sq NS
...............209D
Bouck Av 211A
Bowne St 207C
Boyd Av 204B
Boynton Av......223A
Bradford Av....218A
Bradley St 204A
Brady Av.........216B
Brandt Pl 221A
Bridge St........207C
Briggs Av 209D
Brinsmade Av 218A
Bristow St 222B
Britton St 210D

Broadway ....
...............203C-214D
Bronx & Pelham
Pkwy..............211C
Bronx Bd 204A
Bronx Park E ..210D
Bronx Park S ..216C
Bronx River Av
.....................216D
Bronx River Pkwy ..
...............204A-223A
Bronx St 216D
Bronxdale Av..216B
Bronxwood Av204D
Brook Av 221D
Broun Pl 205D
Brown Pl.........227D
Bruckner Bd ....
...............217D-228C
Bruckner Expwy ..
...............212D-228A
Bruner Av........204B
Brush Av.........217D
Bryant Av........216D
Buchanan Pl ...215C
Buck St...........217A
Buckley St 213B
Buhre Av.........212C
Bullard Av.......204A
Burke Av.........205C
Burnet Pl.........223C
Burnside Av 215C
Burr Av 212A
Bush St 215C
Bussing Av......204B
Bussing Pl 204B
Butler Pl 217B
Buttrick Av......218D
Byron Av.........204C
Caesar Pl 224B
Calhoun Av......218B
Cambreleng Av
.....................215B
Cambridge Av 208D

Cameron Pl......215C
Camp St 204B
Campbell Dr....212D
Canal Pl..........227C
Canal St W......227C
Cannon Pl.......209C
Carlisle Pl.......210B
Carpenter Av ..204A
Carroll Pl........221C
Carroll St 213B
Carter Av 215D
Carver Loop ...205D
Casals Pl 205D
Casanova St....223C
Casler Pl 219C
Castle Hill Av ..217A
Catalpa Pl.......219C
Cauldwell Av ...221D
Cayuga Av 208B
Cedar Av 214D
Cedar La 226B
Cedar Pl 219C
Center St 219A
Centre St 213B
Chaffee Av 219A
Charlotte St 222B
Chatterton Av 217D
Chesbrough Av .....
.....................211D
Chester St 205C
Chisholm St 222B
Choctaw Pl......211C
Cicero Av 224B
Cincinnatus Av.......
.....................217D
City Island Av..213B
City Island Rd..206D
Claflin Av........209C
Claremont Pkwy....
.....................222A
Clarence Av ...218B
Clay Av 221B
Clason Pt La N & S
Av.....................223B

Clementine St 205A
Clifford Pl 221A
Clinton Av.......215D
Clinton Pl 215C
Close Av 223A
Co-Op City Bd 205D
Coddington Av212D
Colden Av........210B
Coles La 215A
Colgate Av 223A
College Av 221B
College Rd 208B
Collis Pl..........219C
Colonial Av......212A
Columbus Sq ..215B
Commerce Av 217B
Commonwealth Av
.....................217C
Compton Av 224B
Concord Av 227B
Concourse Village
E 221D
Concourse Village
W 227A
Connell Pl 212D
Conner St........205A
Continental Av 212C
Cooper Pl........205D
Corlear Av 208D
Cornell Av.......225C
Cornell Pl 212D
Corp I Fisher Pl .....
.....................221A
Corp W J Fufidio
Sq...................223C
Corsa Av 211A
Coster St........223C
Cottage Pl.......221B
Country Club Rd.....
.....................212D
Courtlandt Av..227A
Crames Sq 215C
Cranford Av 204A
Craven St 228B

Crawford Av....205C	Delafield Av ...202D	Earhart La.......212A	Emerson Av ...218D
Crescent Av ...215B	Delafield La ...208B	Earley St 213B	Emmet St 215B
Creston Av 209D	Delafield Pl....202D	East Av 217C	Erdman Pl.......212A
Crimmins Av...227C	Delancey Pl ...217A	E Bay Av 223D	Ericson Pl......212C
Croes Av 216D	Delanoy Av 211B	E Clark St 221A	Erskine Pl......211B
Croes Pl 223B	Delavall Av....205A	E Fordham Rd 215B	Esplanade.......211C
Cromwell Av...221C	Demeyer St 211B	E Kingsbridge Rd ...	Evelyn Pl........215A
Crosby Av 212C	Depot St 220B	.................215A	Evergreen Av ..223A
Cross Bronx Expwy	DeReimer Av ..204B	E Mosholu Pkwy	Exterior St 214B
...........215D-221A	Devanney Sq ..215C	N & S.........209D	Faile St 223C
Cross St 207C	Devoe Av 216D	E Mt Eden Av ..221A	Fairfax Av 212D
Crotona Av 215B	Devoe Ter 215A	E Tremont Av ..215C	Fairfield Av....208D
Crotona Park E......	Dewey Av........218D	Eastburn Av ...221A	Fairmount Av ..212D
.................222B	Deyo St 211A	Eastchester Pl	Fairmount Pl...216C
Crotona Park N	Dickerson Av ..209A	.................205B	Faraday (Isslin) Av..
.................215D	Digney Av 204B	Eastchester Rd	.................202D
Crotona Park S......	Dill Pl 218B	.................204D	Farragut St 223D
.................221B	Ditmars St 213A	Echo Pl 215C	Father Zeiser Pl .....
Crotona Pkwy 216C	Dock St...........217B	Edenwald Av ..204B	.................215A
Crotona Pl 221B	Dr Martin Luther	Edge St 219A	Featherbed La 221A
Cruger Av 210D	King Jr Bd......221C	Edgehill Av 208D	Fenton Av 211A
Cypress Av 227B	Dodgewood Rd	Edgemere St ...206A	Fern Pl 219C
Cypress Pl 227D	.................208B	Edgewater Rd 223C	Ferris Pl........217B
Cyrus Pl 215B	Dogwood Dr....217A	Edison Av 212C	Field Pl 215A
D'Onofrio Sq ..210B	Donizetti Pl....205C	Edsall Av 214A	Fielding St 211A
Daly Pl...........216D	Doris St 217A	Edson Av 204B	Fieldston Rd...202D
Daisy Pl..........219C	Dorothea Pl ...215A	Edward L Grant	Fieldston Ter ..208B
Daniel St 212C	Dorsey St 217A	Hwy 221A	Fillmore St 216B
Dare Pl 219C	Douglas Av 208C	Edwards Av 218A	Findlay Av......221B
Dark St 205A	Dr Theodore	Effingham Av ..225A	Fink Av 217B
Darrow Pl 205C	Kazimiroff Bd ..210C	Eger Pl 219C	Fish Av 211A
Dash Pl 208B	Drainage St 222B	Einstein Loop ESN..	Fleet Ct 225C
David Sheridan Plz	Drake Pk S 223D	.................205D	Fletcher Pl.....215D
.................203C	Drake St 223C	Elder Av 223A	Flint Av 205B
Davidson Av....215C	Dreiser Loop ..205D	Elgar Pl 211A	Folin St 215C
Davis Av 218D	Dudley Av 212D	Elliot Pl 221A	Food Center Dr ......
Dawson St 222D	Duncan St 210B	Ellis Av..........217C	.................223D
De Witt Pl.......211A	Duncomb Av ...210B	Ellison Av 218A	Foote Av 218D
Dean Av 213C	DuPont St 228B	Ellsworth Av....212D	Ford St...........215C
Debs Pl 205D	Duryea Av 205A	Elm Dr 217A	Fordham Pl.....213B
Decatur Av......209D	Dwight Pl 212D	Elm Pl 219C	Fordham Plz....215A
Defoe Pl 205C	Dyre Av...........205A	Elsmere Pl 216C	Fordham St 213A
Dekalb Av 209B	Eagle Av 221D	Elton Av..........221D	Forest Av 221D
DeKruif Pl.......205D	Eames Pl.........215A	Ely Av 204B	Forester Pl 203C

Ft Independence	Gouverneur Pl
St 209C	....
Fort Schuyler Rd	Grace Av ....
.................218A	Graff Av ....
Fowler Av 216B	Grand Av ....
Fox St 222D	Grand Concour
Fox Pl 228A	& Bd 215C–
Fox Ter 211A	Grandview Pl ...
Franklin Av 221D	Grant Av ....
Freeman St......222B	Greene Pl ....
Frisby Av 217B	Grenada Pl ......
Fteley Av.........216D	Greystone Av....
Fuller St 217A	Grinnell Pl.......
Fulton Av 221D	Griswold Av .....
Furman Av 204A	Grosvenor Av..
Gale Pl 209A	Grote St ....
Garden St.......215D	Guerlain St.......
Garfield St 216B	Guion Pl ....
Garrett Pl 205A	Gunther Av .....
Garrison Av 223C	Haight Av ....
Gates Pl 209B	Hall of Fame Te
Geranium Pl ...219C	....
Gerard Av 221C	Hall Pl ....
Gerber Pl 218B	Halleck St ....
Gertland Pl.....205B	Halperin Av ....
Giegerich Pl....219A	Halsey St ....
Gifford St 218A	Hammersley Av
Gilbert Pl........223C	....
Gildersleeve Av	Hampden Pl .....
.................224D	Harding Av .....
Giles Pl 209C	Harlem River D
Gillespie Av ...212D	....
Givan Av 205C	Harper Av ....
Givan Sq 211A	Harrington Av ..
Gleason Av......217D	Harrison Av .....
Glebe Av 217B	Harrod Av ....
Glennon Pl 219C	Harrod Pl ....
Glover St........217B	Hart St ....
Goble Pl 221A	Haskin St ....
Goodridge Av..208B	Hatting Pl ......
Goodwin Ter ..208D	Havemeyer Av
Goulden Av.....209C	Haviland Av ...
Gouverneur Av	Hawkins St .....
.................209A	Hawkstone St

thorne Dr 217A
thorne St 211A
s Sq 223A
Pl 219C
h Av 209C
ncote Av 205A
essy Pl 214D
y Hudson
....202D-209D
y Hudson
E 208B
wood Pl ..215C
g Av 211A
mer Pl ...203D
nany Av ...217D
chell St...217B
tt Pl 222D
s St 210B
Av 204B
an Av 209A
rt Av 211D
Av 222B
nan St...215B
and Av 210B
rs Av....205A
y Pl 219A
wood Av.212D
Pl 209B
e St 222B
er Av 217D
e Av 210B
eywell Av.216C
aday Pl ...216C
on St 213B
mer Av 218D
re Av....225A
ie St 204B
ell St....217A
son Manor Ter
....208D
h J Grant Cir ....
....217C
hes Av ..215B
uenot Av..205A

Hull Av....209D
Hunt Av....216B
Hunter Av 205C
Huntington Av 218A
Hunts Point Av 223C
Husson Av 225A
Hutchinson Av
....205A
Hutchinson River Pkwy 205B-218D
Hutchinson River Pkwy E 211D
Hutchinson River Pkwy W 205D-212C
Huxley Av 202D
Independence Av ..
....202D-214C
Indian Rd 208B
Indian Ter 219C
Intervale Av 222B
Inwood Av 221A
Irvine St 223C
Irwin Av 208D
Iselin Av 208B
Ittner Pl 215D
Ives St 211D
Ivy Pl 219C
Jackson Av 221D
Jarrett Pl 217A
Jarvis Av....212C
Jasmine Pl 219C
Jay Pl 218D
Jefferson Pl 221B
Jennings St 222B
Jerome Av....
....203D-214C
Jesup Av 221A
Jesup Pl 221A
Johnson Av 208D
Kappock St....208D
Katonah Av 204A
Kearney Av....212D
Kelly St 222D
Kennilworth Pl212D

Kepler Av 204C
Kilroe St 207C
Kimberly Pl....209C
King Av 207C
Kings College Pl...
....209B
Kingsbridge Av ...
....208D
Kingsbridge Ter ...
....209C
Kingsland Av ..205C
Kingsland Pl...215C
Kinsella St 217A
Kirby St 207C
Kirk St 217B
Knapp St....211A
Knolls Cres....214A
Knox Pl 209B
Kossuth Av 209B
L. Keane Sq 212C
Lacombe Av 224B
Laconia Av....204D
Ladd Rd 208A
Lafayette Av....217D
Lafontaine Av 215D
Lake View Pl ..208B
Lakewood Pl ..211D
Lamport Pl 218B
Landing Rd 214B
Lane Av 217B
LaSalle Av 212D
Latkin Sq....222B
Latting St 218A
Laurel Dr....217A
Laurie Av 211D
Lawton Av 218D
Layton Av 212D
Lebanon St....216D
Lee St 212C
Leggett Av 222D
Leland Av 217C
Lester St 210D
Libby Pl 211D
Library Av....212D

Liebig Av....202D
Light St 205A
Lincoln Av 227C
Linden Av 219C
Lisbon Pl 209D
Livingston Av ..208B
Locust Av 227D
Lodovick Av ...211B
Logan Av 218B
Lohengrin Pl....212D
Longfellow Av 222B
Longstreet Av 219A
Longwood Av..222D
Loomis St 211D
Lorillard Pl 215B
Loring Pl NS....215C
Lou Gehrig Plz 221C
Louis Nine Bd 222B
Lowell St....223A
Lowerre Pl 204C
Lucerne St 212D
Lurting Av 211A
Lustre St....205A
Lydig Av 211C
Lyman Pl 222B
Lyon Av 217A
Lyvere St 217A
MacDonough Pl...
....212D
Mace Av 210D
Maclay Av 217A
Macomb's Rd...215C
Macy Pl 222D
Magenta St 210B
Magnolia Pl 219C
Mahan Av 212C
Main St 219A
Maitland Av ...218A
Major Deegan
Expwy..203D-227D
Manhattan College
Pkwy....208B
Manida St....223C
Manning St 217A

Manor Av 223A
Mansion St....216D
Mapes Av 216C
Maple Av 219A
Maran Pl....216B
Marcy Pl....221A
Marine St 213B
Marion Av....209D
Marmion Av ...216C
Marolla Pl....205C
Martha Av 204A
Marvin Pl 217A
Mathewson Rd....
....214D
Matilda Av 204A
Matthews Av ..210B
Mayflower Av 212C
McAlpin Av 211D
McClellan St ...221C
McCracken Av ...
....214D
McDonald St ..211D
McGraw Av 217C
McKinley Sq ...221B
Mclean Av 204A
McOwen Av....205A
Mead St 216B
Meagher Av 219A
Melrose Av....221D
Melville St 216D
Merriam Av 221A
Merrill St 216D
Merritt Av....205A
MerryAv....212D
Metcalf Av 216D
Metropolitan Av ....
....217C
Metropolitan Oval ..
....217A
Meyers St....218A
Mickle Av 205C
Middletown Rd....
....212C
Mildred Pl....211D

Miles Av 218D
Milton Pl 219A
Minerva Pl 209D
Minford Pl 222B
Minnieford Av 213B
Miriam St 209D
Mitchell Pl 219A
Mohegan Av ..216C
Monroe Av 215C
Msgr Cahill Pl 210B
Msgr Halpin Pl ....
....219C
Msgr Scanlon Sq....
....217C
Monterey Av ...215C
Montgomery Av.....
....220B
Montgomery Pl .....
....217A
Monticello Av 204B
Morgan Av 211A
Morris Av 209D
Morris Park Av.....
....211D
Morrison Av ...216D
Morton Pl 215C
Mosholu Av....
....202D-209D
Mosholu Pkwy....
....203D-210C
Mt Hope Pl 215C
Mt Eden Pkwy 221A
Mulford Av 211D
Muliner Av 211C
Mullan Pl 219A
Mulvey Av 205A
Mundy La 204B
Murdock Av 204B
Napier Av 203D
Naples Ter 209C
Narragansett Av .....
....211C
Needham Av ..204D
Neill Av 211C

Nelson Av 221C
Neptune Ct.......225C
Neptune La........225C
Nereid Av 204A
Netherland Av 202D
New England
Thrwy (I-95) 205C
Newbold Av 217C
Newell St 210A
Newman Av 225C
Newport Av 211D
Noble Av 216D
Noell Av 205A
North St 215A
N Chestnut St 210B
N Oak Dr.........210B
N Poplar Av 219A
Norton Av 225A
Nuvern Av 205A
O'Brien Sq 215D
O'Brien Av 225A
O'Dell St 217A
O'Neill Pl.........211A
O'Neill Sq 221D
Oak Av 219A
Oak La.............205B
Oak Point Av ..223B
Oak Ter 227B
Oak Tree Pl.....215D
Oakland Pl 215D
Oakley St 204D
Ogden Av 221C
Ohm Av 212D
Olinville Av 210A
Oliver Pl 209D
Olmstead Av...217D
One Lighting Pl.......
............................229A
Oneida Av........203D
Orloff Av 209C
Osborne Pl 214D
Osgood St 204A
Osman Pl 204B
Otis Av.............218B

Outlook Av 212D
Overing St 217A
Oxford Av 208D
Paine St 218A
Palisade Av 208A
Palisade Pl.......221A
Palmer Av 202D
Park Av .215D-227A
Park Dr 205A
Park Dr 206D
Park La 206A
Parkchester Rd .....
............................217C
Parker St 217A
Parkside Pl......209D
Parkview Av.....212C
Parsifal Pl.......212D
Patterson Av ..224B
Paul Av 209C
Paulis Pl 213A
Paulding Av 204D
Pawnee Pl 211C
Peace St..........205B
Pearsall Av 211A
Peartree Av 205A
Pelham Bay Park
W 205B
Pelham Bridge Rd ..
............................206C
Pelham Parkway
NS 211C
Pell Pl 213B
Penfield St 204A
Pennyfield Av 219A
Perot St 209C
Perry Av 209D
Peters Pl 204C
Phelan Pl 215C
Phillip Av.........218B
Pierce Av........217A
Pilgrim Av 212C
Pilot St 213B
Pinchot Pl.......211D
Pine Dr 217A

Pinkney Av 205A
Pitman Av 204B
Plaza Pl 219C
Plimpton Av ...221A
Ploughman's Bush..
............................208A
Plymouth Av....212C
Poe Pl 215A
Polo Pl 212D
Pond Pl 209D
Pontiac Pl.......227B
Ponton Av 217B
Popham Av......221A
Poplar St 217A
Post Rd 203C
Powell Av 217C
Powers Av 227B
Pratt Av...........205A
Prentiss Av......219A
Prospect Av 215D
Prospect Pl 215D
Provost Av 205A
Pugsley Av 217C
Purdy St 217A
Puritan Av 218A
Putnam Av W..209C
Putnam Pl.......209D
Quarry Rd 215D
Quimby Av 217D
Quincy Av 218B
R. Clemente Plz .....
............................227A
Radcliff Av 210B
Radio Dr 212D
Rae St 227A
Randall Av 218C
Randolph Pl ...212D
Rawlins Av 212D
Reed Pl 212D
Reeds Mill Ln..205C
Regina Pl 205A
Reiss Pl............210D
Research Av ...212D
Reservoir Av....209C

Reservoir Oval EW
............................209B
Reservoir Pl 209B
Rev James A Polite
Av.....................222D
Revere Av........218B
Review Pl 209C
Reville St 213A
Reynold St 213B
Reynolds A......219A
Rhinelander Av ......
............................211D
Richardson Av204A
Rider Av 227C
Ridge Pl 205B
Risse St 209D
Ritter Pl..........222B
River Av...........221C
River Rd 208C
Rivercrest Rd..208A
Riverdale Av....202D
Roberts Av 212C
Robertson Pl ..212D
Robertson St ..204A
Robinson Av....218D
Rochambeau Av .....
............................209B
Rochelle St......213B
Rockwood St ..221A
Rodman Pl 216D
Roebling Av 212C
Rogers Pl 222D
Rohr Pl 218C
Rombouts Av...205A
Roosevelt Av ..218B
Roosevelt La ..206B
Roosevelt Pl....206B
Ropes Av 205A
Rosedale Av....217C
Roselle St 217A
Rosewood St...210B
Rowe St 217B
Ruppert Pl.......221C
Ryawa Av 223D

Ryer Av 215C
Sacket Av.......217A
Sagamore St ..216B
St Ann's Av 221D
St Ann's Pl 227D
St Georges Cres.....
............................209D
St Lawrence Av .....
............................217C
St Mary's St 227B
St Ouen St 204A
St Paul Av........212C
St Paul's Pl 221B
St Peters Av....217A
St Raymond Av ......
............................211D
St Theresa Av 212C
Sampson Av ...218D
Sands Pl 212C
Saxon Av 209A
Scenic Pl 208D
Schieffelin Av 204D
Schieffelin Pl..204D
Schley Av 218D
Scholfield St ...213B
Schorr Pl 211A
Schurz Av 218D
Schuyler Pl......212C
Schuyler Ter ...219D
Scott Pl...........218B
Screvin Av 225A
Seabury Av......217B
Seabury Pl 222B
Secor Av 205A
Seddon St 217A
Sedgwick Av ...209C
Selwyn Av 221A
Seminole Av ...211D
Seminole St 211D
Seneca Av 223C
Senger Pl 218C
Seton Av..........204B
Seward Av 217D
Sexton Pl 205C

Seymour Av ....
Shakespeare A
....
Sheridan Av ....
Sheridan Expw
(895).................
Sherman Av ....
Shore Dr ....
Shore Rd ....
Shrady Pl ....
Siegfried Pl ....
Sigma Pl ....
Silver St ....
Simpson St......
Sommer Pl ......
Sound View Av
....
Sound View Dr
....
Soundview Ter
....
S Oak Dr..........
Southern Bd ...
............................215B-
Spencer Av .....
Spencer Dr .....
Spencer Pl ......
Spencer Ter ....
Spofford Av ....
Stadium Av .....
Starling Av ......
Stearns St ......
Stebbins Av ....
Stedman Pl .....
Steenwick Av...
Stell Pl............
Step St ....
Steuben Av ....
Stevens Av......
Stevenson Pl ..
Stickball Bd ...
Stickney Pl......
Stillwell Av ....
Story Av ....

g Av 204D	
ord Av 216D	
g St.........209C	
ban Pl.....222B	
an Pl 218B	
nit Av 221C	
nit Pl 209C	
et Bd.......225C	
et Ter 219C	
rland St..207C	
ton Av.....218B	
more Av..208A	
more Dr..217A	
n Av 203C	
l 217B	
r Av 216D	
Av 221B	
oeck Av..211A	
y Pl 221A	
ce Pl......205B	
ce St......207C	
iot Av 217C	
gmorton Av.....	
...............218B	
gs Neck Bd.....	
...............218B	
gs Neck	
y 218B	
op Av......211A	
aites Pl ..210D	
tt Av 208D	
ut Av 215A	
ann Av ...205C	
St 213A	
ey Pl 219A	
y St 222D	
n St 210B	
son Av....205C	
Hendrick Pl	
...............209C	
son Pl....228A	
n Av........222D	
inson Av ..211C	
ing Av 215C	

Torry Av 225A	Vincent Av 218B	W Mosholu Pkwy S	Yates Av 211A	E 218-19 St......204D
Townsend Av..221A	Vineyard Pl.....216C	...............................209A	Young Av 211A	E 220-21 St 204C
Trafalgar Pl 216C	Vireo Av 204A	W Mt Eden Av 221A	Yznaga Pl 218D	E 222 St............204D
Tratman Av.....217B	Virgil Av 217D	W Tremont Av 215C	Zerega Av.......217B	E 223-26 St 204C
Trinity Av........221D	Virginia Av 217C	Westchester Av......	Zulette Av 212C	E 227-29 St 204D
Truxton St.......223C	Vreeland Av.....218A	.................212C -227B		E 229 Dr N & S 204D
Tryon Av 209B	Vyes Av.........222B	Westchester Sq......	**NUMBERED**	E 230-36 St 204C
Tudor Pl...........221C	Waldo Av 208B	...............................217B	**AV • PL • ST**	E 233 St............203D
Tulfan Ter 208D	Wales Av 227B	Westervelt Av 211B		E 236-38 St 203D
Turnbull Av......217D	Wallace Av....210B	Whalen St........203C	1-2 Av 219A	E 239-43 St 204A
Turneur Av 225A	Walnut Av 227D	Wheeler Av......223A	3 Av ....215D -227A	
Tyndall Av.......202D	Walton Av 215A	White Plains Rd.....	4-5 Av 219A	W 161-68 St 221C
Undercliff Av ...220B	Ward Av 223A	............210D -224B	7 Av 219A	W 169-76 St 221A
Underhill Av 217C	Waring Av 210D	Whitehall Pl.....204A	9 Av 219A	W 177-83 St 215C
Union Av..........222D	Washington Av......	Whitlock Av.....223A	11 Av 219A	W 184 St............215A
Union Pl 221C	...............................215B	Whittier St 223C		W 188 St............215A
Unionport Rd ...216B	Washington Park	Whittmore Av 218A	E 132 St............227C	W 190 St............215A
University Av ...209C	Av.......................221B	Wickham Av ...204B	E 133 St............227D	W 192 St............215A
University Av ...215A	Waterbury ...Av212D	Wilcox Av.......218B	E 134-38 St 227C	W 193 St............214B
Unknown Soldier	Waterloo Pl 216C	Wilder Av.......204B	E 139 St............227D	W 195 St............215A
Plz 215C	Waters Av 211D	Wilkinson Av ...211D	E 140-48 St 227C	W 197 St............209C
Valentine Av....209D	Waters Pl.....211D	Willett Av 210B	E 149 St............227B	W 205 St............209C
Valhalla Pl 212D	Watson Av 217C	William Av 213A	E 150-51 St 226B	W 227-28 St 208D
Valles Av........203C	Watt Av 212D	William Pl 218A	E 152 St............227A	W 229 St............209C
Van Buren St....216D	Wayne Av 209B	Williamsbridge Rd...	E 153 St............226B	W 230-32 St 208D
Van Cortlandt Av E	Webb Av 209C	...............................210D	E 154-55 St 227A	W 233 St............209C
...............................209D	Webster Av......	Willis Av 227A	E 156 St............221D	W 234-40 St 208D
Van Cortlandt Av W	..............204C -221D	Willow Av 227D	E 157-59 St 221C	W 242 St............208B
...............................209C	Weeks Av 215C	Willow La 212C	E 160-61 St 221D	W 244-45 St 208B
Van Cortlandt Park	Weiher Ct 221D	Wilson Av.......211A	E 162-65 St 221C	W 246-49 St 208A
E..........................203D	Wellman Av ...212C	Windward Ln ..213B	E 166 St............221D	W 250-53 St 208B
Van Cortlandt Park	Wenner Pl 218C	Winters St 213B	E 167 St............221C	W 254-55 St 203C
S..........................209A	West Av 217C	Wissman Av......219A	E 168-71 St 221A	W 256-63 St 202D
Van Cortlandt	W Burnside Av.....	Wood Av 217C	E 172 St............216D	
Village Sq 209C	...............................214D	Wood Rd 217C	E 173 St............216C	**FIND A BASIC**
Van Hoessen Av.....	W Clarke Pl 221A	Woodhull Av ...211B	E 174-75 St 215D	
...............................211C	W Farms Rd....216D	Woodmansten Pl.....	E 177 St 215C, 218B	Simply turn to page
Van Nest Av 216D	W Farms Sq....216D	...............................211C	E 178-83 St 215C	and locate the
Vance St..........211B	W Fordham Rd215A	Woodycrest Av	E 184-89 St 215B	basic in grids
Varian Av 205A	W Gun Hill Rd 209B	...............................221C	E 190-93 St 215A	A,B,C or D.
Verveelen Pl....209C	W Kingsbridge Rd ..	Worthen St.......223C	E 194-96 St 211D	
Victor St.........216B	...............................212D	Wright Av........205C	E 197-207 St 209D	MA = Manhattan
Viele Av 223D	W Mosholu Pkwy	Wyatt St 216D	E 208-13 St 209B	BX = The Bronx
Villa Av 209D	N 209B	Wythe Pl.........221A	E 214-17 St 210B	BK = Brooklyn
				QS = Queens
				SI = Staten Island

QUEENS
Abbot Rd..........307D
Aberdeen Rd ...330D
Abigail Adams Av ..
.....................338D
Abingdon Rd ...336B
Adair St..........345D
Adelaide Rd ...345A
Admiral Av 326D
Aguilar Av......329D
Alameda Av ...324B
Albert Rd 342D
Albert Short Sq316B
Albion Av 319C
Alderton St.....327B
Alexander Gray
Triangle 306B
Allendale St ...337B
Almeda Av 367B
Almont Rd.......369D
Alonzo Rd 361D
Alstyne Av 319D
Alwick Rd 343D
Amber St........342C
Amboy La 340B
Amelia Rd 345C
Amory Ct 326C
Amstel Bd......367A
Anchor Dr.......361C
Anderson Rd ..345D
Andrews Av ...326C
Ankener Av 319C
Annandale La 325A
Annapolis St ..369D
Apex Pl 328A
Arcade Av 339C
Arcadia Wk 362C
Arch St 316B
Archer Av 337C
Archway Pl 328D
Ardsley Rd 315C
Arion Rd 342D
Arleigh Rd 315D
Arlington Ter ..344B
Arnold Av 326C
Arthur St........352D
Arverne Bd.....367B
Ascan Av 336B

Ash Av............321B
Ashby Av 322D
Ashford St 332D
Aske St 319B
Aspen Pl 338B
Asquith Cres ..327D
Astoria Bd 309A
Astoria Park S 302C
Atlantic Av 336D
Atlantic Wk ...362B
Aubrey Av 335B
Auburndale La322D
Audley St 336B
Augusta Ct 344B
Augustina Av ..361D
Austell Pl 316B
Austin St327B-336B
Ava Pl 338B
Avery Av 321A
Avon Rd 330D
Avon St 339A
Aztec Pl 369C
Babbage Av ...336B
Bagley Av 322D
Bailey Ct 361C
Baisley Bd 345C
Baisley Legion Sq ..
.....................344D
.....................369A
Baldwin Av 328A
Barbadoes Dr 367A
Barclay Av 321B
Bardwell Av ...340C
Barnett Av 317C
Barnwell Av ...319C
Barrington St ..339A
Barron St 344D
Barrows Ct 324B
Barton Av 322A
Bascom Av 344D
Bath Wk 362B
Battery Rd 361D
Baxter Av 319A
Bay Ct 361C
Bay Dr 315C
Bay Ter 362B
Bay Park Pl ...361C
Bay 24-25 St ..361C

Bay 27-28 St ..361C
Bay 30-32 St ..368B
Bay 32 Pl.......361C
Bay Park Dr ...304B
Bayfield Av 367B
Bayport Pl 361B
Bayside Av 312D
Bayside Dr .....
.............362B, 363B
Bayside La 313D
Bayside Pl 307D
Bayside Wk ...362B
Bayview Av .....
.............315D, 356B
Bayview Wk....362B
Bayswater Av 361C
Bayshore Rd ..315D
Bayswater Ct 361C
Bayway Wk 362B
Beach Channel Dr ..
.............365A-368A
Beach 3-7 St ..369D
Beach 8-9 St ..369B
Beach 11-12 St ....
.....................361D
Beach 13-17 St....
.....................369C
Beach 18-22 St ....
.....................369A
Beach 24 St ...361C
Beach 25-28 St ....
.....................369C
Beach 29-41 St.....
.....................368D
Beach 41 Pl ...368B
Beach 42-46 St.....
.....................368D
Beach 46 Pl ...368D
Beach 46 Wy .368D
Beach 47 St ...368B
Beach 47 Wy .368D
Beach 48 St ...368A
Beach 48 Wy .368C
Beach 48-52 St ....
.....................368C
Beach 53 St ...368A
Beach 54 St ...368C
Beach 56 Pl ...367D

Beach 56-58 St......
.....................367B
Beach 59-72 St......
.....................367D
Beach 73-77 St......
.....................367C
Beach 79-81 St......
.....................367C
Beach 82-89 St......
.....................367A
Beach 90-93 St......
.....................367C
Beach 96-99 St......
.....................366D
Beach 100-02 St....
.....................366D
Beach 102 La 365D
Beach 104-05 St....
.....................368B
Beach 106 La 365B
Beach 106 St ..365B
Beach 108-17 St....
.....................365B
Beach 118-35 St....
.....................365A
Beach 136-46 St....
.....................364B
Beach 145-49 St....
.....................364C
Beach 169 St ..363B
Beach 180 St ..363B
Beach 193 St ..363A
Beach 201 St ..363A
Beach 204 St ..362B
Beach 207-09 St....
.....................362B
Beach 214-21 St....
.....................362B
Beach 222 St ..362A
Beacon Pl 361C
Beatrice Ct 369A
Beaver Rd 337D
Beck Rd 369B
Bedell St 344B
Bedford Av 362B
Beech Av 321B
Beech Ct 305C
Beechknoll Av 325A

Beechknoll Pl 328D
Belknap St 345D
Bell Bd 314B
Bellaire Pl......340A
Belmont Av 342C
Belt Pkwy ......
.............348A-352A
Benham St 319B
Bennet Ct 345D
Bennet St 346D
Bentley Rd 357A
Benton St 345D
Bergen Rd 349C
Berkley Av 325A
Berrian St 303C
Bessemer Rd ..336D
Bessemund Av .....
.....................368B
Beverly Rd 315D
Billings St 332D
Birdsall Av 361D
Birmington Pkwy ..
.....................323D
Blake Av 342C
Bleecker St ...326C
Blossom Av ...321A
Boardwalk ......
.............365B-368D
Boelsen Cres 327D
Bohack Sq 326C
Bolton Rd 361D
Bonnie La 307C
Boody St 310D
Booth Mem Av .....
.....................321C
Booth St 328A
Borage Pl 328D
Borden Av 316A
Borkel Pl 332D
Borough Pl 309D
Boss St 342D
Boulevard 305D
Bourton St 327B
Bow St 328D
Bowden Av 323A
Bowne St 321B
Boyce Av 323A

Braddock Rd .....
Bradley Av ......
Brant Wk ....
Brattle Av ....
Breezy Point B.....
Brevoort Rd ....
Brian Cres ......
Briar Pl ....
Bridgeton St....
Bridgewater A.....
Brinkerhoff Av .....
Brisbin St ....
Bristol Av ....
Britton Av ....
Broad St ....
Broadway ....
Brocher Rd .....
Brookhaven A.....
Brooklyn Quee.....
Expwy (BQE) ...
Brookside St ...
Brookville Bd ..
Brown's Bd .....
Brown Pl ....
Browvale La ....
Brunswick Av..
Bud Pl ....
Buell St ....
Burchell Av .....
Burchell Rd ....
Burden Cres ...
Burdette Pl .....
Burling St ....
Burns St ....
Burrough Pl ....
Burton St ....
Butler Av ....
Butler St ....
Bye Rd ....
Byrd St ....
Byron St ....
C.R. Sohncke S.....
....
Cabot Rd ....
Caffrey Av.......

us Av ...319C
us Cir ...319C
ell Av ...326B
ray St ...320C
ia Av...324B
idge Rd 339A
en Av ...339C
Rd ...369A
La ...353C
Rd ...353C
hristopher
van Plz..310D
annheimer
...322B
Plz ...349D
Service Rd...
...349D
n Pl ...312D
n St ...327B
a Rd ...324B
ter Av ...339C
n St ...352B
l ...324B
t ...319B
wood St..333B
a Av ...334A
Hill Rd ...369B
La ...315D
croft Rd 338B
awn Av 369B
Rd ...343D
Av ...317C
Cargo Rd ...
...349D
Dr..305D-315D
ville St..342B
al Av...334B
l Av...361D
St ...334A
ler St ...361C
el Rd ...358D
ing Rd 361D
l Rd ...307D
l Wk ...362B
Ct ...338B
Pkwy ...338B
cote Ridge...
...338B

Charlotte St ...326C
Charter Rd 329D
Chelsea St 339A
Cheney St 345D
Cherry Av 321A
Cherry St 324B
Chester Wk 362D
Chevy Chase St ...
...330D
Chicot Ct 342D
Christie Av 319D
Church Rd 358D
Claran Ct 326B
Claremont Ter 319D
Claude Av 344B
Clearview Expwy ...
...314D-331A
Clinton Av 326B
Clinton Pl 337B
Clinton Ter 337B
Clinton Wk 362B
Clintonville St...306C
Clio Av 339B
Clover Pl334C, 319B
Cloverdale Bd 323D
Cloverhill Rd...339D
Clyde St 328C
Codwise Pl 319C
Cody Av 334C
Cohancy St...348B
Colden St 321A
Coldspring Rd 361D
Coleman Sq ...348B
Colfax St 340C
College Pl 305A
College Point Bd ...
...305C-321A
Collier Av 369A
Collins Pl 312D
Colonial Av 320D
Columbus Sq ...309A
Commissary Rd349C
Commonwealth Bd
...325C
Como Av 331C
Compass Rd...349D
Conch Rd 368C
Concord St 325A

Congressman
Rosenthal Av ...312D
Continental Av (71
Av) 328C
Cook Av...........335C
Coolidge Av ...337A
Coombs St ...352B
Cooper Av...........327D
Cooper Ter 334B
Corbett Rd 323A
Cornaga Av ...369C
Cornelia St ...334A
Cornish Av 319C
Corona Av......319D
Corona Plz 320D
Corp Kennedy St ...
...314D
Corp Stone St 323A
Couch Pl........311C
Court Sq 316B
Courtney Av ...322C
Courtney La ...363C
Cove Ct 305A
Covert St.........334A
Cowles St 327C
Craft Av......357C
Crandall Av ...345D
Crane St 316C
Cranford St......328D
Cranston St ...351B
Crescent St ...302C
Cresskill Pl ...337C
Crest Rd 369C
Crocheron Av 322B
Crommelin St...321A
Cromwell Cres327D
Cronston Av ...364B
Cross Bay Bd ...
...348B-366B
Cross Bay Pkwy...
...348B-366B
Cross Island Pkwy..
...306D-347D
Croydon Rd ...338B
Crugers Rd......367A
Cryder's La ...307C
Cullman Av ...325C
Culloden Pl......342A

Curtis St 311C
Curzon Rd......336B
Cuthbert Rd ...336B
Cypress Av ...326C
Cypress Hills St ...
...334D
Dahlia Av 321A
Dalny Rd 339A
Dana Ct 327D
Dane Pl 328C
Daniels St 337A
Darren Dr 307C
Dartmouth St ..328C
Davenport Av 332D
Davenport Ct ..348D
Davies Rd 369A
Davis Ct 316B
Davis St 316B
De Costa Av ...367B
De Sota Av 367C
Deauville Wk ..362B
Decatur St 334A
Deepdale Av ...324B
Deepdale Pl ...325A
Deepdene Pl ...336B
Deerfield Rd...369A
Defoe St 345D
DeKalb Av 326C
Delaware Av ...321B
Delevan St 340D
Delong St 321A
Demerest Rd ...367A
Denis St 345D
Denman St ...319B
Depew Av 324B
Depot Rd......322A
Dermody Sq ...323D
Desarc Rd 342D
Devon Wk 362D
Devonshire Rd338B
Dexter Ct 335C
Diane Pl 307C
Dickens St ...361C
Dieterle Cres ...327D
Digby Pl 342A
Dillon St 344B
Dinsmore Av ...369A
Ditmars Bd......302D

Division St 357C
Dix Av 361D
Doncaster Pl ...336B
Dongan Av 319C
Doran Av...........335B
Dorian Ct 369B
Doris La 363A
Dormans Rd ...345B
Dorothy Pl 309B
Douglas Av......338D
Douglas Rd......315D
Douglaston Pkwy...
...324B
Downing St ...312D
Drew St......342A
Dry Harbor Rd 327B
Dumfries Pl ...330D
Dumont Av 342C
Dunbar St 361C
Dunkirk St 339C
Dunlop Av 339C
Dunton Av......339B
Dunton St 331C
Dutch Kills St..316B
Dwight Av 368B
E Gate Plz 345D
E Hangar Rd ...349C
E Williston Av 333D
E.R. Miller Sq...335C
East Dr 315D
East Loop 307D
East Hampton Bd...
...323D
Eckford Av 342D
Edgar G Holmes
Oval 330B
Edgemere Av ...369A
Edgemere Rd ..368D
Edgerton Bd...339A
Edgerton Rd...330D
Edgewater Rd 361C
Edgewood Av 352D
Edgewood St ...353C
Edmore Av 340B
Edsall Av......335A
Effington Av ...322D
Eggert Pl......361C
Egmont Pl 361C

Elbertson St...319B
Elder Av 321C
Eldert La 335C
Eliot Av 326D
Elizabeth Av ...367B
Elizabeth Rd ...367B
Elk Dr......369A
Elkmont Av ...333A
Elks Rd 319C
Ellwell Cres ...327D
Elm Av 321B
Elmere Stubley Sq ..
...322A
Elmhurst Av ...319B
Elmira Av......339C
Elvira Av 369B
Emerald St 342C
Emily Rd 307C
Empire Av 369B
Enfield Pl 323D
Enright Rd......361C
Epsom Course Rd ..
...331C
Ericsson St ...311C
Essex Wk 362D
Estates Dr......307C
Estates La 307C
Eton St 339A
Eveleth Rd ...345C
Everdell Av ...369A
Everitt Pl......345B
Everton St 327D
Exeter St 328C
Faber Ter......361C
Fairbury Av ...340B
Fairchild Av ...322B
Fairview Av ...326C
Fairway Close 336B
Falcon Av 368B
Far Rockaway Bd ..
...368B
Farmers Bd......
...339D-352C
Farrington St ...312D
Federal Cir ...349C
Fern Pl......339C
Ferndale Av ...344B
Fernside Pl...369A

Finnard Av 367A	Gettysburg St..332D	Haddon St 330D	Hillcrest Av.....324B	Ithaca St........319D	Ketcham Pl...
Firwood Pl 339D	Gillmore St 311C	Hague Pl.....351B	Hillcrest Wk ..362B	Ives Ct 361C	Kew Forest
Fitchett St......327B	Gipson St 361C	Haight St.........321A	Hillmeyer Av..367B	Ivy Cl 328D	La ....
Fleet Ct 327D	Gladwin Av 322D	Hamilton Pl....326B	Hillside Av	Jackie Robinson	Kew Gardens
Fleet St 327D	Glassboro Av .343B	Hampton St 319A	......333D-336D, 363B	Pkwy 335A	....
Flushing Av...326B	Gleane St 319A	Hancock St 334A	Hillyer St 319C	Jackson Av ...316B	Kildare Rd....
Foam Pl 369A	Glenmore Av ..342A	Hand Rd 325A	Himrod St 326C	Jackson Mill Rd......	Kildare Wk ...
Foch Bd 343D	Glenn Av 337B	Hanford St 324B	Hobart St 309D	....................311C	Killarney St..
Fonda Av 339C	Glenwood St ..325A	Hannibal St....339D	Hoffman Dr.....319D	Jacobus St 319C	King Rd ....
Foothill Av.....339B	Goethals Av ..329D	Hantz Rd 368B	Holder Pl........328D	Jaegers Av 342D	Kingsbury Av
Forest Av 326D	Gold Rd 342D	Harbour Ct 361C	Holland Av 367C	Jamaica Av ....,	Kingston Pl...
Forest Park Dr 336B	Gold Starr Sq .309C	Haring St 327B	Hollis Av 339C	.................335C-340A	Kissena Bd...
Forest Pkwy ...335C	Goldington Ct..327D	Harman St 326C	Hollis Ct Bd ...322D	Jamaica Wk ..362B	Kneeland Av..
Forest Rd 315D	Goldsmith St ..319C	Harper St 312C	Hollis Hills Ter 331C	James Ct 344B	Kneeland St ..
Forley St 319D	Goodwood Rd 328D	Harris St 361D	Holly Av..........321D	Janet Av 363A	Knollwood Av
Fowler Av 321A	Gorsline St 319D	Harrow St 328C	Hollywood Av..315D	Janet Pl 321A	Kruger Rd ....
Frame Pl 321A	Gotham Rd 343D	Hart St 326C	Hollywood Av ..321C	Jarvis St 369C	Larue Av ......
Francis Lewis Bd	Gotham Wk 362B	Hartland Av 331D	Home Lawn St 338D	Jasmine Av 321B	Laburnum Av
.................313D-353C	Gothic Dr 337B	Haspel St 319C	Honeywell St ..317A	Java Av 367A	Lafayette St ..
Franklin Av 321A	Gouverneur Av 367B	Hassock St......361D	Hook Creek Bd 353D	Jay Av 326B	Lahn St ....
Frankton St....353D	Grace Ct 337D	Hawthorne Av 321B	Hoover Av.......337A	Jefferson Av ..334A	Lakeview Bd ..
Freedom Dr ...335D	Graham Ct 311B	Hawtree Creek Rd ..	Horace Harding	Jewel St 328D	Lakeview La ..
Freeman St 316A	Graham Pl 363A	.................343B	Expwy 330A-324D	Jordan Av 339D	Lakeview St ..
Fremont St 326D	Granada Pl 361C	Hawtree St......342D	Horatio Pkwy ..323D	Jordan Ct 314B	Lakewood Av
Fresh Meadow La ..	Grand Av 319C	Haywood Rd ...339A	Horton Av 361D	Jordan Dr 307C	Lamont Av ....
.................322C	Grand Central Pkwy	Hazen St.........310A	Hovenden Rd ..339A	Jordan St 313D	Lanark Rd ....
Fresh Pond Rd 326D	....310B-328B-325C	Healy Av 361C	Hoxie Dr 323D	Judge St 319D	Lander St .....
Frisco Av........369B	Grandview Av 326C	Hempstead Av 340D	Hoyt Av NS 309A	Julius Rd 305A	Lanett Av .....
Fuller Pl 321A	Granger St 320C	Henderson Av 339C	Hudson Wk 362B	Junction Bd ...311C	Langdale St ..
Fulton Wk 362B	Grannatt Pl.....351B	Hendrickson Pl 338D	Hull Av............326B	Juniper Av 321D	Langston Av ..
Furmanville Av 327C	Grassmere Ter 369A	Henley Rd 338B	Humphreys St 311C	Juniper Bd N .327A	Lansing Av ...
Galasso Pl 326A	Gravett Rd 329A	Henry Av 319C	Hungry Harbor Rd ..	Juniper Bd S .327C	Larkin Av .....
Gale Av 316B	Gray St 327C	Henry Rd.........369B	......................357B	Juniper Valley Rd ..	Larry Muss
Galway Av 339C	Grayson Av 345D	Henry T Tri 313D	Hunter St 308D	....................327C	Memorial Sq
Garden Ct 369B	Greene Av.......326C	Herrick Av (70 Av) ..	Hunters Point Av	Juno St 328C	Latham La ....
Garfield Av 318D	Greenpoint Av 317A	.................328C	.....................316B	Justice Av 319D	Latimer Pl ....
Garland Dr 323D	Greenway Cir..328D	Hessler Av 367B	Hurley Ct.........369A	Kalmia Av 321D	Laurel Hill Bd
Garrett St 345C	Greenway N, S 328D	Hewlett St 325D	Huron St 342D	Kearney St 311C	Lawrence St..
Gaskell Rd 325A	Greenway Ter 328D	Heyson Rd 369C	Huxley St 353C	Keel Ct 305A	Lax Av ....
Gates Av 326D	Grenfell St 336B	Hiawatha Av ..339D	Ilion Av 339C	Keeseville Av .345B	Layton St .....
Gateway Bd ...369A	Grosvenor La ..336B	Hicks Dr 317B	Indiana Av 334B	Kendrick Pl.....338B	Leavitt St .....
Greenway Ter 328D	Grosvenor St ..315D	Hicksville Rd ..369B	Ingram St 328C	Kenilworth Dr 323D	Lee Rd ....
Gen R W Berry Dr ..	Groton St 328C	Higgins St 312C	Inwood St 344A	Kenmore Rd ...315D	Lee St ....
.................307D	Grove St 326D	Highland Av 337B	Iowa Rd 325A	Keno Av 331C	Leeds Rd......
George St 334A	Gull Ct 367A	Highland Bd ...334D	Ireland St 319C	Kent St 330D	Lefferts Bd ...
Georgia Rd 321B	Guinzberg Rd ..337D	Highland Ct 369C	Irving Av 334C	Kessel St 328C	.................336B
Geranium Av ..321D	Guy Brewer Bd	Highland Pl.....363A	Irving Wk 362B	Ketch Ct 305A	Leggett Pl ....
Gerard Pl 328D	.............337D-352A	Hilburn Av 339C	Irwin Pl 345C	Ketcham St 319A	Leith Pl ....

...d ...325A	Manor Rd ...332D	Mexico St ...345B	Newtown Av ..309A	Overhill Rd ...328D	Point Breeze Pl ...
...Rd ...345D	Manse St ...328C	Meyer Av ...344B	Newtown Rd ..309D	Overlook Rd ...325A	...361C
...ch St ...319A	Manton St ...337A	Michael Ct ...307C	Nicolls Av ...320C	Ovid Pl ...345D	Point Breezy Av ...
...Av ...320C	Manville La ...363A	Michael Pl ...307C	Noel Rd ...358D	P. R. Bayer Sq 313C	...362B
...on Av ...345B	Maple Av ...321A	Middlemay Cir328D	Norden Rd ...336B	Page Pl ...326A	Point Cres ...305D
...ay Rd ...368D	Marathon Pkwy	Middlemay Pl..328D	Normal Rd ...337B	Palermo St ...339B	Polo Pl ...327D
...Av ...337D	...325C	Midland Pkwy 330D	Norman St ...334A	Palmer Dr ...362B	Polhemus Av ..339C
...y La ...362B	Marengo St ...331C	Milburn St ...345D	North Dr ...305D	Palmetto St ...326D	Pompeii Av ...339B
...arclay Sq ...	Margaret Pl ...335B	Miller St ...312D	North Loop ...307B	Palo Alto Av ...339A	Pompeii Rd...340A
...311C	Marine Terminal Rd	Minton St ...361D	N Boundary Rd 351D	Palo Alto St ...339A	Pontiac St ...332D
...us Pl ...312D	...310B	Mobile Rd ...369B	N Conduit Av ...352B	Park Cres ...337B	Poplar Av ...321D
...n St ...343D	Marinette St...315D	Moline St ...332D	N Hangar Rd ..351D	Park Dr E ...329C	Pople Av ...321A
...n Wk ...362B	Marion Wk ...362B	Montauk St ...345B	N Service Ct...349D	Park La S ...335D	Poppenhusen Av ...
...Bd	Market St ...363A	Monterey St...340D	N Service Rd ..349D	Park La 315D, 336B	...304B
...342D-347B	Markwood Pl ..336B	Morenci La ...325A	Northern Bd	Park End Pl...328D	Porter Rd ...351D
...Pl ...312B	Marne Pl ...345A	Morgan St ...325A	...312D-324B	Parsons Bd	Powell's Cove Bd ...
...St ...326C	Mars Pl ...345D	Moss Pl ...361D	Norton Av ...368D	...305B-337B	...305A
...a Av ...322C	Marsden St ...345A	Mott Av ...361C	Norton Dr ...361C	Parvine Av ...367B	Power Rd ...358D
...leck Bd 315C	Marshall Av ...362B	Mott Pl ...369A	Nurge Av ...326C	Pearl Rd ...305A	Poyer St ...319C
...leck Pkwy	Martense Av ...320C	Mt Olivet Cres 326D	O'Connell Ct ...319D	Pearson Pl ...316B	Pratt Av ...307D
...315D	Maryland Rd ..324B	Mulberry Av ...321D	O'Donnell Rd ..344B	Pearson St ...316B	President St ...369A
...ool St ...337D	Maspeth Av ...326B	Murdock Av ...340C	Oak Av ...321D	Peartree Av ...328B	Prince St ...312D
...Rd ...344A	Mathewson Ct345D	Muriel Ct ...343C	Oak Dr ...369B	Peck Av ...321D	Princeton St ...344A
...Av ...306D	Mathias Av ...344B	Murray Av ...307C	Oak La ...315D	Peconic St ...342D	Prospect Ct ...352B
...sland Expwy	Maurice Av ...317D	Murray La ...313C	Oakley Pl ...325A	Pelham Wk ...362B	Purves St ...316B
...316A-347B	Mayda Rd ...353C	Murray St ...306D	Ocean Av ...362B	Pell Av ...320B	Putnam Av ...334A
...st ...345C	Mayfair Rd ...336B	Musket St ...332D	Ocean Crest Bd	Pembroke Av ..325A	Pvt John Dwyer Sq
...a Rd ...369A	Mayfield Rd ...338B	Myrtle Av ...334A	...368B	Penelope Av ...327C	...309C
...307C	Mazeau St ...327A	Nameoke St ...361C	Ocean Promenade	Penrod St ...320C	Queens Bd
...t St ...328C	McBride St ...361C	Nansen St ...328C	...365D	Perry Av ...326B	...317A-312D
...ham Pl ..345B	McKenna Sq ..316B	Nasby Pl ...369A	Ocean Wk ...362B	Pershing Cres 337A	Queens Midtown
...Ct ...337D	McIntosh St ...311C	Nashville Bd ...340D	Oceania St ...323C	Perth Rd ...330C	Expwy ...317D
...St ...345D	McLaughlin Av331C	Nassau Bd ...325A	Oceanside Av 362B	Pettit Pl ...319A	Queens St ...316B
...n Av ...339C	Meehan Av ...369B	Nassau Expwy	Officer's Dr ...307C	Phlox Pl ...321B	Queens Plz NS308D
...Pl ...323C	Melbourne Av 329A	...349B-352C	Olcott St ...328C	Phroane Av ...344B	Queens Wk ...362B
...Rd ...334B	Melissa St ...307C	National St ...319D	Old Rockaway Bd ..	Pidgeon Meadow	Quencer Rd ...345B
...an Av ...327C	Melrose La ...315C	Negundo Av ...321D	...351D	Rd ...322C	Quigley St ...357C
...344A	Melvina Pl ...326A	Neilson St ...361D	Old South Rd .349A	Pilot Rd ...349D	Quince Av ...321D
...St ...332D	Memorial Cir ..365A	Nellis St ...345D	Olive Pl ...328D	Pinegrove St ..344A	Race Track Rd
...tosh St ..318B	Memphis Av ...353C	Neponsit Av ...364D	Olive Wk ...362B	Pineville La....345D	...348B
...ish St ...319C	Menahan St ...328C	Nepton St ...345D	Onderdonk Av 326C	Pinson St ...361D	Radar Rd ...351D
...on St ...326D	Mentone St ...353A	Neptune Wk ...363A	Onslow Pl ...336B	Pinto St ...331C	Radcliff Av ...320C
...olia Pl ...321B	Merrick Bd	Nero Av ...331C	Orchard St ...316B	Pitkin Av ...342C	Radnor Rd ...330D
...St ...312D	...338D-353A	New Haven Av 369A	Ordnance Rd ..307B	Plainview Av ..369A	Radnor St ...339A
...Dr ...305B	Merrill St ...345C	Newburg St ...345B	Ostend St ...369A	Plattwood Av ..342D	Rafferty Sq ...316B
...n Av ...345B	Metcalf Av ...322C	Newhall Av ...353C	Otis Av ...320C	Pleasant View St	Raleigh Av ...342D
...a St ...319C	Metropolitan Av	Newport Av ...364B	Otto Rd ...334B	...327C	Range St ...332D
...Rd ...315D	...326C-336C	Newport Wk ..362B	Overbrook Pl ..324B	Plunkett Av ...361C	Ransom St ...332D

Rau Ct 348D
Reads La 369B
Red Cross La .307D
Redding St 342D
Redfern Av 361D
Redfield St 324B
Reeder St 319C
Reeves Av 329C
Reeves Pl 314B
Regatta Pl 314A
Regina Av 369A
Reid Av 363A
Reinhart Rd 368B
Remington St.337C
Remsen Pl 326B
Rene Ct 326C
Review Av 316D
Rex Pl 339C
Ricard St 326C
Richland Av ..331D
Richmond Rd..315D
Rico Pl 342D
Ridge Rd 315D
Ridgedale St..345D
Riis Av 364D
Ring Pl 345C
Rio Dr 339A
Riverside Dr....306D
Riverton St....345D
Riviera Ct 305A
Robard La 340D
Robert Rd 307D
Robin La 307C
Robinson St..321B
Rockaway Beach
Bd 364D-368B
Rockaway Bd
.....342A-356B
Rockaway Frwy
.....367A
Rockaway Point Bd
.....362B
Rockrose Pl....336B
Rocky Hill Rd..323C
Roe Rd 345C
Roman Av 328C
Rome Dr 345B
Romeo Ct 331C

Roosevelt Av
.....319A-322A
Roosevelt St..369B
Roosevelt Wk 362B
Rose Av 321D
Rose St 369B
Rosita Rd 342D
Roxbury Av....363B
Roxbury Bd....363B
Ruby St 342C
Rufus King Av 337D
Ruscoe St 339C
Rushmore Av..324B
Rushmore Ter 325A
Russel Pl.....328D
Russel St 348D
Rust St 326A
Rutledge Av ..335D
Ryan Ct 313A
Rye Pl 339C
Sabre St 332D
Sagamore Av ..339D
Sagamore Rd..339D
Sage St 361D
St Cloud Rd ..367A
St Felix Av 334A
St James Av...319C
St John's Rd..326C
St Nicholas Av334A
Salerno Av 339B
Sancho St.....331C
Sanders Pl.....337C
Sanford Av 321D
Santiago St ..339A
Saull St 321A
Saultell Av 320D
Saunders St..328A
Sawyer Av 331D
Sayres Av 344D
Schaefer St ..334A
Scheer St 367A
Schorr Dr 305A
Seabreeze Wk362B
Seabury St 319D
Seafoam Ct ..367D
Seagirt Av.....368D
Seagirt Bd 369C
Seaside Av 365B

Seasongood Rd
.....328D
Selfridge St ..328C
Selover Rd 345D
Selover Rd 346C
Seneca Av 326C
Sgt Beers Av..307D
Sgt Beers La ..307A
Seward Av 332D
Shad Creek Rd
.....358D
Shaler Av 334B
Shiloh Av 333A
Shore Av 344B
Shore Bd 302C
Shore Front Pkwy ..
.....365B
Shore Rd 307D
Shore Rd 315D
Shorthill Pl ..336B
Shorthill Rd ..336B
Sidway Pl 345D
Sight Test Rd..351D
Sigourney Av..340B
Silver Rd 342D
Simonson St..319C
Sitka St 342D
Skillman Av ..317C
Sloan St 346D
Slocum Cres ..328D
Slocum Ter 328D
Smart St 321B
Smedley St....337B
Smith Pl 369A
Smith St 345C
Soho Dr 339A
Somerset St ..339A
Sound St 309B
South Dr 305D
South Rd 337D
S Conduit Av..352D
S Cargo Rd...349D
S Service Ct..349D
S Service Rd ..349C
Southgate St..346D
Spa Pl 344B
Spencer Av 331D
Spiller Rd 307D

Springfield Bd
.....323D-352D
Springfield La 352D
Spritz Rd 342D
Spruce St 319B
Stafford Av (69 Av)
.....328C
Standish Pl.....328D
Stanhope St ..326C
Starr Av 316D
Starr St 326C
Station Rd.....322A
Steinway Pl ..303C
Steinway St ..303C
Stephen St ..334A
Stewart Rd....331D
Stier Pl 334A
Stockholm St..326C
Story Av 307D
Story Rd 367D
Stratton St ..312D
Strippoli Sq ..309C
Strong Av 320C
Stronghurst Av 332D
Suffolk Dr 345B
Suffolk Wk 362B
Sullivan Rd ..345B
Summer St ..336B
Summerfield St
.....334A
Summit Ct 321A
Summit Pl.....305B
Sunbury Rd....345C
Sunnyside St..361C
Surf Rd 368D
Surrey Pl 330D
Sutphin Bd
.....337D-351B
Sutro St 331C
Sutter Av342C-351A
Suydam St 326C
Swan Rd 367D
Sybilla St 336A
Sylvester La ..307D
Syringa Pl.....321B
Tahoe St 342D
Talbot St 337A
Tennis Pl 328D

Thebes Av 325A
Thetford La....363A
ThomsonAv ..316B
Thornhill Av ..324D
Thornton Pl...328C
Thursby Av 367B
Thurston St ..352B
Tioga Dr 345B
Tioga Wk 362B
Thomson St ..316B
Tonsor St.....326C
Totten St 307C
Totten Av 307D
Traffic Av 326D
Triboro Plz ..309A
Trimble Rd ..318B
Trist Pl 361C
Troon Rd 330D
Trotting Course La..
.....327D
Troutman St ..326C
Troutville Rd ..345C
Tryon Pl.....330D
Tuckerton St ..337D
Tudor Rd 330D
Turin Dr 345B
Twombly Pl....337D
Tyler Av 317D
Ulmer St 312B
Underhill Av ..322C
Underhill Rd ..307D
Underwood Rd 328D
Union Hall St ..337D
Union St 312D
Union Tpk 329D
Upland Rd.....325A
Upshaw Rd....336B
Ursina Rd 345D
Ursula Wk 336A
Utica Wk 362B
Utopia Pkwy
.....307C-338B
Van Brunt Rd ..367A
Van Cleef St ..320D
Van Dam St ..316B
Van Doren St ..320D
Van Horn St ..319C
Van Kleek St..319C

Van Loon St ..
Van Sicklen S
Van Wyck Exp
(678).....
Van Zandt Av
Vanderveer S
Vaux Rd.....
Vernon Bd .....
Veterans Men
Veterans Sq ..
Victoria Dr ....
Victoria Rd ....
Vietor Av .....
Village Rd .....
Virginia St....
Vleigh Pl .....
Wainwright C
Walden Av .....
Waldron St ....
Walnut St .....
Walter Reed F
Waltham St ..
Walton Rd.....
Wareham Pl...
Warren St .....
Warwick Av ..
Warwick Cres
Water Gate D
Waterloo Pl ..
Waterview St
Watjean Ct ...
Watson St .....
Weaver Av ....
Webe Pl .....
Weeks La .....
Weimar St ....
Weirfield St ..
Weller Av .....
Weller La .....
Welling Ct.....
Wendover Rd.
West Dr.....
West Rd .....
West St.....
W Alley Rd ....
West End Dr ..

...ngar Rd ..349C	**NUMBERED**	16 Av 306D-314B	29 St 302D-316B	41 Dr 317B	54 Dr 317C
...rket St ..362B	**AV • PI • ST**	16 Dr 306D-313A	30 Av 309A-314D	41 Rd 319B, 321A	54 PI 326C
...gate St 352B		16 Rd 305D-314A	30 Dr 309A	41 St 310A-317A	54 Rd 317C
...ourne Av361C	1 St 302C, 348D	17 Av 305D-314B	30 PI 316B	42 Av 319B-324B	54 St 309D-326C
...noreland PI....	1 St...............357C	17 Rd 305D-314A	30 Rd 309A-309D	42 PI 309C	55 Av 316A-326A
...............315C	2 Av 305B-306A	18 Av 305D-314B	30 St 308D	42 Rd 308D-322B	55 Dr 326A
...noreland St	2 Av 302D, 316A	18 St 302C-309A	31 Av 309A	42 St 310A-317A	55 Rd 326B-327A
...............325A	2 St...............357C	19 Av 303C-314B	31 Dr 309A-312D	43 Av 308C-325A	55 St 309D-326B
...side Av....320C	3 Av 305B-306A	19 Dr 310B	31 PI 316B	43 Rd 308C-322B	56 Av 318C-324C
...way Rd 307D	3 St 302C, 357C	19 Rd 310B	31 Rd	43 St 310A-317C	56 Dr 317C-326C
...erole St ..328A	4 Av 305B-306A	19 St 302D	...309A, 312C, 315C	44 Av 308C-325A	56 PI 309D
...ord Ter ...339A	4 Av 362B	20 Av 302D	31 St 302D-316B	44 Dr 308C	56 Rd 317C-326B
...tley St ...361D	4 St 302C	20 Rd 302D	32 Av 310D-313D	44 Rd 308C	56 St 309D-326C
...ler Av 307D	5 Av 305A-306A	20 St 302D	32 Av (Vista Av)	44 St 310A-317C	56 Ter 326A
...hall Ter ..331D	5 Av 362B	21 Av 302D-314C	...............314C	45 Av 308C-322B	57 Av 319D-325C
...law St ...342D	5 St 316A	21 Dr 302D	32 PI 317A	45 Dr 322D	57 Dr 324D-326B
...stone Expwy	6 Av 305A-306B	21 Rd 302D-312B	32 Rd 313D	45 Rd 308C-322D	57 PI 326A
...............305D	6 Rd 306B	21 St 302D-316B	32 St 302D-309C	45 St 310A-317A	57 Rd 321C-326A
...ey Av 319B	7 Av 305A-306A	22 Av 312A	33 Av 309A-314D	46 Av 308C-324A	57 St 309D-326C
...ton St ...336B	7 Av 362B	22 Dr 302D-311A	33 Rd 308D-314A	46 Rd 308C-322D	57 St 334C
...ow PI.....339A	8 Av 304D-306C	22 Rd 302D-312B	33 St 302D-317A	46 St 310A-317C	58 Av 319D-325C
...s Point Bd	8 Av 362B	22 St 308D	34 Av 309A-320B	47 Av 316A-324C	58 Dr 326A
...............320B	8 St 302C-309A	23 Av 302D-314D	34 Rd 312D-314D	47 Rd 316A	58 La 317D
...s St 307D	8 Rd 305D-306D	23 Dr 302D	34 St 309C-317A	47 St 310A-318A	58 PI 317D-326A
...m Ct 369A	9 Av 305D-306D	23 Rd	35 Av 308D-323A	48 Av 316A-324A	58 Rd 321C-326B
...mson Av 345D	9 Av 362B	...309B, 311C, 314B	35 Rd 319A	48 St 310A-326A	58 St 309D-318C
...ghby Av 326C	9 Rd 305C	23 St 302D-316B	35 St 309C	49 Av 316A-324C	59 Av 319D-325C
...v St 324B	9 St 302C-308C	23 Tr 302C	36 Av 308D-321A	49 La 326C	59 Dr 326D
...ester Bd 332D	10 Av 305C-307C	24 Av 302D-314D	36 Rd 321A	49 PI 326A	59 PI 317D-326B
...r St 328D	10 Av 362B	24 Dr 302C	36 St 310A-317A	49 Rd 323D	59 Rd 326B
...off St 340D	10 St 308B	24 Rd	37 Av 308D-312D	49 St 310A-326A	59 St 318Dt-326B
...St 345A	11 Av 305C-307C	...302C, 313C, 314C	37 Dr 320A	50 Av 316A-324C	59 St 334C
...bine St ..326D	11 PI 316A	24 St 302D-308D	37 Rd 318B	50 St 309D-326A	60 Av 319D-325C
...haven Bd	11 St 308BC	25 Av 311C-314C	37 St 310A-317A	51 Av 316A-325A	60 Ct 326D
...............327D	12 Av 305C-306D	25 Dr 313C	38 Av 308C-324A	51 Dr 319C	60 Dr 326D
...haven Ct	12 Av 362B	25 Rd 302C, 312B	38 Dr 324B	51 Rd 317D-319C	60 La 326B
...............342C	12 Rd 305D-314A	25 St 316B	38 St 315D	51 St 309D	60 PI 326D
...hull Av ...339D	12 St 302C-309A	26 Av 302C-314C	38 St 310A-317A	52 Av 317D-325A	60 Rd 325C-327B
...side Av ..318D	13 Av 305C-306D	26 Rd 309A	39 Av 308D-324B	52 Ct 319C	60 St 309D-326D
...ward Av 326C	13 Rd 305D, 313A	26 St 302D	39 Dr 317B	52 Dr 317D-327A	60 St 334A
...PI 339C	13 St 308BD	27 Av 309A-314D	39 PI 317A	52 Rd 317D-325A	61 Av 325C
...off Av 334A	14 Av 304D-306D	27 Rd 309A	39 Rd 315D	52 St 317B-318B	61 Dr 327B
...St 320C	14 PI 302C	27 St 302D-316B	39 St 317A	53 Av 318D-324D	61 Rd 321C-327C
...Rd 344B	14 Rd 304D, 313A	28 Av 309A-314D	40 Av 308D-324B	53 Dr 318D-326B	61 St 309D-326D
...vstone Bd	14 St 302C	28 Rd 312D-315C	40 Dr 319B	53 PI 309D	61 St 334B
...............328B	15 Av 304D-314B	28 St 302D-316B	40 Rd 308D, 319B	53 Rd 325A	62 Av 321C-325C
...t 324B	15 Dr 305D-314B	29 Av 309A-314D	40 St 317A	53 St 326C	62 Dr 320D-327C
...Rd 345D	15 Rd 305D-314B	29 Rd 312D	41 Av 308D-324B	54 Av 316A-324D	62 Rd 317B-328A

62 St 309D-334B	71 Rd 325C-336A	82 Rd 333C-337A	93 Rd.....337C, 340B	107 St 311C-342D	120 Rd 345D-
63 Av 321C-325C	71 St 310C334B	82 St 310D-348A	93 St 319B-328A	108 Av 340D-342A	120 St 304D-
63 Dr 327B-328A	72 Av 325C-328D	83 Av 333C-335B	94 Av 340D-342A	108 Dr 344D	121 Av 344D
63 Pl.........326B	72 Pl 319C-335A	83 Dr 335B, 337A	94 Dr.........340B	108 Pl.........344B	121 St 304D-
63 Rd 321C-326A	72 Cres 329C	83 Pl.........327B	94 Pl.........342D	108 Rd 338D, 339C	122 Av 344D-
63 St 318D-326D	72 Dr 328D-336A	83 Rd.........337A	94 Rd.........340A	108 St 311C-342B	122 Pl..........
64 Av 321C-325C	72 Rd 325C-336A	83 St 310D-348A	94 St 311A-348B	109 Av 340D-342A	122 St 311D-
64 Cir.........330B	72 St 310C-335A	84 Av.........337B	95 Av 341A-342A	109 Dr.........344B	123 Av ....
64 La.........334B	73 Av 325D-335B	84 Dr 333C-338A	95 Pl.........342D	109 Rd....339D, 344A	123 St 305C-
64 Pl.........334B	73 Pl 319C-335A	84 Pl.........327B	95 St 342D-348B	109 St 320A-342B	124 Av 344D-
64 Rd 327B-329A	73 Rd.........331B	84 Rd 333C-338A	96 Av.........341A	110 Av 340D-344B	124 Pl..........
64 St 318B-334B	73 St 310C-335A	84 St 310D-348A	96 Pl.........342D	110 Rd 339D-345A	124 St 305C-
65 Av 328A-324D	73 Ter.........329C	85 Av 333D-335D	96 Rd.........340B	110 St 304D-343B	125 Av 344D-
65 Cres 331A	74 Av 325D-335B	85 Dr.........335C	96 St 311C-348B	111 Av 340D-343C	125 St 305C-
65 Dr 327C-328C	74 Pl.........335C	85 Rd 331C-339B	97 Av 341A-342A	111 Rd 339D-346A	126 Av 345C-
65 La.........326D	74 St 310C-335A	85 St 310D-348A	97 Pl.........319D	111 St 304D-343A	126 Pl 311D,
65 Pl 317D-334B	75 Av 333B-334A	86 Av 333C-335C	97 St 311C-348B	112 Av....340D, 344B	126 St 305C-
65 Rd.........327B	75 Pl.........327C	86 Cres 337B	98 Av.........340B	112 St 304D-343A	127 Av ....
65 St 318B-334B	75 Rd.........329C	86 Dr 335D-336C	98 Pl.........319D	113 Av 340C-344B	127 Pl..........
66 Av 324C-328A	75 St 310C-335A	86 Rd 331C-338B	98 St 311C-350A	113 Dr.........340D	127 St 305C-
66 Dr.........327C	76 Av 332A-335B	86 St 310D-348A	99 Av.........339D	113 Rd.........345B	128 Av 344D-
66 Pl.........334B	76 Dr.........328D	87 Av 333C-335C	99 Pl 342D, 350A	113 St 304D-343A	128 Dr..........
66 Rd.........327C	76 Rd.........328D	87 Dr 333C, 339A	99 St 311C-350A	114 Av.........340D	128 Rd.........
66 St 318C-334B	76 St 310C-342A	87 Rd 333C-338B	100 Av 339D-340B	114 Dr 345B-347B	128 St 305C-
67 Av 324D-334A	77 Av 325D-335A	87 St 310D-348A	100 Dr.........340D	114 Pl....343D-350A	129 Av 344C-
67 Dr.........327C	77 Cres 333A	87 Ter.........333D	100 Pl.........341C	114 Rd....344B, 347B	129 Rd 347D-
67 Pl.........334B	77 Pl.........327A	88 Av 333C-335C	100 St 311C-350A	114 St 304D-350A	129 St 305C-
67 Rd.........327C	77 Rd.........336B	88 Dr.........333C	101 Av 340D-342A	114 Ter.........347B	130 Av 344C-
67 St 318B-334B	77 St 310D-348A	88 La.........335B	101 Rd.........342B	115 Av 343D-347A	130 Dr..........
68 Av 324D-334A	78 Av 329C-334A	88 Pl.........335B	101 St 311C-350A	115 Dr 344B, 346B	130 Pl 344C-
68 Dr.........328B	78 Cres 336B	88 Rd 333C, 335C	102 Av 340D-342A	115 Rd 344B-347C	130 Rd 345D-
68 Pl.........334B	78 Dr.........329C	88 St 310D-348A	102 Rd 342A-343B	115 St 304D-350A	130 St 305C-
68 Rd 327C-334A	78 Rd 329C-335A	89 Av 335D-341A	102 St 311C-350A	116 Av 343D-347A	131 Av 343D-
68 St 309D-334B	78 St 310D-348A	89 Rd 337C, 340A	103 Av 340D-342A	116 Dr.........344D	131 Rd..........
69 Av 335A-325C	79 Av 333B-334A	89 St 310D-348A	103 Dr.........342B	116 Rd 344D-347A	131 St 305C-
69 Dr.........335A	79 La.........335A	90 Av 335C-341A	103 Rd.........339C	116 St 304D-350A	132 Av 351A-
69 La.........326B	79 Pl.........335A	90 Ct.........340A	103 St 311C-350A	117 Rd 343D-347A	132 Rd 345D-
69 Pl 318D-334B	79 St 310D-348A	90 Pl.........310D	104 Av 339C-340D	117 St 340D-349A	132 St 305C-
69 Rd 328D-336A	80 Av 333B-334A	90 Rd.........335C	104 Rd.........338D	118 Av 344D-347A	133 Av 342C-
69 St 310C-334B	80 Dr.........330D	90 St 310D-348A	104 St 311C-342D	118 Rd 344D-346B	133 Dr..........
70 Av 324D-334A	80 Rd 330D-336B	91 Av 335C-341A	105 Av 340D-343B	118 St 304D-350A	133 Pl..........
70 Dr.........336A	80 St 310D-348A	91 Pl.........319D	105 Pl.........342B	119 Av 344D-347A	133 Rd 345D-
70 Rd 328D-336A	81 Av 333B-335B	91 Rd 332D-340B	105 St 311C-342D	119 Dr.........344D	133 St 312C,
70 St 310C-334B	81 Rd.........335B	91 St 310D-348B	106 Av 340D-342A	119 Rd 344D-346B	134 Av 342D-
71 Av 325C-334A	81 St 310D-348A	92 Av 332D-335D	106 Rd.........339C	119 St.........304B	134 Pl..........
71 Cres 330B	82 Av 333C-335B	92 Rd 332D-340B	106 St 311C-342D	120 Av 343D-347A	134 Rd 342D-
71 Dr.........336A	82 Dr.........333C	92 St 310D-348B	107 Av 340D-342A		134 St 321C-
71 Pl.........335A	82 Pl.........327B	93 Av 335D-340B	107 Rd.........343B		135 Av 343C-

Street	Grid
r	342D
l	343D
d	342D-353B
t	305C-351A
v	351B-353B
d	345B-353B
t	305C-337C
v	351B-353A
l	321D
d	346D-353D
t	305C-329C
t	352B-353C
l	305D
d	346D
t	305C-351A
v	352B
d	352B
t	305D-337C
v	351B
t	305C-351A
v	352B
	329C
d	352B
t	305D-344A
v	351B
d	352B
t	305D-344A
v	352B
	305D
d	352A
t	305D-351A
v	351B
r	351B
l	337C
d	351B
t	305D-351A
v	351D
r	351D
l	305D-312D
d	351D
t	305D-351A
v	352C
	351D
r	351D
l	305D-321C
d	351D
t	312D-351A
er	352C

Street	Grid
147 Av	352C
147 Dr	353C-357B
147 Pl	305B-338C
147 Rd	353C
147 St	305B-351A
148 Av	351D-357B
148 Dr	357AB
148 Pl	321C
148 Rd	351D-357B
148 St	305B-351C
149 Av	342C-357B
149 Dr	357A
149 Pl	305B, 313C
149 Rd	352C, 357B
149 St	305B-357B
150 Av	349D-352C
150 Dr	352C
150 Pl	306B
150 Rd	342D
150 St	305B-351C
151 Av	342C
151 Dr	352C
151 Pl	306C, 351B
151 St	306B
152 Av	349A-350B
152 St	306D-344D
153 Av	342C-348A
153 Ct	351B
153 La	351B
153 Pl	351A
153 St	306D-351B
153 Wy	351B
154 Pl	306B, 321D
154 St	306D-351B
155 Av	342C
155 St	306D-351B
156 Av	348A
156 Pl	337D
156 St	306D-351B
157 Av	348A
157 St	306D-351B
158 Av	348A
158 St	306D-351B
159 Av	348A
159 Rd	348B
159 St	306D-352A
160 Av	348A
160 St	307C-352A

Street	Grid
161 Av	348C
161 Pl	345C
161 St	306D-352A
162 Av	348C
162 St	307C-337B
163 Av	348C
163 Dr	348D
163 Pl	322C
163 St	307C-338D
164 Av	348C
164 Dr	348D
164 Pl	329D
164 Rd	348D
164 St	307C-345C
165 Av	348C
165 Pl	338D
165 St	307C-346C
166 Pl	346C-352A
166 St	307C-352A
167 St	313D-352A
168 Pl	338D
168 St	313D-352A
169 St	313D-352A
170 Pl	322D
170 St	313D-352A
171 Pl	322D-345A
171 St	313D-352A
172 St	313D-352A
173 St	330A-352A
174 Pl	345C
174 St	330B-352A
175 Pl	322D
175 St	330D-352C
176 Pl	345C
176 St	330B-352B
177 Pl	345D-352A
177 St	330C-352C
178 Pl	339C-352A
178 St	330D-346C
179 Pl	339C
179 St	330D-352A
180 Pl	339C
180 St	330D-352B
181 Pl	339C-352B
181 St	330D-352C
182 Pl	339A
182 St	330D-352D
183 Pl	339C

Street	Grid
183 St	330B-352D
184 Pl	339C
184 St	322D-352D
185 St	322D-352B
186 La	330B
186 St	322D-339C
187 Pl	339A
187 St	322D-339C
188 St	322D-339C
189 St	322D-346B
190 La	330B
190 Pl	339D
190 St	314D-346B
191 St	322B-346B
192 St	322B-346B
193 La	331A
193 St	322B-346D
194 La	331A
194 St	322D-346B
195 La	331A
195 Pl	339B
195 St	322D-346B
196 Pl	322D
196 St	322D-346B
197 St	322D-346B
198 St	322D-346B
199 St	323D-346B
200 St	307C-346B
201 Pl	346B
201 St	307C-346B
202 St	307C-347A
203 Pl	314D
203 St	314C-347A
204 St	314C-347A
205 Pl	340C
205 St	314D-347A
206 St	314D-323C
207 St	314D-347A
208 Pl	314B
208 St	314B-347A
209 Pl	314D-340C
209 St	314A-347A
210 Pl	314D-340A
210 St	314D-340D
211 Pl	340A
211 St	314D-340D
212 Pl	331D-340D
212 St	314B-340D

Street	Grid
213 St	314D-340D
214 La	323A
214 Pl	314D, 340B
214 St	314D-340D
215 St	315C-340B
215 St	307D-340D
216 St	307D-340D
217 La	340D
217 Pl	340D
217 St	307D-352B
218 Pl	331D-340B
218 St	315C-352D
219 St	323B-352B
220 Pl	323B-353A
220 St	323B-352D
221 Pl	332D
221 St	331D-352D
222 St	323B-352D
223 Pl	332A
223 Rd	323B-332A
223 St	323B-352D
224 St	323D-352D
225 St	323D-352D
226 St	323D-352D
227 St	341C-352D
228 St	323D-352D
229 St	323D-352D
230 Pl	352D
230 St	323D-352D
231 St	323D-352D
232 St	323D-352D
233 Pl	324B
233 St	324B-353C
234 Pl	353A
234 St	324B-353A
235 Ct	332D
235 St	324B-353B
236 St	332D-357A
237 St	332D-353B
238 St	332D-347D
239 St	332D-341A
240 Pl	324D
240 St	324B-353C
241 St	324B-357A
242 St	324B-357A
243 St	324B-357A
244 St	324B-353B
245 La	325C

Street	Grid
245 Pl	325C
245 St	324B-353C
246 Cres	325C
246 Pl	325C
246 St	325C-353C
247 St	324B-353C
248 St	324B-353C
249 St	324B-357A
250 St	324B-353C
251 St	325A
251 Pl	325A
252 St	325A
253 Pl	353C
253 St	325A-341B
254 St	315C-357A
255 St	315A-357A
256 St	325A-357A
257 St	333B-357B
258 St	333B-357B
259 St	333B-357B
260 Pl	325C
260 St	325A-333B
261 St	325C-333B
262 Pl	357B
262 St	325A-333B
263 St	325A-333B
264-65 St	333B
266-67 St	325C-333B
268-69 St	333B
270-71 St	325D
E 1 Rd	358B
E 3-5 Rd	358B
E 6-10 Rd	358B
E 12 Rd	358D
E 14 Rd	358D
E 16 Rd	358D
E 18 Rd	358D
E 20 Rd	358D
E 21 Rd	366B
W 5 Rd	358D
W 8-20 Rd	358D
W 22 Rd	358D

BROOKLYN	Aster Ct............438C	Battery Av 426D	Bedford Pl 416A	Bragg St 437D	Bristol St........
Abbey Ct.....445B	Atkins Av 419A	Baughman Pl..429D	Beekman Pl 416C	Branton St 424C	Broadway.......
Aberdeen St....412D	Atlantic Av	Bay Av..........429C	Belmont Av 419A	Brevoort Pl.....416A	Brookdale Plz
Abraham Miller Sq	........407C-418B	Bay St 414D	Belt Pkwy	Brevoort Pl......416A	Brooklyn Av ..
.........424A	Atlantic Av 442C	Bay Pkwy 428D	.........425C-446A	Bridge St 407A	Brooklyn Rd ..
Adams St 407C	Atwater Ct 443A	Bay 7-8 St.....435A	Belvidere St ...405C	Bridge Plz Ct ..407A	Brooklyn-Que◄
Adelphi St....407D	Auburn Pl 407D	Bay 10-11 St..435A	Bennett Ct 426B	Bridgewater St........	Expwy (BQE)..
Adler Pl........413D	Aurelia Ct 429A	Bay 13-14 St..435A	Benson Av 435A	.........403C	.........402D-
Agate Ct 416B	Autumn Av 413D	Bay 16-17 St..435A	Bergen Av 430B	Brigham St 437D	Broome St ....
Ainslie St 404B	Av A-B..........424A	Bay 19-20 St..435C	Bergen Ct 430B	Brighton Ct....443B	Brown St ......
Aitken Pl.....407C	Av C 422D	Bay 22-23 St..435D	Bergen Pl 420C	Brighton 1 Pl ..443D	Bryant St ......
Alabama Av ..418B	Av D 424A	Bay 25-26 St..435D	Bergen St 407C	Brighton 1 Rd..443D	Buckingham Rd
Albany Av	Av F 428B	Bay 28-29 St..435D	Berkeley Pl.....415A	Brighton 1 St ..443D	Buffalo Av......
.....416B-429B	Av H 428B	Bay 31-32 St..435D	Berriman St ...419A	Brighton 1 Wk 443B	Bulwer Pl ......
Albee Sq........407C	Av I 428D	Bay 34-35 St..435D	Berry St 402D	Brighton 2 St ..443B	Burnett St .....
Albee Sq W ...407C	Av J-M 424D	Bay 37-38 St..435D	Bethel Loop ...425A	Brighton 2 Wk 443B	Bush St ....
Albemarle Rd..421D	Av N 424D-436B	Bay 40 St 435D	Beverley Rd ...422C	Brighton 3 Rd..443B	Bushwick Av .
Albemarle Ter 422D	Av O 430C-436B	Bay 41 St.......436C	Bevy Ct 438C	Brighton 3 St ..443D	Bushwick Pl ..
Alben Mem Sq421C	Av P 429D	Bay 43 St.......436C	Bijou Av 438C	Brighton 3 Wk 443B	Butler Pl ....
Alice Ct.........416B	Av R 429D	Bay 44 St 443A	Billings Pl 436B	Brighton 4 Rd..443D	Butler St ....
Allen Av 437D	Av S 430C-436B	Bay 46-47 St..443A	Bills Pl.........421D	Brighton 4 St ..443B	Cadman Plz E◄
Alton Pl.......429D	Av T-W ..430D-436D	Bay 49-50 St..443A	Blake Av 417D	Brighton 4 Ter 443B	....
Amber St 419B	Av X-Y 431C	Bay 52-54 St..442B	Blake Ct 443B	Brighton 4 Wk 443B	Calder Pl ......
Amboy St 417D	Av Z 443A	Bay 56 St.......443C	Blake Sq........417D	Brighton 5 St ..443D	Calhoun St ....
Amersfort Pl..429A	Aviation Rd......447A	Bay Cliff Ter ..426A	Bleecker St ...405C	Brighton 5 Wk 443B	California Pl ...
Ames La 424A	Bainbridge St..417D	Bay Ridge Av ..426B	Bliss Ter 426A	Brighton 6 St ..443D	Calyer St ....
Amherst St....444D	Balfour Pl 416D	Bay Ridge Pkwy.....	Boardwalk 443C	Brighton 7 St ..443B	Cambridge Pl.
Amity St 407C	Baltic St 406D	.........426B	Boardwalk E ..443D	Brighton 7 Wk 443B	Cameron Ct ...
Anchorage Pl..407A	Bancroft Pl....417B	Bay Ridge Pl ..426B	Boardwalk W ..443C	Brighton 8 St ..443B	Campus Pl ....
Anna Ct........424B	Bank St 424B	Bayard St 402D	Bocchino D Mem	Brighton 10 Ct 443B	Campus Rd....
Anthony St 403C	Banker St 402D	Bayview Av 442D	Plz 427A	Brighton 10 La 443B	Canal Av ....
Apollo St......403C	Banner Av 443B	Bayview Pl 424C	Boerum Pl.....407C	Brighton 10 Path	Canarsie Rd ..
Applegate Ct ..436B	Barberry Ct....413C	Beach Wk 443D	Boerum St 405C	.........443B	Canton Ct .....
Archie C Ketchum	Barbey St 413C	Beach 37 St ...442B	Bogart St 405C	Brighton 10 St 444B	Carlton Av ....
Sq 436B	Barlow Dr NS 439A	Beach 38 St ...442B	Bokee Ct........443B	Brighton 10 Ter........	Carroll St ......
Ardsley Loop ..425A	Barnwell Ct 434A	Beach 40 St ...442C	Bond St 407C	.........443B	Cary Ct ....
Argyle Rd 422C	Bartel Pritchard Sq	Beach 42-51 St 442C	Border Av 425C	Brighton 11 St 443B	Cass Pl ....
Arion Pl......405C	.........415C	Beacon Ct 445B	Borinquen Pl ..404B	Brighton 12-14 St....	Catharine St...
Arkansas Dr....438B	Bartlett Pl 445B	Beadel St 403C	Bouck Ct 443A	.........444B	Cathedral Pl...
Arlington Av ..413C	Bartlett St......404D	Beard St 414A	Boulevard St ..436D	Brighton 15 St 443D	Caton Av ....
Arlington Pl ..416B	Baruch Pl 407D	Beaumont St ..444D	Bowery St......443C	Brighton Beach Av	Caton Pl ....
Ascenzi Sq.....404B	Bassett Av 439A	Beaver St 405C	Bowne St 414A	.........443D	Cedar St ....
Ash St 402B	Bassett Wk 438B	Bedell La........424C	Box St 402B	Brightwater Av........	Cedar St ....
Ashford St ...418B	Batchelder St 437B	Bedford Av	Boynton Pl 443A	.........444D	Celeste Ct......
Ashland Pl 407D	Bath Av 435A	.........404A-437C	Bradford St ...418B	Brightwater Ct 443D	

r Dr	415D
al Av	405C
e St	414B
nel Av	438C
el St	407A
es Pl	405C
es W Boyce	430D
e Ct	424C
ncey St	412C
ver Pl	406D
y St	403C
er Av	421D
er Ct	422B
ter St	417D
nut Av	429C
nut St	413C
topher Av	418C
h Av	422C
ch La	424C
St	421D
ndon Rd	423D
St	407A
son Av	422B
on Av	404C
r Pl	410D
St	402B
St	407D
ont Av	407D
land St	419A
rd Pl	402D
n Pl	410D
n Av	407C
on St	407C
Rd	416D
St	404C
k Ct	443C
y St	414A
y Ct	443A
man St	429D
idge St	444D
s St	414B
Pl	436D
ge Pl	407A
nial Ct	426A

Colonial Gardens	426C
Colonial Rd	426C
Columbia Hts	407A
Columbia Pl	406D
Columbia St	406D
Columbus Pl	417A
Commerce St	414A
Commercial St	402B
Concord St	407A
Coney Island Av	422C-444A
Congress St	406D
Conklin Av	424D
Conover St	414A
Conselyea St	404B
Conway St	418A
Cook St	405C
Cooke Ct	412C
Cooper St	412D
Corbin Pl	444D
Cornelia St	412A
Corporal Witshire Sq	437A
Cortelyou Rd	422C
Court St	407C
Coventry Rd	424C
Covert St	412C
Cox Pl	413D
Coyle St	437B
Cozine Av	425A
Cranberry St	407A
Crawford Av	437C
Creamer St	414A
Crescent St	413D
Crooke Av	422B
Cropsey Av	435D
Crosby Av	412D
Croton Loop	425A
Crown St	416D
Crystal St	419A
Cumberland St	407D
Cunningham Sq	422C

Cypress Av	405B
Cypress Av	442C
Cypress Ct	413D
Cyrus Av	445C
Dahill Rd	421D
Dahl Ct	428C
Dahlgren Pl	434B
Dakota Pl	439A
Dale Pl	425A
Danforth St	413D
Dank Ct	443A
Dare Ct	445B
De Koven Ct	428B
De Witt Av	424B
Dean St	407C
Debevoise Av	403C
Debevoise St	405C
Decatur Av	445C
Decatur St	411D
Degraw St	406D
DeKalb Av	405D
Delamere Pl	429C
Delavan St	414A
Delmar Loop	425A
Delmonico Pl	404D
Dennet Pl	414B
Denton St	415A
DeSales Pl	412D
Desmond Ct	437C
Devoe St	404B
Devon Av	438C
Dewey Pl	417B
Diamond St	402B
Dickinson St	405A
Dictum Ct	438C
Dikeman St	414A
Dinsmore Pl	413D
Ditmars St	411B
Ditmas Av	422D
Division Av	404C
Division Pl	403C
Dobbin St	402D
Dock St	407A
Dodworth St	411B
Dooley St	444B

Dorchester Rd	422D
Dorman Sq	429C
Dorset St	424C
Doscher St	419A
Doughty St	407A
Douglass Ct	407C
Douglass St	407C
Dover St	444C
Downing St	410D
Drew St	419B
Driggs Av	402D
Duffield St	407B
Dumont Av	417C
Dunham Pl	404A
Dunne Ct	444A
Dunne Pl	445A
Dupont St	402B
Durland Pl	424C
Duryea Ct	427D
Duryea Pl	422D
Dwight St	414A
Dyker Pl	426D
Eagle St	402B
E New York Av	416D
East Dr	415D
East Lake Dr	422B
Eastern Pkwy	416D
Eaton Ct	445B
Ebony Ct	438C
Eckford St	402D
Eldert La	413D
Eldert St	412D
Elizabeth Pl	407A
Ellery St	404D
Elm Av	429C
Elm Pl	407C
Elmer E Bennett Jr Mem Sq	413C
Elmira Loop	425A
Elm Pl	407C
Elmwood Av	428D
Elton St	419C
Emerald St	419B
Emerson Pl	410B
Emmanuel Av	445B

Emmons Av	444B
Empire Bd	416C
Engert Av	402D
Erasmus St	422D
Erskine St	425B
Esplanade	444D
Essex St	413C
Estate Rd	436B
Etna St	413C
Euclid Av	413D
Evans St	407B
Everett Av	438C
Everett St	407A
Evergreen Av	411B
Exeter St	444D
Fair Pl	407C
Fairview Pl	423A
Falmouth St	444D
Fanchon Pl	418A
Fane Ct	437D
Farragut Pl	423C
Farragut Rd	423C
Father Kehoe Sq	429C
Fayette St	405C
Fenimore St	416D
Ferris St	414A
Ferry Pl	406D
Fillmore Av	430D
Fillmore Pl	404A
Fiske Pl	415D
Flatbush Av	407A-438B
Flatbush Av Ext	409A
Flatlands 1-2 St	424B
Flatlands 3-10 St	425C
Flatlands Av	424D
Fleet Al	407A
Fleet St	407C
Florence Av	438D
Florida Pl	439A
Flushing Av	

	404C-407B
Folsom Pl	419A
Forbell St	419B
Force Tube Av	413C
Ford St	417C
Ford St	437B
Forest Pl	426D
Forrest St	405C
Fort Greene Pl	407D
Ft Hamilton Pkwy	421D
Fort Hill Pl	434B
Foster Av	423C
Fountain Av	419A
Fox Sq	407C
Frank Ct	445B
Franklin Av	410D
Franklin St	402B
Fraser Sq	429C
Freeman St	402A
Freeport Loop	425A
Friel Pl	422C
Front St	407A
Frost St	403C
Fuller Pl	422C
Fulton Mall	407C
Fulton St	410D-418A
Furman Av	412C
Furman St	407A
Gain Ct	445B
Gallatin Pl	407C
Garden Pl	406D
Garden St	405C
Gardner Av	403C
Garfield Pl	415A
Garibaldi Sq	436C
Garland Ct	437D
Garnet St	414A
Gates Av	411C
Gatling Pl	426D
Gaylord Dr NS	439A
Gelston Av	426D
Gem St	402D
Geneva Loop	425A

George St 405C	Gunther Pl 418A	Henry Peter Sq	Hunterfly Pl ...417A	Joval Ct...........438C	Lamont Ct ....
Georgia Av 418B	Hale Av 413C	.................426B	Huntington St..414B	Judge St........405A	Lancaster Av ..
Gerald Ct 444A	Hall St 410A	Henry St 406D	Hunts La 407C	Juliana Pl......404C	Landis Ct......
Gerald H Chambers	Halleck St 414C	Herbert St....402D	Huron St 402B	Junius St........418C	Langham St ...
Sq 444D	Halsey St 411C	Herkimer Ct ..416B	Hutchinson Ct 436D	Just Ct..........445B	Laurel Av ......
Gerritsen Av...437B	Hamilton Av ..406D	Herkimer Pl ..416B	Hyman Ct 445B	Kane Pl 417A	Lawn Ct........
Gerry St 404D	Hamilton Pl...414D	Herkimer St ..416B	Imlay St........414A	Kane St 406D	Lawrence Av ..
Gilmore Ct 444A	Hamilton Wk ..426C	Herzl St........417D	Independence Av ..	Kansas Pl......439A	Lawrence St...
Girard St 444D	Hampshire Pl..439A	Hewes St 404D	................435C	Karweg Pl......413D	Lawton St ......
Glen St 413D	Hampton Av ..444B	Heyward St ...404D	India St 402B	Kathleen Pl....444A	Lee Av..........
Glendale Ct ...430A	Hampton Pl ..416B	Hicks St........408C	Indiana Pl......439A	Kaufman Pl....424D	Lefferts Av ....
Glenmore Av ..418B	Hancock St....411C	High St 407A	Ingraham St....405C	Kay Ct 445A	Lefferts Pl.....
Glenwood Rd ..424C	Hanover Pl 407C	Highland Av ..442C	Ira Ct...........438C	Keap St 404D	Legion Sq .....
Gold St 407A	Hanson Pl.....407D	Highland Bd ..413C	Irving Av 405D	Keen Ct 445B	Legion St ......
Goodwin Pl....411D	Harbor Ct 434A	Highland Pl...413C	Irving Pl 410D	Keily Pl 413D	Leif Ericsson S
Gotham Av 438D	Harbor La 426A	Highland View Av ..	Irving St........406D	Kenilworth Pl..429A	
Gowanus Expwy	Harbor View Ter...	.................443C	Irvington Pl...428B	Kenmore Pl ...422B	Lenox Rd.......
.................414B	................426A	Highlawn Av ..436C	Irwin St.........445C	Kenmore Ter ..422B	Leonard St ....
Grace Ct 406D	Harden St 429D	Hill St 419A	Ivan Ct..........445B	Kensington St 445C	Lester Ct.......
Grace Ct Al...407C	Haring St 437B	Hillel Pl 429A	Ivy Hill Rd 403C	Kensington Wk....	Lewis Av ....
Grafton Av 417D	Harkness Av ..445A	Himrod St.....405D	Jackie Robinson	.................443C	Lewis Pl ....
Graham Av (Av of	Harman St 405D	Hinckley Pl ..422C	Pkwy............412D	Kent Av..402C-410C	Lexington Av ..
Puerto Rico)...404B	Harrison Al....407B	Hinsdale St...418B	Jackson Ct ...434A	Kent St 402B	Liberty Av .....
Grand St 410B	Harrison Av ...404D	Hitchings Av ..445A	Jackson Pl.....415C	Kermit Pl.......422C	Lincoln Av .....
Grand St 402C	Harrison Pl....405C	Holly St 419C	Jackson St.....403C	Kimball St......429D	Lincoln Pl .....
Grand Army Plz	Hart Pl.........443A	Holmes La 424D	Jaffray St......445C	King St 414A	Lincoln Rd.....
.................415B	Hart St 405D	Homecrest Av 437C	Jamaica Av 413C	Hwy	Lincoln Ter .....
Granite St 412D	Harway Av 442B	Homecrest Ct..436D	Jardine Pl......418A	.......417D-436A	Linden Bd ......
Grant Av 413D	Harwood Pl ...423D	Hooper St......404D	Java St 402B	Kings Pl........436D	.............423A-
Grant Sq 416A	Hastings St...444D	Hope St........404D	Jay St 407C	Kingsland Av ..403C	Linden St ......
Granville Payne Av	Hattie Jones Ct	Hopkins St 404D	Jefferson Av ..411C	Kingston Av ...416B	Linwood St.....
.................418D	................417A	Hopkinson Av..412C	Jefferson St...405C	Knapp St........437D	Little Nassau St
Grattan St....405C	Hausman St ...403C	Horace Ct 422A	Jerome Av 444B	Knickerbocker Av ..	
Gravesend Neck	Havemeyer St 404D	Hornell Loop...425C	Jerome St......418B	.................405D	Little St ....
Rd 436D	Havens Pl......418A	Howard Al 407A	Jewel St........402B	Knight Ct.......445A	Livingston St ..
Greene Av........	Hawthorne St 423A	Howard Av 411D	Jewell McKoy La ..	Kosciuszko St 411B	Livonia Av......
....405D-410D	Hazel Ct.......438C	Howard Pl 422A	.................417A	Kossuth Pl 411B	LLoyd Ct ....
Green St 402B	Heath Pl 412D	Hoyt La 424D	Jewell Sq......418A	Krier Pl 424C	Lloyd St ....
Greenpoint Av 402B	Hefferman Sq..421C	Hoyt St 407C	Jodie Ct 423D	Lacon Ct 445A	Locust Av ......
Greenwood Av 421B	Hegeman Av ..419C	Hubbard Pl ...429D	John St 407A	Lady Moody Sq..436D	Locust St.......
Grove Pl 407C	Hemlock St....413D	Hubbard St....444A	Johnson Av ...405C	Lafayette Av	Logan St ....
Grove St 411B	Henderson Wk443C	Hudson Av...407BD	Johnson Pl.....422B	.......407D-411D	Lois Av ....
Guernsey St...402D	Hendrickson Pl438B	Hull St...........418A	Johnson St.....407A	Lafayette Wk ..426C	Lombardy St....
Guider Av 443B	Hendrickson St 429D	Humboldt St...402D	Jones Wk 443C	Lake Pl 436C	Lorimer St......
Gunnison Pl ...445A	Hendrix St 418B	Hunter Av 442B	Joralemon St..407C	Lake St 436D	Loring Av ....

ne St 414B	Marion St 412C	Miller Av......418B	New Lots Av ..418D	Opal Ct 445B	Peter Trust Sq ......
e Ter 445A	Marine Av 434A	Miller PI......412D	New Utrecht Av	Orange St......407A	......430C
Av 418C	Marlborough St 422B	Milton St......402B	......427D	Orient Av 405A	Pierrepont PI ..406B
I 429D	Marshall St ...407A	Minna St......421D	New York Av	Oriental Bd......444D	Pierrepont St ..407A
t 422B	Martense Ct...422B	Moffat St 412D	......416D-429B	Osborn St 418C	Pilling St 412D
PI 417B	Martense St...422B	Monaco PI 418A	Newel St......402D	Otsego St 414C	Pine St 413D
a St......421D	Martin Luther King	Monastery Sq 426C	Newkirk Av ...423C	Overbaugh PI..429D	Pineapple St ..407A
e Ter......426A	Jr PI......404D	Monitor St ...402B	Newport St......417D	Ovington Av ...426B	Pineapple Wk 407A
ana Av ..424B	Maspeth Av ...403C	Monroe PI 407A	Newton St 402D	Ovington Ct ...427D	Pioneer St 414A
La 407A	Matthews Ct ..422C	Monroe St 411C	Nichols Av ...413D	Owls Head Ct..426A	Pitkin Av......417D
m PI 416C	Matthews PI ..431A	Montague St ..407A	Nixon Ct 443B	Oxford St......445C	Plaza St EW ...415B
er St 414B	Maujer St ...404B	Montague Ter 406B	Noble St 402B	Pacific St 407C	Pleasant PI......418A
Av 442C	Mayfair Dr NS 439A	Montana PI 439A	Noel Av......445B	Paerdegat Av N	Plumb 1 2 St...437D
n St 404D	McClancy PI ..418D	Montauk Av ...419A	Nolans La 424A	......430A	Plumb 3 St......445A
Donough St......	McDonald Av..421B	Montauk Ct ...444A	Noll St......405C	Paerdegat Av S	Plumb Beach Av 445B
......411D	McDonald Sq..426D	Montgomery PI	Norfolk St 445C	......430B	Plymouth St ...407A
Dougal St 417B	McGuiness Bd......	......415D	Norman Av ...402D	Paerdegat 1 St430B	Poe PI......404D
ay PI 426A	......402B	Montgomery St	N Conduit Av ..419B	Paerdegat 2-11 St ..	Polhemus PI...415D
Kenzie St 445C	McGuiness Bd S ...	......416C	N Elliot PI 407B	......430B	Poly PI......434B
n St 411C	......402B	Montieth St ...405C	N Henry St ...402B	Paerdegat 12-15 St	Poole La......444B
eline Ct ..426B	McKeever PI ..416C	Montrose Av ..404D	N Oxford St ...407B	......431A	Poplar Av 442C
son PI......437B	McKibben St ..405C	Moore PI......437A	N Portland Av 407B	Paidge Av ...402B	Poplar St......407A
son St......411C	McKinley Av ..413D	Moore St......405C	Norwood Av ...413C	Palm Ct......416D	Portal St......417C
c Av 445B	Meadow St ...405A	Morgan Av ...403C	Nostrand Av	Palmetto St ...412A	Porter Av 403C
St......407A	Meeker Av ...403C	Morton St 404C	......410D-437D	Parade PI 422B	Post Ct......445B
one St ..416D	Melba Ct......445B	Mother Gaston Bd..	Nova Ct......445B	Park Av......404C	Powell St......418C
olm X Bd 411D	Melrose St ...405C	......418A	O'Brien PI......413D	Park Cir......422A	Powers St......404B
a St 424B	Memorial Sq ...405A	Moultrie St......402B	Oak St 402C	Park PI......415A	Prescott PI......417B
attan Av 402B	Menahan St....411B	Mt Carmel Sq..402D	Oakland PI ...422D	Park St......405C	President St......406B
attan Av 442C	Merit Ct......445B	Murdock Ct ...443B	Ocean Av	Parkside Av ...422A	Preston Ct......424C
attan Ct..443B	Mermaid Av ...442D	Myrtle Av......	......422D-444D	Parkside Ct...422B	Prince St......407A
r Ct 444A	Meserole Av ...402D	......405D-411B	Ocean Ct......443B	Parkville Av ...428B	Prospect Av ...422A
sfield PI...429C	Meserole St...404D	Narrows Av ...426A	Ocean Pkwy	Parkway Ct...443B	Prospect Expwy ......
e Av 442C	Metropolitan Av......	Nassau Av ...402D	......422C-444C	Parrott PI 426D	......415C
e St......416D	......402C	Nassau St 407A	Oceanic Av......442C	Patchen Av ...411D	Prospect Park SW.
oro Sq ..436B	Meucci Sq 436C	National Dr......438B	Oceanview Av 442C	Pearl St......407A	......422A
oni PI ..418A	Miami Ct 416D	Nautilus Av ...442C	Oceanview Av 443B	Pearson St ...430D	Prospect Park W ...
us Garvey Bd	Micieli PI 421D	Navy St......407B	Ohio Wk 430D	Pembroke St ..445C	......415D
......411C	Middagh St ...407A	Nelson St 414B	Old Fulton St ..407A	Penn St......404D	Prospect PI ...415A
y Av 404D	Middleton St ..404D	Neptune Av ...442D	Old Mill Rd ...419C	Pennsylvania Av	Prospect St ...407A
inal St ..420B	Midwood St...416D	Nevada PI......439A	Old New Utrecht	......418D	Provost St......402B
inal St EW	Milford St 419A	Nevins St 407C	Rd 428A	Percival St ...414D	Pulaski St 411C
......418B	Mill Av......430D	New Dock St ..407A	Olean St 429C	Peri La......430D	Putnam Av ...411C
ne Av 434A	Mill La......430D	New Jersey Av	Olive St 405A	Perry PI......416B	Quay St......402C
ne Pkwy ..437B	Mill St......414B	......418D	Oliver St 426C	Perry Ter......426A	Quentin Rd ...429D

Street	Grid	Street	Grid	Street	Grid
Quentin St	445C	Royce Pl	430B	Sea Pl	442D
Quincy St	411C	Royce St	430B	Seabreeze Av	443D
Rabbi J Teitelbaum Pl	404C	Ruby St	419B	Seabreeze Wk	443D
Radde Pl	418A	Rugby Rd	422D	Seabring St	414A
Raleigh Pl	423C	Russell St	402B	Seacoast Ter	444D
Ralph Av	411D-430B	Rutherford Pl	435A	Seaview Av	425A
Randolph St	405B	Rutland Rd	416D	Seaview Ct	431A
Rapelye St	414B	Rutledge St	404D	Seaview Loop	425B
Red Cross Pl	408B	Ryder Av	436B	Seawall Av	445C
Red Hook La	407C	Ryder Sq	430A	Seba Av	445B
Reed St	414A	Ryder St	429D	Sedgwick Pl	420C
Reeve Pl	422A	Ryerson St	410A	Sedgwick St	406D
Regent Pl	422D	Sackett St	406D	Seeley St	421D
Remsen Av	417C	Sackman St	418A	Seigel St	405C
Remsen St	407A	St Anton Rd	445A	Senator St	426B
Revere Pl	416B	St Andrews Rd	416B	Seton Pl	428B
Rewe St	403C	St Charles Pl	416A	Sgt Joyce Kilmer Sq	437A
Richards St	414A	St Edwards St	407B	Sharon St	405A
Richardson St	403C	St Felix St	407D	Sheepshead Bay Rd	437C
Richmond St	413C	St Francis Pl	416A	Sheffield Av	418B
Ridge Bd	426C	St James Pl	410D	Shell Bank Av	445A
Ridge Ct	426C	St Johns Pl	415A	Shell Rd	443C
Ridgecrest Ter	426A	St Jude Pl	431A	Shepherd Av	413C
Ridgewood Av	413D	St Marks Av	415B	Sheridan Av	419D
Ridgewood Pl	412A	St Marks Pl	415A	Sherlock Pl	418A
Riegelmann Boardwalk	442D	St Paul's Ct	422B	Sherman St	422A
River St	402C	St Paul's Pl	422B	Shore Bd	444B
Riverdale Av	417D	St Nicholas Av	405D	Shore Ct	426C
Robert Pl	413C	Sandford St	410D	Shore Pkwy (Belt Pkwy)	435C-444B
Robert St	413C	Sands St	407B	Shore Pkwy (Leif Ericsson Dr)	426A
Rochester Av	417C	Saratoga Av	412C	Shore Rd	420C-442B
Rock St	405C	Schaefer St	412D	Sidney Pl	407C
Rockaway Av	417B	Schenck Av	418B	Sigourney St	414C
Rockaway Pkwy	417D-432A	Schenck St	431B	Skidmore Av	431A
Rockwell Pl	407D	Schenectady Av	423B	Skidmore La	424C
Roder Av	428D	Schermerhorn St	407C	Skidmore Pl	431A
Rodney St	404B	Scholes St	404D	Skillman Av	403C-410B
Roebling St	402B	School La	424C	Skillman St	410B
Rogers Av	416C	Schroeders Av	425A	Sloan Pl	436D
Roosevelt Pl	417B	Schweickerts Wk	443C	Slocum Pl	422C
Ross St	404C	Scott Av	403C-405B		
Rost Pl	424D	Sea Gate Av	442C		

Street	Grid	Street	Grid	Street	Grid
Smith St	407C	Sullivan St	414A	Turner Pl	
Smiths La	424C	Summit Pl	406D	Twin Pines Dr	
Snediker Av	418D	Sumner Pl	405C	Underhill Av	
Snyder Av	423A	Sumpter St	417B	Union Av	
Somers St	418A	Sunnyside Av	413C	Union St	406D-
S Conduit Av	419B	Sunnyside Ct	413C	University Plz	
S Elliott Pl	407D	Sunset Ct	442C	Utah Wk	
S Oxford St	407D	Surf Av	442C	Utica Av	
S Portland Av	409D	Sutter Av	417D	Van Brunt St	
S Lake Dr	422B	Sutton St	403C	Van Buren St	
South Shore Plz	430B	Suydam Pl	417A	Van Dam St	
Southgate Ct	436D	Suydam St	405D	Van Dyke St	
Spencer Ct	410D	T Raymond Nutley Sq	402D	Van Sicklen St	
Spencer Pl	416A	Taaffe Pl	410B	Van Siclen Av	
Spencer St	404D	Tabor Ct	427A	Van Sinderen A	
Stagg St	404C	Tampa Ct	416D	Vandalia Av	
Stanhope St	405D	Tapscott St	417D	Vanderbilt Av	
Stanley Av	419D	Taylor St	404C	Vanderbilt St	
Stanton Rd	445A	Tech Pl	407A	Vanderveer Pl	
Stanwix St	405C	Tehama St	421D	Vanderveer St	
Starr St	405D	Temple Ct	422A	Vandervoort Pl	
State St	407C	Temple Sq	407D	Vandervoort Av	
Stephens Ct	422D	Ten Eyck St	404B	Varet St	
Sterling Pl	415A	Tennis Ct	422D	Varick Av	
Sterling St	416D	Terrace Pl	421B	Varick St	
Steuben St	410B	Thames St	405C	Varkens Hook ▸	
Stewart Av	403C	Thatford Av	417D	Verandah Pl	
Stewart St	418A	Thomas St	403C	Vermont Av	
Stillwell Av	436C	Thornton St	404D	Vermont Ct	
Stillwells Pl	424D	Throop Av	404D	Vermont Pl	
Stockholm St	405D	Tiemans La	424D	Vermont St	
Stockton St	411A	Tiffany Pl	406D	Vernon Av	
Stoddard Pl	416C	Tilden Av	422D	Verona Pl	
Stone Av	412D	Tillary St	407A	Verona St	
Story St	421D	Times Plz	407D	Veronica Pl	
Stratford Rd	422C	Tompkins Av	411C	Veterans Av	
Strauss St	417D	Tompkins Pl	407C	Victor Rd	
Strickland Av	430D	Townsend St	403C	Village Ct	
Strong Pl	406D	Troutman St	405D	Village Rd E, N,	
Stryker Ct	436D	Troy Av	423B		
Stryker St	436D	Troy Pl	430A		
Stuart St	437B	Trucklemans La	424D		
Stuyvesant Av	411D	Truxton St	418A		
Sullivan Pl	416D	Turnbull Av	424B	Vine St	

ia Pl 416B	Westminster Rd .....
tion Pl ...414A	............422C
Pl 426B	Westshore Av 442B
ies Av 444B	Wharton Pl....413D
man Pl...420C	Whipple St 404D
orf Ct 428B	White St 405C
r St 425A	Whitman Dr ...438B
bout St ...404D	Whitney Av ...438C
ston Ct ..427D	Whitney Pl ...436D
h Ct 428B	Whitty La 423D
on St 404D	Whitwell Pl....415A
vorth St...404D	Will Pl 424B
en Pl 406D	William Ct 444B
en St 406D	Williams Av ..418B
off Pl 404D	Williams Pl ..418A
vick St ...418B	Williamsburgh Pl ..
nington Av	............404C
............410C	Williamsburgh St
nington Park	E & W 404C
............407D	Willmohr St ..424A
nington Plz	Willoughby Av 405D
............404A	Willoughby St 407C
nington St407A	Willow Pl 406D
r St 407A	Willow St 407A
rbury St .405A	Wilson Av 405D
ins St 418C	Wilson St 404C
erly Av 407B	Windsor Pl ...415C
ster Av ...428B	Winthrop St ..417C
ster Pl 415C	Withers St 403C
field St ...412C	Wogan Ter ...434B
lon St......413D	Wolcott St 414A
ngton Ct..428B	Wolf Pl 436D
s St 419A	Wood Pl 422B
t Av 443B	Woodbine St .412A
t Dr 415D	Woodhull St ..414B
t St 402A	Woodpoint Rd 405A
ighton Av443D	Woodruff Av ..422B
Coffey Sq 426D	Woodside Av ..436B
Hennesy Sq	Wortman Av ..425A
............443D	Wyckoff Av 405D
t Lake Dr..422A	Wyckoff St 407C
odney St .404C	Wyona St 418B
sbury Ct..422B	Wythe Av 402C
t End Av ..444B	Wythe Pl 404C
erly La ...426A	York St..........407A

NUMBERED AV • Pl • ST

1 Av 420C	18 St 414D	80 St 426D-436A	E 76 St.............430B
1 Ct 436B	19 Av 428B	81 St 426D-436C	E 76-85 St 424C
1 Pl 414B	19 La 435C	82-86 St ..426C-436C	E 86-89 St 424A
1 St 414B	19 St 414D	87-96 St 426C	E 91-96 St 424A
2 Av 420D	20 Av 428B	97-101St 434A	E 98-103 St 424D
2 Pl 414B	20 Dr 435C	157 Av 419D	E 100 St 424D
2 St 414B	20 La 435C		E 100-01 St 424B
3 Av 415A-426D	20 St 414D	E 1 St 436D	E 104 St 424D
3 Pl 414B	21 Av 428D	E 2-4 St 421D	E 105 Wk 424B
3 St 414B	21 Dr 435C	E 5 St 422C	E 105-08 St 424B
4 Av 415C-426D	21 La 435C	E 7-8 St 422A	
4 Pl 414B	21 St 414D	E 9-10 St 422C	N 1 St 402C
4 St 414B	22 St 414D	E 12-15 St 428D	N 3-9 St 402C
5 Av 415C-426D	23 Av 435D	E 16-17 St 422B	N 10-15 St 402D
5 St 414B	23 St 414D	E 18-19 St 422D	
6 Av 415C-426D	24 Av 435D	E 21-24 St 429A	S 1-6 St 404A
6 St 415C	24 St 421A	E 25 St 422D	S 8 St 404A
7 Av 415C-426D	25 Av 435D	E 26-29 St 423C	S 9-11 St 404C
7 St 415C	25 St 421A	E 31 St 423A	
8 Av 415C-427A	26 Av 436C	E 32 St 423A	W 1 St 436B
8 St 415C	26 St 421A	E 33 St 437B	W 2 Pl 443D
9 Av 421C-427A	27 Av 443A	E 34-35 St 423A	W 2-4 St 436B
9 St 414B	27 St 421A	E 35 St 423A	W 5-7 St 436D
10 Av 421C	28 Av 443A	E 36 St 429B	W 8 St 436C
10 St 415C	28-33 St 421A	E 37-40 St 423A	W 8 St 414B
11 Av 421C-434B	34 St 420B	E 41 St 430C	W 9 St 436C
11 St 415C	35-36 St 421A	E 42 St 423A	W 10-13 St 436C
12 Av 421D-435A	37 St 420B	E 43 St 423B	W 15-17 St 443A
12 St 415C	38-39 St 421A	E 45-46 St 417C	W 19 St 443A
13 Av 427D	40 St 420B	E 48 St 423B	W 20-22 St 442B
13 St 415C	41-42 St 421A	E 49 St 417C	W 23-25 St 442D
14 Av 427B	43-45 St 420B	E 51-52 St 423B	W 27-33 St 442D
14 St 415C	46 St 420D	E 53 Pl 438B	W 35-37 St 442D
15 Av 427B	47 56 St 420D	E 53-56 St 423B	
15 St 415C	57 Dr 438B	E 57 Pl 438B	
16 Av 427B	57-64 St 420D	E 57 St 423D	
16 St 415C	65 St 420C-436A	E 58 St 423B	
17 Av 427B	66 St 426B	E 59 Pl 438B	
17 Ct 435C	67-68 St ..420C-436A	E 59 St 423B	
17 St 414D	69 St 436A	E 60 Pl 430D	
18 Av 428B	70-71 St ..426A-436A	E 60-61 St 430D	
	72 St 426A	E 63-71 St 430D	
	72-78 St ..426A-436A	E 72-73 St 430B	
	79 St 426D-436A	E 74 St 430D	

FIND A BASIC

Simply turn to page
and locate the
street in grids
A,B,C or D.

Long avenues,
roads and streets
are indicated by a
range: 426A-436A

STATEN ISLAND
A-B Row 502D
Abbey Rd 521D
Abbott Pl..........513B
Abby Pl 506D
Abingdon Av ...521D
Abingdon Ct 521D
Acacia Av.........529D
Academy Av ...536A
Academy Pl 507A
Ackerman St ...530C
Acorn St 523C
Ada Dr 509A
Ada Pl 512B
Adam Ct 515D
Adams Av.........517D
Addison Av.......533B
Adelaide Av 523C
Adele Ct 513A
Adelphi Av 532D
Adlai Cir 529C
Adlers La 536D
Admiralty Loop 533C
Adrianne Pl 503C
Adrienne Pl 529B
Advance Pl.......517A
Agda Av 523D
Agda St............524C
Agnes Pl 519C
Ainsworth Av...530B
Akron St 509D
Alabama Pl.......511A
Alan Loop 512D
Alaska Pl 521A
Alaska St 505D
Alban St 506D
Albany Av 502D
Albee Av...........528D
Albert Ct 503C
Albert St 511B
Alberta Av 514C
Albion Pl 505C
Albourne Av 533A
Albourne Av E 533B

Albourne Ct 533A
Albright St 518B
Alcott St 527A
Alden Pl 506B
Alderwood Pl..518B
Alexander Av ..521C
Alexandra Ct ..521C
Alexandra Pl ..511C
Algonkin St......534A
Alice St 532B
Allegro St 534B
Allen Ct 505D
Allen Pl 534B
Allendale Rd ...519A
Allentown La ...532A
Allison Av 523B
Allison Ct 524A
Almond St........527B
Alpine Av 512B
Alpine Ct 511A
Altamont St 517C
Alter Av 518B
Altoona Av 523A
Alverson Av 527C
Alverson Loop 527C
Alvine Av 528D
Alysia Ct 533A
Amador St 509A
Amanda Ct.......520D
Amaron La 536D
Amber St 523A
Amboy Rd ....
.................523C-536B
Amelia Ct 506B
Amherst St 523D
Amity Pl..........503C
Amity St 513C
Amsterdam Av509C
Amsterdam Pl 515A
Amy Ct............515C
Amy La 515B
Anaconda St ...527D
Anderson Av ...505C
Anderson Pl 503C

Anderson St....513A
Andes Pl 511C
Andrea Pl 503C
Andrease St.....513A
Andrews Av 523A
Andrews St 519A
Andros Av 503A
Androvette Av 533B
Androvette St..526C
Anita St............509B
Ann St 505A
Annadale Rd ...521C
Annfield Ct 518B
Anthony St 527C
Appleby Av.......519A
Arbutus Av 534A
Arbutus Way ...534A
Arc Pl 523A
Arcadia Pl 505D
Archwood Av...528D
Arden Av 527B
Ardmore Av 510D
Ardsley St........522B
Area Pl 511C
Argonne Av 519A
Arielle La 521B
Arkansas Av 521D
Arlene Ct 509A
Arlene St..........509C
Arlington Av 503A
Arlington Ct 503A
Arlington Pl 502B
Arlo Rd 512B
Armand St 509B
Armour Pl........533D
Armstrong Av 521D
Arnold St 507A
Arnprior St 503D
Arrowood Ct ...527A
Arthur Av 519A
Arthur Ct..........505D
Arthur Kill Rd ....
................520D-537A
Arthur Pl 529C

Ascot Av...........523A
Ash Pl 510D
Ashland Av.......533A
Ashland Av E ..533B
Ashley La 526D
Ashton Dr 527B
Ashwood Ct 522D
Ashworth Av ...515A
Asp Pl 536D
Aspen Knolls Way ..
..........................520D
Aspinwall St 536C
Astor Av 509A
Atkins St 533D
Atlantic Av 518B
Atmore Pl 523C
Auburn Av 509D
Augusta Av 529A
Aultman Av 523A
Ausable Av 506D
Austin Av 519B
Austin Pl 507C
Av B 505A
Averill Pl 532C
Aviston Av 523D
Avon Green 527C
Avon La............510B
Avon Pl 507C
Aye Ct 509A
Aymar Av 511D
Azalea Ct 527A
Bach St 530B
Bache Av 523B
Bache St 505C
Baden Pl..........524B
Bailey Pl 502B
Baker Pl 506D
Baldwin Av......530B
Balfour St 519A
Ballard Av 527D
Balsam Pl........527A
Baltic Av 512D
Baltic St 507D

Baltimore St....529B
Bamberger La 529C
Bancroft Av 517D
Bang Ter 513D
Bangor St 515D
Bank Pl 518B
Bank St 507A
Barb St 529C
Barbara St 523A
Barclay Av 534B
Barclay Cir 528B
Bard Av 506B
Bard Pl 512A
Baring Pl..........512B
Barker St 505D
Barlow Av 521C
Barnard Av 532C
Baron Bd 514B
Barrett La 505B
Barrett Av 505C
Barrow Pl 527A
Barry St 527A
Bartlett Av 521C
Barton Av 517D
Bartow Av 536B
Bartow St 530B
Bascom Pl 509D
Bass St 510D
Bates St 514B
Bath Av 518B
Bathgate St 534B
Baxter St 532B
Bay St 507B
Bay Ter 530B
Bayard St 529C
Baylor St..........532D
Bayne Av 532B
Bayonne Bridge Plz
..........................503D
Bayview Av 533C
Bayview Pl 507C
Bayview Ter 534B
Beach Av 523B
Beach La 530C

Beach Rd ....
Beach St..................
Beachview Av ....
Beacon Av ....
Beacon Pl................
Bear St ....
Beard St ....
Beaver St ....
Beckman St ....
Bedell Av ....
Bedell St..................
Bedford Av ....
Bee Ct ....
Beebe St...................
Beecher Pl ....
Beechwood Av ....
Beechwood Pl..........
Beekman Cir ....
Beekman St ....
Beethoven St ....
Behan Ct...................
Belair Rd...................
Belden St ....
Belfast Av ....
Belfield Av ....
Belknap St ....
Bell St ....
Belle Dr....................
Bellhaven Pl.............
Belmar Dr E ....
Belmar Dr W ....
Belmont Pl ....
Bement Av ....
Bement Ct ....
Benedict Av ....
Benedict Rd ....
Benjamin Dr ....
Benjamin Pl ....
Bennet Pl ....
Bennett Av ....
Bennett St ....
Bennington St..........
Benson St.................
Bent St ....

ey St......536A	Blue Heron Dr 529C	Bridgetown St 515D	Butler Pl 513A	Carnegie Av ...509C	Champlain Av..523C
n Av 518B	Blythe Pl 522D	Brielle Av 517A	Butler St 532D	Caro St 510D	Chandler Av ...511A
n Ct 523C	Boardwalk Av 534B	Brighton Av 506D	Butler Ter 507C	Carol Ct 533C	Channel View Ct ....
ger Av 507A	Bodine St 505D	Brighton St.......536C	Butterworth Av	Carol Pl 503C	......523A
sford Av ..514C	Bogert Av 517A	Bristol Av 511D	......511D	Carolina Ct 517A	Chapin Av 518A
und Av ..509C	Bogota St 515D	Britton Av 512D	Buttonwood Rd	Carolina Pl 511A	Chappell St.....505D
ey St......529C	Bolivar St 511C	Britton St 505D	......517B	Caroline St 505D	Charles Av 503B
uda Pl ..518D	Bombay St 527C	Broad St 507D	Byrd Pl 530C	Carpenter Av ..515B	Charles Ct......517C
e Pl 527C	Bond St 505C	Broadway......505D	Byrne Av.........510D	Carreau Av 515A	Charles Pl......503C
Av 521C	Boone St 510D	Bromley Av 532B	C-D Row 502D	Carroll Pl......507A	Charleston Av 526D
Ct 527A	Booth Av 529C	Brook Av 523D	Cable Wy 503C	Carteret St 536C	Charter Oak Rd.......
a Pl 512B	Borman Av 515B	Brook St 507A	Cabot Pl 513D	Cartledge Av ..514D	......517D
am Av ..534A	Borough Pl......507B	Brookfield Av..521D	Cady Av 532B	Cary Av 505D	Chatham St 520D
ick Pl ..512A	Boscombe Av 532B	Brooks Pl 505C	Calcutta St 532D	Cascade St......517D	Chelsea Rd 508D
in La 505D	Bosworth St...505D	Brooks Pond Pl	Caldera Pl......506D	Case Av 533C	Chelsea St 536C
Pl 529B	Botany Pl 532D	......505D	Call St 523A	Cassidy Pl......506B	Chemical La 526B
l Av 532C	Boulder St 527D	Brookside Av..511A	Callan Av 518A	Castleton Av ..503B	Cherokee St...525A
rly Av ..512A	Boundary Av ..524A	Brown Av 529B	Calvin Pl 507C	Castleton Ct ..507C	Cherry Pl......517A
rly Rd	Bovanizer St...529C	Brown Pl 513D	Cambria St 519A	Castor Pl......527D	Cherrywood Ct ......
......315D, 336B	Bowden St 517D	Brownell St 513A	Cambridge Av 509D	Caswell Av 509B	......522D
a Ct 520D	Bowdoin St ...515D	Browning Av ..517A	Camden Av......536B	Caswell La 509A	Cheryl Av 521C
ell Av ..510B	Bowen St 513A	Bruckner Av...503C	Camden St 513A	Catherine Ct...505C	Chesebrough St ......
s St 520D	Bower Ct 527A	Brunswick St..515D	Cameron Av 519A	Catherine St...502B	......529C
u St 528D	Bowles Av 503D	Bryan St 536C	Campbell Av...505B	Catlin Av 507C	Chesire Pl......512A
Av 536C	Bowling Green Pl....	Bryant Av 524A	Campus Rd 512B	Cattaraugus St......	Chester Av 534C
a Av 519A	......515A	Bryson St......509B	Canal St 507C	......511D	Chester Pl......507C
Av 506D	Boyce Av 523C	Buchanan Av..510D	Candon Av 526D	Cayuga Av 511D	Chesterton Av 523C
La 527B	Boyd St 507C	Buel Av 518C	Candon Ct 526B	Cebra Av 507C	Chestnut Av ...513A
Rd 503C	Boylan St 521C	Buffalo St 523C	Cannon Av 514A	Cedar Av......519A	Chestnut Cir ...520D
ard Av ..510D	Boyle Pl 523A	Buffington Av..528D	Cannon Bd 523B	Cedar Grove Av	Chestnut Pl......506D
p Av 523A	Boyle St 517C	Bunnell Ct......527B	Canoe Pl 525A	......524D	Chestnut St 512B
arck Av ..507A	Boynton Av 533A	Bunnell St......527B	Canon Dr 521B	Cedar St 507C	Chicago Al 513C
arck Ct ..507C	Brabant St 503C	Burbank Av 524A	Canton Av......527C	Cedar Ter 512D	Chicago Av......519A
ford Av ..503D	Bradford Av ..533A	Burchard Ct 528D	Capellan St...534A	Cedar Wood Ct......	Chisholm St ...533B
e Ct 505D	Bradley Av 511C	Burden Av 503D	Cardiff St 527D	......503C	Christine Ct ...534A
Pl 534A	Bradley Ct 517A	Burgher Av 518B	Carlin St 526C	Cedarcliff Rd ..512B	Christopher La 509D
er Pl......515A	Braisted Av 515D	Burke Av 514B	Carlton Av 527D	Cedarview Av 523C	Christopher St 503A
Pl 532D	Brandis Av 521C	Burnside Av 510B	Carlton Bd 527B	Celina La 536D	Church Av 514B
St 523C	Brehaut Av 532C	Burr Av 532B	Carlton Ct 527D	Celtic Pl......524C	Church La 513B
nfield Av 508D	Brenton Pl 511B	Burton Av 533C	Carlton Pl 512C	Center Av 512B	Church St......505A
ningdale Rd	Brentwood Av 506B	Burton Ct 517C	Carly Ct 532D	Center Pl......524D	Churchill Av ...532B
......526D	Brewster St 507C	Bush Av 503C	Carlyle Green..527D	Center St 522B	Cicero Av 521D
om La ...536B	Briarcliff Rd 519A	Butler Av 536A	Carmel Av......510D	Central Av 507B	Cindra Av 530C
erry La ..535A	Briarwood Rd..503C	Butler Bd 536D	Carneaux Av..527B	Champ Ct 532D	Circle Loop......513A

Street	Grid	Street	Grid	Street	Grid
Circle Rd	518A	Cody Pl	527A	Cooper Pl	533D
City Bd	506D	Coke St	532B	Cooper Ter	515A
Claire Ct	512B	Cole St	532D	Copley St	515D
Claradon La	513C	Colfax Av	517D	Copperflag La	517D
Clarence Pl	523C	Colgate Pl	523D	Copperleaf Ter	517D
Clarendon Av	532C	College Av	510B	Corbin Av	521D
Clark Av	522B	College Pl	517B	Cordelia Av	533C
Clark La	507C	Collfield Av	509B	Cornelia St	518B
Clark Pl	510B	Collyer Av	528D	Cornell Av	505D
Claude St	532C	Colon Av	521D	Cornell Pl	512B
Clawson Av	523C	Colon St	534A	Cornell St	505C
Clawson St	523D	Colonial Av	515B	Cornish St	530C
Clay Pit Rd	526D	Colonial Ct	505D	Cornwall Av	518A
Clayboard St	524C	Colony Ct	524D	Corona Av	522D
Clayton St	513D	Colorado St	511A	Correll Av	526D
Clearmont Av	533A	Colton St	513C	Corson Av	506D
Clermont Av	536D	Columbia Av	513C	Cortelyou Av	521D
Clermont Pl	511C	Columbus Pl	510B	Cortelyou Pl	506B
Cletus St	518D	Combs Av	523C	Cortlandt St	505C
Cleveland Al	513C	Comely St	534A	Cosmen St	532B
Cleveland Av	529B	Commerce St	509C	Cottage Av	530C
Cleveland Pl	513C	Commodore Dr	533C	Cottage Pl	505A
Cleveland St	507A	Community La	534A	Cotter Av	522D
Cliff Ct	513D	Comstock Av	509B	Cottonwood Ct	522D
Cliffside Av	512B	Concord La	518A	Coughlan Av	511B
Cliffwood Av	517C	Concord Pl	512D	Country Dr ENSW	515C
Clifton Av	513A	Confederation Pl	503C	Country La	527A
Clifton St	509C	Conger St	519B	Country Woods La	522D
Clinton Av	506B	Congress St	507C	Coursen Ct	513A
Clinton Ct	506B	Conklin Av	503D	Coursen Pl	513A
Clinton Pl	503D	Connecticut St	536C	Court Pl	522D
Clinton Rd	530A	Connor Av	523A	Court St	507C
Clinton St	507C	Conrad Av	515D	Coventry Loop	527D
Clinton B Fiske Av	510B	Constant Av	511A	Coventry Rd	517D
Cloister Pl	523C	Continental Pl	503C	Coverly Av	511D
Clove Lake Pl	505D	Convent Av	527C	Coverly St	523A
Clove Rd	505D	Conyingham Av	506D	Cowen Pl	503A
Clove Way	511B	Cooke St	509A	Cozzens Bd	532D
Cloverdale Av	529D	Coonley Av	503C	Crabbs La	514C
Clovis Rd	529C	Coonley Ct	503A	Crab Tree Av	526D
Clyde Pl	507A	Cooper Av	518C	Crafton Av	510D
Coale Av	511A			Craig Av	536A
Coddington Rd	523B				

Street	Grid	Street	Grid	Street	Grid
Crane Av	514B	Daleham St	521D	Delmar Av	
Cranford Av	523A	Dalemere Rd	518A	Delmore St	
Cranford Ct	523A	Dallas St	511B	Delphine Ter	
Cranford St	530B	Dalton Av	523A	Delwit Av	
Crescent Av	507A	Damon St	532D	Demopolis Av	
Crest Loop	529D	Dana St	506D	Demorest Av	
Creston Pl	507C	Daniel Low Ter		Denise Ct	
Creston St	533C		507A	Denker Pl	
Crist St	513C	Darcy Av	509D	Dennis Toricell	
Crittenden Pl	503B	Darlington Av	527D	St	
Croak Av	511C	Darnell La	526D	Dent Rd	
Crocheron Av	509D	David Pl	503D	Denton Pl	
Crocker Ct	527A	David St	529D	Depew Pl	
Croft Ct	523C	Davidson Ct	503A	Deppe Pl	
Croft Pl	509C	Davidson St	503A	Derby Ct	
Cromer St	521D	Davis Av	506A	Deserre Av	
Cromwell Av	518B	Davis Ct	505B	Detroit Av	
Cromwell Cir	517D	Dawson Cir	509C	Devens St	
Cross St	507D	Dawson Ct	509C	Devine St	
Crossfield Av	521C	Dawson Pl	518D	Devon Loop	
Crosshill St	506D	Dawson Dr	510D	Devon Pl	
Croton Av	512A	Dayna St	513C	Dewey Av	
Croton Pl	509C	De Groot Pl	505D	Dewey Pl	
Crowell Av	511A	De Hart Av	503C	Dewhurst St	
Crown Av	527D	De Noble La	511D	Di Marco Pl	
Crown Pl	527D	De Ruyter Pl	503C	Di Renzo Ct	
Crystal Av	509B	De Soto Pl	507C	Diana's Trail	
Cuba Av	523D	Deal Ct	513C	Diane Ct	
Cubberly Pl	523B	Dean Av	514D	Diaz Pl	
Cunard Av	512B	Debbie St	509D	Diaz St	
Cunard Pl	512B	Decatur Av	509D	Dickie Av	
Currie Av	523C	Decker Av	505C	Dierauf St	
Curtis Av	511A	Deems Av	511A	Dina Ct	
Curtis Ct	506B	Deerpark Pl	511D	Dinsmore St	
Curtis Pl	507A	Deisius St	534A	Disosway Pl	
Cypress Av	511B	Dekalb St	512D	Ditson St	
Cypress Crest La	509B	DeKay St	506D	Dix Pl	
Cypress Loop	527A	Delafield Av	505C	Dixon Av	
Daffodil Ct	527B	Delafield Pl	506A	Dixwell Av	
Daffodil La	515C	Delaware Av	518B	Doane Av	
Dahlia St	527D	Delaware Pl	511A	Dobbs Av	
Dakota Pl	511A	Delaware St	518A	Dock St	
Dale Av	523B	Delford St	512B	Doe Ct	
		Dellwood Rd	518B	Doe Pl	

ood Dr...527B	Dumont Av 518B	Edgewater St..513B	Elm Pl 512A	Eugene Pl 534A	Field St 515B
ood La...513C	Dunbar St.......522D	Edgewood Rd.........	Elm St 505B	Eunice Pl........503C	Fieldmeyers La 514C
St.........534B	Duncan Rd 507C	.........................529D	Elm Tree Av 524B	Eva Av 523D	Fields Av 516B
n Pl 502D	Duncan St 518B	Edinboro Rd ...522B	Elmbank St 534B	Evan Pl 528B	Fieldstone Rd...509C
in St 509A	Dunham St 533A	Edison St 524A	Elmhurst Av....511D	Evans St 515D	Fieldway Av 530A
d Pl 506B	Durant Av 523C	Edith Av 534C	Elmira Av 511A	Evelyn Pl.........513D	Figurea Av 529A
an Av ...511A	Durges St 518B	Edstone Dr 506D	Elmira St 523D	Everett Av 533C	Filbert Av 518D
an St ...505C	Dustan St 524D	Edward Ct 515D	Elmwood Av....529D	Everett Pl 533C	Filer St............529A
an Hills Av	Dutchess Av ..518B	Edward Curry Av	Elmwood Park Dr ..	Evergreen Av..518B	Filipe La...........530C
.............518D	Dwarf St 502D	.........................508D	.........................515C	Evergreen St ..522D	Fillat St 510D
ey Av ...513C	Dyson St 507C	Edward G Baker Sq	Elson Ct...........509A	Everton Av 527B	Fillmore Pl 513D
a Ct 515C	E-F Row 502D	.........................507B	Elson St............509A	Everton Pl 527B	Fillmore St 506B
St.........510B	Eadie Av 534C	Edwin St 529C	Eltinge St 512D	Excelsior Av....533C	Filmore Av 510D
Ct.....505D	Eadie Pl..........507A	Egbert Av 511A	Eltingville Bd...521C	Exeter St..........530A	Fine Bd 511C
en Dr...503C	Eagan Av 529C	Egbert Pl.........513D	Elverton Av.....521D	Eylandt St 529C	Fingal St 529C
hea Pl ...523A	Eagle Rd 510A	Egbert Sq.........503D	Elvin St 511C	Faber St 505C	Finlay Av 533C
hy St ...516B	Earl Av............510B	Egmont Pl........507A	Elwood Pl........506D	Fabian St 529C	Finlay St 536C
al Av ...521C	Earley Pl 536A	Elaine Ct 518A	Ely Av 528D	Fahy Av............509A	Finley Av 524C
al Pl 521C	E Augusta Av ..529B	Elbe Av 512D	Ely St 507A	Fairbanks Av ..523C	Firth Rd 509C
Av.........519B	E Brandis Av ...521D	Elder Av 533C	Emeric Ct 503B	Fairfield St 521D	Fisher Av..........532C
las Av ...511B	E Broadway 523A	Eldridge Av 510B	Emerson Av 512D	Fairlawn Av 530B	Fitzgerald Av 530C
las Rd...512D	E Buchanan St507A	Eleanor La 529D	Emerson Ct......512C	Fairlawn Loop 530B	Flagg Ct 517D
Green ..527B	E Figurea Av ...529B	Eleanor Pl........503C	Emerson Dr 512D	Fairmont Av 506D	Flagg Pl............517D
es Av ...527D	E Gurley Av 521D	Eleanor St 523A	Emily La 520D	Fairview Pl 517B	Flagship Cir 533D
hey Pl ...503C	E Loop Rd 517D	Elias Pl 511A	Emmet Av 523C	Fairway Av 523A	Fletcher St 513C
e Av.....511A	E Macon Av 521D	Elie Ct 515C	End Pl 521C	Fairway La 512A	Flint St 523D
er Pl 515A	E Raleigh Av....505D	Elise Ct 522D	Endor Av 512C	Falcon Av 523C	Florence Pl......533C
den Pl ...511D	E Reading Av....521D	Elizabeth Av 506A	Endview St 529C	Fancher Pl 502B	Florence St......530C
er Av.....509D	E Scranton Av 529B	Elizabeth Ct 532D	Enfield Pl 523A	Fanning St 511C	Florida Av 519B
s St.......529D	E Stroud Av 529B	Elizabeth Pl 533D	Engert St..........527A	Farraday St 509B	Florida Ter 517C
goole Rd E.....	E Tenafly Av 529C	Elizabeth St 505D	Englewood Av 532B	Farragut Av 509A	Flower Av 536D
.............527D	Eastentry Rd ..517D	Elizabeth Grove Rd	Erastina Pl 503A	Father Capodanno	Floyd St............505C
goole Rd W....	Eastman Av 515B	.........................502D	Eric La 521D	Bd 519C	Foch Av 519A
.............528D	Eastman St 529C	Elk Ct 523C	Erie St 533A	Fayette St 518B	Fonda Pl 533A
La.........519B	Eastwood Av ...532D	Elkhart St 521D	Errington Pl 513A	Fayann La 536D	Fontaine Pl 529B
en Ct 505C	Eaton Pl 503B	Elks Pl 527C	Escanaba Av ...529B	Federal Pl 502B	Foote Av 512B
dale St ...516B	Ebbitts St 523D	Ella Pl 523D	Esmac Ct NW 517B	Felton St 509A	Ford Pl.............505D
n Pl 503C	Ebey La 527B	Ellicott Pl.........506B	Essex Dr 515D	Fenway Cir 521D	Forest Av 502D
is Av ...505C	Ebony St 523A	Ellington St.......512B	Essex St 509A	Fern Av 529B	Forest Ct 503C
ey Av ...511B	Echo Pl 509B	Ellis Rd 526C	Estelle Pl..........536B	Ferndale Av 515C	Forest La..........536C
Av.........519B	Eddy St 507C	Ellis St 532C	Esther Depew St	Ferndale Ct......515A	Forest Rd 517B
La.........507C	Edgar Pl 512D	Ellsworth Av...527D	.........................517C	Ferry St 505A	Forest Green 527B
dale St ...523D	Edgar Ter 507C	Ellsworth Pl 511A	Etna St 515B	Ficarelle Dr.....533C	Forest Hill Rd...515B
Pl 511C	Edgegrove Av 527D	Ellwood Av 515C	Eton Pl 509C	Fiedler Av 507C	Fornes Pl..........529C

STATEN ISLAND   Forrestal Av – Heusden St

Page
Grid

Forrestal Av 521C
Forrestal Ct 528B
Fort Hill Cir 507A
Fort Pl 507A
Foss Av 523D
Foster Av 517A
Foster Rd 527C
Four Corners Rd.....
.............517B
Fox La 531A
Fox Hill Ter 513C
Fox Hunt Ct.....511B
Foxbeach Av 531A
Foxholm St 523B
Francesca La ..503C
Francine Ct....523B
Francine La 509B
Francis Pl 518A
Franklin Av 507A
Franklin La 521B
Franklin Pl....511C
Franklin D Roosevelt
Boardwalk 519C
Fraser St....515D
Frean St 507C
Frederick St 511A
Freeborn St ...524B
Freedom Av 515A
Freeman Pl....505D
Fremont Av....517D
Fremont St 507A
Fresh Kill Rd....520B
Front St 507D
Fuller Ct 522D
Fulton St 513A
Furman St 529C
Furness Pl 515D
Futurity Pl 521C
G-H Row 502D
Gadsen Pl 515A
Gales La 505A
Galesville Ct....519B
Galloway Av....503D
Gansevoort Bd511C

Garden Ct 517B
Garden St 511C
Gardenia La 515C
Garfield Av 513D
Garibaldi Av ...524C
Garretson Av ..518B
Garretson La ..512D
Garrick St 509A
Garrison Av 510B
Garson Av 513D
Garth Ct 522D
Gary Ct 509C
Gary Pl 515A
Gary St 520D
Gaspar Av 514B
Gateway Dr 512D
Gaton St 532A
Gauldy Av 509A
Gaynor St 532B
Geigerich Av ..536B
Geigerich Pl ...536D
Geldner Av 523B
Genesee Av 529A
Genesee St 511B
Georges La 533C
George St 536D
Gervil St 527B
Getz Av 521C
Geyser Dr 527B
Gibson Av 522D
Giffords Glen ..529B
Giffords La 521D
Gigi St 503D
Gil Ct 529A
Gilbert Pl 533C
Gilbert St 522B
Giles Pl 512D
Gillard Av 529C
Gilroy St 527C
Giordan Ct 503A
Girard St 532C
Gladwin Av....526D
Gladwin St 532B
Glascoe Av....510B

Glen Av 507C
Glen Rd 515B
Glen St 508D
Glencoe St 521D
Glendale Av 518B
Glenwood Av ..511B
Glenwood Pl ..511A
Globe Av 509A
Glover St....530C
Goethals Av 532B
Goethals Rd 509A
Goethals Rd N 502D
Goff Av 533A
Gold Av 521C
Golf View Ct ...515D
Goll Ct 518B
Goller Pl 509C
Goodall St....530C
Goodell Av 511A
Goodwin Av 511A
Gordon Pl 503D
Gordon St 513A
Gorge Rd 518A
Gothic Pl 529A
Governor Rd....511A
Gower St....511C
Grace Ct 506B
Grace Rd 523A
Grafe St 527A
Graham Av 509C
Graham Bd 524B
Grandview Av 503A
Grandview Ter 530C
Granite Av 503D
Grant Pl 524A
Grant St....507C
Grantwood Av 528B
Grasmere Av ..512D
Grasmere Dr ..513C
Grattan Av 530B
Graves St 511C
Gray St 507C
Grayson St 523D
Great Kills La ..531A

Great Kills Rd..530A
Greaves Av 521D
Greaves Ct 530A
Greeley Av 517D
Green Ct 505C
Green St 506C
Green Valley Rd
.............527B
Greencroft Av 530B
Greenfield Av ..513A
Greenfield Ct ..513A
Greenleaf Av ..505C
Greenport St ..518B
Greentree La ..509C
Greenway Av ..515B
Greenway Dr ..512A
Greenwood Av
.............506D
Gregg Pl 506D
Gregory La 521B
Greta Pl....512B
Gridley Av 503C
Grille Ct 526D
Grimsby St 524B
Grissom Av....515A
Griswold Ct 506D
Groton St 529D
Grove Av 505A
Grove Pl 503B
Grove St 507C
Grymes Hill Rd512B
Guilford St 519B
Gulf Av 502D
Gunda St....515B
Gunton Pl 527A
Gurdon St 510D
Gurley Av 521D
Guyon Av 523D
Hafstrom St ..523C
Hagaman Pl ...503D
Hagedorn Av ..510B
Hale St 532C
Hales Av 529D
Hall Av....509D

Hallister St 533A
Halpin Av 527B
Hamden Av 517D
Hamilton Av 507A
Hamilton Pl....514A
Hamilton St 512B
Hamlin Pl....505C
Hammock La ..527B
Hampton Green
.............527B
Hampton Pl ...527A
Hancock St 518B
Hank Pl 533D
Hannah St....507C
Hanover Av 512D
Hanover Av 533D
Harbor La 504D
Harbor Loop 503C
Harbor Rd 503C
Harbor View Pl E,
N, & S 513D
Harbor View Ct......
.............507C
Harbour Ct 530C
Hardin Av 505D
Hardy Pl 529B
Hardy St 513A
Hargold Av 532B
Harold Av 534B
Harold St 511C
Harriet Av 533D
Harriet St 517A
Harris Av....510D
Harris La 526D
Harrison Av 503B
Harrison Pl 505D
Harrison St....513A
Harrower St ...510B
Hart Av 506D
Hart Bd 506D
Hart Loop 523C
Hart Pl 532C
Hartford Av 511B
Hartford St 530C

Harvard Av ....
Harvest Av ....
Harvey Av ....
Harvey St ....
Hasbrouck Rd
Hastings St ....
Hatfield Pl....
Hathaway Av .
Haughwout Av
Haven Av ....
Haven Espl ....
Havenwood Rd
Hawthorne Av
Hay St ....
Haynes St....
Hays Pl ....
Haywood St ...
Hazen St ....
Heafy St ....
Heaney Av ....
Heenan Av ....
Heberton Av ..
Hecker St ....
Heffernan St...
Heinz Av ....
Helena Rd ....
Helene Ct ....
Helios Pl ....
Hemlock Ct....
Hemlock La ....
Hemlock St ...
Hempstead Av
Henderson Av
Henderson Ct.
Hendricks Av .
Henning St ....
Henry Pl ....
Herbert St....
Hereford St ...
Herkimer St ...
Herrick Av ....
Hervey St ....
Hett Av ....
Heusden St....

t Av 512D	Holsman Rd ...512D	Ilyssa Way 520D	Jeannette Av ..529C	Kathleen Ct ...536B	Knesel St 527A
ry Av 519A	Holten Av 533D	Ina St.............523D	Jefferson Av ..517D	Kathy Pl.......515C	Knollwood Ct ..503C
ry Cir 527B	Home Av 513D	Indale Av 533C	Jefferson Bd ..527B	Keating Pl....515B	Knox Pl 511B
ry Ct......527A	Home Pl 509B	Independence Av ..	Jefferson St...518C	Keating St....533D	Knox St 533C
St 513D	Homer St......507C	...................521A	Jeffrey Pl 536B	Keats St 530A	Koch Bd 529C
and Av ...512B	Homestead Av 505C	Industrial Loop	Jennifer La ...524C	Keegans La ...530B	Kraft Pl 529C
and La ...530C	Honey La 536B	..................526B	Jennifer Pl ...509C	Keeley St 513B	Kramer Av ...526D
and Rd ...530A	Hooker Pl 503D	Industry Rd....508C	Jerome Av ...519A	Keiber Ct.....511A	Kramer Pl 505C
nount Rd 529B	Hooper Av 523C	Inez St..........533D	Jerome Rd ...518D	Kell Av.........510D	Kramer St.....519C
oint Rd ..518A	Hope Av 513D	Ingram Av......510D	Jersey St 507A	Kelly Bd 515D	Kreischer St...532A
iew Av.....507A	Hopkins Av ...523C	Innis St.........503D	Jewett Av 505C	Kelvin Av 530B	Kruser St 524A
ook Ct...513C	Hopping Av ...536A	Inwood Rd 512D	Joan Pl 511A	Kemball Av...511A	Kunath Av ...526B
ook Dr ...513C	Housman Av .503B	Iona St........525A	Joel Pl 523A	Ken La 520D	Kyle Ct.........520D
est Av ...529B	Houston La ...503D	Ionia Av.........527C	Johanna Loop 533D	Kenilworth Av 520D	Labau Av......512C
est Ct 513C	Houston St ...503D	Iowa Pl.........510B	John St 503B	Kenmore St ...521C	Lacon St 521D
est Rd ...512B	Howard Av ...507C	Irma Pl........512A	Johnson Av ...536A	Kennebeck Av 514B	Laconia Av ...518D
est St ...529D	Howard Cir ...507C	Iron Mine Dr ..517D	Johnson Pl...518B	Kenneth Pl ...533C	Ladd Av 521C
est Ter ...513C	Howard Ct ...505B	Ironwood St...522D	Johnson St...526A	Kennington St 521D	Lafayette Av ..506C
le Ct 513C	Howton Av ...522D	Iroquois St ...524B	Johnston Ter ..533C	Kensico St 523A	Lafayette St ...536A
St 529C	Hoyt Av 506D	Irving Pl......512B	Joline Av 536B	Kensington Av 519A	LaForge Av ...503D
an Av 509C	Hudson Pl....503D	Irvington St...534C	Joline La 536D	Kent St 517C	LaForge Pl ...505C
ge Ct 513C	Hudson St....507C	Isabella Av ...523D	Jones St 509C	Kenwood Av ...534B	LaGrange Pl ...503D
le Av 512B	Huguenot Av .527A	Isben Av 528B	Joseph Av ...516B	Keppel Av 536A	LaGuardia Av .511C
le Ter....529B	Hughes Av ...508D	Isernia Av ...523D	Joseph La 513C	Kermit Av 519A	Lake Av 503D
o Pl 529D	Hull Av........517D	Islin Pl.......505C	Josephine St ..511C	Kerry La 536B	Lake Dr 513D
o Rd 529D	Humbert St...519A	Islington St...521D	Journeay St ...503C	Kesselman Av 517A	Lakeland Rd ...511B
o Ter......517B	Hunt La 517B	Ismay St 516B	Joyce La 536A	Keune Ct......518D	Lakeview Ter ..513C
ew La 518A	Hunter Av ...517D	Isora Pl 523D	Joyce St 518D	King St 529D	Lakewood Rd..506D
ew Pl 518A	Hunter Pl 506D	Ivy Ct.........527A	Jules Dr 509A	Kingdom Av ...534A	Lamberts La
od Ct....513C	Hunter St ...512D	Jackson Av ...519B	Julie Ct 511C	Kinghorn St ...534B	...........508B,509A
n St........520D	Hunton St ...518B	Jackson St....507C	Julie Pl 532C	Kingsbridge Av......	Lamberts St ...509A
cock Av .523A	Hurlbert St ...518B	Jacob St......536B	Jumel St 521D	...................509A	Lamoka Av ...529A
Pl 528D	Huron Pl 506D	Jacques Av ...523B	Juni Ct........515D	Kingsland St...533D	Lamont Av......
es Pl 511A	Hurst St......505C	Jaffe St........510B	Juniper Pl.....517D	Kingsley Av ...511A	...........528A-533A
rnt Ct....505C	Husson Av ...517D	James Ct 503D	Juno Av 531B	Kingsley Pl ...507C	Lamped Loop ..515C
mb Av ...527B	Hyatt St......507B	James Pl......513C	Jupiter La 503C	Kinsey Pl......502D	Lamport Bd ...519A
n Bd 511C	Hygeia Pl ...507C	Jamie La 520D	Justin Av 530B	Kirby Ct......506B	Lander Av 509A
idge Av ..534B	Hylan Bd	Jansen Ct.....534A	Kaltenmaier La	Kirshon Av ...509A	Landis Av 519A
te St 509D	.........513B-536D	Jansen St......533B	.................513A	Kissam Av ...523D	Langere Pl 513A
ay Dr 510A	Ida Ct......527D	Jardine Av ...509C	Kalver Pl 503D	Kissel Av......506B	Lansing St ...519B
ay Wy....510A	Idaho Av ...533A	Jarvis Av......534C	Kansas Av ...513C	Kiswick St ...524B	Larch Ct 527A
Av........529D	Idlease Pl ...524B	Jasper St 516B	Karen Ct 511A	Klondike Av ...515A	Laredo Av 529A
Pl 523A	Ilion Pl........523A	Jay La 520D	Katan Av 529A	Knapp St......515A	Larkin St 505A
St 518B	Ilsye Ct 523C	Jay St 524B	Katan Loop ...530A	Knauth Pl 519A	LaSalle St......503B

Latham Pl 527C	Lily Pond Av 519B	Loring Av 528B	Madison Av 509B	Marianne St....510B	McCully Av ......
Lathrop Av 510B	Lincoln Av 517D	Loring Ct.........509D	Madsen Av......532D	Marie Pl 512D	McDermott Av
Latimer Av 514B	Lincoln Pl 513D	Lorrain Av.......529C	Magnolia Av ...518D	Marie St.........518B	McDivitt Av ....
LaTourette St .533C	Lincoln St 511C	Lorraine Loop 526D	MaGuire Av 527C	Marine Dr 533C	McDonald St ..
Laurel Av 512B	Linda Av 519B	Lortel Av 511C	MaGuire Ct.....533A	Marine Way 524C	McKee Av ......
Lava St 519A	Lindbergh Av ..523B	Lotus Av 534A	Maiden La 532C	Mariners La 503A	McKinley Av ...
Law Pl 505D	Linden Av 503C	Louis St 507C	Main St 536A	Marion Av 507C	McLaughlin St
Lawn Av 523A	Linden St 506B	Louise La 511D	Maine Av 510B	Marion St 505C	McVeigh Av ....
Lawrence Av ..506D	Lindenwood Av	Louise St........534A	Majestic Av 526B	Marisa Cir 526D	Meade Loop....
Layton Av 507A	.....................529B	Lovelace Av 529A	Major Av.........519A	Mark St 518B	Meade St ....
Leason Pl 515D	Lindenwood Pl529B	Lovell Av 515B	Malden Pl.......523D	Market St 505D	Meadow Av ....
Ledyard Pl 519A	Linton Pl 521D	Low St............532D	Mallard La 526D	Markham Pl 511A	Meadow Ct ....
Lee Av 532C	Linwood Av 519A	Lowell St.........516D	Mallory Av 519A	Marne Av 529A	Meadow Pl......
Leeds St 523D	Lion St...........532C	Lucille Av 526B	Mallow St.......527C	Marscher Pl ...533D	Medford Rd ....
Legate Av 528B	Lipsett Av 529C	Ludlow St 528B	Malone Av 523C	Marsh Av 515C	Medina St.......
Leggett Pl 509C	Lisa La 527B	Ludwig La 503C	Malvine Av......526D	Marshall Av 517A	Meeker Av .....
Legion Pl 513C	Lisa Pl 509C	Ludwig St 505D	Manchester Dr527D	Martha St 512D	Meisner Av ....
Leigh Av 509A	Lisbon Pl 517D	Luigi Ct 523A	Mandy Ct 526D	Martin Av 510D	Melba St.........
Lenevar Av 527C	Lisk Av 503C	Luigi Pl 523B	Manee Av.......533A	Martin Luther King	Melhorn Rd .....
Lenhart St.....532C	Liss St 529D	Luke Ct 522D	Manhattan St..536C	Jr Expwy.......503D	Melissa St ......
Lennon Ct......521D	Little Clove Rd 511D	Luna Cir 534B	Manila Av........523D	Martineau St ..502B	Melrose Av .....
Lenore Ct 509B	Littlefield Av ...529D	Lundi Ct..........515C	Manila Pl.........524D	Martling Av 511A	Melrose Pl .....
Lenzie St 534D	Livermoore Av 510B	Lundsten Av 526D	Manley St 526C	Marvin Rd........533A	Melville St .....
Leo St 509B	Livingston Av ..511C	Luten Av 533B	Mann Av..........510D	Marx St...........511D	Melvin Av ....
Leola Pl 534B	Livingston Ct ..506A	Lyle Ct 523C	Manor Ct 522B	Mary St 512D	Melyn Pl ....
Leon St 509A	Llewelyn Pl 505C	Lyman Av 513D	Manor Rd 511A	Maryland Av ...513B	Memo St ....
Leona St 509C	Lloyd Ct 505D	Lyman Pl 512D	Manorville Ct ..513C	Maryland Pl 511A	Memphis Av....
Leonard Av.....509B	Lockman Av 503C	Lynch St 534B	Mansion Av 530D	Mason Av 518D	Mena St ....
Leonard St 534A	Lockman Loop 503C	Lyndale Av 529D	Manton Pl.......513C	Mason Bd.......526D	Mendelsohn St
Leroy St 514B	Lockwood Pl ..510B	Lyndale La 529C	Maple Av 505A	Mason St 518B	
Leslie Av 518B	Locust Av 523B	Lynhurst Av 513A	Maple Ct 527B	Massachusetts St ..	Mercer Pl ......
Lester St 511C	Locust Pl 529B	Lynn Ct 503D	Maple Pkwy 503C	....................536C	Mercury La .....
Leverett Av....521D	Logan Av 511D	Lynn St 523D	Maple Ter 524D	Mathews Av ...506D	Meredith Av ....
Levit Av 509B	Lois Pl 506B	Lynnhaven Pl...505D	Mapleton Av ...524B	Maxwell Av 533D	Merkel Pl ......
Lewiston St 515D	Lola St 525A	Lyon Pl 529C	Maplewood Av......	May Av 509A	Merle Pl ....
Lexa Pl 527D	Lombard Ct.....527A	MacArthur Av 529A	....................523A	May Pl 529C	Merrick Av .....
Lexington Av ..505C	London Ct.......523A	Mace St 522B	Maplewood Pl524A	Mayberry	Merrill Av ....
Lexington La ..521D	London Rd 516D	MacFarland Av	Marble St 510B	Promenade 535A	Merriman Av ...
Leyden Av......503C	Long Pond La..513A	....................519A	Marc St 509B	Maybury Av 530A	Merry Mount S
Liberty Av 518D	Longdale St 509A	MacGregor St 533D	Marcy Av 527D	Maybury Ct 530B	
Lighthouse Av 522B	Longfellow Av 512B	Macon Av 521C	Maretzek Ct ...533A	Mayer Av 517A	Mersereau Av
Lightner Av.....511D	Longview Rd ...512D	Macormac Pl..502B	Margaret St 530A	McBaine Av 526D	Metcalfe St ....
Lilac Ct 503C	Loret Ct 505D	Madera St 533B	Margaretta Ct 511A	McClean Av 519A	Metropolitan A
Lillian Pl 529D	Loretto St 536D	Madigan Pl......512D	Maria La 529A	McCormick Pl 518B	....

r La 513D	Moreland St...524B	Nathan Ct......533A	Nolan Av........529B	Oak Ct 530A	Orchard La 515C
elle Ct....503C	Morgan La 509C	Natick St 523A	Nome Av........515C	Oak La 520D	Orchard La 534B
elle La 524C	Morley Av 523A	Naughton Av ..518D	Norden St.......517B	Oak St 513A	Orchard St 529A
e Loop Rd529A	Morningstar Rd	Nautilus Ct ...513D	Norma Pl 506D	Oakdale Av 518B	Ordell Av 505C
nd Av....517D	..................503D	Nautilus St ...513D	Normalee Rd ..519A	Oakdale St 529C	Oregon Rd 518B
nd Rd....530A	Morris Pl 530C	Navesink Pl ...524C	Norman Pl 533D	Oakland Av 505D	Orinoco Pl 503A
ay Pl 518B	Morris St 527A	Neal Dow Av ..510B	North Av........509B	Oakland Ter 512B	Orlando St 519A
nk Rd 524C	Morrison Av ...505D	Neckar Av 512D	North Ct 530D	Oakley Pl 523B	Ormond Pl 513A
rn St 523A	Morrow St 502D	Nedra La 527B	North Dr 513C	Oakville St 517A	Ormsby Av 533D
n Av....512D	Morse Av 517A	Nehring Av 515C	North St 505A	Oakwood Av ..506D	Osage La 534B
ed Av....514B	Morton St 523A	Neilsen Av 526C	N Bridge St 532A	Oban St 534B	Osborn Av 529D
Av....521D	Mosel Av 512D	Nelson Av 529D	N Burgher Av..505B	Oberlin St 519A	Osborne St 529C
d Av....511D	Mosel Loop 513C	Neptune Pl 509D	N Gannon Av..510D	Occident Av ...507C	Osgood Av 512B
d Dr....511D	Mosley Av 529C	Neptune St.....524D	N Mada Av......506D	Ocean Av 519B	Oswald Pl 533D
d....523D	Motley Av 511D	Nesmythe Ter 512B	N Pine Ter 528D	Ocean Rd 530A	Oswego St 511D
d Av....517A	Mott St 529A	Netherland Av 503C	N Railroad Av 518B	Ocean Ter 511D	Otho St 521D
St....511A	Mountainside Rd	Neutral Av 524C	N Railroad St..527D	Oceanic Av 535A	Otis Av 523B
Av....519B	..................518D	Nevada Av 517C	N Randall Av ..506D	Oceanside Av 519C	Otsego Av 511D
Av....523D	Mountain View Av..	New Dorp La ..523B	N Rhett Av 530A	Oceanview Av 534D	Outerbridge Av..
sa La....527A	..................511D	New Dorp Plz NS...	N St Austin's Pl	Oceanview La 511D	..................532A
va Av....532D	Mulberry Av ...515A	..................523B	..................506D	Oceanview Pl 529D	Ovas Ct 529A
va Pl....507A	Mulberry Cir ...515A	New La 513D	N Tremont Av..503D	Oder Av 512D	Overlook Av ....
St....518B	Muldoon Av ...520D	New St 505C	Northentry Rd 517B	Odin St 523B	..................503C-518B
rne St..507B	Muller Av 510B	New York Pl ...511A	Northern Bd....511D	Ogden St 529C	Overlook Ct....513C
rn Av....527C	Mundy Av 505C	Newark Av 503B	Northfield Av ..503A	Ohio Pl 511A	Overlook Dr 512D
e Av....523A	Murdock Pl 503D	Newberry Av ..518B	Northfield Ct ..502B	Old Amboy Rd 529B	Overlook Ter....513C
tt St....529C	Muriel St 526C	Newfolden Pl..532D	Northport La ...515C	Old Farmers La	Ovis Pl 530B
Pl 511D	Murray Hulbert Av..	Newkirk Av 505C	Norwalk Av 511C	..................518A	Ox Ct 515A
St....532A	..................507D	Newton St 534B	Norway Av 519A	Old Mill Rd	Oxford Pl........507C
nan Av..515D	Murray Pl 507C	Newvale Av 521B	Norwich St......516B	..........521B-531A	Oxholm Av 512A
e Av....507A	Murray St 532D	Niagara Av 511B	Norwood Av ...513A	Old Town Rd...518B	Pacific Av 529D
e Pl....517A	Myrna La 527B	Nicholas Av ...503B	Norwood Ct ...507C	Oldfield St 524B	Page Av 532D
y Pl....503D	Myrtle Av 505D	Nicholas St ...507A	Nostrand Av ...509C	Olga Pl 513C	Palace Ct 518A
uk Pl....509D	Nadal Pl 509C	Nicolosi Dr 534C	Notre Dame Av	Olive St 505C	Palisade St 519B
ll St....505C	Nadine St 523A	Nicolosi Loop.534D	..................529D	Olive St 532C	Palma Dr 513C
rey Av..529A	Nahant St 522D	Nightingale St 517C	Notus Av 528B	Oliver Pl 509C	Palmer Av 505C
omery Av.....	Nancy Ct........530A	Niles Pl 516B	Nugent Av 518D	Olympia Bd 519A	Pamela Dr 512D
..................507A	Nancy La 536B	Nina Av 509D	Nugent St 523A	Oneida Av 512D	Pan St 532D
ello Ter 529D	Narrows Rd NS	Nina Av 510C	Nunley Ct 513A	Ontario Av 511B	Paradise Pl.....536A
eal Av....523C	..................513C	Nippon Av 527C	Nutly Pl 506C	Opp Ct 521C	Parish Av 514A
vale Pl..529B	Nash Ct 530C	Nixon Av 507C	Nutwood Ct ...522C	Orange Av 503D	Park Av 505C
Pl....506B	Nashville St ...532C	Noble Ct 518A	O'Connor Av ...510D	Orangeburg Av.....	Park Ct 506D
St....522B	Nassau Pl 532C	Noble Pl 505D	O'Gorman Av ..523C	..................534B	Park Dr N 515A
St....509C	Nassau St.......507A	Noel St 534B	Oak Av 523D	Orchard Av 532C	Park Dr E & W514D

Park Dr S 520B	Percival Pl 533C	Pleasant Valley Av ..	Princewood Av 533B	Ravenna St......534B	Richmond Ct .
Park Hill Av 513A	Perine Av 518D	......................512B	Prol Pl 535A	Ravenhurst Av 511A	Richmond Rd .
Park Hill Cir 513A	Perine Ct 518D	Plymouth Rd 515A	Promenade Av 523D	Rawson Pl 514D	Richmond Ter
Park Hill Ct 513A	Perkiomen Av 529A	Poe St 536B	Property St.......529B	Ray St 529C	Richmond Hill
Park Hill La 513A	Perry Av 511C	Poets Cir 527B	Prospect Av 506B	Raymond Av 511A	....
Park La 512B	Pershing Cir ...507B	Poi Pl 515C	Prospect Pl 523B	Raymond Pl 505D	Richmond Pkw
Park Pl 507A	Pershing St 519A	Poillon Av 534A	Prospect St 507C	Reading Av 529A	....
Park Rd 529D	Perth Amboy Pl	Point St 530C	Providence St 518B	Rebecca Ct ...532B	Richmond Pkw
Park St 523A	.......................536C	Poland Pl 511C	Pulaski Av 503C	Rector St.......505C	....
Park Ter 529B	Peru St 517A	Pommer Av 507C	Purcell St 505D	Red Cedar La ..526D	Richmond Vall
Parker St.........532C	Peter Av 523D	Pompey Av 529A	Purdue Ct 515C	Redgrave Av ..530B	....
Parkinson Av ..518B	Peter St.........509B	Pond St 527A	Purdue St 515C	Redmond St 518A	Ridge Av ....
Parkview Loop 509D	Petersburg Av 534B	Pontiac St.......503D	Purdy Av 510D	Redwood Av ..522D	Ridge Ct ....
Parkview Pl 512A	Petersons La ..533A	Poplar Av 527A	Purdy Pl 533D	Redwood Loop	Ridge Loop ....
Parkwood Av ..533A	Petrus Av 529C	Poplar La 526D	Purroy Pl.......507C	......................527A	Ridgecrest Av
Parsons Pl 506D	Phelps Pl 507A	Port Richmond Av ..	Putnam Pl 507C	Regal Wk 509A	Ridgefield Av
Patten St.........536C	Philip St 534A	.......................503D	Putnam St 529C	Regan Av 506D	Ridgeway Av
Patterson Av ..519C	Phyllis Ct.......526D	Portage Av 517A	Putters Ct 512A	Regent Cir 527B	Ridgewood Av
Patty Ct 529A	Piave Av 519A	Portland Pl 506D	Queen St.........511C	Regina La 528B	Ridgewood Pl
Paulding Av 509C	Pickersgill Av 519A	Portsmouth Av 511D	Queensdale St 533B	Regis Dr 509A	Riedel Av ......
Pauw St 507A	Piedmont Av....513C	Posen St 529C	Quincy Av 519C	Reid Av 518B	Rieglemann S
Pavillion Hill Ter	Pierce St.........512B	Post Av 505C	Quinlan Av 511C	Reiss La 518A	Riga St ....
......................507C	Pierpont Pl 515D	Post La 503A	Quinn St 513A	Remsen St 518B	Rigby St ....
Paxton St 507C	Pierre Pl 534A	Potter Av 511A	Quintard St 519C	Rene Dr 523C	Riley Pl ....
Peare Pl 534B	Pike St 507C	Pouch Ter 513C	Racal Ct 515C	Renee Pl 509C	Ring Rd ....
Pearl Pl 532C	Pilcher St 516B	Poughkeepsie Av ..	Radcliff Rd 519A	Renfrew Pl 503D	River Rd ....
Pearl St 507C	Pine Pl.............513A	.......................534B	Radford St 515A	Reno Av 523B	Rivington Av ..
Pearsall St 519A	Pine St 507C	Poultney St......524A	Radigan Av 526D	Rensselaer Av 527C	Roanoke St....
Pearson St 514D	Pine Ter 529C	Powell La 527C	Rae Av 529C	Renwick Av 511B	Roberts Dr ....
Peck Ct 522D	Pinewood Av ..523A	Powell St 527C	Railroad Av 519B	Reon Av 511C	Robin Rd ....
Peel Pl 523C	Pinto St 525A	Prall Av 533B	Raily Ct 527A	Retford Av 529D	Robin Ct ....
Pelton Av 506C	Pitney Av 532B	Pratt Ct 527A	Rainbow Av 505C	Retner Av 519B	Robinson Av...
Pelton Av 506D	Pitt Av 517A	Prescott Av 517D	Ralph Av 529C	Revere La 521B	Rochelle Pl ....
Pelton Pl 506A	Pittsville Av ...536C	President St 510D	Ralph Pl 512D	Revere St 506D	Rochelle St....
Pemberton Av 521D	Plank Rd 509C	Presley St.......529D	Ramapo Av 527C	Reynaud St.....519C	Rockaway St
Pembine St.....532B	Platinum Av ...515C	Preston Av 529D	Ramble Rd 530D	Reynolds St ...513C	Rockland Av...
Pembrook Loop	Platt St 523C	Prices La 514B	Ramblewood Av......	Rhett Av 530A	Rockne St .....
......................526D	Plattsburg St ..518B	Primrose Pl 523D	.......................529D	Rhine Av 512D	Rockport St ...
Penbroke Av ..506D	Plaza Av 532C	Prince La 526D	Ramona Av 527C	Rice Av 511A	Rockville Av ...
Pendale St 523C	Pleasant Ct 513A	Prince St 513A	Ramsey Pl 512B	Richard Av 532D	Rockwell Av .
Pendleton Pl ..507A	Pleasant Pl.....513A	Princess La 503D	Randall Av 506D	Richard La 509D	Rodeo La ......
Penn Av 523D	Pleasant Plains Av	Princess St......503D	Rankin St 529C	Riche Av 514B	Roderick Av ...
Penn St 511C	......................532D	Princeton Av ..523B	Raritan Av 518B	Richmond Av	Rodman St ...
Penton St 533C	Pleasant St.....529B	Princeton La ..527B	Rathbun Av.....527C	......................503D–529D	Roe St ....

St 512B	Sable Av 512D	Saxon Av 515A	Shadow La 523A	Signs Rd 509C	S Drum St 533A
s Pl 529C	St Adalbert Pl 503D	Saybrook St ...509C	Shady Pl 511D	Silver Beech Rd	S Gannon Av .510D
y Pl 506B	St Albans Pl ...529D	Scarboro Av...513D	Shadyside Av..533C	..................512D	S Goff Av 533C
g Hill Green....	St Andrews Pl 532C	Scarsdale St ...529B	Shafter Av 503B	Silver Ct 506D	S Greenleaf Av..511A
..................527B	St Andrews Rd	Scenic La 513A	Shale St 515D	Silver Lake Park Rd	S Mann Av 511C
Av 524C	..................522B	Scheffelin Av..516D	Shamrock Av ..526D	..................506D	S Railroad Av .....
n Av 509A	St Anthony Pl..510B	Schley Av 530A	Sharon Av 506D	Silver Lake Rd 506D	..............518B-530B
n Ct 536D	St Austin's Pl ..506D	Schmeig Av ...532A	Sharon La 533A	Simmons La ...514B	S Railroad St .527D
Av 512D	St George Dr ..517B	Schmidts La ...511C	Sharpe Av 503B	Simonson Av ..503C	S St Austin's Pl ...
r Rd 517B	St George Rd ..523A	Schoharie St ...511B	Sharrett Pl ...505C	Simonson Pl...505C	..................506D
d Av 503D	St James Av...517B	School Rd 513D	Sharrott Av ...533C	Simpson St....518D	S Service Rd ..532B
velt Av .511C	St John Av ...510B	School St 529B	Sharrotts Rd ..526C	Sinclair Av 532C	Sowall Av 532C
velt St...511C	St John's Av ...513C	Schubert St ...513C	Shaughnessy La	Singleton St ...533C	Spar Av 527C
velt St...512D	St Josephs Av 503B	Schuyler St ...507B	..................513A	Sioux St 524A	Spark Pl 509C
Av 523B	St Julian Pl...507D	Scott Av 519A	Shaw Pl 510B	Sky Dr 513A	Sparkill Av 518B
Ct 506D	St Lukes Av ...526B	Scranton Av...529A	Shawnee St ...506D	Skyline Dr 513A	Spartan Av 503C
La 534A	St Marks Pl ...507A	Scranton St ...518B	Sheffield St ...505D	Slaight St 503B	Speedwell Av..509C
ank Pl...513B	St Mary's Av ..513A	Scribner Av ...507A	Sheldon Av ...527C	Slater Bd 518D	Spencer St 508C
iff Rd ...503C	St Paul's Av ...507C	Scudder Av ...533A	Shelley Av 514B	Slayton Pl 515C	Sperry Pl......527C
ale Av ...527C	St Peters Pl ...507A	Sea Gate Rd...513D	Shelterview Dr..507C	Sleepy Hollow Rd ..	Sprague Av ...536B
vood Pl ..507C	St Stephens Pl523B	Sea View Av ..518D	Shenandoah Av	..................515A	Spratt Av......523C
Av 523B	Sala Ct 534A	Sea Breeze La536D	..................514B	Sleight Av 536C	Spring St......512D
La 529C	Salamander Loop ..	Seacrest Av...535A	Shepard Av ..515A	Sloane Av 517C	Springfield Av 510B
ille Av ...527C	..................526D	Seacrest La ...536D	Sheraden Av ..510D	Slosson Av 511A	Springhill Av ..506B
ell Av ...514D	Sampson Av...530A	Seafoam St ...524D	Sheridan Av...512D	Slosson Ter ...507B	Spruce La 526D
Pl.........528B	Samuel Pl ...503C	Seaver Av......517D	Sheridan Ct ...523C	Smith Av 511A	Spruce St 523A
n Av 518D	Sanborn St ...534B	Seaver St 524D	Sheridan Pl...529C	Smith Ct 510B	Stack Dr 527B
ry St ...503C	Sand La..........519A	Seeley La 529D	Sherman Av ...507A	Smith Pl 503D	Stafford Av ...527C
Oak Rd ..511B	Sandalwood Dr	Seguine Av....533D	Sherwood Av..533C	Smith St 513A	Stage La 513A
stein St 513C	..................522D	Seguine Pl ...529C	Sherwood Pl ..529B	Smith Ter 507C	Stanley Av 506D
rd St 524A	Sanders St ...503D	Seidman Av ...529C	Shiel Av 526D	Smyrna Av 528B	Stanley Cir 529B
Av 512B	Sandgap St ...534B	Seldin Av 509A	Shift Pl.......527C	Sneden Av 529C	Stanwich St ...512D
es St 534A	Sands St 507C	Selkirk St 527A	Shiloh St 515A	Snug Harbor Rd	Star Ct 529A
a Pl 527A	Sandy La..........536D	Selvin Loop ...509A	Shirley Av 534B	..................506B	Starbuck St ...512D
on Rd ...521B	Sandywood La526D	Seneca Av 511B	Shirra Av 515B	Sobel Ct 512B	Stark Ct 507C
t Av 516B	Sanford Pl ...511B	Seneca St 505C	Shore Acres Rd	Sommer Av....509C	Starlight Rd ...512D
k Dr 527C	Sanford St ...536D	Serrell Av 529A	..................513D	Sommers La ...511C	Starr Av 511B
ll St 529D	Sanilac St...524A	Service Rd EW..520D	Shore Av 534C	Sonia Ct 532B	State St 505D
Pl 529B	Satterlee St ...536C	Seth Ct 512B	Shore Rd 536C	Soren St 516B	Staten Island Bd ....
I 519A	Saturn La 515C	Seven Gables Rd	Short Pl......533B	South Av 503C	..................511D
t 510B	Saunders St...512D	..................512D	Shotwell Av ...528B	South Ct 530C	Staten Island
n Av 527B	Savin Ct 518B	Seward Pl.......510B	Sideview Av ...509C	South St 505D	Expwy 509A
Pl 534B	Savoy St 523C	Sewell St 532C	Siersema Av...517A	S Beach Av ...519A	Station Av 532D
v 529C	Sawyer Av 511A	Seymour Av ...503D	Signal Hill Rd ..512B	S Bridge St....532C	Stebbins Av ...506A

Stecher Av	534C	Surf Av	536C	Tennyson Dr.	530C
Stecher St	534A	Surfside Pl	536D	Teri Ct	515B
Steele Av	524A	Susan Ct	513A	Terrace Av	533A
Steers St	516B	Sussex Green	527A	Terrace Ct	523A
Steinway Av	515A	Sutton Pl	527B	Thames Av	506D
Stephen Loop	515C	Suzanna La	528B	Thayer Pl	530B
Stepney St	515D	Swaim Av	534C	The Blvd	510B
Sterling Av	523B	Swan St	507C	The Oval	517D
Stern Ct	530A	Sweet Brook Rd		The Plaza	517D
Steuben St	512C		529A	Theatre La	513A
Stevenson Pl	533C	Sweetwater Av		Thelma Ct	513A
Stewart Av	509B		530C	Theresa Pl	512B
Stieg Av	521D	Swinnerton St	536C	Thollen Av	523C
Stobe Av	517D	Sycamore St	529C	Thomas Pl	523D
Stone La	521B	Sydney Pl	523B	Thomas St	523A
Stone St	507C	Sylva La	513B	Thompson Pl	513C
Stonecrest Ct.	530A	Sylvan Ct	536B	Thompson St	507D
Stonesgate Dr.	512D	Sylvan Pl	503A	Thornycroft Av	
Storer Av	526C	Sylvaton Ter	513B		529D
Stratford Av	512B	Sylvia St	529C	Thurston St	509B
Stratford Ct.	515C	Tabb Pl	503D	Tiber Pl	511D
Strauss St	513C	Tacoma St	518B	Tiger Ct	510A
Strawberry La	535A	Taft Av	507A	Tilden St	507A
Stroud Av	529A	Taft Ct	510D	Tillman St	511C
Studio La	513A	Talbot Pl	513A	Tilson Pl	513A
Sturges St	511A	Tallman St	529C	Timber Ridge Dr.	
Stuyvesant Av	529C	Tanglewood Dr.			530A
Stuyvesant Pl.	507A		521B	Tioga St	511D
Suffolk Av	511C	Tappen Ct	507C	Titus Av	523D
Summer St	513D	Targee St	512B	Todd Pl	531B
Summerfield Pl.		Tarlee Pl	530C	Toddy Av	515A
	503C	Tarlton St	531A	Todt Hill Ct	517D
Summit Av	517C	Tarring St	523C	Todt Hill Rd	511C
Summit Pl	529C	Tarrytown Av	523D	Token St	521C
Summit Rd	536A	Tate St	503D	Tompkins Av	513A
Sumner Av	509B	Tatro St	523C	Tompkins Cir	507A
Sumner Pl	507C	Taunton St	530A	Tompkins Ct	505B
Sunfield Av	521C	Taxter Pl	507C	Tompkins Pl	507C
Sunnyside Ter	512B	Taylor Ct	505D	Tompkins St	513A
Sunrise La	534B	Taylor St	505D	Tone La	513C
Sunrise Ter	507C	Teakwood Ct	521D	Tonking Rd	517C
Sunset Av	510D	Teleport Dr	508D	Topping St	524D
Sunset La	536D	Temple Ct	514B	Totten St	527A
Sunset Hill Dr.	512A	Tenafly Pl	528B	Tottenville Pl.	536C

Towers La	514B	Utica St	533A	Vincent Av	
Townley Av	511D	Utter Av	511A	Vine St	
Townsend Av	513A	Uxbridge St	510D	Vineland Av	
Tracy Av	532C	Vail Av	533C	Vinton St	
Trantor Pl	503D	Valdemar Av	533B	Virginia Av	
Travis Av	514B	Valencia Av	506D	Virginia Pl	
Treadwell Av	503B	Valleyview Pl.	511D	Vista Av	
Treetz St	511A	Van Allen Av	529A	Vista Pl	
Tremont Av	509B	Van Brunt St.	529C	Vogel Av	
Trent St	530D	Van Buren St	506B	Vogel La	
Trenton Ct	533D	Van Cordtland Av		Vogel Loop	
Tricia Way	536D		512B	Vogel Pl	
Trinity St	505D	Van Duzer St	507C	Von Braun Av	
Trossach Rd	507C	Van Duzer St Ext		Vreeland St	
Trout Pl	534C		507D	Vulcan St	
Troy St	521D	Van Name Av	503C	Wade St	
Truman St	536D	Van Pelt Av	503C	Wadsworth Av	
Trumbull Pl	507C	Van Riper St	503D	Wadsworth Rd	
Tuckahoe Av	533B	Van St	505B	Wadsworth Ter	
Tudor St	522D	Van Tuyl St	507A	
Tulip Cir	527B	Van Wyck Av	533D	Wagner St	
Turf Ct	515D	Vanderbilt Av	513A	Wahler Pl	
Turf Rd	515D	Vassar St	515C	Waimer Pl	
Turner St	526D	Vaughn St	513C	Wainwright Av	
Tuscany Ct	519A	Vedder Av	503D	Wakefield Av	
Tuttle St	510B	Veith Pl	534C	Wakefield Rd	
Twin Oak Dr.	512D	Veltman Av	505C	Walbrooke Av	
Twombley Av	523C	Venice Av	512C	Walch Pl	
Tyler Av	511B	Venus La	515D	Walcott Av	
Tynan St	521C	Vera St	518D	Walden Av	
Tyndale St	534B	Vermont Av	513C	Waldo Pl	
Tyron Av	528B	Vermont Ct	511C	Waldron Av	
Tyrrell St	536C	Vernon Av	527C	Wales Pl	
Tysen Ct	522B	Vespa Av	527B	Walker Ct	
Tysen St	506B	Veterans Rd EW		Walker Dr.	
Tysens La	523A		514C	Walker Pl	
Uncas Av	533A	Victor St	533A	Walker St	
Union Av	503C	Victoria Rd	527B	Wall St	
Union Ct	503C	Victory Bd		Wallace Av	
Union Pl	507C		507B-514B	Walloon St	
University Pl.	506D	Victory Bd Ext.	514D	Walnut Av	
Upton St	518B	Villa Av	503D	Walnut Pl	
Urbana St	518B	Villa Nova St	515C	Walnut St	
Utah St	536A	Village La	529C	Walsh St	

rs St 511B	Weser Av 512D	Wieland Av 527C	Windom Av 519B	Woodvale Loop..533C	**NUMBERED HIGHWAYS**
n Av 514C	West St............505D	Wilbur Pl.........510D	Windsor Av 523A	Woodward Av 510D	
el Av ...512B	W Buchanan St	Wilbur St 533D	Windsor Ct 511D	Wooley Av 510B	Highway names appear alphabetically in each borough street list.
er Av ...532A	...........................506B	Wilcox St 503C	Windsor Rd 511C	Wrenn St 533B	
Av 507C	W Castor Pl ...527C	Wild Av 514A	Windy Hollow Way	Wright Av 503B	
s Point Av	W Cedarview Av	Wilder Av 523A	..........................517D	Wright St 507C	
............536C	...........................522B	Wildwood La ..536D	Winfield Av 518B	Wygant Pl........505C	1 ....157C-205C
well Av ..510B	W Fingerboard Rd ..	Wiley Pl 523A	Winfield St 519C	Wyona Av 509D	9A 128A-202A
g Av 528B	...........................518D	Willard Av 510D	Wingham St 513D	Xenia St 519A	25 ....308D-340A
er Av ...527C	W Raleigh Av...505D	Willard Pl 510B	Winham Av 524C	Yale St 503C	25A 309C-324B
en Hill St 513A	West Shore Expwy	William Av 529D	Winslow Pl 529C	Yates Av 517A	27 ....422A-353D
vick Av ...510D	..............508D-526D	William St 507C	Winston St 520D	Yeomalt Av 534C	87 ....203D-226B
ington Av.........	W Willow Rd ..509B	Willis Av 507C	Winter Av 507A	Yetman Av 536A	95 ....157C-205C
............516B	Westbrook Av 503D	Willow Av 513A	Winthrop Pl 511A	Yona Av 509D	278 ....224B-502C
ington Pl 505C	Westbury Av ...506B	Willow Rd E & W ...	Wirt Av 526B	York Av 507A	295 ....218B-314B
nogue Rd.509B	Westcott Bd 511A	..........................509B	Wirt La 526D	York Ter 507A	440 ....503D-532B
r St 507D	Westentry Rd..517D	Willow St 507C	Witteman Pl 511D	Young St 512B	495 ....316B-325B
rbury Av 533A	Western Av 502B	Willow Pond Rd	Wolcoff La 503C	Yucca Dr..........527B	678 ....218C-349B
rford ..519B	Westervelt Av 507A	..........................517B	Wolcott Av 529A	Yukon Av 521A	695 ....218B
rs Av ...509B	Westfield Av ..526B	Willowbrook Ct	Wolf St 533D	Zachary Ct 505C	895 ....223A
rside Pkwy.......	Westminster Ct	..........................510B	Wolverine St ...523C	Zebra Pl 526B	
............530D	...........................518A	Willowbrook Rd	Wood Av 532C	Zeck Ct 509B	**ABBREVIATIONS**
rside St ...524D	Westport La ...515C	..........................509B	Wood Ct 527A	Zeni Pl 524A	
ins Av 521C	Westport St ...515C	Willowood La..522D	Woodbine Av ..509D	Zephyr Av 534D	Al ....Alley
on Av 514B	Westwood Av 509D	Wills Pl 519A	Woodbridge Pl	Zev Pl 513C	Av ....Avenue
ner St ...532A	Wetmore Rd....512D	Wilson Av 529C	..........................510B	Zoe St 518D	Bd, Blvd Boulevard
St 507D	WhalleyAv 529C	Wilson St 518B	Woodcliff Av ..502D	Zwicky Av 524A	Cir ....Circle
crest St..524D	Wheeler Av 511C	Wilson Ter 512D	Woodcrest Rd		Cl ....Close
rly Pl ...512B	Wheeling Av ..533B	Wiman Av 530C	..........................503C	**NUMBERED**	Cres ....Crescent
e St 505B	Whitaker Pl 518B	Wiman Pl 513B	Woodcutters La	**CT • ST**	Ct ....Court
ylan St ...521C	White Ct 529C	Winans St.........532D	..........................530B		Dr ....Drive
er St ...534B	White Pl 505D	Winant Av 527C	Wooddale Av ..511D	1 Ct 534B	Expwy Expressway
ter Av ...507C	White St 513D	Winant Pl 526C	Woodhaven Av	1 St 523B	Ft ....Fort
Av 523D	White Hall St ..523D	Winant St 503B	..........................517B	2 Ct 534B	Hts ....Heights
er St ...532D	White Oak La ..526D	Winchester Av	Woodhull Av ..533B	2 St 523B	Hwy ....Highway
Av 533C	White Plains Av	..........................529D	Woodland Av ..530A	3 Ct 534B	La ....Lane
La 532C	...........................513A	Windemere Av	Woodlawn Av 519A	3 St 523B	Pkwy ....Parkway
rook Av ..511C	Whitewood Av	..........................523C	Woodrow Rd ..527B	4 Ct 534B	Pl ....Place
s Ct ...506D	...........................512A	Windemere Rd	Woodruff La ...505B	4 St 523B	Plz ....Plaza
ington Ct..515C	Whitlock Av ...517B	..........................513C	Woods of Arden Rd	6 St 531A	Pt ....Point
ple St ...503C	Whitman Av ...530C	Windham Loop	..........................534B	7 St 523B	Rd ....Road
y Dr 534A	Whitney Av 518B	..........................521B	Woodside Av ..512B	8 St 523D	Sq ....Square
ock St...503D	Whitwell Pl......517B	Winding Woods	Woodstock Av 507C	9 St 523B	St ....Street
worth Av 519C	Wiederer Pl 512B	Loop 536D	Woodvale Av ..533C	10 St 523D	Ter ....Terrace
					Tri.................Triangle
					Wk....................Walk

EMERGENCIES

AAA Road Service
800-222-4357

Ambulance, Fire, Police 911

Animal Bites
212-676-2483

Animal Med. Ctr
212-838-8100

Arson Hotline
718-722-3600

Battered Women
800-621-4673

Coast Guard
800-735-3415

Child Abuse
800-342-3720

Dental Emergency
212-677-2510

Domestic Violence
800-621-4673

Drug Abuse
800-395-3400

Emergency Children's Services
212-966-8000

Emergency Medical Technician Info
718-416-7000

Hazardous Materials
718-699-9811

Locksmith (24hr)
212-247-6747

Park Emergencies
(24hr) 800-201-7275

Pharmacy (24hr)
212-541-9708

Poison Control Center (24hr)
212-764-7667

Rape Hotline
212-577-7777

Runaway Hotline
212-966-8000

Sex Crimes Reports
212-267-7273

Suicide Prevention
212-532-2400

Victim Services Hotline
212-577-7777

ESSENTIALS

AAA
212-757-2000

B & B Reservations
212-737-7049

ChequePoint USA
212-869-6281

Convention & Visitor's Bureau
212-484-1222

Customs (24hr)
800-697-3662

Directory Assistance 411

Foreign Exchange Rates 212-883-0400

Immigration
800-375-5283

Hotel Reservations
800-444-7666

Jacob Javits Convention Center
212-216-2000

Lost Travelers Checks
• AMEX
800-221-7282
• Citicorp
800-645-6556
• VISA
800-227-6811

Movies
212-777-FILM

NYC On Stage
212-768-1818

Passport Info
718-834-3052

Post Office
212-967-8585

Telegrams
800-325-6000

Time
212-976-1616

Traveler's Aid
212-577-7700

UN Information
212-963-1234

Wake-Up Call
212-540-9000

Weather
212-976-1212

TOURS & EXCURSIONS

All American Stage Tours
800-735-8530

Art Tours
212-239-4160

Big Apple Greeter
212-669-2896

Big Onion Tours
212-439-1090

Bronx Heritage Trail 718-881-8900

Brooklyn Historical Society
718-254-9830

City Walks
212-989-2456

Circle Line
212-563-3200

Doorways to Design
718-339-1542

Ellis Island Ferry
212-269-5755

GrayLine Tours
212-397-2600

Harlem Visitors & Convention Assoc.
212-862-8497

Hoboken Ferry (NJ)
201-420-4422

Liberty Helicopters
212-967-6464

NY Apple Tours
800-876-9868

NY Gateway Tours
212-967-6008

NY Waterway
800-53-FERRY

The Petrel (1938)
877-693-6131

Seaport Music Cruises
212-630-8888

Seastreak
800-262-8743

Spirit Cruises
212-727-2789

Urban Explorations
718-721-5254

Walking Tours of Chinatown
212-619-4785

Wild Foods & Ecology Tours
718-291-6825

World Yacht Cruises
212-630-8100

92nd St. YM–YWHA
212-996-1100

TRANSPORT

Airlines–Domestic
• American
800-433-7300
• Continental
800-523-3273
• Delta
800-221-1212
• Northwest
800-441-1818
• TWA
800-221-2000
• United
800-241-6522
• USAir
800-428-4322

Airlines–Foreign
• Aeromexico
800-237-6639

• Air Canada
800-776-3000
• Air France
800-321-4538
• ANA–ALL Nip
800-235-9262
• British Airwa
800-247-9297
• Lufthansa
800-645-3880

Bus & Subway
• Main
718-330-1234
•Access -Disab
718-596-8585
• Greyhound
800-231-2222
• Hampton Jitn
800-936-0440

Ferries
• Ellis Island
212-269-5755
• Harbor Shutt
888-254-RIDE
• NY Waterwa
800-53-FERRY
• Seastreak
800-262-8743
• Staten Island
718-815-BOAT
• Statue of Libe
212-269-5755

**George Washi
Bridge Bus Sta**
212-564-1114

Helicopter
• Helicopter Fli
Services
212-355-0801
• Liberty
212-487-4777

Airport
in
244-4444

ardia Airport
in
476-5000
ry
54-FERRY
king
533-3850

usine Service
728-2838

ark Airport
in
361-6000
king
623-6334

assenger Ship inal
246-5451

Authority Bus inal
564-8484

sevelt Island
212-832-4543

ns
trak
523-8720
582-6875
ng Island
oad (LIRR)
217-5477
tro North
638-7646
Transit
626-7433
TH
234-7284

rboro Airport
288-1775

BUSINESS & CONSUMER
Better Bus. Bureau
212-533-6200

Chamber of Commerce
BK 718-875-1000
BX 718-829-4111
MA 212-493-7400
QS 718-898-8500
SI 718-727-1900

Consumer Affairs
212-487-4444

Gas, Electric, Water Complaints
800-342-3377

Small Business Administration (SBA) 212-264-4354

Taxi Complaints
212-221-8294

GOVERNMENT
Borough President
BK 718-802-3700
BX 718-590-3500
MA 212-669-8300
QS 718-286-3000
SI 718-816-2236

City Council
212-788-7100

Mayor's Office
212-788-7585

Tax Info
• City Tax (24hr)
718-935-6736
• Federal (IRS)
800-829-1040
• State Tax
800-225-5829

HEALTH & HUMAN
AIDS Hotline
800-462-6787

Alcoholics Anonymous
212-647-1680

All Night Pharmacy
212-541-9708

Bail 212-669-2879

Domestic Violence Hotline
800-621-4673

Department for the Aging
212-442-1000

Disabled Info
212-229-3000

Health Info (24hr)
212-434-2000

Legal Aid Society
212-577-3300

Medicaid
718-291-1900

Medicare
800-MEDICARE

Parents League of NY 212-737-7385

Salvation Army
212-337-7200

Senior Citizens
212-442-1000

Salvation Army
212-337-7200

Social Security
800-772-1213

LIBRARIES
The Bronx
718-579-4200

Brooklyn
718-230-2100

Brooklyn Business
718-623-7000

NY Public
212-340-0849

NY Science, Industry & Business (SIBL)
212-592-7000

Queens
718-990-0700

Staten Island
718-442-8560

PARKING & TRAFFIC
Parking Violations
212-477-4430

Potholes
718-225-5368

Registration Plates
212-645-5550

Sidewalks
718-225-5368

Towed-Away ?
212-869-2929

UTILITIES
Bell Atlantic
890-1550

Brooklyn Union (Keyspan)
718-643-4050

ConEdison
800-75-CON-ED

WEBSITES NY
All internet addresses listed are assumed to begin with "www."

Brooklyn Botanic Gardem
bbg.org

Brooklyn Children's Museum
bchildmus.org

Brooklyn Information & Culture
brooklynx.org/tourism

The Brooklyn Museum of Art
brooklynart.org

Brooklyn Public Library
brooklynpublic
library.org

Central Park
centralpark.org

Citysearch NY
citysearch.com

Metrobeat
metrobeat.com

Official City of New York Web Site
ci.nyc.ny.us/
home.html

NYC Reference a.k.a.Clay Irving's Home Page
panix.com/~clay/

New York Sidewalk
sidewalk.com

The New York Times
nytimes.com

The New York Web
nyw.com

NYC Beer Guide
nycbeer.org

Prospect Park.
prospectpark.org

VanDam, Inc.
vandam.com

Village Voice
villagevoice.com

NOTES

ATTRACTIONS

Abyssinian Baptist Church
132 W 138 St, MA
212-862-7474 **149**B

American Craft Museum
40 W 53 St, MA
212-956-6047 **125**B

American Museum of Natural History
CPW @ 79 St, MA
212-769-5000 **133**A

The Apollo Theater
253 W 125 St, MA
212-749-5838 **149**C

Battery Park City Esplanade **102**A

Bloomingdale's
1000 Third Av, MA
212-705-2000 **130**D

Brighton Beach
Btwn Ocean & West End Avs, Coney Island, BK **443**D

The Bronx Museum of the Arts
1040 The Grand Concourse, BX
718-681-6000 **221**C

Bronx Zoo – Int'l Wildlife Conservation Park
Bronx River Pkwy @ E Fordham Rd, BX, 718-367-1010 **216**A

Brooklyn Academy of Music (BAM)
30 Lafayette Av, BK
718-636-4100 **407**D

Brooklyn Botanic Gardens
1000 Washington Av BK, 718-622-4433 **415**D

Brooklyn Bridge
Enter @ City Hall Park, MA or Adams St, BK **105**A-**408**B

Brooklyn Heights Promenade **406**B

Brooklyn Museum of Art (BMA)
200 Eastern Pkwy BK, 718-638-5000 **415**D

Carnegie Hall
881 Seventh Av, MA
212-247-7800 **125**A

Cathedral Church of St. John the Divine
Amsterdam Av @ 112 St, MA
212-662-2133 **144**D

Central Park **129**A

Chelsea Market **116**D

Children's Museum of Manhattan
212 W 83 St, MA
212-721-1223 **132**B

Chinatown, Manhattan **107**C

Chrysler Bldg
E 42 St @ Lexington Av MA **126**D

Circle Line
W 42 St @ 12 Av, MA
212-563-3200 **120**A

The Cloisters
Fort Tryon Pk, MA
212-923-3700 **158**B

Columbia University
W 116 St @ Broadway, MA
212-854-1754 **144**B

Coney Island USA
1208 Surf Av, BK
718-372-5159 **443**C

Cooper-Hewitt National Design Museum
2 E 91 St, MA
212-849-8300 **137**D

El Museo del Barrio
1230 Fifth Av, MA
212-831-7272 **141**B

Ellis Island Nat'l Monument
Take ferry from Battery Park, MA
212-363-3200 **102**C

Empire State Bldg
350 Fifth Av, MA
212-736-3100 **121**D

FAO Schwarz
767 Fifth Av, MA
212-644-9400 **129**D

Federal Hall Nat'l Memorial
26 Wall St, MA
212-264-8711 **103**C

Flatiron Bldg
Fifth Av @ 23 St, MA **117**B

Fraunces Tavern Museum
54 Pearl St, MA
212-425-1778 **103**A

Frick Collection
1 E 70 St, MA
212-288-0700 **130**B

Grant Nat'l Mem
Riverside Dr @ W 122 St, MA
212-666-1640 **144**A

Guggenheim (SoHo)
575 Broadway @ Prince St, MA
212-423-3500 **109**B

Int'l Center of Photography (ICP)
1135 Fifth Av, MA
212-860-1777 **137**B

ICP Midtown
6 Av @ W 43 St, MA
212-768-4680 **125**D

Intrepid Sea-Air-Space Museum
W 46 St @ 12 Av, MA
212-245-0072 **124**C

Isamu Noguchi Garden Museum
32-37 Vernon Bd, QS
718-204-7088 **308**B

Jamaica Bay Nat'l Wildlife Refuge
Broad Channel & First St, QS
718-318-4300 **358**B

Jewish Museum
1109 Fifth Av @ E 92 St, MA
212-423-3200 **137**B

Lincoln Center for the Performing Arts
Broadway @ 65 St, MA
212-875-5000 **128**D

Little Italy

Lower East Side Tenement Museum
90 Orchard St, M
212-431-0233

Macy's Herald S
151 W 34 St, MA
212-695-4400

Madison Sq Gar
4 Penn Plz, MA
212-465-6741

The Metropolita Museum of Art
5 Av @ E 82 St, M
212-535-7710

Morgan Library
29 E 36 St, MA
212-685-0610

Museum for African Art
593 Broadway, M
212-966-1313

Museum of American Folk A
2 Lincoln Sq, MA
212-977-7298

Museum of the of New York
1220 Fifth Av, M.
212-534-1672

Museum of Chin in the Americas
70 Mulberry St, M
212-619-4785

The Museum of Jewish Heritage
18 First Pl, MA
212-968-1800

um of Modern
(MoMA)
53 St, MA
08-9480   **125**B

Museum of
ision & Radio
52 St, MA
21-6600   **125**B

Museum of the
ican Indian
ms House @
ng Green, MA
25-6700   **102**D

Academy
um
Fifth Av
9 St, MA
69-4880   **137**D

Studio Tour
ckefeller Plz,
212-664-4000
125D

Museum of
emporary Art
roadway, MA
19-1222   **109**B

quarium
St
rf Av, BK
65-3400   **443**C

otanical Garden
t @ Southern
X
17-8700   **210**C

all of Science
111 St, QS
99-0005   **320**B

ublic Library
@ 5 Av, MA
61-7220   **122**A

**NY Stock Exchange
(NYSE)**
20 Broad St, MA
212-656-5165   **102**B

The Plaza Hotel
768 Fifth Av @
Central Park S, MA
212-759-3000   **129**D

**Queens Museum
of Art (QMA)**
Flushing Meadows–
Corona Park, QS
718-592-9700   **320**D

**Queens Theatre
in the Park**
Flushing Meadows
Corona Park, QS
718-760-0064   **320**D

**Radio City
Music Hall**
Sixth Av @ W 50 St,
Rockefeller Ctr, MA
212-247-4777   **125**B

Riverside Church
490 Riverside Dr
@ W 120 St, MA
212-222-5900   **144**A

Rockefeller Center
Bet. Fifth–Sixth Avs
& 48–51 Sts, MA
212-698-2950   **125**D

**Rose Center for
Earth & Science**
CPW @ W 81 St,
212-769-5900   **133**A

**St Patrick's
Cathedral**
Fifth Av @ E 50 St,
MA, 212-753-2261
125B

St Paul's Chapel
B'way @ Fulton St,
MA, 212-602-0872
104D

Seagram Bldg
375 Park Av, MA
212-572-7000   **126**B

Shea Stadium
Flushing Meadows
Corona Pk, QS
718-507-8499   **320**B

**Snug Harbor
Cultural Center**
1000 Richmond Ter,
SI, 718-448-2500
506B

**Socrates
Sculpture Park**
B'way @ Vernon Bd,
Long Island City, QS
718-956-1819   **308**B

**Solomon R
Guggenheim
Museum (Uptown)**
1071 Fifth Av, MA
212-423-3500   **138**C

**Sony Wonder
Technology Lab**
550 Madison Av
@ 56 St, MA
212-833-8100   **126**B

SoHo
Houston–Canal Sts
& SixthAv– Lafayette
St, MA   **109**D

**South Street
Seaport Museum**
Seaport Plz
207 Front St, MA
212-748-8600   **105**C

Staten Island Ferry
Take ferry from
Battery Park, MA
212-363-3200   **103**C

**Statue of Liberty
Liberty Island**
212-363-3200 Ferry,
212-269-5755   **102**C

**Studio Museum in
Harlem**
144 W 125 St, MA
212-864-4500   **145**C

Tiffany & Co.
727 Fifth Av, MA
212-755-8000   **126**A

Times Square   125C

Trinity Church
89 B'way @ Wall St,
MA, 212-602-0872
102B

Trump Tower
725 Fifth Av
@ E 56 St, MA
212-832-2000   **126**A

United Nations
First Av @ E 45 St,
MA, 212-963-1234
127C

**Van Cortlandt
Mansion Museum**
B'way @ 246 St, BX
718-543-3344   **209**A

**Verrazano Narrows
Bridge   434**A

**Waldorf–Astoria
Hotel**
301 Park Av, MA
212-355-3000   **126**B

**Warner Bros.
Studio Store**
Fifth Av @ 57 St, MA
718-754-0300   **129**D

**Washington Square
Park, MA   113**C

Wave Hill
675 W 252 St, BX
718-549-3200   **208**A

**Whitney Museum
of American Art**
945 Madison Av, MA
212-570-3600   **134**D

Woolworth Bldg
233 Broadway, MA
104D

**World Financial
Center (WFC)**
Liberty St @ the
Hudson River, MA
212-945-0505   **104**C

**World Trade Center
Observation deck**
WTC 2 @ Liberty St,
MA, 212-435-7000
104A

Yankee Stadium
161 St & River Av, BX
718-760-6200   **221**C

TO FIND A TOP 100

Simply turn to page
and locate the
attraction in grids
A,B,C or D.

MA = Manhattan
BX = The Bronx
BK = Brooklyn
QS = Queens
SI = Staten Island

ATTRACTIONS

BUSINESS

ADVERTISING

Interpublic Group of Companies
1271 Sixth Av, MA
212-399-8000 **126**A

Ogilvy & Mather
309 W 49 St, MA
212-237-4000 **125**C

OmniCom Group
437 Madison Av, MA
212-415-3600 **130**D

Saatchi & Saatchi
375 Hudson St, MA
212-463-2000 **108**B

WPP Group USA
309 W 49 St, MA
212-632-2200 **125**C

CONSUMER GOODS

Avon
1345 Sixth Av, MA
212-282-5000 **126**A

Bristol-Meyers Squibb Company
345 Park Av, MA
212-546-4000 **126**B

Colgate Palmolive
300 Park Av, MA
212-310-2000 **126**D

Estée Lauder
767 Fifth Av, MA
212-572-4200 **129**D

Kinney Shoe Corp
233 Broadway, MA
212-720-3700 **104**D

Pfizer
235 E 42 St, MA
212-573-2323 **123**A

MAFCO
36 E 63 St, MA
212-688-9000 **130**D

Philip Morris
120 Park Av, MA
212-880-5000 **122**A

RJR Nabisco
1301 Sixth Av, MA
212-258-5600 **126**A

Seagram
375 Park Av, MA
212-572-7000 **126**B

Unilever
390 Park Av, MA
212-888-1260 **126**B

Venator Group, Inc.
233 Broadway, MA
212-553-2000 **104**D

FINANCIAL SERVICES

American Express
200 Vesey St, MA
212-640-2000 **104**C

Bank of NY
1 Wall St, MA
212-495-1784 **102**B

Bear Stearns
245 Park Av, MA
212-272-2000 **126**D

Chase Manhattan Bank
270 Park Av, MA
212-270-6000 **126**D

Citigroup
399 Park Av, MA
212-559-1000 **126**B

Deutsche Bank
31 West 52 St,
212-469-8000 **126**A

Donaldson, Lufkin & Jenrette
277 Park Av, MA
212-892-3000 **126**D

Ernst & Young
787 Seventh Av, MA
212-773-3000 **125**A

Federal Reserve Bank of NY
33 Liberty St, MA
212-720-5000 **105**C

Fortis
1 Chase Manhattan Plz, MA
212-859-7000 **103**A

Goldman Sachs
85 Broad St, MA
212-902-1000 **103**A

HSBC Bank
452 Fifth Av, MA
212-525-5000 **122**A

KPMG Peat Marwick
345 Park Av, MA
212-758-9700 **126**B

JP Morgan
60 Wall St, MA
212-483-2323 **103**A

Lehman Brothers
3 WFC
@ 200 Vesey St, MA
212-526-7000 **104**D

Merrill Lynch
N & S Tower, WFC,
MA, 212-449-1000
104C

Morgan Stanley, Dean Witter, Discover & Co
1585 Broadway, MA
212-761-3000 **125**C

PaineWebber Group
1285 Sixth Av, MA
212-713-3000 **125**B

Prudential Securities
199 Water St, MA
212-214-1000 **105**C

Salomon Smith Barney
388 Greenwich St,
MA, 212-816-6000
106C

INSURANCE

Axa Financial Equitable
1290 Sixth Av, MA
212-554-1234 **125**A

Empire Blue Cross & Blue Shield
622 Third Av, MA
212-476-1000 **122**B

Guardian Life
201 Park Av S, MA
212-598-8000 **118**D

Marsh & McLennan
1166 Sixth Av, MA
212-345-5000 **126**C

Met Life
1 Madison Av, MA
212-578-2211 **118**A

MONY Life
1740 Broadway, MA
212-708-2000 **125**A

NYLCare Health Plans
1 Liberty Plz, MA
212-437-1000 **104**D

NY Life
51 Madison Av, MA
212-576-7000 **118**B

Teachers Insura and Annuity As of America
730 Third Av, M
212-490-9000

Reliance Group Holdings
55 E 52 St, MA
212-909-1100

MEDIA

ABC
77 W 66 St, MA
212-456-7777

Bertelsmann
1540 Broadway
212-782-1000

CBS
51 W 52 St, MA
212-975-4321

FOX
205 E 67 St, MA
212-452-5555

Hearst
959 Eighth Av, N
212-649-2000

NBC
30 Rockefeller Plz
212-664-4000

News America Holdings
1211 Sixth Av, N
212-852-7000

Sony Corp
550 Madison Av
212-833-6800

Time Warner
75 Rockefeller Pl
MA, 212-484-80(

er Corporation
ludson St, MA
29-6000 **108**B

om
Broadway, MA
58-6000 **125**C

LISHING

nce
ications
es Sq,
86-2860 **125**C

es & Noble
ifth Av, MA
33-3300 **118**C

é Nast
es Sq,
86-2860 **125**C

's NY Business
42 St, MA
10-0100 **122**A

Jones
iberty St, MA
16-2000 **102**B

er & Jahr
exington Av, MA
99-2000 **122**B

erCollins
53 St, MA
07-7000 **126**B

ette Filipacchi
Broadway, MA
67-6000 **125**A

st Magazines
V 55 St,
49-2000 **126**A

raw Hill
Sixth Av, MA
12-2000 **125**A

New York Times
229 W 43 St. MA
212-556-1234 **125**A

Penguin Putnam
375 Hudson St, MA
212-366-2000 **109**A

Random House East
201 E 50 St, MA
212-751-2600 **127**A

Random House West
1540 Broadway, MA
212-354-6500 **125**C

St Martin's Press
175 Fifth Av, MA
212-674-5151 **118**A

Simon & Schuster
1230 Sixth Av, MA
212-698-7000 **125**D

von Holtzbrinck
123 W 18 St, MA
212-674-5151 **117**D

Warner Books
1271 Sixth Av, MA
212-522-7200 **125**A

REAL ESTATE DEVELOPMENT

Forest City Ratner
1 MetroTech BK,
718-722-3500 **408**D

Helmsley–Spear
60 E 42 St, MA
212-687-6400 **122**B

Loews
667 Madison Av, MA
212-521-2000 **130**D

Mitsui & Co USA
200 Park Av, MA
212-878-4000 **126**D

Trump Organization
725 Fifth Av, MA
212-832-2000 **126**B

TECHNOLOGY

AT&T
32 Sixth Av, MA
212-387-5400 **106**B

Bell Atlantic
1095 Sixth Av, MA
212-395-2121 **126**C

Dover Corp.
280 Park Av, MA
212-922-1640 **126**C

ITT Corp
1330 Sixth Av, MA
212-258-1000 **126**A

Mitsubishi Int'l
520 Madison Av, MA
212-605-2000 **126**B

Nissho Iwai
1211 Sixth Av, MA
212-704-6500 **125**A

Siemens
1301 Sixth Av, MA
212-258-4000 **126**A

Toshiba America
1251 Sixth Av, MA
212-596-0600 **125**A

UTILITIES & TRANSPORT

Con Edison
4 Irving Pl, MA
212-460-4600 **118**D

MTA
347 Madison Av, MA
212-878-7000 **126**D

Keyspan Energy (Brooklyn Union)
1 MetroTech Ctr, BK
718-403-2000 **408**D

BUSINESS IMPROVEMENT DISTRICTS (BIDS)

Alliance for Downtown, NY
120 Broadway, MA
212-566-6700 **102**B

Fashion Center
249 W 39 St, MA
212-764-9600 **121**A

Fifth Av
600 Fifth Av, MA
212-265-1310 **126**C

Fulton Mall Assoc.
356 Fulton St, BK
718-852-5118 **407**C

Grand Central Partnership
6 E 43 St, MA
212-818-1777 **122**A

Lincoln Square
10 Columbus Cir, MA
212-974-9100 **129**C

Madison Av
903 Madison Av, MA
212-249-4095 **130**B

MetroTech
4 MetroTech, BK
718-488-8200 **409**C

Times Square
1560 Broadway, MA
212-768-1560 **125**C

14 St/Union Sq
223 E 14 St, MA
212-674-1164 **118**D

34 St Partnership
6 E 43 St, MA
212-818-1913 **122**A

CHAMBERS OF COMMERCE

The Bronx
226 E Fordham Rd,
BX, 718-829-4111 **215**C

Brooklyn
7 MetroTech Center,
BK, 718-875-1000 **409**C

NYC Partnership
1 Battery Park Plz, MA
212-493-7400 **121**C

Queens
75-20 Astoria Bd, QS
718-898-8500 **310**D

Staten Island
130 Bay St, SI
718-727-1900 **507**B

CONVENTIONS

Jacob Javits
11 Av @ 36 St, MA
212-216-2000 **120**A

NY Convention Pier
Pier 92, MA **124**A

TO FIND A TOP 100

Simply turn to page
and locate the
company in grids
A,B,C or D.

MA = Manhattan
BX = The Bronx
BK = Brooklyn
QS = Queens
SI = Staten Island

DINING

AMERICAN

Aureole $$$$
34 E 61 St, MA
212-319-1660 **130**D

Gramercy Tavern $$$$ 42 E 20 St, MA
212-477-0777 **118**D

March $$$$
405 E 58 St, MA
212-754-6272 **131**C

New Prospect Cafe $$ 393 Flatbush Av, BK, 718-638-2148
415B

Union Sq Cafe $$$
21 E 16 St, MA
212-243-4020 **118**C

BISTRO

Balthazar $$$
80 Spring St, MA
212-965-1414 **109**B

L'Actuel $$$
145 E 50 St, MA,
212-583-0001 **127**B

Raoul's $$$
180 Prince St, MA
212-966-3518 **109**A

CHINESE

Canton $$$
45 Division St, MA
212-226-4441 **107**C

Chin Chin $$$
216 E 49 St, MA
212-888-4555 **127**C

Joe's Shanghai $$
136-21 37 Av, QS
718-539-3838 **321**A

Shun Lee Palace $$$
155 E 55 St, MA
212-371-8844 **126**B

Tse Yang $$$
34 E 51 St, MA
212-688-5447 **126**B

CONTINENTAL

Eleven Madison Park $$$
11 Madison Av, MA
212-8898-0905 **118**A

Four Seasons $$$$
99 E 52 St, MA
212-754-9494 **126**B

Marylou's $$$
21 W 9 St, MA
212-533-0012 **113**A

One if by Land, TIBS $$$$ 17 Barrow St, MA, 212-228-0822
113C

Petrossian $$$$
182 W 58 St, MA
212-245-2214 **130**C

Peacock Alley $$$
Waldorf-Astoria
301 Park Av, MA
212-872-4895 **126**D

21 Club $$$
21 W 52 St, MA
212-582-7200 **125**B

DELI/KOSHER

Barney Greengrass $$
541 Amsterdam Av, MA, 212-724-4707
136D

Carnegie Deli $
854 Seventh Av, MA
212-757-2245 **125**A

Katz's $
205 E Houston St, MA
212-254-2246 **110**B

Ratners $$
138 Delancy St, MA
212-677-5588 **110**B

2nd Av Deli $
156 Second Av, MA
212-677-0606 **114**A

DINER

Bright Food Shop $$ 218 Eighth Av,
212-243-4433 **117**C

Coffee Shop $$
29 Union Sq W, MA
212-243-7969 **118**C

Empire Diner $$
210 Tenth Av, MA
212-243-2736 **116**B

Juniors $
386 Flatbush Ext. Av
BK, 718-852-5257
409C

Market Diner $$
572 Eleventh Av, MA
212-695-0415 **120**B

Vynl Diner $
824 Ninth Av, MA
212-974-2003 **124**D

FRENCH

Daniel $$$$
60 E 65 St, MA
212-288-0033 **130**B

Chanterelle $$$$
2 Harrison St, MA
212-966-6960 **104**B

La Bouillabaisse $$
145 Atlantic Av, BK
718-522-8275 **408**C

La Côte Basque $$$$ 60 W 55 St, MA
212-688-6525 **126**A

Le Cirque 2000 $$$$
455 Madison Av, MA
212-303-7788 **126**B

Le Gans $$$
46 Gansevoort St, MA,
212-675-5224 **112**B

FUN FOOD

Brooklyn Diner USA $$ 212 W 57 St, MA
212-581-8900 **125**A

Hard Rock Cafe $$
221 W 57 St, MA
212-489-6565 **125**A

Official All Star Cafe $$ 1540 B'way, MA
212-840-TEAM **125**C

Planet Hollywood $$ 140 W 57 St, MA
212-333-7827 **126**B

Tavern on the Green $$$ CPW & 67 St, MA
212-873-3200 **129**A

FUSION

Cendrillon $$
45 Mercer St, MA
212-343-9012 **109**D

Jo Jo $$$
160 E 64 St, MA
212-223-5656 **130**D

Verbena $$$
54 Irving Pl, MA
212-260-5454 **118**D

Le Colonial $$$
149 E 57 St, MA
212-752-0808 **130**D

GREEK, MIDDLE EASTERN

Agrotikon $$
322 E 14 St, MA
212-473-2602

Karyatis $$
35-03 Broadway
718-204-0666

Moustache Pitza $
405 Atlantic Av,
718-852-5555

Oznots Dish $$
79 Berry St, BK
718-599-6596

Periyali $$$
35 W 20 St, MA
212-463-7890

Telly's Taverna $
28-13 23 Av, QS
718-728-9194

INDIAN

Baluchi's $$
193 Spring St, MA
212-226-2828

Bay Leaf $$
49 W 56 St, MA
212-957-1818

Dawat $$$
210 E 58 St, MA
212-355-7555

Jackson Diner $$
37-03 74 St, QS
718-672-1232

Shaan $$$
57 W 48 St, MA
212-977-8400

Tabla $$$
11 Madison Av,
212-889-0667

DINING

...AN

Bondi $$$
0 St, MA
91-8136 **117D**

a $$$$
58 St, MA
58-1479 **131C**

Mio $$$
arren St, MA
71-5555 **104B**

Mino $$$$
3 St, MA
73-3783 **113C**

o $$$
53 St, MA
53-8450 **127A**

$$$
114 St, MA
22-6709 **147C**

NESE

ki $$
9 St, MA
73-3327 **114A**

$
econd Av, MA
77-0361 **115C**

$$$$
udson St, MA
19-0500 **106C**

e Sushi $
ompson St, MA
77-9346 **109A**

ICAN/ MEXICAN

ing Horse
Mexicano $$
ghth Av, MA
63-9511 **117C**

Santa Fe $$
72 W 69 St, MA
212-724-0822 **129A**

Zarela $$$
953 Second Av, MA
212-644-6740 **127B**

OLDE NEW YORK

Café des Artistes $$$ 1 W 67 St, MA
212-877-3500 **129A**

Fanelli $
94 Prince St, MA
212-226-9412 **109B**

Fraunces Tavern $$$
54 Pearl St, MA
212-269-0144 **103A**

Gage & Tollner $$$
372 Fulton St, BK
718-875-5181 **408B**

Old Bermuda Inn
$$$ 2512 Arthur Kill
Rd, SI, 718-948-7600 **526B**

Old Homestead $$$
56 Ninth Av, MA
212-242-9040 **117C**

PIZZA

John's Pizzeria $
278 Bleecker St, MA
212-243-1680 **113C**

Lombardi's $$
32 Spring St, MA
212-941-7994 **110C**

Mario's $$
2342 Arthur Av, BX
718-584-1188 **215B**

Patsy Grimaldi's $
19 Old Fulton St, BK
718-858-4300 **407A**

SEAFOOD

Aquagrill $$$
210 Spring St,
212-274-0505 **109A**

Bridge Cafe $$
279 Water St, MA
212-227-3344 **105C**

Le Bernardin $$$$
155 W 51 St, MA
212-489-1515 **125A**

Le Pescadou $$$
18 King St, MA
212-924-3434 **108A**

Oceana $$$$
55 E 54 St, MA
212-759-5941 **126B**

River Café $$$$
1 Water St, BK
718-522-5200 **406B**

Water's Edge $$$
44 Dr & E River, QS,
718-482-0033 **308C**

SOUTHERN & SOUL FOOD

Jezebel $$$
630 Ninth Av, MA
212-582-1045 **124D**

Mekka $$
14 Av A, MA
212-475-8500 **114D**

Miss Ann's $
86 S Portland St, BK
718-858-6997 **407D**

Shark Bar $$
307 Amsterdam Av,
212-874-8500 **132D**

Sylvia's $$
328 Lenox Av, MA
212-996-0660 **149D**

SPANISH/TAPAS

El Cid $$
322 W 15 St, MA
212-929-9332 **117C**

Marichu $$$
342 E 46 St, MA
212-370-1866 **127C**

STEAK

Palm & Palm Too $$$
837 Second Av, MA
212-687-2953
212-697-5198 **127C**

Peter Luger $$$$
178 Broadway, BK
718-387-7400 **404A**

Post House $$$$
28 E 23 St, MA
212-935-2888 **130D**

Smith & Wollensky
$$$ 797 Third Av, MA
212-753-1530 **126D**

Sparks $$$$
210 E 46 St, MA
212-687-4855 **127C**

THAI

Jai-Ya Thai $$
396 Third Av, MA
212-889-1330 **118B**

Planet–Thailand $
141 N 7 St, BK
718-599-5758 **404A**

Vong $$$
200 E 54 St, MA
212-486-9592 **127A**

TROPICAL

Asia de Cuba $$$
237 Madison Av, MA
212-726-7755 **122B**

Bambou $$$
243 E 14 St, MA
212-505-1180 **118D**

Brawta $
347 Atlantic Av, BK
718-855-5515- **406C**

Calle Ocho $$$
466 Columbus Av
(81/82 St),
212-873-5025 **132B**

Circus $$$
808 Lexington Av, MA,
212-223-2965 **130D**

Tropica Bar & Seafood House $$$
200 Park Av, MA
212-867-6767 **126D**

Casa Brasil $$
316 E 53 St, MA
212-355-5360 **127A**

VEGETARIAN

Angelica Kitchen $
300 E 12 St, MA
212-228-2909 **114A**

Hangawi $$$
12 E 32 St, MA
212-213-0077 **122C**

Mavalli Palace $$
46 E 29 St, MA
212-679-5535 **118B**

Quantum Leap $
88 W 3 St, MA
212-677-8050 **113C**

Souen $$
28 E 13 St, MA
212-627-7150 **113B**

TO FIND A TOP 100

Simply turn to page and locate the restaurant in grids A,B,C or D.

MA = Manhattan
BX = The Bronx
BK = Brooklyn
QS = Queens
SI = Staten Island

EDUCATION

ARTS

Culinary

French Culinary Institute
462 Broadway, MA
212-219-8890 **109**D

NY Restaurant School
75 Varick St, MA
212-226-5500 **109**C

Performing

Alvin Ailey American Dance Center
211 W 61 St, MA
212-767-0940 **128**D

American Academy of Dramatic Arts
120 Madison Av, MA
212-686-9244 **122**D

Harlem School of the Arts (HSA)
645 St Nicholas Av, MA, 212-926-4100 **153**C

Joffrey Ballet School
434 Sixth Av, MA
212-254-8520 **113**A

The Juilliard School
60 Lincoln Center, MA
212-799-5000 **128**B

Manhattan School of Music
120 Claremont Av, MA
212-749-2802 **144**A

Mannes College of Music
150 W 85 St, MA
212-580-0210 **132**B

Martha Graham School
316 E 63 St, MA
212-838-5886 **131**C

School of American Ballet
165 W 65 St, MA
212-877-0600 **128**E

Steller Adler Conservatory
419 Lafayette St, MA
212-260-0525 **113**D

Visual & Design Arts at University Settlement
184 Eldridge St, MA
212-674-9120 **110**B

Nat'l Academy of Design School of Fine Art
5 E 89 St, MA
212-996-1908 **137**D

Fashion Institute of Technology (FIT)
227 W 27 St, MA
212-217-7999 **117**A

Parsons School of Design
2 W 13 St, MA
212-229-8900 **113**A

Pratt Institute
• Manhattan
259 Lafayette St, MA
212-925-8481 **110**A
• Brooklyn
200 Willoughby St, BK
718-636-3669 **410**B

School of Visual Arts
209 E 23 St, MA
212-679-7350 **118**B

COLLEGES & UNIVERSITIES

Audrey Cohen College
75 Varick St, MA
800-338-4465 **106**A

Bank Street College
610 W 112 St, MA
212-875-4467 **144**C

Barnard College
3009 Broadway, MA
212-854-5262 **144**A

Baruch College (CUNY)
17 Lexington Av, MA
212-802-2000 **118**B

Benjamin N Cardozo School of Law
55 Fifth Av, MA
212-790-0200 **113**B

Berkeley College
3 E 43 St, MA
212-996-4343 **126**E

Boricua College
186 North 6 St, BK
718-782-2200 **404**B

Boro of Manhattan Community College (CUNY)
199 Chambers St, MA
212-346-8000 **104**A

Bronx Community College (CUNY)
181 St & University Av, BX 718-289-5100 **215**C

Brooklyn Law
250 Joralemon St, BK, 718-625-2200 **408**D

Brooklyn College (CUNY)
2900 Bedford Av, BK
718-951-5000 **429**A

City College (CUNY)
Convent Av @ 138 St, MA, 212-650-7000 **148**B

College of Insurance
101 Murray St, MA
212-962-4111 **104**B

College of Mount Saint Vincent
6301 Riverdale, BX
718-405-3200 **202**D

College of Staten Island (CUNY)
2800 Victory Bd, SI
718-982-2000 **509**D

Columbia University
W 116 St , MA
212 854-1754 **144**B

Cornell University Medical College
1300 York Av, MA
212-746-5454 **131**B

Cooper Union
30 Cooper Sq, MA
212-254-6300 **114**A

CUNY Law
65-21 Main St, QS
718-575-4200 **329**A

CUNY Graduate Center
365 Fifth Av, MA
212-817-7000 **122**C

Fordham University
Rose Hill
441 E Fordham Rd, BX
718-817-1000 **215**B

Fordham Univer School of Law
140 W 62 St, MA
212-636-6000

Health Science Center (SUNY)
450 Clarkson Av
718-270-1000

Hebrew Union College
1 W 4 St, MA
212-674-5300

Hostos Commun College (CUNY)
475 Grand Concourse, BX
718-518-4444

Hunter College (CUNY)
695 Park Av, MA
212-772-4000

John Jay Colleg Criminal Justic
899 Tenth Av, M
212-237-8000

Kingsborough Community Coll
2001 Oriental Bd
718-368-5000

La Guardia Community Coll
31-10 Thomson A
718-482-7200

Lehman College (CUNY) Bedford
Park Bd W, BX
718-960-8000

Long Island University (LIU)
1 University Plz,
718-488-1000

EDUCATION

attan College
Manhattan
...e Pkwy, BX
...2-8000 **208**B

...mount
...attan College
...71 St, MA
...7-0400 **131**A

...ar Evers
...)
Bedford Av, BK
...0-4900 **416**C

...ve College
Jerome Av, BX
...6-6676 **215**A

School Univ.
...12 St, MA
...9-5600 **113**A

York City
...ical College
...ay St, BK
...50-5000 **408**C

NY College of
...tric Medicine
...24 St, MA
...0-8000 **146**B

York Law
...orth St, MA
...31-2100 **104**B

York
...rsity (NYU)
...ington Sq, MA
...98-4636 **113**D

...University
...e Plz, MA
...46-1200 **105**C

...echnic
...rsity
...roTech Ctr, BK
...60-3100 **409**C

Queens College (CUNY)
65-30 Kissena Bd, QS
718-997-5411 **329**A

Queensborough Community College (CUNY)
222-05 56 Av, QS
718-631-6262 **323**D

Rockefeller University
1230 York Av, MA
212-327-8000 **131**B

St Francis College
180 Remsen St, BK
718-522-2300 **408**D

St John's University
800 Utopia Pkwy, QS
718-990-6132 **330**C

St Joseph's College
245 Clinton Av, BK
718-636-6800 **410**C

Schuyler Maritime College (SUNY)
Fort Schulyer, BX
718-409-7200 **219**D

Teacher's College
525 W 120 St, MA
212-678-3000 **144**B

University of the Streets
130 E 7 St, MA
212-254-9300 **114**D

Wagner College
631 Howard Av, SI
718-390-3100 **512**B

Yeshiva University
500 W 185 St, MA
212-960-5400 **157**A

York College (CUNY)
94-20 Guy R Brewer
Bd, Jamaica, QS
718-262-2000 **337**D

LIBRARIES

Bronx
Fordham Library Ctr
2556 Bainbridge Av,
BX, 718-579-4200
215A

Brooklyn
Grand Army Plz, BK
718-780-7700 **415**D

Brooklyn Business
280 Cadman Plz W
BK, 718-722-3333
408B

Donnell Library Center
20 W 53 St, MA
212-621-0618 **126**B

The Kurdish Library Museum
144 Underhill Av, BK
718-783-7930 **415**B

The Langston Hughes Community
102-09, Northern
Bd, Corona ,QS
718-651-1100 **320**A

Pierpont Morgan
29 E 36 St, MA
212-685-0610 **122**D

NY Public
455 Fifth Av, MA
212-661-7220 **122**A

NY Public Library for the Performing Arts 40 Lincoln
Center Plz, MA
212-870-1630 **128**D

NY Science, Industry & Business (SIBL)
188 Madison Av, MA
212-592-7000 **122**D

Queens
89-11 Merrick Bd,
Jamaica, QS
718-990-0781 **338**D

Staten Island
St George Center, SI
718-442-8560 **507**B

SPECIAL HIGH SCHOOLS

Bronx HS of Science
75 W 205, BX
718-817-7700 **209**C

Brooklyn Technical
Brooklyn Tech Pl, BK
718-858-5150 **409**D

Campus Magnet
207-01 116 Av
Cambria Heights, QS
718-978-6432 **347**A

HS of Fashion Industries
225 W 24 St, MA
212-255-1235 **117**A

HS of Graphic Communication Arts
439 W 49 St, MA
212-245-5925 **124**D

Manhattan Center for Science & Math
E 116 & FDR Dr, MA
212-876-4639 **147**D

Murray Bergtraum HS for Business Careers
411 Pearl St, MA
212-964-9610 **105**A

St George School
450 St Marks Pl, SI
718-273-3225 **507**A

Aviation
45-30 36 St, LIC, QS
718-361-2032 **317**A

Samuel Gompers
455 Southern Bd, BX
718-665-0950 **227**B

Stuyvesant
345 Chambers St, MA
212-312-4800 **104**A

TECHNICAL

College of Aeronautics
La Guardia Airport,
QS, 718-429-6600
310D

College of Technology
320 W 31 St, MA
800-225-8246 **121**C

College of Optometry (SUNY)
33 W 42 St, MA
212-780-4900 **122**B

NY Institute of Technology
1855 Broadway, MA
212-261-1500 **129**C

TO FIND A TOP 100

Simply turn to page
and locate the
college or school in
grids **A,B,C** or **D**.

MA = Manhattan
BX = The Bronx
BK = Brooklyn
QS= Queens
SI = Staten Island

GOVERNMENT

BOROUGH & CITY HALLS

The Bronx
851 Grand Concourse
718-590-3500 **221**C

Brooklyn
209 Joralemon St
718-802-3700 **408**D

Manhattan
Municipal Bldg
212-669-8300 **105**A

Queens
120-55 Queens Bd,
Kew Gardens
718-286-3000 **337**A

Staten Island
10 Richmond Ter
718-816-2236 **507**B

City Hall, MA
• City Council
212-788-7100 **105**A
• Mayor's Office
212-788-3000 **105**A

BUSINESS SERVICES

NYC Department of Business Services
110 Williams St, MA
212-513-6300 **105**C

Small Business Administration (SBA)
26 Federal Plz, MA
212-264-4354 **105**A

US Customs
6 WTC, MA
800-697-3662 **104**D

COURTS
The State & City court system is undergoing a major overhaul in the year 2000. Here is a short key to the jurisdictions of the current system.

• Civil–for disputes under $25,000
• Criminal–for misdemeaners
• Family–for child custody issues
• Surrogate–for probation of wills
• Supreme–civil cases over $25,000, divorce and felony cases.

Municipal– Bronx County
Civil
851 Grand Concourse
212-791-6000 **221**C

Criminal
215 E 161 St
718-374-5880 **221**C

Family
900 Sheridan Av
718-590-3321 **221**C

Supreme–Bronx Co
851 Grand Concourse
718-590-3723 **221**C

Surrogate's
851 Grand Concourse
718-590-3618 **221**C

Small Claims
851 Grand Concourse
212-791-6000 **221**C

Kings County
Civil
141 Livingston St
718-643-5069 **408**D

Criminal
120 Schermerhorn St
718-643-4044 **408**D

Family
283 Adams St
718-643-2652 **408**D

Supreme–Kings Co
360 Adams St
718-643-8076 **408**D

Surrogate's
2 Johnson St
718-643-5262 **408**D

Small Claims
141 Livingston St
408D

New York County
Civil
111 Centre St
212-791-6000 **106**D

Criminal
100 Centre St
212-374-5880 **105**A

Family–NYS & Co
60 Lafayette St
212-374-8743 **105**A

Supreme– New York Co
60 Centre St
212-374-4422 **107**C

Surrogate's
31 Chambers St
212-374-8233 **105**A

Small Claims
111 Centre St
212-374-5776 **106**D

Queens County
Civil
120-55 Queens Bd
718-643-5069 **337**A

Criminal
125-01 Queens Bd
212-374-5880 **337**A

Family
89-14 Parsons Bd
718-520-3991 **337**D

Supreme– Queens Co
88-11 Sutphin Bd
718-520-3713 **337**D

Surrogate's
88-11 Sutphin Bd
718-520-3132 **337**D

Small Claims
120-55 Queens Bd
212-791-6000 **336**B

Richmond County
Civil
927 Castleton Av
212-791-6000 **506**C

Criminal
67 Targee St
212-374-5880 **507**C

Family
100 Richmond Ter
718-390-5462 **507**A

Supreme– Richmond Co
18 Richmond Ter
718-390-5352 **507**B

Surrogate's
18 Richmond Ter
718-390-5400 **507**B

Small Claims
927 Castleton Av
718-390-5421 **506**C

State– Supreme Civil
60 Centre St, M
212-374-8359

Criminal
100 Centre St, N
212-374-5880

Family
60 Lafayette St,
212-374-8743

Supreme Appe
• First Division
27 Madison Av,
212-340-0400
• Second Divisi
45 Monroe Pl, E
718-875-1300

Surrogate's
31 Chamber St,

Small Claims
111 Centre St, M

Federal– US Bankruptcy
1 Bowling Gree
MA, 212-688-28

US Court of Appeals
40 Foley Sq, MA
212-857-8500

US District–
• Southern
500 Pearl St, M.
212-805-0136
• Eastern
225 Cadman Plz ▶
718-260-2600

US Int'l Trade
1 Federal Plz, M
212-264-2800

**RGENCY &
ORCEMENT**

Guard
oast Guard Dr
3-354-4037
513D

**Enforcement
istration**

th Av, MA
7-3900 **116**B

**al Bureau of
igation (FBI)**
eral Plz, MA
4-1000 **105**A

ept Hdqtrs
roTech Ctr BK,
9-2000 **409**C

**Dept Hdqrs
tral Booking
ronx**
9 St
0-2804 **221**A

lyn
hermerhorn St
5-6586 **409**A

attan
ce Plz
4-3838 **105**A

is
Queens Bd,
ardens
8-4523 **337**A

Island
hmond Ter
6-8490 **507**A

**GRATION &
RALIZATION**
eral Plz, MA
6-6500 **105**A

**MOTOR
VEHICLE**

DMV
The Bronx
2265 E Tremont Av
212-645-5550 **217**A

Brooklyn
• 481 Hudson Av
718-966-6155 **409**C
• 2875 W 8 St,
Coney Island
718-966-6155 **443**C

Manhattan
• 155 Worth St
212-645-5550 **105**A
• 2110 Adam
Clayton Powell Bd
212-645-5550 **149**C

Queens
• 92-35 165 St,
Jamaica, QS
718-966-6155 **338**C
• 168-35 Rockaway Bd
Springfield Grdns
718-966-6155 **352**C
• 30-56 Whitestone
Expwy, Flushing
718-966-6155 **312**D

Staten Island
2795 Richmond Ter
800-368-1186 **503**A

Parking Violations
770 Broadway, MA
212-477-4430 **113**B

*Read the signs for
street cleaning and
alternate side park-
ing times carefully.*

*Errors can cost
$200.00 or more!*

**Tow-Away Lots
(DOT)**
The Bronx
745 E 145 St **227**B

Brooklyn
Navy Yard **409**A

Manhattan
• 203 Ninth Av. **116**B
• 38 St & 12 Av **120**A

Queens
129-05 31 Av **312**C

Staten Island
350 St Marks Pl
718-876-5307 **507**A

Traffic Violations
The Bronx
2455 Sedgwick Av
718-488-5710 **214**B

Brooklyn
• 30 Rockwell Pl
718-488-5710 **409**C
• 2875 W 8 St
718-488-5710 **443**C

Manhattan
• 19 Rector St
718-488-5710 **102**B
• 2110 Adam Clayton
Powell Jr. Bd
718-488-5710 **149**C

Queens
• 168-35 Rockaway
Bd, Springfield Grdns
718-488-5710 **352**C
• 30-56 Whitestone
Expwy, Flushing
718-488-5710 **312**D

Staten Island
2795 Richmond Ter
718-488-5710 **503**A

PASSPORT

NY Passport Office
376 Hudson St, MA
212-206-3500 **108**B

**SOCIAL
SERVICES**

**Alcoholism &
Substance Abuse**
55 W 125 St, MA
212-961-8471 **149**D

Aging
2 Lafayette St, MA
212-442-1322 **106**D

Family & Children
80 Maiden La, MA
212-383-1825 **104**D

Medicaid
330 W 34 St, MA
718-291-1900 **121**C

Human Rights
40 Rector St, MA
212-306-7500 **102**B

Victim Services
2 Lafayette St, MA
212-577-7700 **106**D

Youth & Community
156 William St, MA
212-442-5900 **105**C

Social Security
• 26 Federal Plz, MA
212-264-8819 **105**A
• 226 161 St, BX
718-537-4637 **204**C
• 59-07 175 Pl, Fresh
Meadows, QS
718-357-8805 **330**B
• 200 Montague St,
BK, 718-330-7861
408D

TAXES

**Internal Revenue
Service (IRS)**
The Bronx
3000 White Plains Rd
800-829-1040 **210**D

Brooklyn
10 MetroTech Center
800-829-1040 **409**C

Manhattan
• 110 W 44 St
800-829-1040 **125**D
• 55 W 125 St
800-829-1040 **149**D

Queens
1 Lefrak City Plz
800-829-1040 **319**D

Staten Island
45 Bay St
718-488-8432 **507**B

City Tax Offices
25 Elm Pl, BK
718-935-6739 **409**C

State Tax Info
Albany, NY
800-225-5829

TO FIND A TOP 100

Simply turn to page
and locate the
agency in grids
A,B,C or D.

MA = Manhattan
BX = The Bronx
BK = Brooklyn
QS = Queens
SI = Staten Island

GOVERNMENT

HOTELS

AIRPORTS

The Crowne Plaza LaGuardia $$$
104-04 Ditmars Bd, QS 800-692-5429
311C

JFK Airport Hilton $$$
138-10 135 Av, QS 800 HILTONS
351A

LaGuardia Marriott $$
102-05 Ditmars Bd, QS
718-565-8900
311C

Sheraton LaGuardia East $$
135-20 39 Av, QS
718-460-6666
321A

BED & BREAKFAST

All B & B's require reservations prior to arrival.

Baisley House $
294 Hoyt St, BK
718-935-1959
414B

The Gracie Inn $$
502 E 81, MA
212-628-1700
135B

Le Refuge Inn $$
620 City Island, BX
718-885-2478
207C

NY B&B $
134 W 119 St, MA
212-666-0559
146A

SoHo $$
167 Crosby St, MA
212-925-1034
114C

MANHATTAN

Downtown

Best Western Seaport Inn $$
33 Peck Slip, MA
212-766-6600
105C

Holiday Inn Downtown $$
138 Lafayette St, MA
212-966-8898
106B

Marriott Financial Center $$$
85 West St, MA
212-385-4900
102B

Marriott WTC, New York $$$
3 WTC, MA
212-938-9100
104D

Millenium Hilton $$$
55 Church St, MA
800-835-2220
104D

Regent Wall Street $$$$$
55 Wall St, MA
212-308-0601
103A

SoHo & Village

The Larchmont $
27 W 11 St, MA
212-989-9333
113A

The Mercer $$$
147 Mercer St, MA
212-966-6060
109B

Off-SoHo Suites $
11 Rivington St, MA
212-979-9808
110A

SoHo Grand $$$
310 W Broadway, MA
212-965-3000
106B

Washington Sq $
103 Waverly Pl, MA
212-777-9515
113A

Chelsea & Gramercy Park

Chelsea $$
222 W 23 St, MA
212-243-3700
117A

Gramercy Park $$
2 Lexington Av, MA
800-221-4083
118B

Inn at Irving Place $$
56 Irving Pl, MA
212-533-4600
118D

Southgate Tower $$
371 Seventh Av, MA
212-563-1800
121C

Midtown East

Beekman Tower $$
3 Mitchell Pl, MA
212-355-7300
127C

The Benjamin $$$$
125 E 50 St, MA
212-753-2700
126B

Crowne Plaza UN $$
304 E 42 St, MA
212-986-8800
123A

The Doral Park Av $$
70 Park Av, MA
212-687-7050
122B

Dumont Plaza Suite $$$
150 E 34 MA
800-ME-SUITE **122**D

Eastgate Tower Suite $$
222 E 39 St, MA
800-ME-SUITE **123**A

The Fitzpatrick $$$
687 Lexington Av, MA
212-355-0100
126B

The Four Seasons $$$$$
57 E 57 St, MA
212-758-5700
130D

Grand Hyatt NY $$$
Park Av @ 42 St, MA
800-228-9000
122B

Helmsley Middletowne $$
148 E 48 St, MA
800-221-4982
126C

Hotel Élysée $$
60 E 54 St, MA
212-753-1066
126B

Hotel Inter-Continental NY $$$
111 E 48 St, MA
800-327-0200
126D

Kitano $$$$
66 Park Av, MA
212-885-7000
122B

Loews NY $$
569 Lexington Av, MA
212-752-7000
126B

Morgans $$$
237 Madison Av, MA
800-686-0300
122D

NY Helmsley $$$
212 E 42 St, MA
800-221-4982
122B

The NY Palace $$$$
445 Madison Av, MA
212-888-7000
126B

Omni Berkshire Place $$$
21 E 52 St, MA
800-THE-OMNI **125**B

Pickwick Arms $$
230 E 51 St, MA
212-355-0300
127A

Regal UN Plaza $$$$
1 UN Plz, MA
800-222-8888
127C

The Roger Will $$$
131 Madison, MA
212-488-70

Roger Smith $$
501 Lexington A
212-755-1400

St Regis $$$$$
2 E 55 St, MA
800-759-7550

San Carlos $$
150 E 50 St, MA
800-722-2012

Shelburne $$
303 Lexington A
800-689-5200

Swissôtel NY, The Drake
440 Park Av, MA
800-63-SWISS

Vanderbilt YM
224 E 47 St, MA
212-756-9600

The W Court $$
130 E 39 St, MA
800-685-1100

The W Tuscany
120 E 39 St, MA
800-686-1600

The W New Yo
541 Lexington A
MA, 212-755-1

The Waldorf–Astoria $$$
301 Park Av, MA
800-WALDORF

The Waldorf To
100 E 50 St, MA
800-WALDORF

town West

Algonquin *SSS*
44 St, MA
648-0345 **125D**

Western
assador
W 45 St, MA
821-7600 **125C**

Western
ident *S*
W 48 St, MA
826-4667 **125C**

Western
hattan *SS*
32 St, MA
736-1600 **121C**

vne Plaza
hattan *SSS*
Broadway, MA
227-6963 **125A**

x House *SSS*
CPS, MA
484-5100 **129C**

pshire Hotel &
es *S*
W 47 St, MA
768-3700 **125C**

Hilton NY *SSS*
Sixth Av, MA
HILTONS **125B**

l Edison *S*
W 47 St, MA
840-5000 **125C**

-Continental-
ral Park South
112 CPS, MA
757-1900 **129D**

arker Meridien
118 W 57 St, MA
543-4300 **125B**

The Mansfield *SS*
12 W 44 St, MA
212-944-6050 **125D**

Marriott Marquis
SSS 1535 B'way, MA
800-228-9290 **125C**

Michelangelo *SSS*
152 W 51 St, MA
800-237-0990 **125A**

The Millennium
Broadway *SSS*
145 W 44 St, MA
800-622-5569 **125C**

Paramount *SS*
235 W 46 St, MA
800-225-7474 **124C**

The Peninsula NY
SSSS 700 Fifth Av, MA
800-262-9467 **126A**

The Plaza *SSS*
768 Fifth Av, MA
800-759-3000 **129D**

Quality Hotel &
Suites *S*
59 W 46 St, MA
212-719-2300 **125D**

Rihga Royal *SSS*
151 W 54 St, MA
800-937-5454 **125A**

The Royalton *SSS*
44 W 44 St, MA
800-635-9013 **125D**

St Moritz
on-the-Park *SS*
50 CPS, MA
800-221-4774 **129D**

Sheraton NY Hotel
& Towers *SS*
811 Seventh Av, MA
800-325-3535 **125A**

The Shoreham *SSS*
33 W 55 St, MA
212-247-6700 **125B**

The Warwick *SSS*
65 W 54 St, MA
212-247-2700 **125B**

The Wyndham *SS*
42 W 58 St, MA
212-753-3500 **129D**

Upper Eastside
The Carlyle *SSSS*
35 E 76 St, MA
212-744-1600 **134D**

The Franklin *SS*
164 E 87 St, MA
212-369-1000 **139C**

The Lowell *SSSS*
28 E 63 St, MA
800-221-4444 **130D**

The Mark *SSSS*
25 E 77 St, MA
800-THE-MARK **133D**

Plaza Athénée *SSSS*
37 E 64 St, MA
800-734-9100 **130B**

The Regency *SSSS*
540 Park Av, MA
212-759-4100 **130D**

The Pierre *SSSS*
5 Av @ E 61 St, MA
800-332-3442 **129D**

Sherry–Netherland
SSSSS 781 Fifth Av,
MA, 800-247-4377
129D

The Stanhope *SSSS*
995 Fifth Av, MA
800-828-1123 **133B**

Surrey *SSS*
20 E 76 St, MA
212-288-3700 **133D**

92nd St YMCA *S*
de Hirsch Residence
1395 Lex Av, MA,
800-858-4692 **139A**

Upper Westside
Beacon Hotel *SS*
2130 Broadway, MA
800-572-4969 **132D**

Empire Hotel
SS 44 W 63 St, MA
212-265-7400 **128D**

Inn New York City
SS 266 W 71 St, MA
212-580-1900 **128B**

Mayflower Hotel
on the Park *SS*
15 Central Park W,
MA, 800-223-4164
129C

NY Int'l American
Youth Hostel *S*
891 Amsterdam Av,
@ W 103, MA
212-932-2300 **140D**

Trump International
Hotel & Tower *SSSS*
1 Central Park W,
MA, 800-44TRUMP
129C

63rd St YMCA *S*
5 W 63 St, MA
212-787-4400 **129C**

OUTER BOROS
Comfort Inn
Brooklyn *SS*
8315 Fourth Av, BK
800-447-3467 **426D**

New York Marriott
Brooklyn *SSS*
333 Adams St, BK
718-246-7000 **408D**

The Staten Island
Hotel *SS*
1415 Richmond Av, SI
800-532-3532 **510C**

RESERVATIONS
At Home in NY
800-692-4262

City Lights B & B
212-737-7049

NY by Phone
888-NYC-APPLE

New World
800-443-3800

Urban Ventures
212-594-5650

PRICE KEY

S = less than $100
SS = $100–$200
SSS = $200–$300
SSSS = $300–$400
SSSSS = $400–$500

Price ranges given
are for single occu-
pancy midweek.
It's smart to call for
weekend specials
and promotional
rates.

MA = Manhattan
BX = The Bronx
BK = Brooklyn
QS = Queens
SI = Staten Island

MUSEUMS

Abigail Adams Smith House Museum
421 E 61 St, MA
212-838-6878 **131**C

African–American Wax Museum
316 W 115 St, MA
212-678-7818 **145**C

Alice Austen House
2 Hylan Bd, SI
718-816-4506 **513**B

Alternative Museum
594 Broadway
Suite #402, MA
212-966-4444 **109**C

American Academy of Arts & Letters
633 W 155 St, MA
212-368-5900 **152**B

American Craft Museum
40 W 53 St, MA
212-956-6047 **125**B

American Museum of the Moving Image (AMM)
35 Av @ 36 St, QS
718-784-4520 **309**C

American Museum of Natural History
21 Central Park
West @ 79 St, MA
212-769-5000 **133**C

American Numismatic Society
Audubon Ter, MA
212-234-3130 **152**B

The Americas Society
680 Park Av, MA
212-249-8950 **130**B

The Asia Society
725 Park Av, MA
212-288-6400 **130**B

Asian American Art Centre
26 Bowery, MA
212-233-2154 **107**C

Bartow–Pell Mansion Museum
Shore Rd N, BX
718-885-1461 **206**D

The Black Fashion Museum
155 W 126 St, MA
212-666-1320 **149**D

The Bronx Museum of the Arts
1040 Grand
Concourse, BX
718-681-6000 **221**C

Brooklyn Children's Museum
145 Brooklyn Av, BK
718-735-4432 **416**B

Brooklyn Historical Society
128 Pierrepont St, BK
718-624-0890 **408**B

Brooklyn Museum of Art (BMA)
200 Eastern Pkwy, BK
718-638-5000 **415**D

Children's Museum of the Arts
182 Lafayette St, MA
212-941-9198 **109**B

Children's Museum of Manhattan
212 W 83 St, MA
212-721-1223 **132**B

China Institute in America
125 E 65 St, MA
212-744-8181 **130**B

The Cloisters
Fort Tryon Pk, MA
212-923-3700 **158**B

Cooper–Hewitt National Design Museum
2 E 91 St, MA
212-849-8300 **137**D

Dahesh Museum
601 Fifth Av, MA
212-759-0606 **125**D

Dia Center for the Arts
548 W 22 St, MA
212-989-5912 **116**B

The Drawing Center
35 Wooster St, MA
212-219-2166 **109**D

Dyckman Farmhouse Museum
4881 Broadway, MA
212-304-9422 **159**A

Edgar Allan Poe Cottage
Grand Concourse &
E Kingsbridge Rd, BX
718-881-8900 **215**A

El Museo del Barrio
1230 Fifth Av
@ E 104 St, MA
212-831-7272 **141**B

Ellis Island Immigration Museum
Ellis Island, MA
212-363-7620 **102**C

Exit Art / The First World
548 Broadway, MA
212-966-7745 **109**B

Federal Hall
26 Wall St, MA
212-825-6888 **103**A

Federal Reserve Bank of NY
33 Liberty St, MA
212-720-6130 **105**C

Forbes Magazine Galleries
62 Fifth Av, MA
212-206-5548 **113**A

Fraunces Tavern
54 Pearl St, MA
212-425-1778 **103**A

Frick Collection
1 E 70 St, MA
212-288-0700 **130**B

Garibaldi Meucci Museum
420 Tompkins Av, SI
718-442-1608 **513**A

Guggenheim Museum–SoHo
575 Broadway
@ Prince St, MA
212-423-3500 **109**B

The Hispanic Society of America
613 W 155 St, MA
212-690-0743 **152**B

Historic Richmond Town
441 Clarke Av, S
718-351-1611 **5**

Int'l Center of Photography, (ICP) Uptown
1130 Fifth Av, M
212-860-1777 **1**

ICP Midtown
6 Av @ W 43 St,
212-768-4680 **1**

Intrepid Sea–Air Space Museum
W 46 St @ 12 Av,
212-245-0072 **1**

Isamu Noguchi Garden Museum
32-37 Vernon Bd,
718-204-7088 **3**

Jacques Marcha Museum of Tibetan Art
338 Lighthouse Av
718-987-3500 **5**

Jamaica Arts Center
161-04 Jamaica
QS, 718-658-7400
3

Japan Society
333 E 47 St, MA
212-832-1155 **1**

Jewish Museum
1109 Fifth Av, M
212-339-3430 **1**

The John A Nob Collection
1000 Richmond Te
718-447-6490 **5**

MUSEUMS

Judaica
...eum
...Palisades Av, BX
...548-1006 **202D**

...Manor
...eum
... Park, QS
...523-0029 **337D**

...sland
...estead (Queens
...rical Society)
...35 37 Av, QS
...939-0647 **312D**

...Kurdish
...ry Museum
...Inderhill Av, BK
...783-7930 **415B**

...Liberty
...nce Center
...rty State Pk, NJ
...200-1000 **104C**

...er East Side
...ment Museum
...rchard St, MA
...431-0233 **110D**

...Metropolitan
...eum of Art
... Fifth Av, MA
...535-7710 **133B**

...gan Library
...36 St, MA
...685-0610 **122B**

...ris-Jumel
...sion
...umel Ter, MA
...923-8008 **154D**

...eum for
...can Art
...Broadway, MA
...966-1313 **109C**

**Museum of Amer.
Financial History**
28 Broadway, MA
212-908-4110 **102B**

**Museum of
American Folk Art**
2 Lincoln Sq, MA
212-977-7298 **128B**

**Museum of
Amer. Illustration**
128 E 63 St, MA
212-838-2560 **130D**

**Museum of
Bronx History**
3309 Bainbridge Av,
BX, 718-881-8900
209D

**Museum of
the City of NY**
1220 Fifth Av, MA
212-534-1672 **141B**

**Museum of
Jewish Heritage**
18 First Pl, MA
212-968-1800 **102D**

**Museum of Modern
Art (MoMA)**
11 W 53 St, MA
212-708-9480 **125B**

**Museum of Chinese
in the Americas**
70 Mulberry St, MA
212-619-4785 **107C**

**Museum of TV
& Radio**
25 W 52 St, MA
212-621-6600 **125B**

**National Academy
Museum**
1083 Fifth Av, MA
212-369-4880 **137D**.

**National Museum of
the American Indian**
1 Bowling Green, MA
212-825-6700 **102D**

**New Museum of
Contemporary Art**
583 Broadway, MA
212-219-1222 **109B**

NYC Fire Museum
278 Spring St, MA
212-691-1303 **109C**

NY Hall of Science
47-01 111 St, QS
718-699-0005 **320B**

**New–York
Historical Society**
170 CPW, MA
212-873-3400 **133A**

NY Public Library
42 St @ Fifth Av, MA
212-661-7220 **122A**

NY Transit Museum
Boerum Pl, BK
718-243-3060 **408D**

**Nicholas Roerich
Museum**
319 W 107 St, MA
212-864-7752 **140A**

North Wind Museum
610 City Island Av, BX
718-885-0701 **207A**

**Old Merchant's
House**
29 E 4 St, MA
212-777-1089 **114C**

**Pieter Claeson
Wyckoff House
Museum**
5816 Clarendon Rd, BK
718-629-5400 **424C**

Police Museum
235 E 20 St, MA
212-477-9753 **118D**

PS 1
22-25 Jackson Av, QS
718-784-2084 **316B**

**Queens County
Farm Museum**
73-50 Little Neck
Pkwy, QS
718-347-3276 **333A**

**Queens Museum
of Art (QMA)**
Flushing Meadows–
Corona Park, QS
718-592-9700 **320D**

**Rose Center for
Earth & Science**
CPW @ W 81 St,
212-769-5900 **133A**

**Rose Museum @
Carnegie Hall**
154 W 57 St, MA
212-247-7800 **125A**

Skyscraper Museum
closed for renovation
212-968-1961 **103A**

**Snug Harbor
Cultural Center**
1000 Richmond Ter,
SI, 718-448-2500 **506B**

**Socrates
Sculpture Park**
B'way @ Vernon Bd
Long Island City, QS
718-956-1819 **308B**

**Solomon R
Guggenheim
Museum (Uptown)**
1071 Fifth Av, MA
212-423-3500 **138C**

**Sony Wonder
Technology Lab**
550 Madison Av, MA
212-833-8100 **126B**

**South Street
Seaport Museum**
207 Front St
Seaport Plz, MA
212-748-8600 **105C**

**Staten Island
Children's Museum**
1000 Richmond Ter, SI
718-273-2060 **506B**

**Staten Island
Institute of Arts
and Sciences**
75 Stuyvesant Pl, SI
718-727-1135 **507B**

**Studio Museum
in Harlem**
144 W 125 St, MA
212-864-4500 **145B**

**Theodore Roosevelt
Birthplace**
28 E 20 St, MA
212-260-1616 **118C**

Ukrainian Museum
203 Second Av, MA
212-228-0110 **114A**

**Van Cortlandt
Mansion Museum**
B'way @ 246 St, BX
718-543-3344 **209A**

**Whitney Museum of
American Art**
945 Madison Av, MA
212-570-3600 **134D**

**Whitney Museum
at Philip Morris**
120 Park Av, MA
917-663-2550 **122B**

**TO FIND A
TOP 100**

Simply turn to
page to locate
museums in grids
A,B,C or D.

MA = Manhattan
BX = The Bronx
BK = Brooklyn
QS = Queens
SI = Staten Island

NATURE 3

AQUARIA & ZOOS

Bronx Zoo–Int'l Wildlife Conservation Park
Bronx River Pkwy @ E Fordham Rd, BX, 718-367-1010 **216AB**

Central Park Zoo Wildlife Conservation Ctr
830 Fifth Av, MA
212-439-6500 **129D**

Prospect Park Wildlife Conservation Ctr
450 Flatbush Av, BK
718-339-7339 **415D**

NY Aquarium
W 8 St & Surf Av, BK
718-265-3400 **443D**

Queens Wildlife Conservation Ctr
53-51 111 St, QS
718-271-7761 **320D**

Staten Island Zoo
614 Broadway, SI
718-442-3100 **512A**

BEACHES

Brighton BK **443D**
Coney Island BK **443C**
Great Kills SI **530D**
Jacob Riis QS **364C**
Manhattan BK **444D**
Ferry Point BX **218D**
Orchard BX **206D**
Rockaway QS **365C**

CEMETERIES

The Bronx
St Raymonds **218D**
Woodlawn **203D**

Brooklyn
Canarsie **424D**
Friends **422A**
Greenwood **421A**
Holy Cross **423C**
Washington **428D**

Manhattan
African Burial Grounds **104A**
St Paul's **104D**
Trinity **152B**

Queens
Calvary **317C**
Cemetery of the Evergreens **334C**
Cypress Hills **334B**
Flushing **322C**
Lutheran **326D**
Montefiore **347C**
Mt Carmel **334D**
Mt Hebron **329A**
Mt Lebanon **335A**
Mt Judah **334D**
Mt Olivet **326B**
Mt Zion **317D**
New Calvary **317D**
St John's **327D**
St Michael's **310C**

Staten Island
Baron Hirsch **510A**
Moravian **517C**
Ocean View **522D**
Snug Harbor **506B**
Resurrection **533C**
United Hebrew **522D**

GARDENS

Botanical
Brooklyn Botanic
1000 Washington Av
BK, 718-622-4433 **416C**

New York Botanical
200 St & Southern Bd BX
718-817-8700 **210D**

Queens Botanical
4350 Main St, QS
718-939-0647 **321C**

Staten Island Botanical
1000 Richmond Ter, SI
718-273-8200 **506B**

Wave Hill
675 W 252 St, BX
718-549-3200 **208A**

Community
Through fortitude and grit, New Yorkers have taken over 700 vacant lots and transformed them into beautiful and productive gardens that help strengthen their communities.

Aided by Green Thumb, city gardeners get access to city land and horticultural training. Here are a few of the finest in the five boroughs.

Brisas La Caribe
237 E 3 St, MA **114D**

Howard
750 Howard Av, BK **417B**

Joe Holzka
1171 Castleton Av, SI **506C**

The One Love
Inwood St, QS **344A**

Taqwa
90 W 164 St, BX **221C**

Youth & Senior
Surf Av @ 32 St, BK **442D**

6th & B
624 E 6 St, MA **115A**

Special
Biblical Garden
St John the Divine, MA **144D**

Cloisters
Ft Tryon Pk, MA **158B**

Peace
UN Plz, MA **127C**

Conservatory
Central Pk, MA **141D**

St Luke's-in-the-Field
487 Hudson St, MA **112D**

Sterling Park
Brooklyn Heights, BK **408A**

Shakespeare
Central Park, MA **133C**

Strawberry Fields
Central Park, MA **129A**

INTERPRETIVE CENTERS

Alley Pond Park Environmental
228-06 Northern Douglaston, QS
718-229-4000 **3**

Brooklyn Center for the Urban Environment
Tennis House, Prospect Park, B
718-788-8549 **4**

Charles A Dana Discovery
Lenox Av & 110 St ,MA
212-860-1370 **1**

Clay Pits Ponds State Preserve
83 Nielsen Av, SI
718-967-1976 **5**

Henry Luce Nature Observat
Belvedere Castle Central Park, MA
212-772-0210 **1**

High Rock Conservation
200 Nevada Av, S
718-667-6042 **5**

Jamaica Bay Na Wildlife Refuge
Cross Bay Bd, QS
718-318-4340 **3**

Urban Ecology
Inwood Pk, MA
212-304-2365 **1**

Urban Forest Ecolo
Van Cortlandt Pk,
718-548-0912 **20**

PARKS

KS
Bronx

K 210C
e Hill 225A
mont 221B
na 216C
Point...........218D
Sigel 226B
en 205C
Mullaly ...221C
mb's Dam ......
...............221C
am Bay ...206A
ley's Creek 225A
dale 208A
rto Clemente....
...............214D
ary's 227B
a Falls ...205C
d View ...223D
Cortlandt ...203C
Creek ...219A

klyn

en Beach...431C
rsie Beach ....
.................431A
Offerman 442B
r Beach ..434B
re Fulton Ferry
.................407A
Greene ...407D
land 413C
hland 409A
nattan Beach....
.................445A
ne 438D
arren 402D
s Head ...426A
b Beach ..445B
pect 415D
g Creek 425B
et 421C
Whitman 407A

Manhattan

Battery 102D
Bryant.............122A
Carl Schurz 139D
Central ...129A-142A
City Hall 105C
Corlears Hook 111D
East River 111B
Fort Tryon......158D
Fort Washington
.........................156D
Gramercy..........118D
Inwood Hill 160D
Isham 161C
Harlem River Drive
................153D-159A
High Bridge......154B
Jackie Robinson
.........................153C
Jeaneatte..........103C
John Jay 135D
Liberty 102B
Madison Sq......117B
Marcus Garvey ...
.........................146B
Morningside ...144B
Paley 126B
Randalls Is 302B
Riverbank State 148A
Riverside 132A-144A
Robert F Wagner Jr.
.........................102A
Rockefeller 104B
St Nicholas 148B
Thomas Jefferson....
.........................147C
Tompkins Sq ...114B
Union Sq 118D
James J Walker ....
.........................108D
Wards Island....302C
Washington Sq ....
.........................113C

Queens

Alley Pond ...324B
Astoria 302C
Baisley Pond ..351B
Bayswater 369B
Bowne 313C
Breezy Point ..362C
Brookville 352D
Clearview 314A
Crocheron 315C
Cunningham ...331A
Dr Charles Andrew
Memorial 344C
Douglaston 325C
Flushing Meadows–
Corona 320D
Edgemere 360D
Forest 336B
Fort Tilden 363D
Francis Lewis ..305B
Frank Golden
Memorial 306C
Gateway Nat'l 358A
Glen Ridge 334B
Grover Cleveland ...
.........................358B
Hamilton Beach ....
.........................358B
Herman MacNeil ....
.........................305B
Jacob Riis 364C
John Golden
Memorial...........315C
Juniper Valley 327C
Kings 337D
Kissena 321D
Liberty 339C
Little Bay 307C
Queens Bridge 308C
Rainey 308B
Rockaway 365C
Springfield 352D
Spring Creek...348B

Staten Island

Austen House ..513B
Bloomingdale ..533A
Blue Heron 534B
Clay Pits Pond 526D
Clove Lakes ...511B
Conference House ..
.........................536C
Deere 511D
Eibs Pond 513C
Evergreen 522C
Frasier 505A
Fresh Kills ...515C
Great Kills 530B
Hero 507C
High Rock 517C
J. Lyons City ...507D
Latourette 521B
Lemon Creek ..533D
Miller Field 524A
Silver Lake 506D
South Beach ...506D
Arthur Von Briessen
.........................513D
Walker 506A
Willow Brook...509D
Wolfe's Pond...533D

PRESERVES

Dubos Pt Wildlife
Sanctuary, QS...368A
Plumb Beach,
BK 446B
Prall's Island,
SI.......................508C
Thomas Pell
Wildlife Refuge &
Sanctuary, BX...206C
Udall's Cove Park,
QS 315D
William T Davis
Wildlife Refuge,
SI.......................515A

THINGS TO DO
Birding
The Ramble,
Central Pk, MA **133C**
E & W Ponds,
Jamaica Bay Nat'l
Wildlife Refuge
QS **358B**
Hunter Island,
Pelham Bay Park
BX **206B**
Alley Pond Pk,
QS **324B**
Greenbelt, SI....**517C**

Butterflying
Floyd Bennett Field,
BK **439C**
Inwood Hill Park,
MA **160D**
Jamaica Bay,
QS **358B**
Gerike Farm, SI**526D**
Van Cortlandt Pk,
QS **209A**

Fishing
City Island, BX **213B**
Fort Tilden, QS **363D**
Prospect Park Lake
BK **422A**

TO FIND A TOP 100

Simply turn to page
and locate a park or
garden in grids
A,B,C or D.

MA = Manhattan
BX = The Bronx
BK = Brooklyn
QS = Queens
SI = Staten Island

NIGHTLIFE

BLUES, FOLK, ROCK & SOUL

Venues may offer many styles of music. Call for more details.

Arlene Grocery
95 Stanton St, MA
212-358-1633 **110B**

Arthur's Tavern
57 Grove St, MA
212-675-6879 **112D**

Baby Jupiter
170 Orchard St, MA
212-982-2229 **110B**

The Baggot Inn
82 W 3 St, MA
212-477-0622 **113C**

BAM Cafe
30 Lafayette Av, BK
718-636-4139 **407D**

Bitter End
147 Bleecker St, MA
212-673-7030 **113D**

The Blue Lounge
625 Broadway, MA
212-473-8787 **113D**

Bottom Line
15 W 4 St, MA
212-228-7880 **113D**

Brownies
169 Av A, MA
212-420-8392 **114B**

CBGB
315 Bowery, MA
212-982-4052 **114C**

Chicago B.L.U.E.S.
73 Eighth Av, MA
212-924-9755 **112B**

The Cooler
416 W 14 St, MA
212-645-5189 **112B**

Fez (Time Café)
380 Lafayette St, MA
212-533-2680 **114C**

Galapagos
70 North 6 St, BK
718-782-5188 **402C**

Irving Plaza
17 Irving Pl, MA
212-777-6800 **119D**

Knitting Factory
74 Leonard St, MA
212-219-3055 **106D**

Le Bar Bat
311 W 57 St, MA
212-307-7228 **129C**

Mercury Lounge
217 E Houston St, MA,
212-260-4700 **114D**

Rebar
127 Eighth Av, MA
212-627-1680 **117C**

Sidewalk Cafe
94 Av A, MA
212-473-7373 **114D**

Terra Blues
149 Bleecker St, MA
212-777-7776 **113C**

Tonic
107 Norfolk St, MA
212-358-7503 **110B**

West End Gate
2911 Broadway, MA
212-662-8830 **144C**

Wetlands Preserve
161 Hudson St, MA
212-966-4225 **106A**

CABARET

Bemelmans Bar
35 E 76 St, MA
212-744-1600 **134D**

Chez Josephine
414 W 42 St, MA
212-594-1925 **120B**

Danny's Skylight Room
346 W 46 St, MA
212-265-8133 **125C**

Don't Tell Mama
343 W 46 St, MA
212-757-0788 **125C**

The Duplex
61 Christopher St, MA
212-255-5438 **113A**

Judy's Chelsea
169 Eighth Av, MA
212-929-5410 **117C**

Mother
432 W 14 St, MA
212-366-5680 **112A**

The Oak Room
59 W 44 St, MA
212-840-6800 **125D**

Superfine @ Between the Bridges
63 York St, BK
718-243-9005 **407A**

Triad
158 W 72 St, MA
212-799-4599 **128B**

COMEDY CLUBS

Boston Comedy
82 W 3 St, MA
212-477-1000 **113C**

Caroline's
1626 Broadway, MA
212-757-4100 **125A**

Comedy Cellar
117 MacDougal St, MA, 212-254-3480
113C

Comic Strip
1568 Second Av, MA,
212-861-9386 **135A**

Chicago City Limits
1105 First Av, MA
212-888-5233 **131C**

Dangerfield's
1118 First Av, MA
212-593-1650 **131C**

Gotham
34 W 22 St, MA
212-367-9000 **117C**

NY Comedy Club
241 E 24 St, MA
212-696-LAFF **118B**

Stand-Up NY
237 W 78 St, MA
212-595-0850 **132D**

DANCE CLUBS

Au Bar
41 E 58 St, MA
212-308-9455 **130D**

Centro-Fly
45 W 21 St, MA
212-627-7770 **118A**

Cheetah
12 W 21 St, MA
212-206-7770 **118B**

Club El Flamingo
547 W 21 St,
212-307-7171 **116B**

Copacabana
617 W 57, MA
212-582-2672 **124A**

Jimmy's Bronx Cafe
281 W Fordham Rd,
BX, 718-329-2000 **214B**

The Latin Quarter
2551 Broadway, MA
212-864-7600 **136B**

Life
158 Bleecker St
212-420-1999

Mother
432 W 14 St, MA
212-366-5680

Nell's
246 W 14 St, MA
212-675-1567

Pyramid Club
101 Av A, MA
212-473-7184

Roseland
239 W 52 St, MA
212-247-0200

S.O.B.'s
204 Varick St, M
212-243-4940

Soca Paradise
205-20 Jamaica A
718-464-3600

Webster Hall
125 E 11 St, MA
212-353-1600

HOUSE

Baktun
418 W 14 St, MA
212-206-1590

Exit
610 W 56 St, MA
212-582-8282

The Roxy
515 W 18 St, MA
212-645-5156

Tunnel
220 W 12 Av, MA
212-695-4682

Twilo
530 W 27 Av, MA
212-268-1600

udson St, MA
43-1379 **109**C

**Z &
NDARDS**

nquin
44 St, MA
40-6800 **125**D

and
V 44 St, MA
81-3080 **125**C

Blue Note
W 3 St, MA
75-8592 **113**C

ery Ballroom
ancey St, MA
33-2111 **110**A

& Bear
Av @ 49 St, MA
72-4900 **126**D

Carlyle
76 St, MA,
44-1600 **134**D

ur
E 13 St, MA
33-6212 **114**B

**stein's @
Regency**
Park Av, MA
39-4095 **130**D

efront
W 54 St, MA
60-2271 **125**A

um
V 63 St, MA
82-2121 **128**D

Bar
First Av, MA
28-0444 **114**B

Internet Cafe
82 E 3 St, MA
212-614-0747 **114**C

The Jazz Standard
116 E 27 St, MA
212-576-2232 **118**B

Jules
65 St Marks Pl, MA
212-477-5560 **114**A

Knitting Factory
74 Leonard St, MA
212-219-3055 **106**D

Lenox Lounge
288 Lenox Av, MA
212-722-9566 **145**B

Michael's Pub
57 E 54 St, MA
212-758-2272 **126**B

Metronome
915 Broadway, MA
212-505-7400 **118**B

Opaline
85 Av A, MA
212-475-5050 **114**D

St. Nick's Pub
773 St. Nicholas Av,
MA, 212-283-9728
152D

Small's
183 W 10 St, MA
212-929-7565 **140**A

Smoke
2751 Broadway, MA
212-864-6662 **140**A

Sol
229 DeKalb Av, BK
718-222-1510 **407**D

Sweet Basil
88 Seventh Av S, MA
212-242-1785 **113**C

Up Over Jazz Cafe
351 Flatbush Av, BK
718-398-5413 **415**B

Village Vanguard
178 Seventh Av S, MA
212-255-4037 **112**B

Well's
2247 Seventh Av, MA
212-234-0700 **149**A

Zinc Bar
90 W Houston, MA
212-477-8337 **109**A

LATE NIGHT EATS

Around the Clock
8 Stuyvesant St, MA
212-598-0402 **114**C

Blue Ribbon
97 Sullivan St, MA
212-274-0404 **109**A

Brasserie
(Seagrams Bldg)
100 E 53 St, MA
212-751-4840 **126**B

Carnegie Deli
854 Seventh Av, MA
212-757-2245 **125**A

Coffee Shop
26 Union Sq W, MA
212-243-7969 **118**C

Florent
69 Gansevoort St, MA
212-989-5779 **112**A

L'Actuel
145 E 50 St, MA
212-583-0001 **127**A

**New York
Noodle Town**
28 1/2 Bowery, MA
212-349-0923 **107**C

The Odeon
145 W Broadway, MA
212-233-0507 **106**D

Pravda
281 Lafayette St, MA
212-226-4696 **109**B

Raoul's
180 Prince St, MA
212-966-3518 **109**A

Uncle George's
33-19 Broadway, QS
718-626-0593 **309**C

Wollensky's Grill
205 E 49 St, MA
212-753-0444 **127**C

PUBS & BARS

Bowery Bar
40 E 4 St, MA
212-475-2220 **114**C

**The Campbell
Apartment**
17 Vanderbilt Av, MA
212-980-9476 **122**B

Double Happiness
173 Mott St, MA
212-941-1282 **107**A

57–57
Four Season Hotel
57 W 57 St, MA
212-758-5700 **130**D

The G Lounge
223 W 19 St, MA
212-929-1085 **117**C

**Greatest Bar
on Earth**
1 WTC 107th fl, MA
212-524-7011 **104**A

Joe's Pub
425 Lafayette St, MA
212-239-6200 **114**C

King Cole Bar
St. Regis Hotel
2 E 55 St, MA
212-350-8741 **126**A

Lansky Lounge
102 Norfolk St, MA,
212-677-9489 **110**B

**McSorley's Old
Ale House**
15 E 7 St, MA
212-473-9148 **114**C

Standard
158 First Av, MA
212-387-0239 **114**B

White Horse Tavern
567 Hudson St, MA
212-243-9260 **112**B

SUPPER CLUBS

Laura Belle
120 W 43 St, MA
212-819-1000 **126**C

The Rainbow Grill
30 Rockefeller Plz,
65th floor, MA
212-632-5000 **126**A

Supper Club
240 W 47 St, MA
212-921-1940 **125**C

151
151 E 50 St, MA
212-753-1144 **126**B

TO FIND A TOP 100

Simply turn to page
and locate a club or
pub in grids
A,B,C or D.

MA = Manhattan
BX = The Bronx
BK = Brooklyn
QS = Queens
SI = Staten Island

PERFORMING

Aaron Davis Hall
CUNY, W 135 St @
Convent Av, MA
212-650-7100 **148**B

Alice Tully Hall
Lincoln Center, MA
212-875-5000 **128**B
Chamber Music Society

American Opera Projects
463 Broome St, MA
212-431-8102 **109**D

Amato Opera
319 Bowery, MA
212-228-8200 **110**A

Avery Fisher Hall
Lincoln Center, MA
(212) 875-5030 **128**B

Bargemusic, Ltd
Fulton Ferry
Landing, BK
718-624-4061 **406**B

Beacon Theater
B'way @ 74 St, MA
212-307-7171 **132**D

Belmont Italian American Playhouse
2385 Arthur Av, BX
718-364-4700 **215**C

Billie Holiday Theatre
1368 Fulton St, BK
(718) 636-0918 **416**B

Brecht Forum
122 W 27 St, MA
212-242-4201 **117**D

The Bronx County Historical Society
3309 Bainbridge Av
BX, 718-881-8900 **209**D

Bronx Opera Co.
5 Minerva Pl, BX
718 365-4209 **209**D

Brooklyn Academy of Music (BAM)
30 Lafayette Av, BK
718 636-4100 **407**B

Brooklyn Center for Performing Arts
Campus Rd
@ Hillel Pl, BK
718-951-4500 **429**A

Brooklyn Heritage House
581 Mother Gaston
Bd, BK, 718-385-1111 **418**C

The Center for Art & Culture of Bedford Stuyvesant
1368 Fulton St, BK
718-636-6948 **416**B

CSC Repertory
136 E 13 St, MA
212-677-4210 **114**A

CAMI Hall
165 W 57 St, MA
212-841-9650 **129**C

Carnegie Hall
881 Seventh Av
@ W 57 St, MA
212-903-9600 **125**A

Circle in the Square
1633 Broadway, MA
212-307-2700 **125**A

City Center
131 W 55 St, MA
212-581-1212 **125**B

Colden Center for the Performing Arts
65-30 Kissena Bd, QS
(718) 793-8080 **329**B

Danspace at St Mark's Church-in-the-Bowery
131 E 10 St, MA
212-674-8194 **114**A

Dance Theater Workshop (DTW)
219 W 19 St, MA
212-924-0077 **117**C

Delacorte Theater Shakespeare in the Park
Central Park, MA
212-861-PAPP **133**A

Dia Center
548 W 22 St, MA
212-989-5912 **116**B

En Foco
32 E Kingsbridge Rd
BX, 718-584-7718 **215**A

Ensemble Studio
549 W 52 St, MA
212-247-4982 **124**C

FIT, Haft Auditorium
227 W 27 @ 7 Av, MA
212-307-2700 **117**A

Flea Theatre
41 White St, MA
212-226-0051 **106**B

Florence Gould Hall
Alliance Française
55 E 59 St, MA
212-355-6160 **130**D

Gowanus Arts Exchange
295 Douglass St, BK
718-596-5250 **415**A

The Greek Cultural Center
27-18 Hoyt Av S, QS
718-726-7329 **309**A

Hammerstein Ballroom
311 W 34 St, MA
212-279-7740 **121**C

The Harvey
651 Fulton St, BK
718-636-4181 **407**D

Henry St. Settlement
Louis Abrams Arts
Center,
466 Grand St, MA
212-598-0400 **111**C

HERE
145 Sixth Av, MA
212-647-0202 **109**A

Historic Richmond Town
441 Clarke Av, SI
718-351-1611 **522**B

Hostos Performing Arts Center
500 Grand
Concourse, BX
718-518-4300 **227**A

Irish Arts Center
553 W 51 St, MA
212-757-3318 **124**C

Jamaica Arts Center
161-04 Jamaica Av
QS, 718-658-7400 **337**D

The Joseph Pap Public Theater
425 Lafayette St
212-260-2400

Joyce Theater
175 Eighth Av, N
212-242-0800

Joyce SoHo
155 Mercer St, N
212-431-9233

Juilliard Theatre
Lincoln Center, A
(212) 799-5000

The Kitchen
512 W 19 St, MA
212-255-5793

Langston Hughe Community Arts
102-09 Northern
QS, 718-651-110

La MaMa E.T.C.
74 1/2 E 4 St, MA
(212) 475-7710

Lehman College Center for the Performing Arts
250 Bedford Par
Bd W, BX
718 960-8232

Lincoln Center
Lincoln Center, N
212-875-5400

Manhattan Scho of Music
120 Claremont Av,
212-749-2802

Merkin Concert
129 W 67, MA
212-362-8719

etropolitan
m of Art
fth Av, MA
5-7710 **133B**

etropolitan
House
Center, MA
2-6000 **128D**
n Ballet Theatre
politan Opera

Theater–
bia Univ
@ 116 St, MA
4-1754 **144B**

lewhouse
Center, MA
2-7600 **128B**

ictory Theater
42 St, MA
4-4222 **125C**

York
cal Society
W, MA
3-3400 **133C**

ew York
Library for
rforming Arts
@ 65 St, MA
0-1630 **128B**

heater
Center, MA
0-5570 **128D**
let • NYC Opera

ican Poets

St, MA
5-8183 **114D**

Downtown
er
ce St, MA
6-1715 **105C**

**Pan Asian
Repertory Theater**
423 W 46 St, MA
212-505-5655 **124D**

Performing Garage
33 Wooster St, MA
212-966-3651 **109D**

P.S. 122
150 First Av, MA
212-477-5288 **114B**

**Queens Theater
in the Park**
Flushing Meadows
QS, 718 760-0064
320D

Regina Opera Co.
65 St @ 12 Av, BK
718-232-3555 **427C**

Riverside Church
490 Riverside Dr, MA
212-222-5900 **145A**

**Radio City
Music Hall**
Sixth Av @ 50 St, MA
212-247-4777 **125B**

**St Ann's Center
for Restoration
and the Arts**
157 Montague St, BK
718-834-8794 **408C**

**St Mark's Church–
in–the–Bowery**
131 E 10 St, MA,
212-674-8194 **114B**

**The Spanish
Institute**
684 Park Av, MA
(212) 628-0420 **130B**

**Snug Harbor
Cultural Center**
1000 Richmond Ter, SI
718-448-2500 **506B**

**The Studio Museum
in Harlem**
144 W 125 St, MA
(212) 864-4500 **145A**

**The Sylvia & Danny
Kaye Playhouse–
Hunter College**
Park Av @ 68 St, MA
212-772-4448 **130B**

Symphony Space
2537 Broadway, MA
212-864-5400 **136B**

TADA!
120 W 28 St, MA
212-627-1732 **117B**

**Theatre for the
New City**
155 First Av, MA
212-254-1109 **114B**

**Thelma Hill
Performing Arts
Center**
University Plz, BK
718-875-9710 **409C**

**Thalia Spanish
Theater**
41-17 Greenpoint Av,
Sunnyside, QS
718-279-3880 **317A**

Town Hall
123 W 43 St, MA
212-840-2824 **125C**

**Tribeca Performing
Arts Center**
199 Chambers St, MA
212-346-8510 **104A**

**Vivian Beaumont
Theater**
Lincoln Center
150 W 65 St, MA
212-362-7600 **128B**

**Walter Reade
Theater**
Lincoln Center, MA
212-875-5600 **128B**

Westbeth Theatre
151 Bank St, MA
212-741-0391 **112D**

**Winter Garden at
the WFC**, MA
212-945-0505 **104C**

92nd St Y & YWCA
1395 Lex. Av, MA
212-996-1100 **139A**

FILM

**American Museum
of the Moving Image**
35 Av @ 36 St, QS
718-784-0077 **309C**

AMNH
CPW @ 79 St, MA
212-769-5650 **133C**

Angelika Film Center
18 W Houston St, MA
212-995-2000 **113D**

Anthology
32 Second Av, MA,
212-505-5110 **114C**

BAM Rose Cinemas
30 Lafayette Av, BK
718-623-2770 **407D**

Film Forum
209 W Houston St,
MA, 212-727-8110
109A

French Institute
55 E 59 St, MA
212-355-6160 **130D**

MoMA
11 W 53 St, MA
212-708-9400 **125B**

NY Film Academy
100 E 17 St, MA
212-674-4300 **118D**

NYU Cantor Film Ctr
36 E 8 St,
212-998-8872 **113B**

Donnell Media Ctr
20 W 53 St, MA
212-621-0618 **126A**

Screening Room
54 Varick St,
212-334-2100 **106A**

Sony IMAX
1998 Broadway
@ 68 St, MA
212-336-5000 **128B**

Walter Reade Theatre
Lincoln Center, MA
212-875-5600 **128B**

YMCA Cine-Club
610 Lex. Av, MA
212-755-4500 **126B**

The Ziegfeld
141 W 54 St, MA
212-765-7600 **125B**

TO FIND A TOP 100

Simply turn to page
and locate a cinema
or theater in grids
A,B,C or D.

MA = Manhattan
BX = The Bronx
BK = Brooklyn
QS = Queens
SI = Staten Island

ARTS & FILM

SHOPPING

ART & PAPER

Alphabets
115 Av A, MA
212-475-7250 **114B**

The Art Store
1 Bond St, MA
212-533-2444 **113D**

Kate's Paperie
561 Broadway, MA
212-941-9816 **109B**

Papyrus
852 Lex Av, MA,
212-717-0002 **130D**
plus 3 locations
citywide.

Pearl Paint
308 Canal St, MA
212-431-7932 **106B**

Poster America
138 W 18 St, MA
212-206-0499 **117D**

BOOKS & MUSIC

Argosy
116 E 59 St, MA
212-753-4455 **130D**

Barnes & Noble
33 E 17 St, MA
212-253-0810 **118D**
plus 9 locations
citywide.

B&N - Main
105 Fifth Av, MA
212-807-0099 **118C**

Borders WTC
5 WTC, MA
212-839-8037 **104D**
plus 2 locations
citywide.

Coliseum
1771 Broadway, MA
212-757-8381 **129C**

Colony Records
1619 Broadway, MA
212-265-2050 **125C**

Empire State News
Empire State Bldg,
MA, 212-279-9153 **121D**

HMV
1280 Lex. Av, MA
212-348-0800 **139C**
Plus 4 citywide

Hudson News
Penn Station, MA
212-971-6800 **121C**

Rizzoli International
454 W B'way, MA
212-674-1616 **109B**

St Mark's Book Shop
31 Third Av, MA
212-260-7853 **114A**

Shakespeare & Co.
716 Broadway, MA
212-529-1330 **113D**

The Strand
828 Broadway, MA
212-473-1452 **113A**

Subterranean Records
5 Cornelia St, MA
212-463-8900 **113B**

Tower Records
692 Broadway, MA
212-505-1500 **113D**

Universal News
484 Broadway, MA
212-965-9042 **109D**

Virgin Megastore
1540 Broadway, MA
212-921-1020 **125C**

DESIGNERS

Agnès B.
116-18 Prince St, MA
212-925-4649 **109B**

Anna Sui
113 Greene St, MA
212-941-8406 **109B**

Armani
760 Madison Av, MA
212-988-9191 **130D**

Betsey Johnson
138 Wooster St, MA,
212-995-5048 **109B**

Calvin Klein
654 Madison Av, MA
212-292-9000 **130D**

Comme des Garçons
116 Wooster St, MA
212-219-0660 **109B**

Helmut Lang
80 Greene St, MA
212-925-7214 **109B**

Paul Smith
108 Fifth Av, MA
212-627-9770 **117D**

Ralph Lauren
867 Madison Av
@ 72 St, MA
212-606-2100 **130B**

Todd Oldham
123 Wooster, MA
212-219-3531 **109B**

Tocca
161 Mercer, MA
212-343-3912 **109D**

Yohji Yamamoto
103 Grand St, MA
800-803-4443 **106B**

DEPARTMENT STORES

Barneys NY
660 Madison Av, MA
212-826-8900 **130D**

Bergdorf Goodman
754 Fifth Av, MA
212-753-7300 **130C**

Bloomingdale's
1000 Third Av, MA
212-705-2000 **130D**

Brooks Brothers
346 Madison Av, MA
212-682-8800 **126D**

Canal Jean
504 Broadway, MA
212-226-1130 **109D**

Century 21
22 Cortlandt St, MA
212-227-9092 **104D**

Felissimo
10 W 56 St, MA
212-247-5656 **126A**

Henri Bendel
712 Fifth Av, MA
212-247-1100 **126A**

Jeffrey NY
449 W 14 St, MA
212-206-1272 **116C**

Lord & Taylor
424 Fifth Av, MA
212-391-3344 **122A**

Macy's–Herald Sq
151 W 34 St, MA
212-695-4400 **121C**

Pearl River
277 Canal St, M
212-219-8107

Saks Fifth Ave
Fifth Av @ 49 S
212-753-4000

Syms
42 Trinity Pl, M
212-797-1199

Takashimaya
693 Fifth Av, M
212-350-0100

Terra Verde
122 Wooster S
212-925-4533

ELECTRONIC

Harvey's
888 Broadway,
212-228-5354

J&R Music W
23 Park Row, N
212-238-9000

Stereo Exchan
627 Broadway,
212-505-1111

GIFTS & TOY

Enchanted For
85 Mercer St, D
212-925-6677

FAO Schwarz
767 Fifth Av, M
212-644-9400

Forbidden Plan
B'way @ 13 St,
212-473-1576

Little Rickie
49 1/2 First Av,
212-505-6467

RMET

Wines &
s
r Pl, MA
4-7500   **114A**

ci's
th Av, MA
3-2600   **113A**

Greengrass
nsterdam Av,
2-724-4707
136D

Bakery
Broadway, MA
4-2525   **106D**

lla
roadway, MA
4-0383   **132D**

& DeLuca
oadway, MA
1-1691   **109B**

ay Market
roadway, MA
5-1888   **132D**

ay Market
vn)
welfth Av, MA
4-3883   **148C**

Markets
7-3220
n Sq, MA **118D**
ugh Hall, BK
408D

et Garage
oome St, MA
1-5850   **109D**

Pickle Products
ex St, MA
4-4477   **110D**

Patisserie Lanciani
414 W 14 St, MA
212-989-1213   **112B**

Sherry–Lehmann
679 Madison Av, MA
212-838-7500   **130D**

Russ & Daughters
179 E Houston St, MA,
212-475-4880   **110A**

Zabar's
2245 Broadway, MA
212-787-2000   **132B**

HOME & DESIGN

ABC-Home & Carpet
888 Broadway, MA
212-473-3000   **118C**

Ad Hoc Softwares
410 W B'way, MA
212-925-2652   **106B**

Bed Bath & Beyond
Sixth Av @ 18 St, MA
212-255-3550   **117D**

Crate & Barrel
650 Madison Av, MA
212-308-0011   **130D**

**Chelsea
Antiques Market**
110 W 25 St, MA
212-929-0909   **117C**

Depression Modern
150 Sullivan St, MA
212-982-5699   **109A**

Moss
146 Greene St, MA
212-226-2190   **109B**

Prince Lumber
15 St @ Ninth Av, MA
212-777-1150   **116D**

Shabby Chic
93 Greene St, MA
212-274-9842   **109B**

Smith & Hawken
394 W B'way, MA
212-925-0687   **109C**

**The Terence
Conran Shop**
415 E 57 St, MA
212-755-9079   **131C**

Urban Archaeology
285 Lafayette St, MA
212-431-6969   **109B**

INSTRUMENTS–MUSICAL

Sam Ash
160 W 48 St, MA
212-719-2299   **125C**

Manny's
156 W 48 St, MA
212-819-0576   **125C**

The Music Store
44 W 62 St, MA
212-541-6236   **128D**

JEWELRY

Bulgari
730 Fifth Av, MA
212-315-9000   **126A**

Cartier
725 Fifth Av,
Trump Tower, MA
212-308-0843   **126A**

Harry Winston
718 Fifth Av, MA
212-245-2000   **126A**

Tiffany & Co.
727 Fifth Av, MA
212-755-8000   **126A**

Tourneau
12 E 57 St, MA
212-758-7300   **130D**

Van Cleef & Arpels
744 Fifth Av, MA
212-644-9500   **126C**

PERSONAL CARE & VANITY

**Astor Place Hair
Designers**
2 Astor Pl, MA
212-475-9854   **113B**

Elizabeth Arden
691 Fifth Av, MA
212-546-0200   **126A**

Gauntlet
144 Fifth Av, MA
212-229-0180   **117D**

Georgette Klinger
501 Madison Av, MA
212-838-3200   **126B**

Jason Croy
632 Hudson St, MA
212-691-8299   **112B**

Kiehl's
109 Third Av, MA
212-677-3171   **114A**

**Russian &
Turkish Baths**
268 E 10 St, MA
212-505-0665   **114A**

Vidal Sassoon
767 Fifth Av, MA
212-535-9200   **129D**

SPORTS

Blades– 6 locations
120 W 72 ST, MA
212-787-3911   **128B**

NikeTown, NY
6 E 57 St, MA
212-891-6453   **130D**

Paragon
867 Broadway, MA
212-255-8036   **118C**

THEME STORES

The Disney Store
711 Fifth Av, MA
212-702-0702   **125C**

**Warner Bros.
Studio Store**
1 E 57 St, MA
800-223-6524   **129D**

WORLD MARKETS

Arthur Av, BX
(Italian) **215B**

Main St. Flushing,
QS, (Chinese) ..**321A**

La Marqueta,
Park Av @ 110-118
Sts, MA **146C**

Fulton Mall, BK ......
(Hip-Hop) **409B**

Harlem USA,
125 St, MA (African
American) **145A**

74 St & 37 Av, QS
(Indian/Pakistani) ....
...........................**319A**

Manhattan Av, BK
(Polish) **402B**

**Roosevelt Av @ 74–
110 St**, QS (Latino) ..
...........................**318A**

149 St
Third Av @ 149 St,
BX (Latino) **227A**

SPORTS 3

ARENAS & STADIUMS

Aqueduct Race Track
Rockaway Bd
@ 110 St, QS
718-641-4700 **343**C

Belmont Park Race Track
Hempstead Tpk @
Plainfield Av, QS
718-641-4700 **341**C

USTA National Tennis Center
Flushing Meadow–
Corona Pk, QS
718-760-6200 **320**B
US OPEN (Sep)

Continental Airline Arena
The Meadowlands,
NJ, 201-935-3900
NY Nets (Nov-Apr) **120**A
NJ Devils (Oct-Apr)

Glants Stadium
The Meadowlands,
NJ, 201-935-8222
Giants (Sep-Jan) **120**A
Jets (Sep-Jan)
Metrostars (Apr-Sep)

Madison Sq Garden
7 Av @ W 32 St, MA
212-465-6741 **121**C
NY Cityhawks (Apr-Jul)
NY Liberty (Jun-Aug)
NY Knicks (Nov-Apr)
NY Rangers (Oct-Apr)
WTA Tennis (Nov)

Meadowlands Race Track
The Meadowlands,
NJ, 201-438-3100
120A

Shea Stadium
Flushing, QS
718-507-8499 **320**B
Mets (Apr-Oct)

Yankee Stadium
161 St & River Av,
BX, 212-760-6200
Yankees (Apr-Oct) **121**C

CITY LINKS

18 Holes

Douglaston
6320 Marathon Pkwy,
QS, 718-428-1617
325C

Dyker Beach
Seventh Av @ 86 St,
BK, 718-836-9722
434B

LaTourette
1000 Richmond Hill
Rd, SI, 718-351-1889
516C

Mosholu
Van Cortlandt Pk, BX
718-655-9164 **209**B

Pelham/Split-Rock
Shore Rd, BX
718-885-1258 **206**A

Bucket of Balls
Chelsea Piers
12 Av @ 23 St, MA
212-336-6400 **116**C

Family Golf Center
Randall's Island, MA
212-427-5689 **302**B

Golden Bear
Alley Pond Park, QS
718-225-9187 **324**A

Turtle Cove
1 City Island Rd, BX
718-885-2646 **206**D

FIELD OF DREAMS

Baseball
Dyker Beach Park
BK **434**B

Alley Pond Park
QS **332**B

Batting Practice
Chelsea Piers
12 Av @ 23 St, MA
212-336-6500 **116**C

Hackers, Hitters & Hoops
123 W 18 St, MA
212-929-7482 **117**D

Randall's Island Practice Center
MA, 212-427-5689
302B

Cricket
Randall's Island
MA **302**B

Softball
Canarsie Beach Park, BK **431**A

GOTHAM GRID IRON

Football Pick Up
Harris Park
BX **209**C

Central Park
MA **133**A

Marine Park
BK **438**A

Hurling
Gaelic Park
BX **208**D

Rugby
Randall's Island
MA **302**B

GYM FOR A DAY

Asphalt Green
555 E 90 St, MA
212-369-8890 **139**D

Club La Raquette
119 W 56 St, MA
212-245-1144 **125**B

Crunch Fitness
54 E 13 St, MA
212-475-2018 **113**B

Eastern Athletic
43 Clark St, BK
718-625-0500 **408**B

NY Health & Racquet
• 20 E 50 St, MA
212-593-1500 **126**B
• 39 Whitehall St, MA
212-269-9800 **103**C
(7 locations in MA)

NY Sports Club
1635 Third Av, MA
212-987-7200 **139**C

Printing House Fitness & Racquet
421 Hudson St, MA
212-243-7600 **108**B

Sports Center at Chelsea Piers
12 Av @ 23 St, MA
212-336-6000 **116**C

World Gym
232 Mercer St, MA
212-780-7407 **113**D

YM & YWCA
• 610 Lex. Av, MA
212-755-4500 **126**B
• 42-07 Parsons Bd,
QS, 718-353-4553
321B

HOOP DREA

*There are a n
of courts in M
where great
street basketb
can be experie
indoors and o
Here's a samp
the best:*

Indoors
Gaucho's Gym
478 Gerard Av
@ 149 St, BX

IS 8
Merrick Bd @
108 Av, QS

Outdoors
"The Cage"
W 4 St, MA

Fort Tryon Park
Margaret Corb
MA

"The Garden"
Surf Av @ 25 S

Holcombe Rucker Park
155 St @ Eight
MA

Kingston Park
Atlantic Av
@ Kingston Av

St Albans Park
Merrick Bd
@ 172 St, QS

Walker Park
Bard Av @
Livingston Ct, S

RECREATION

MARATHON FITNESS

Road Runners
Fred Lebow Pl, ... St, MA
...60-4455 **137D**

...Y Marathon is ... runners ...ing through ...boroughs on ...st weekend in ...mber. Starts ... Verrazano ... and ends in ...al Park.
513D-129A

...QUETS
...is

... National ...s Center
...ing Meadows–
...a Park, QS
...60-6200 **320B**

...ealth & ...uet Tennis
...St @ Piers 13
...MA
...22-9300 **103C**

...ports Club
...Vernon Bd, QS
...37-2381 **308C**

...Courts
...al Park
...& West Dr, MA
...30-0205 **137A**

...ect Park
...ide Av
...rk Cir, BK **422A**

...ortland Park
...dway @ 241 St,
...**209A**

GLOBAL GOALS
Soccer Pick-Ups
Marine Park
BK **438A**

East River Park, MA
Sunday 11am **111D**

Flushing Meadows
QS, Sunday 11am
320D

Red Hook, BK
Sunday 11am **414A**

SKATING – ICE

Lasker Rink
110 St & Lenox Av,
MA, 212-534-7639
141B

Kate Wollman Rink
Prospect Park, BK
718-965-8904 **422B**

Rockefeller Center
MA, 212-332-7654
125B

Sky Rink
Chelsea Piers, MA
212-336-6100 **116C**

Staten Island War Memorial
Clove Lakes Park, SI
718-720-1010 **511D**

Wollman Rink
S Central Park, MA
212-396-1010 **129D**

World's Fair Rink
Flushing Meadows–
Corona Park, QS
718-271-1996 **320D**

South St Seaport
Seaport Plz, BK
212-732-7678 **105D**

STREET WHEELS
Bikes
119 miles of bike routes exist today, with plans for 781 more miles:

Central Park
MA **129A**

Forest Park Dr
QS **336A**

Mosholu/Pelham Greenway
BX **209B**

Shore & Marine Pkwys
BK **426A-439C**

Bay St, SI **507B**

Blades
Empire Skate Club of NY (ESCNY)
MA 212-592-3674

NY Skate Patrol
MA 212-439-1234

Central Park
MA **129B**

Battery Park Esplanade
MA **104C**

Brooklyn Bridge
MA **105A**

Shore & Marine Pkwys
BK **426A**

Boards
Brooklyn Bridge
@ Park Row, MA
105A

Central Park
The Mall, MA **129A**

URBAN HOOVES
Stables
Claremont Riding Academy
175 W 89 St, MA
212-724-5100 **136D**

Jamaica Bay Riding Academy
7000 Belt Pkwy, BK
718-531-8949 **431A**

Lynne's Riding School
88-03 70 Rd, QS
718-261-7679 **336A**

Riverdale Riding Academy
Van Cortland Pk, BX
718-548-4848 **203C**

Pelham Bay Stable
9 Shore Rd, BX
718-885-0551 **206C**

VOLLEYBALL
Big City Volleyball League
212-288-4240

NY Urban Professional Athletic League
212-877-3614

Central Park
on 68 St, MA **129B**

Dalton Gym
E 87 St @ Third Av
MA **139C**

HS Environmental Studies
444 W 56 St, MA
124B

Lost Battalion Hall
Rego Park, QS **328A**

WATER SPORTS
Canoe & Kayak
Metropolitan Canoe & Kayak Club
MA, 212-724-5069

Sebago Canoe Club
Paedergat Basin,
BK, 718-241-3683
431A

Dyckman Marina
W 254 St, BX **208A**

NY Kayak Co
601 W 26 St, MA
116A

Sail
Manhattan Sailing School
North Cove, MA
212-786-0400 **104C**

Great Hudson Sailing Center
Chelsea Piers, MA
212-741-7245 **116A**

Swim
Indoors–

63 St YMCA
5 W 63 St, MA
212-787-1301 **129C**

Asphalt Green
555 E 90 St, MA
212-369-8890 **139D**

Vanderbilt YMCA
224 E 47 St, MA
212-756-9600 **127C**

Outdoors–

Hamilton Fish Pool
128 Pitt St, MA
212-387-7687 **111A**

THEATRE

ON BROADWAY

Ambassador
215 W 49 St, MA
212-239-6200 **125**C

Americn Airlines
1530 Broadway, MA
212-719-9393 **125**C

Belasco
111 W 44 St, MA
212-239-6200 **125**D

Booth
222 W 45 St, MA
212-239-6200 **125**C

Broadhurst
235 W 44 St, MA
212-239-6200 **125**C

Broadway
1681 Broadway, MA
212-239-6200 **125**A

Brooks Atkinson
256 W 47 St, MA
212-307-4100 **125**C

Circle in the Square
1633 Broadway, MA
212-239-6200 **125**A

Cort
138 W 48 St, MA
212-239-6200 **125**C

Criterion Center
1530 Broadway, MA
212-764-7903 **125**C

Ethel Barrymore
243 W 47 St, MA
212-239-6200 **125**C

Eugene O'Neill
230 W 49 St, MA
212-239-6200 **125**C

Gershwin
222 W 51 St, MA
212-586-6510 **125**A

Golden
252 W 45 St, MA
212-239-6200 **125**C

Helen Hayes
240 W 44, MA
212-307-4100 **125**C

Imperial
249 W 45 St, MA
212-239-6200 **125**C

Longacre
220 W 48 St, MA
212-239-6200 **125**C

Lunt-Fontanne
205 W 46 St, MA
212-575-9200 **125**C

Lyceum
149 W 45 St, MA
212-239-6200 **125**C

Majestic
247 W 44 St, MA
212-239-6200 **125**C

Marquis
1535 Broadway, MA
212-382-0100 **125**C

Martin Beck
302 W 45 St, MA
212-239-6200 **125**C

Minskoff
200 W 45 St, MA
212-869-0550 **125**C

Music Box
239 W 45 St, MA
212-239-6200 **125**C

Nederlander
208 W 41 St, MA
212-307-4100 **121**A

Neil Simon
250 W 52 St, MA
212-757-8646 **125**A

Palace
1564 Broadway, MA
212-730-8200 **125**C

Plymouth
236 W 45 St, MA
212-239-6200 **125**C

Richard Rodgers
226 W 46 St, MA
212-307-4100 **125**C

Royale
242 W 45 St, MA
212-239-6200 **125**C

St James
246 W 44 St, MA
212-239-6200 **125**C

Shubert
225 W 44 St, MA
212-239-6200 **125**C

Virginia
245 W 52 St, MA
212-239-6200 **125**A

Vivian Beaumont
Lincoln Center, MA
212-239-6200 **128**B

Walter Kerr
219 W 48 St, MA
212-239-6200 **125**C

Winter Garden
1634 Broadway, MA
212-239-6200 **125**A

OFF & OFF-OFF

American Jewish
307 W 26 St, MA
212-633-9797 **117**A

American Place
111 W 46 St, MA
212-840-2960 **125**D

Actors Playhouse
100 Seventh Av, MA
212-239-6200 **117**C

Astor Place
434 Lafayette St, MA
212-254-4370 **113**B

Atlantic
336 W 20 St, MA
212-239-6200 **117**C

Beacon
2124 Broadway, MA
212-307-7171 **132**D

Bouwerie Lane
330 Bowery, MA
212-677-0060 **114**C

**Castillo Cultural
Center**
500 Greenwich St,
MA, 212-941-1234
106A

Century
111 E 15 St, MA
212-239-6200 **118**D

Cherry Lane
38 Commerce St, MA
212-239-6200 **113**C

City Center Stage
131 W 55 St, MA
212-581-1212 **125**A

Classic Stage
136 E 13 St, MA
212-677-4210

Currican
154 W 29 St, MA
212-736-2533

Douglas Fairba
432 W 42 St, MA
212-239-4321

Duffy
1553 Broadway
212-695-3401

Duo
62 E 4 St, MA
212-598-4320

**Ensemble Stud
Theatre**
549 W 52 St, MA
212-247-3405

**Ford Center for
Performing Arts**
214 W 43 St, MA
212-307-4100

Greenwich Hou
27 Barrow St, MA
212-242-4140

Harold Clurman
412 W 42 St, MA
212-594-2370

Helen Hayes
240 W 44 St, MA
212-944-9450

Irish Repertory
132 W 22 St, MA
212-727-2737

Cocteau
tory
owery, MA
677-0060   **114C**

sh Repertory
91 St, MA
831-2000   **139C**

Houseman
42 St, MA
54-2220   **120B**

Anderson
42 St. MA
54-7853   **120B**

aMa E.T.C.
E 4 St, MA
475-7710   **114C**

's
44 St, MA
97-1780   **125C**

ng Glass
57 St, MA
07-9467   **124B**

e Lortel
hristopher St,
212-239-6200
112D

n Kaufmam
42 St, MA
39-6200   **120B**

tta Lane
netta La, MA
20-8000   **113C**

Amsterdam
42 St, MA
07-4100   **125C**

New Dramatist
424 W 44 St, MA
212-757-6960   **124D**

**New Perspectives
Theater Co**
750 Eighth Av, MA
212-730-2030   **125C**

New Victory
209 W 42 St, MA
212-564-4222   **125C**

NY Theatre Workshop
79 E 4 St, MA
212-460-5475   **114C**

Orpheum
126 Second Av, MA
212-477-2477   **114A**

**The Joseph Papp
Public Theater**
425 Lafayette St, MA
212-239-6200   **113D**

Pearl Theatre Co
80 St Marks Pl, MA
212-598-9802   **114A**

Playwrights Horizons
416 W 42 St, MA
212-279-4200   **120B**

Promenade
2162 Broadway, MA
212-239-6200   **132D**

St Luke's Church
308 W 46 St, MA
212-246-3540   **125C**

Samuel Beckett
410 W 42 St, MA
212-594-2370   **120B**

Signature Theater
555 W 42 St, MA
212-244-7529   **120B**

SoHo Playhouse
15 Vandam St, MA
212-691-1555   **109A**

SoHo Repertory
46 Walker St, MA
212-334-0962   **106B**

Stardust
51 St @ B'way, MA
212-239-6200   **125A**

**Sullivan Street
Playhouse**
181 Sullivan St, MA
212-674-3838   **109A**

Synchronicity Space
55 Mercer St, MA
212-343-1181   **109D**

Theatre East
211 E 60 St, MA
212-838-0177   **131C**

**Theater for the
New City**
155 First Av, MA
212-254-1109   **114B**

Theatre Four
424 W 55 St, MA
212-239-6200   **124B**

Theatre Off Park
224 Waverly Pl, MA
212-627-2556   **112B**

Ubu Repertory
15 W 28 St, MA
212-679-7540   **117B**

Union Square
100 E 17 St, MA
212-505-0700   **118D**

Variety Arts
110 Third Av, MA
212-239-6200   **114A**

Westside
407 W 43 St, MA
212-239-6200   **120B**

Westside Repertory
252 W 81 St, MA
212-874-7290   **132B**

Wings
154 Christopher St,
MA, 212-627-2961
112D

WPA
519 W 23 St, MA
212-206-0523   **116B**

13th St Repertory
50 W 13 St, MA
212-675-6677   **113A**

22 West
22 W 135 St, MA
212-862-7770   **149B**

28th St Theatre
120 W 28 St, MA
212-727-7722   **117B**

45 St
354 W 45 St, MA
212-333-7421   **125C**

55 Grove St Cabaret
55 Grove St, MA
212-366-5438   **112D**

ON or OFF?
*Because you are
within a few blocks
of Broadway does
not mean you are
ON Broadway.*

*ON Broadway the-
aters generally offer
500 seats or more,
and are under con-
tract to produce ON
"Broadway plays."*

*TKTS
For half-price
tickets to same day
performances head
to the TKTS booth
@ Broadway &
West 46 St.*

Telecharge
212-239-6200

Teletron
212-340-4171

Ticketmaster
212-307-4100

TO FIND A TOP 100

Simply turn to page
and locate the
theatre in grids
A,B,C or **D.**

MA = Manhattan
BX = The Bronx
BK = Brooklyn
QS = Queens
SI = Staten Island

THEATRE

1898

Amusing the Masses

No Biz Like Show Biz

HARLEM ON MY MIND

GETTING IT UP

To Be Or Not To Bop

We
you ho
here to th
twenty pages,
got here from
points in each o
century, New Y
we look at ou
and how the
has shap
glol

TRUTH IS WHAT SELLS

GREED IS GOOD

own
et from
the next
w you how we
how, at crucial
decades of this
hanged the way
s Americans,
ss of change
emporary
re.

HOW FAR TO GO TOO FAR?

THE PROMISED LANDSCAPE?

FREEDOM TO DRIP

If, at the end of the 20th Century, New York is becoming a theme park, it is just one more proof that what goes around comes around.

At century's start, New Yorkers built on the innovations of world's fair producers to create the first permanent theme park for mass entertainment. Between 1895 and 1904, in fact, four competing theme parks opened at Coney Island, with Ferris wheels and carousels, freak shows, thrill rides, and recreations of exotic or fantastic worlds (including "Selenian" midgets on a green– cheese moon, transplanted Inuit in Alaska, and premature ba not to mentic unplanned lo trict for booz bling, and wl

Coney Island & the Inven

photo © Brown Brothers

Amusing

(See Lucy, the Colossal Elephant at right.) By the time the subway reached Coney Island in 1920, upwards of a million people jammed the parks and beaches every summer Sunday.

Lucy, the Colossal Elephant of Coney Island

Lucy may have been inspired by Jumbo, the elephant P. T. Barnum brought from London to NYC, an immediate hit with New Yorkers (she stands in comparison, beneath Lucy).
Lucy was a seven-story wooden structure with a tin skin. Though conceived as a hotel, and later an auditorium, rumors have it that Lucy was really a brothel. Customers would enter through a door at the right hind leg.

the American Theme Park

1904

e Masses

No Biz like Show Biz **1915**

From the 1890s Yiddish theaters and music halls of the Lower East Side, Jewish entertainers, artists, and entrepreneurs moved uptown and created Show Biz.

By 1915, Broadway and Tin Pan Alley had industrialized the production and distribution of the nation's entertainment, using African-American, Jewish, Irish, and Italian immigrant idioms to lampoon, dissect, and ultimately transform American culture.

Talent and content assembled for the Ziegfeld Follies and its competitors, including the Shubert Brothers' The Passing Show and Jerome Kern's Princess Theater Shows, were dispatched throughout the country via the vaudeville circuit, through which the performers and material became an integral part of the life of heartland America.

In direct lines of succession the system gave rise to the modern Broadway musical (Kern's "Show Boat" in 1927), to Hollywood comedy and musical films, to radio and television variety shows, to the pop music industry, and to the distinct Yiddishization of the American comic sensibility in an unbroken line from the Marx Brothers to Billy Crystal.

"And if anyone, on hearing Jerome Kern say that Irving Berlin IS American music, is then so famous to object on the ground that he was born in Russia, it might be pointed out that if the musical interpreter of American civilization came over in the foul hold of a ship, so did American civilization."

Alexander Woolcott

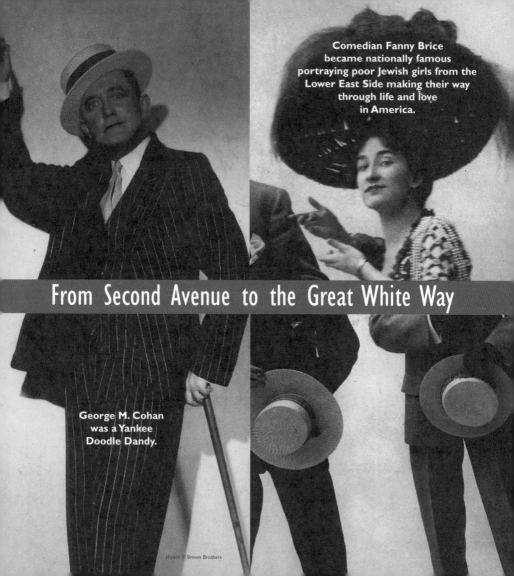

Comedian Fanny Brice became nationally famous portraying poor Jewish girls from the Lower East Side making their way through life and love in America.

From Second Avenue to the Great White Way

George M. Cohan was a Yankee Doodle Dandy.

HARLEM ON

Jazz-age Harlem was ground zero for an explosion of creativity among African–Americans, a modernist urban expression of cultural roots in the rural South, the Caribbean, and Africa. The blues and other ancestral forms were made contemporary in the Harlem Renaissance, just as Picasso and other Europeans were drawing inspiration from African art. The poems of Langston Hughes and Countee Cullen, the music of Duke Ellington, the murals of Aaron Douglas, the stories of Zora Neale Hurston, the novels and plays of Claude McKay—all spoke a new language that informed a new political consciousness exemplified by such Harlem-based political figures as Adam Clayton Powell and Marcus Garvey. And white folks had to pay attention.

Langston Hughes
Poet, essayist, playwright, novelist he championed the blues and the language of the common man as literature.

The Weary Blues
"...To the tune o' those Weary Blues.
With his ebony hands and each ivory key
He made that poor piano moan with melody
O Blues!"

I, Too
They'll see how beautiful I am
And be ashamed –
I, too, am America.

BLACK IS BEAUTIF

MIND: 1926

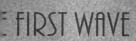

...odoo in America

...writer Zora Neale Hurston, like the ...cer Katherine Dunham after her, was ...ned in anthropology. She refused to ...ntenance the notion of race based on ...color, and instead focused on the ...ts of culture, producing both field ...dies and literary works based on the ...lore of the rural South and African and ...ibbean carryovers in the spiritual ...of African Americans, including ...odoo" (voodoo) traditions in ...v Orleans.

...il Rights by Copyright

...rston was before her time... ...Billie Holiday and Bessie Smith, ...followed her own road, believed ...er own gods, pursued her own ...ms, and refused to separate ...elf from 'common' people.. ...was a cultural revolutionary ...ly because she was ...ys herself..."   **Alice Walker**

E FIRST WAVE

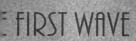
© World Wide

Skyscrapers as a Badge of Cityhood

1990s, after seeing the sterility the glass box had led to, Philip Johnson himself went post-modern

Questioned in 1996, Johnson had this to say: "What do I know that I didn't know before? I didn't know about this wonderful material out there, using concrete."

1931

GET

Is the Skyscraper tolerable?

Lewis Mumford

Modern vs Moderne Architecture

Even while the economy sank toward rock bottom in the Great Depression, American architecture was reaching from Manhattan bedrock toward the stars. Ignoring the European modernism that would resurface after World War II as the International Style of glass-and-steel boxes, the New York skyscraper went "moderne," or deco — not just tall and sleek, but goddam glamorous.

William Van Alen, architect of the Chrysler Building (left), and his former partner, H. Craig Severance, became bitter rivals when each was commissioned to design the world's tallest building. In 1931, as the Chrysler tower seemed likely to top out at 925 feet, the builders of the Bank of Manhattan Company structure at 40 Wall Street decided to halt their operations at 927 feet.

Meanwhile, workers were secretly assembling the rustless steel sections of the Chrysler spire which, when lifted through the dome and bolted into place, brought the building to its triumphant height of 1,048 feet. The triumph was short-lived. Lamb's Empire State Building was completed later that year, at 1,250 feet.

But the seeds of minimalist dogma were even then being planted in New York. The young Philip Johnson co-

UP

ING IT

To Be or Not to Bop
Jazz goes classic on 52nd St

BOP [bebop, rebop]

America was flush with success from World War II when bebop took 52nd Street by storm. The new music arrived on the street fully formed, complete with its own fashions, manners and attitude.

First developed in the early 40s by Dizzy Gillespie, Charlie Parker, Bud Powell, Thelonious Monk, Kenny Clarke, and Max Roach, bop is shorthand for the syllables bebap and rebop commonly used in scat singing to accompany the distinctive two note rhythm shown here.

bä - o - ä - ü - lä - dä

be bäp

bä de ba ba

DIZZYMANIA

These guys were among the best dressed men in America, but Dizzy Gillespie was the kingpin and object of mass adulation.

THE LATIN CONNECTION

"I thought he (Dizzy) was the greatest thing I had ever heard. The difference was he came with a new approach and confirmations and a different pattern than the old jazz. In it there was the evolution of American music ..."

MARIO BAUZA
The gran'daddy of Latin Jazz

BENDIN' THE HORN

"The truth is it was an accident. I could have pretended that I went into the basement and thought it up, but it wasn't that way. It was an accident ..."

DIZZY GILLESPIE

BIRD & DIZ

"I had never seen anything like it. Charlie would end his solo on a particular note and John [Dizzy] would start with that same note and go with it some totally different place."

BUD JOHNSON

JAZZ AS ART

Bop opened the four-to-the-bar beat to allow the utmost in improvisational freedom. The drummer follows and justifies the soloist.

It was a new music, in the words of Quincy Jones, "like nitroglycerine, sheer electricity."

It took jazz from the dance floor to the concert hall, from entertainment to art.

1951: BYE, BYE, BOP

"Right now it's rough. Everybody wants you to play what they call dance music. What they mean is that ticky-ticky-tick stuff. Man, that ain't dance music!"

DIZZY GILLESPIE

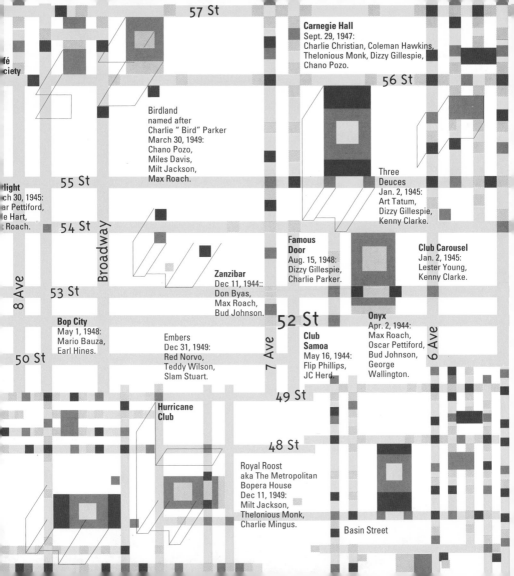

57 St

Carnegie Hall
Sept. 29, 1947:
Charlie Christian, Coleman Hawkins,
Thelonious Monk, Dizzy Gillespie,
Chano Pozo.

56 St

fé
ciety

Birdland
named after
Charlie " Bird" Parker
March 30, 1949:
Chano Pozo,
Miles Davis,
Milt Jackson,
Max Roach.

Three
Deuces
Jan. 2, 1945:
Art Tatum,
Dizzy Gillespie,
Kenny Clarke.

light
ch 30, 1945:
ar Pettiford,
le Hart,
Roach.

55 St

Broadway

54 St

Famous
Door
Aug. 15, 1948:
Dizzy Gillespie,
Charlie Parker.

Club Carousel
Jan. 2, 1945:
Lester Young,
Kenny Clarke.

Zanzibar
Dec 11, 1944::
Don Byas,
Max Roach,
Bud Johnson.

53 St

8 Ave

Bop City
May 1, 1948:
Mario Bauza,
Earl Hines.

Embers
Dec 31, 1949:
Red Norvo,
Teddy Wilson,
Slam Stuart.

52 St

7 Ave

**Club
Samoa**
May 16, 1944:
Flip Phillips,
JC Herd.

Onyx
Apr. 2, 1944:
Max Roach,
Oscar Pettiford,
Bud Johnson,
George
Wallington.

6 Ave

50 St

49 St

**Hurricane
Club**

48 St

Royal Roost
aka The Metropolitan
Bopera House
Dec 11, 1949:
Milt Jackson,
Thelonious Monk,
Charlie Mingus.

Basin Street

FREEDOM TO DRIP 1951

Cold War Culture Wars

The US Government's need to convince European elites that America was not only a military and economic superpower, but also a cultural one, required an American school of painting. In the freedom of Jackson Pollack's Action Painting and the "all-over-style" Abstract Expressionism, the State Department found a powerful weapon in its Cold War culture war with the Soviet Union.

Action Painting in the Atomic Ag

Pollack's drip paintings exemplified the anxiety of the nuclear era and expressed the dreadful power of the unseen. For the avant–garde, abstraction was the only way to deal with a society grown accustomed to the image of the mushroom cloud and children diving under their desks.

"They know themselves better than artists who over–intellectualize their work."
Harold Rosenberg,
Art critic of the New Yorker

*Inspired by the ideas of Serge Guilbaut

"The American Century"
as proclaimed by
Henry Luce,
founder of *Time*.

 **vs**

When Is a Picture Complete?

The New York School was bent on freeing color and line. If the ultimate goal of art is to resolve the differences between form and content, for the New York School form became content.

"The conclusion forces itself that the main premises of western art have at last migrated to the United States, along with the center of gravity of industrial and political power."

Clement Greenberg,
Art critic of the Nation, and Author of "Avant Garde and Kitsch"

Bigger Is Better

The movement's preference for dramatically large canvases and its desire to give spontaneous expression to the unconscious was used by liberals of the **Vital Center** to prove American superiority in the struggle between free western democratic man versus the alleged Eastern communist drone.

Goodbye Paris

US Government–sponsored exhibitions skillfully turned this avowedly apolitcal movement of pure paint into a cultural weapon of the Cold War and virtually assured New York's place as the art capital of the world.

The Promised L

The Powerbroker
Robert Moses, city planner, parks commissioner, and mega–builder extraordinaire, parlayed a series of seemingly obscure appointive jobs in city and state government into an empire that overwhelmed mayors and governors.

Moses on Jacobs
Dear Bennett,
 I am returning the book (The Death & Life of Great American Cities by Jane Jacobs) you sent me... Aside from the fact that it is intemperate, and inaccurate, it is also libelous. Sell this junk to someone else. RM

From a letter to Benn Cerf, co-founder of Random House.

1961: How the Great Moses was wiped out by Jane Jacob

Bulldozer Diplomacy
Even as Moses created an impressive network of parks, highways, housing projects, beaches, and bridges (see graphic), he destroyed stable neighborhoods (such as the South Bronx) and accelerated middle–class flight to the then undeveloped suburbs. When he proposed "urban renewal" for Greenwich Village, Jane Jacobs took him on.

The Moses Motto:
"If the end doesn't justify the means, what does?"

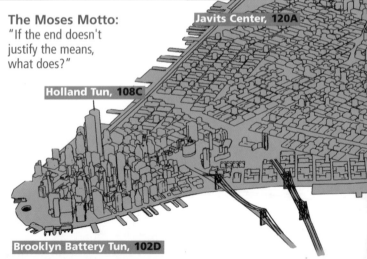

ndscape ?

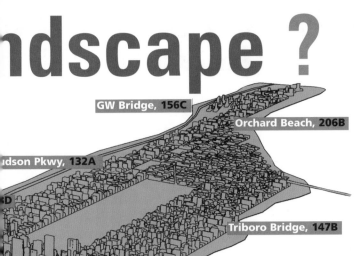

GW Bridge, **156C**

Orchard Beach, **206B**

udson Pkwy, **132A**

Triboro Bridge, **147B**

sewife, editor and apostle of cities

United Nations, **127C**

Midtown Tun, **127C**

The Apostle

Jane Jacobs, housewife and community activist, stood up to Moses and the planning titans who thought the car supreme. With her ground-breaking book, The Death & Life of Great American Cities, Jacobs fought for diverse neighborhoods, and successfully challenged the modernist dogma's claim that planned, geometric urban spaces would improve society. City planning was never quite the same again.

photo © Mayanne Hogbin

Paradigm Shift

"Jane was the first and probably the best and most incisive critic of the plague that modern architecture and urban renewal have visited upon our cities. What a pleasure to salute her." Norman Mailer

On The Death & Life...

It's one of those rare books that make a difference in world history" Rudolf Flesch

"The abattoir for sacred cows" Charles Abrams

"Her common sense was what made her such a radical thinker." Erik Wensberg

"What a dear sweet character she isn't!" Roger Starr

Jacobs on Winning

"...The 2nd time I got arrested I enjoyed the ride...We won it without a filing system. Everything we needed was always near the top!"

If the history of modern Western painting is one of a continuing series of conceptual erasures, of taking away what was heretofore considered the essence of art (nature, beauty, authorship, and paint), as Arthur Danto has argued, then Andy Warhol's Brillo Box may well mark the end of the master narrative that has defined modern Western painting.

Andy "Candy" Warhol

Whatever.

Here's what Andy said:

"I like painting on a square, because you don't have to decide whether it should be longer–longer, or shorter-shorter, or longer-**shorter.**"

"Paintings are too hard... I want to be like a machine..."
Andy Warhol

FAR
low

to sell his semen in a limited edition.

Gee..

"I'm using silkscreens now. I think somebody should be able to do all my paintings for me...

I think it would be so great if more people took up silkscreens so that no one would know whether my picture was mine or somebody else's.

"I'd prefer to remain a mystery. I never like to give my background and, anyway, I make it all up different every time I'm asked."

GREED IS GOOD

'86 –the Age
of Milken...

1998
Even
the s
millic
recer
reign
issue
at th

We know, or think we do, when art slides
into commerce. But when does commerce
itself become art? At what point, does it so
infuse and change culture that it can be said
to be the dominant aesthetic?

Put it somewhere around 1980, three years after
Michael Milken first understood the leverage that
could be obtained from debt, making something
out of less than nothing, and artists of the deal
began to use his insight to redraw the world.

By the end of the decade Milken, Ivan Boesky,
Martin Siegel, Dennis Levine, Charles Keating, and
others whom Tom Wolfe dubbed "Masters of the
Universe" had landed in jail–but from Moscow to
Bejiing the whole world now dances to the siren
song they sang.

Ivan Boes
sentenced to 3
settles SEC char
$100 millio

oms

ken is supposedly barred from
dustry for life (he just paid $48
a probation violation on the
ner–Turner merger), junk still
19 billion in junk bonds were
riple the amount sold in 1986
he age of Milken.

Michael Milken is ... a man of pure intellect and virtue, incapable of committing any but the slightest of sins or misdemeanors... **Jude Wanniski**, memo to Frank Rich 12/17/96

Rapid progress is unsettling.. These leaps of progress cause rapid change, and in rapid change there are always people who loose.... **Robert Bartley**, editor of the Wall Street Journal 5/17/92

is Levine
d to 2 years,
62.000 in fines
penalties

Judge Kimba Wood

Michael Milken
sentenced to 10 years, and
$600 million in fines and
restitutions. Barred from the
securities industry for life.

TRUTH IS W

"It was a [Bronx] DJ style which helped to create the lifestyle which came to be known as hip-hop." **David Toop,** Author of The Rap Attack

It goes back to Africa...it was the Dillard storyteller that would tell the stories through hand clappin' and congas... at the same time, they would be getting their history and they would be getting the news. **KRS-1,** Rap Pioneer

"...Rap is Black People's CNN..." **Chuck D,** Public Enemy

"...The revolution will not be televised..." **Gil Scott-Heron**

"...Don't push me 'cause I am close the edge. I'm tryin' not to lose my head..." **Grandmaster Flash & the Furious Five**

"...I'll wet you like I never met you..." **Lil' Kim**

"You're Nobody (Til Somebody Kills You) **The Notorious B.I.G.**

"They are the style—setters" **Betsey Johnson,** Fashion designer

---

* the truth as sold by **Stuart Ewen,** author of "All Consuming Images"

HAT SELLS*

 DA BRONX
OPS POP WORLDWIDE

photo © André Grossman

98

| Rockin' it - say it loud............... |

1969–**James Brown** records Funky Drummer whose syncopated drumbeat becomes the most sampled track in Hip Hop history. It's Got the Beat!

"...Hip Hop saved the Funk..." **George Clinton,** Funkadelics

1981 Can you all get Funky!
–Rap transcends the Bronx
–Charlie Ahern's movie "Wildstyle."

1984–Hip Hop goes global via Hollywood through the movies Beatstreet and Crush Groove.

| Gangsta Bandwagon................. |

1986–**Ice T** creates a furor with the song "Cop Killaz" – **NWA's** "Fuck tha Police" takes gangsta mainstream– prompting Education Secretary **Bill Bennett** to push Time-Warner to divest itself of Interscope Records, the leading rap label.

1993–Fashion designers **Donna Karan** & **Tommy Hilfiger** cash in on the hip-hop craze

1997–**Tupac Shakur** and the **Notorious B.I.G.** (Biggie Smalls) are gunned down.

1998–Estimated worldwide rap record & CD sales top $12 Billion.

CREDITS

THE MAN

Van Dam *is an award–winning graphic designer, cartographer and information architect. He holds several patents in the field of paper engineering and origami map folding.*

Van Dam's maps and packaging designs have been honored by the AIGA, the Industrial Design Society of America, the editors of ID Magazine and been featured on national television.

Among Van Dam's clients are American Express, Chase Manhattan Bank, Bertelsmann AG, Forbes, Getty Oil, LACVB, The Marvel Entertainment Group, The Metropolitan Museum of Art, NYCVB, St Martin's Press, Warner Brothers and the Walt Disney Company.

Stephan Van Dam, AIGA
Publisher, General Editor
& Creative Dictator

Staff
Cartographic Design
Gerry Krieg, Günter Vollath
& Stephan Van Dam

Editorial
Fred Lafontaine, *Director*

Proof Reading
George Delury, Patrick
Pardo, Ruth Houston

Photography
André Grossmann

Cover
Yang Zhao

Production Management
Kenneth Kern,
Tomasz Tomaszewski,
Desktop Publishing

Marketing & Distribution
Victor A. Garrido, *Director*

Contributing Editors
Ron Dorfman, David
Henderson, Gail Pellett

VanDam, Inc.
The VanDam Bldg.
11 W 20 St, NYC 10011

vox:	212-929-0416
fax:	212-929-0426
toll-free:	1-800-UNFOLDS
e-mail:	stephan@ vandam.com
web:	www.vandam.com

SPECIAL THANKS

We would like to thank the following people for their insight, suggestions and help in producing Manhattan@tlas.

Schuyler Chapin,
    Cultural Affairs
    Commissioner NYC
Stuart & Elizabeth Ewen
Mike Feller,
    NYC Parks Dept.
Arthur Gelb,
    New York Times
Serge Guilbault,
    UBC
Andrew Heiskell
Mary Holloway,
    ABNY
Nigel Holmes
Alice Hudson,
    NYPL
Jane Jacobs
Richard Kaplan
Robert Macdonald,
    Museum of the City
    of New York
Brendan Sexton,
    Times Square Bid
Jane Weisman,
    Green Thumb
Richard Saul Wurman
    The one and only

printed in China